BETWEEN *Legitimacy* AND *Violence*

A book in the series *Latin America In Translation* /
En Traducción / *Em Tradução*
Sponsored by the Duke–University of North Carolina
Program in Latin American Studies

BETWEEN *Legitimacy* AND *Violence*

A HISTORY OF COLOMBIA, 1875–2002

Marco Palacios

Translated by Richard Stoller

Duke University Press | Durham and London 2006

2nd printing, 2007

© 2006 Duke University Press

All rights reserved

Printed in the United States of America on acid-free paper ∞

Designed by Heather Hensley

Typeset in Centaur by Tseng Information Systems, Inc.

Library of Congress Cataloging-in-Publication Data

appear on the last printed page of this book.

I firmly believe that all of us here today, and all of us who belong to this unfortunate generation, can say with pride that we have witnessed Colombia's last civil war. Our grandchildren, who will be born after this cycle of horrors, will find it hard to understand what kind of insanity led to such bloodshed among brothers. But we will be able to tell them, from our old age, exactly how and why the last representatives of this cruel and intransigent political fanaticism had the sad privilege of witnessing the final hurricane in all its terrible devastation. It lasted over a thousand days and left nothing standing, either materially or morally, as it hurled Colombians into furious battle against one another. We may not find absolution from our descendants, but if the fatal inheritance does not reach them, it will be because we took all the blame upon ourselves, so as to spare them.

RAFAEL URIBE URIBE
DECEMBER 31, 1902

Contents

Tables

Acknowledgments

I would like to extend special thanks to my colleagues who supported the publication of this work in English, especially Ann Farnsworth-Alvear, who encouraged me to approach Duke University Press with the proposal. My thanks also to the press's anonymous readers, for their useful comments.

MARCO PALACIOS
MEXICO, D.F., JUNE 2005

Prologue to the Second Colombian Edition

Between Legitimacy and Violence sets out a historical synthesis of Colombia's trajectory, from the 1870s through the present. The story begins with the notable increase in commercial, technological, and intellectual activity in the North Atlantic region after the mid-nineteenth century. The dynamism of the capitalist revolution gave Colombia's ruling classes a stark choice: integrate the country into the modern industrial world or perish in a backwater of barbarism. To incorporate the country into the world system they would again have to look to the institutional, political, and economic models of Europe and the United States.

This was a more difficult and controversial project than it might appear. There was, to start, no consensus about the real content of those models, and the models were constantly changing. Colombia's rulers and thinkers had been divided on political issues since the Enlightenment. But if consensus could be reached and if the challenges of applying the models to Colombia could be met, the rewards would be enormous.

This was, to be sure, not a new challenge: Colombia had been wrestling with modernity since the eighteenth century. The achievement of independence in 1819, by eliminating the formal obstacles to the embrace of modernity, laid bare the real obstacles: the immensity of Colombia's territory in comparison with its population, its overwhelming poverty, and the inadequacy of its public administration. By examining each of these elements of adversity and the unusual ways in which they combined over time and place, we can better understand the history of the years since the mid-nineteenth century.

Colombia's geography was a formidable obstacle to prosperity and democracy, and the difficulties it posed were exacerbated by technological backwardness, low economic product per inhabitant, and the corrosive concentration of wealth. High transportation costs gave day-to-day viability to sleepy regions and enclaves, which remained as self-sufficient and disconnected from one another as they were before independence. In the early twentieth century this characteristic was seized upon by business leaders, who wanted a national market, and by political leaders, who wanted a national electorate.

Social and ethnic inequalities, which probably increased over the course of the nineteenth century, produced economic and political effects. On the economic side, the small aggregate demand for goods and services combined with the unlimited supply of unskilled labor created a vicious circle of poverty that gave rise to open social conflict in the 1920s and thereafter. As the Colombian economy modernized, fitfully after 1880 and more decisively after 1910 with the rise of coffee, the ingredients were there for a Darwinian explosion: the survival of the fittest, as determined by the market and by recourse to violence.

Colombian capitalism, born as it was of waves of agricultural colonization, reinforced cultural patterns of agrarian individualism that were resistant to solidarity and collective responsibility—important features of modern society. Perhaps for this reason, the socialist appeal (as far back as the utopian socialism espoused by Manuel Murillo Toro in the mid–nineteenth century) had little resonance in Colombia. Catholic social thought (of the sort pioneered by Pope Leo XIII) had a better reception, since it could be locally rooted and led or manipulated by recognized local leaders; but it was at best a palliative for the indignities and deprivations wrought by an ostentatiously exclusionary society.

The role of statist nationalism, which was so central to the economic modernization of many Latin American countries, has been muted in Colombia. Colombia's leaders cast their lot with the model of modern capitalism represented by the United States rather than Europe, and in keeping with that model (and with preexisting notions of economic liberalism), the economic role of the Colombian state has been relatively passive and reactive. Even during the period of active state support of industrialization (c. 1945–90), the government was largely an agent of compromise between the interests of coffee growers, importers, and bankers on the one hand and industrialists on the other. Without strategic initiatives of its own (and without, perhaps, even the means to conceive of any), the Colombian state limited its interventions to cases in which social peace required government action, such as the strikes of the 1930s and 1940s and the rural unrest of the 1920s and 1930s. In the second half of the twentieth century, policies on such issues as agrarian reform, urban housing, and social services such as health and education obeyed the same dynamic of necessity. At the same time, the urban and rural popular organizations that helped put these reforms on the government agenda were contained through co-optation or destroyed through repression.

The social and regional fragmentation of the country and the corrosive effects of partisan conflict have combined to produce a weak state. Between the letter of the law and its effective application is a huge chasm. The state's weakness is apparent in the fragility of its fiscal base: large-scale tax evasion restricts revenues, corruption and clientelism distort spending, and archaic values prevent the achievement of necessary social goals via the national budget. Public education is the most important example of this negative phenomenon, and throughout the book we will make reference to its progress.

Colombian geography strengthened the dominance of local political bosses and formed the basis for regionalist discourse on everything from cultural identity to electoral practices. The creation of a national state that could achieve meaningful goals such as economic growth and social peace had to face regionalist headwinds at every turn, and the consistent winners were local and regional brokers who were the only effective links between the citizen and the state. This situation set the stage for apathy and sometimes for disobedience, because there was no way for the popular sectors to partake of a sense of belonging to the nation when the promise of civic equality was so patently unfulfilled.

The national scope and vertical integration of the two parties simultaneously masked and attenuated the effects of social fragmentation. The system of partisan identities and conflict that came out of the nineteenth century came with a historical mythology that could incite and funnel the political loyalties of most Colombians well into the twentieth century. The relationship between this all-encompassing (and all-dividing) party system and the modernizing impulse to expand citizens' rights and democratic competition has unequal dimensions. The parties progressively increased participation in the electoral system until universal adult suffrage was attained in 1957, but the dominance of local party bosses and clientelism have effectively closed off genuine competition, creating an environment in which political leaders are never called to account for their actions. The main problem, in short, is that representative democracy has not reached maturity in Colombia, and neither has public administration.

The post–Cold War vogue of the concepts of civil society and participatory democracy (as opposed to representative democracy) shows that many Colombians recognize these failings and would like to overcome them. However, as noted in the Epilogue to this book, much recent thinking on the future path of Colombian democracy (expressed most cogently in the 1991 Constitution) has been insufficiently reflective and perhaps too quick to copy models from other countries with different economic, social, and political contexts.

I will leave it to the reader to make his or her own judgments about the achievements and mistakes of Colombia's ruling classes during the years covered in this book. I will take the liberty of citing one enormous error here: in the 1930s and 1940s large landowners were permitted to block any and all initiatives on land reform. The issue could not be addressed until the early 1960s, and then only weakly, in the context of counterinsurgency and the Alliance for Progress. The consequences for Colombia have been disastrous, not just for the countryside but for the entire country. Two opportunities to achieve social peace were lost, and the accumulation of errors has come to dominate the dark social and political panorama that Colombia faces as it moves into the twenty-first century.

Although I have tried to stick to a chronological rendering, in accordance with the usual reader expectations and intuitions about a work of history, sometimes the strands of society, economy, politics, and culture move at different rhythms. If a date permits us to close one period and open another (and that is how historians usually operate), the question inevitably arises: Is the period cultural, political, social, or economic? If all of these aspects are part of our narrative, which should have priority in the overall periodization?

There are various solutions to this problem. I have chosen to resolve it by weighing the relative importance of the four aspects of each epoch, and political periodization has generally gone by the wayside. For instance, this book does not follow the conventional division of Colombian history into a Conservative Republic from 1886 to 1930, a Liberal Republic from 1930 to 1946, and a Conservative (or quasi-Conservative) Dictatorship from 1948 to 1958.

Chapter 1 examines an era in which public discourse was dominated by politics and constitutional forms: federalist radicalism versus centralist conservatism. The struggle between these two political visions occupied center stage and managed to absorb all other questions, including those related to the overriding "civilizational" issue described at the outset, how to create a stable export-based economy. Against the prevailing (political) periodization, I believe the story starts in the mid-1870s, with clear signs of decay in the Radical Olympus regime forged by Colombian Liberals in the early 1860s, which culminated in the wartime coup of 1900. The era of the Regeneration (1878–1900) is, I think, best understood when it is separated from the explicitly Conservative Republic that followed.

Chapter 2 considers the 1903–1930 period in a similar light. The treaties that ended the last great partisan civil war (1899–1902) were elite pacts to make recourse to arms illegitimate once and for all. This was the necessary basis for the definitive rise of coffee in the Colombian economy, and for the ever more hegemonic presence of the United States in Colombian life, until it became what President Marco Fidel Suárez would call the North Star. It was a period of social change in a decidedly capitalist direction, sporadically opposed by Catholicism on the one hand and by the working class on the other. It was an essentially optimistic period that combined, more or less tranquilly, economic liberalism and political conservatism.

Chapter 3 starts with the decisive year of 1930. That year saw the confluence of two crises: the Conservative collapse that permitted the return of the Liberal party to power after half a century and a global economic depression that put an end to Colombia's "dance of the millions," the easy credit that propelled the country's development in the previous decade. The new era would be one of social and political mobilization, and of a somewhat strengthened state. The social and cultural demands that accumulated during the previous period were partially addressed by government, but the new struggle would be between the imperative of widening access to effective citizenship and the reality of a new plutocratic elite that was somewhat less bound by partisan identities. The elite won: while bankers, coffee growers, and industrialists united when they needed to, the popular sectors were divided by competing mobilizations and by political sectarianism. Because of the importance of the Violencia in the overall history of Colombia, and in order not to impose its distinctive periodization (c. 1945–64) on the wider narrative, I have chosen to discuss it in Chapter 4.

Because of the Violencia, but also because of this historical victory of the new unified elite against the challenge of popular mobilization, Colombia never went through a full-fledged populist stage of the sort proposed by the Liberal caudillo Jorge Eliécer Gaitán in the years before his assassination in 1948. Chapter 5, which begins with the bipartisan National Front agreement of 1958, focuses on the consequences of this absence for the creation of political legitimacy and a modernized state. In the intervening decades Colombia has teetered between this ideal and the creeping reality of "savage capitalism," whose most recent protagonists have included drug traffickers and organized criminals of other kinds. This is the basis for Chapter 6 and the Epilogue, which take the story through the so-called 8,000 Case in the 1990s: this scandal, which involved President Ernesto Samper and a host of important figures inside and outside the world of politics, illustrated the corruption and exhaustion of Colombia's political and judicial institutions and of public discourse itself.

MARCO PALACIOS
MEXICO CITY, NOVEMBER 2002

Chapter 1

FROM LIBERAL DECAY
TO REGENERATION

*F*our national civil wars (1876–77, 1885–86, 1895, and 1899–1902) provide ample evidence of disagreement among the Colombian elite about how to structure the state's relationships with the individual, the Catholic Church, and the regions. The final war, known as the War of the Thousand Days, brought about the secession of Panama and starkly illustrated the consequences of a political culture characterized by extreme political partisanship on the one hand and on the other by a growing gap between the political elites and the common people concerning the meaning and development of political citizenship.

Radical liberalism came out of the 1876 war gravely wounded, and it was smashed in the 1885 war. From that war emerged the Regeneration (1878–1900), whose symbol was the constitution of 1886: centralist, confessional, presidentialist, and a bit easier to reform than the prior one. Like its predecessor, the 1886 constitution arose not from popular suffrage but rather from an unholy alliance forged during the armed struggle — in this case, between Conservatives and a varied group of Liberals known as the Independents, both of which were excluded from the "Radical Olympus" regimes. The political history of the period is a record of both the fragile alliance between these groups and the discord that was sown in each of the two traditional parties.

Liberals and Conservatives both credited international commerce with opening the doors of civilization. Poverty and backwardness were seen as the consequences of Colombia's isolation from the vigorous currents of trade, capital, labor, and technology in the Atlantic Basin in the second half of the 1800s. The political conflict only marginally impinged on the liberal economic model. The most important and controversial question of political economy during this period was whether the state should control the monetary system. But the basic orientation of the export economy remained uncontested, pulled along by coffee cultivation and by the rebound of gold and silver mining, activities that in turn promoted, albeit in fitful and disorderly fashion, the development of a railway system. The recurring crises generated by the export of tobacco in the 1870s and of quinine in the 1880s contributed to political instability.

The restrictions of the colonial era continued to limit Colombia's long-term economic growth: a very low level of per capita income, with the poverty and lack of education that it implied; the dispersion of the population in pockets isolated from one another and from the exterior; the precariousness of all sorts of infrastructure; the primitive character and techniques of finance and business in general; and last but not least, the shortage of capital. To all this we can add the rivalries between towns, regions, and parties.

Some elements of this picture slowly changed with the development of the coffee sector. Concentrated first in the eastern mountains and spreading to the west, coffee promoted commercial capitalism and land colonization. The oscillations in the international price brought cycles of bonanza (1862–75 and 1888–95) and depression (1889–99), which were felt in public finances and were an important reason for the crises of the final years of the century. Coffee increased agricultural productivity, created employment, and integrated new regions in Colombia's temperate zones into the economy. But its effects would be felt fully only in the second decade of the twentieth century.

An Empty, Mixed-Race Country

Today Colombia has around 44 million inhabitants. More or less on the same territory, exclusive of Panama, the population in 1870 was a mere 2.6 million, of whom 80,000 were classified as "savage Indians." By 1920 the population had doubled, but there were marked regional variations owing to different migration rates and infant mortality. Taking as a base the censuses of 1851 and 1912, one notices a clear contrast between Antioquia and Santander, in the western and eastern mountains respectively. Antioquia's share of the national population rose from 11.2 percent to 23 percent, while Santander's fell from 18.6 percent to 12 percent. These figures can be deceiving because they include not only natural increase but also in- and out-migration, and we know through historical studies that Colombians from Cauca, Tolima, and the central regions of Cundinamarca and Boyacá were important participants in the colonizing of Antioquian lands in the late nineteenth century, while there was some emigration from Santander toward the Caribbean coast and even the neighboring Venezuelan province of Táchira.

Most Colombians in the late 1800s lived dispersed in relatively self-sufficient rural communities. Of 734 *municipios* (townships), only 21 had more than 10,000 inhabitants. In each of them, from the wealthiest to the most miserable, one's place depended on blood ties, wealth, and education. The feeble supply of educational opportunities rose irregularly, and demand for them—the key determinant of supply, in the absence of government policy—came mostly from urban males. If we are to believe the census of 1870, at the height of the pro-education Radical Liberal period, 64 percent of schools were public, and they accounted for 79 percent of enrollment. The 82,561 students registered throughout the country represented only 12 percent of the school-age population, and the female share of the total was only 27 percent. During the post-1885 Conservative regimes the relative weight of public education increased, as did the attendance rates of both boys and girls. In 1899, right before the War of the Thousand Days, some 140,000 children were enrolled in primary schools throughout the country. Attendance through 1930 (when the figure reached 438,000) also continued to expand under Conservative regimes.

Bogotá and Medellín were the only urban centers with more than 20,000 residents, and together they represented 2.5 percent of the national population—a tiny figure in comparison with similar "urban primacy" measurements of 21 percent in Cuba (1877), 11 percent in Chile (1875), and 7 percent in Venezuela (1873). The 1851 and 1912 censuses both confirm the preponderance of the mixed-race population: 47 percent and 49 percent respectively. In the 1912 census male respondents made their own racial classifications (in earlier censuses the census taker made the judgment), and perhaps for that reason we see evidence of "whitening": the white category went from 17 percent to 34 percent, while Indians fells from 14 percent to 6 percent and blacks/mulattos fell from 17 percent to 10 percent. In the southwestern department of Cauca, however, the picture differed remarkably: there only 19 percent classified themselves as mestizo, while larger numbers chose Indian, white, or black.

In contrast to the situation in countries with large indigenous populations such as Mexico, Guatemala, Ecuador, Peru, Bolivia, and Paraguay, questions of the legal status of indigenous communities, their access to land, and their incorporation in national society were of limited and regionally circumscribed importance in Colombia. Neither did the country experience the massive influx of European immigrants seen during this period in Argentina, Brazil, and Uruguay. The numerical weight of the mestizo population lent viability to the notion of political participation based on formal principles of civic equality.

It strengthened nationally integrated networks of political leadership and patronage long before any national integration of the economy. Although true racial democracy was a civic myth, the notion of a harmonious mestizo-based society was widely diffused. But skin color and all the features associated with it were still strongly correlated with occupation and income.

Once slavery was abolished in 1851, black and mulatto communities presented fewer problems of a legal-institutional sort, since republican institutions did not reserve for them anything like the *resguardos* (community lands) held by some indigenous populations. Afro-Colombians remained concentrated in dispersed pockets of the Pacific coast and in the old mining regions of the colonial period; on the Caribbean coast; and in the Cauca, Magdalena, and Patía river basins. They were the majority in Cartagena and in Chinú in the north, in Chocó, Tumaco, and Barbacoas in the west, and in several important regions of inland Cauca in the southwest. In Antioquia they were concentrated in Medellín and in mining zones to the north and northeast. The white Bogotá geographer Rufino Gutiérrez wrote in 1917 that in the mining towns "the blacks and mulattos rarely hear Mass, save for those enrolled in school," and he observed that the workers at the British-owned Segovia mines "live like draft animals without souls," in an environment of "permanent hostility" toward the white management. The formal marriage rate was the lowest in the country, as unions outside the ecclesiastical and civil frameworks were the norm.

Some Afro-Colombian communities of the Pacific coast and the southwest, abandoned to their fate, suffered from high crime rates and even higher rates of malaria and yellow fever. In 1916 the Panama Canal administration had to ask Colombia to put the port of Buenaventura (an important stop for canal-bound shipping) under quarantine because of its sanitary crises. The same level of official indifference existed toward the indigenous people of La Guajira in the extreme northeast, where as late as 1943 a malaria epidemic claimed 3,000 lives. Both Afro-Colombians and indigenous peoples were called rebellious and quarrelsome by racially pessimistic (and overwhelmingly white) elites, even though the "whitest" towns of Antioquia and Santander had higher murder rates — in many of those towns, revolvers and machetes were almost universally worn by adult men, and were used with some regularity.

A Mosaic of Isolated Regions

Colombia around 1900 still largely followed late-colonial settlement patterns, although there was substantial recent settlement from the three mountain ranges down toward temperate regions in the Cauca and Magdalena river basins. In the late 1800s and early 1900s several new population centers also arose along the Caribbean coast. Still, the overall picture was one of many distinct populated regions with little or no communication between them. The four great economic regions—Antioquia, the Caribbean coast, the east-central region, and the southwest, including the marginalized Pacific coast—had very different levels of internal political and cultural cohesion and of ethnic composition and homogeneity. At the start of the twentieth century the distinctive cultural profile of each region was not at all clear, and the persistent clichés and stereotypes of a half-century earlier tended to obscure the changes constantly occurring within each region.

The case of Cauca in the southwest illustrates the internal complexity of the four overarching regions. Gran Cauca ("Greater Cauca," including the modern departments of Cauca and Nariño) was extremely diverse in racial composition, traditions and idiosyncrasies, ecosystems, and productive sectors. In the south, the agricultural plateaus of Pasto, Túquerres, and Ipiales had a strongly indigenous cast, in contrast to zones farther north that had a clear split between white proprietors and Afro-Colombian majorities. But these same populations were all fragmented spatially and politically, as we can see by comparing the provinces of Barbacoas and Patía with Chocó or the Cauca Valley.

From independence through the civil war of 1876–77, Cauca was consistently the principal theater of conflict against a backdrop of economic decline, particularly in gold mining. Although the underlying elements of politicization have not yet been extensively studied, it is clear that the tradition of popular mobilization and frequent appeals to arms in a region where the racist legacy of slavery met postindependence ideologies of radical egalitarianism was bound to produce situations of turmoil and violence. In the background we also find the old rivalry between Popayán and Cali, the principal towns of central Cauca. The old Popayán elite fought their final battle as national protagonists in the wars of 1860–62 and 1876–77, as Cali emerged as the more important economic center. It would be a mistake to assume that, along European lines, Popayán represented an aristocracy and Cali a capitalist bourgeoisie. Despite the abolition of slavery, in both urban centers society continued to revolve around values based on the hitherto slave-based hacienda and mining sectors. But social insecurity, a real phenomenon further exaggerated by Conservatives, and geographical isolation turned all of Cauca into what one observer called "an economic Paraguay." The mid-century novel *María*, a crowning example of Latin American literary romanticism set in the Cauca Valley, offers a rather disingenuous view of regional society: in the Cauca depicted by Jorge Isaacs, blacks were part of a poetic natural landscape, displaying obsequiousness, rustic Christianity, and musical talent. One would never guess that this same region would erupt in social and racial violence just a few years after the novel's publication.

Although the war delayed Cali's rise to regional leadership, geographical isolation was a greater factor: as late as 1880 the road from Cali to the port of Buenaventura was impassible for part of the year. Popayán, like the similarly decaying cities of Cartagena and Tunja, continued to send more congressmen and ministers to Bogotá, and its elite knew how to take advantage of the prestige and influence of their poets and polemicists and of their tradition-bound university.

A Peasant Nation

Rural poverty, more grinding (and certainly more preponderant) than urban poverty, was not widely noted as a problem even though it was a severe constraint on economic development. Eventually there would be an avalanche of rural migration to the cities, which in the twentieth century would find its voice in populism. The agrarian structure was characterized by concentration of property and underutilization of the best lands, and by low productivity overall; a large percentage of the rural population worked shallow and eroded mountainside soils. Unemployment and underemployment were very high, especially during the "dead times" of the agricultural calendar, though it should be noted that women worked consistently throughout the year. The diet was poor in protein and barely rose above subsistence level for most poor rural Colombians. But on the plus side, between roughly 1890 and 1920 there was a clear congruence — never equaled before or since — between the local manufacture of agricultural tools and the needs of local cultivators.

Climate and soil fertility, as always, determined production and labor options. The rhythms of life of a majority of the population could be altered at any time by droughts or infestations. The rainy season brought regular flooding to the Caribbean coast, where a fifth of the territory consists of rivers, swamps, or other wetlands. The pre-Columbian cultivation calendar was still widely followed for traditional products, and techniques were barely changed from those of the seventeenth century. Land was cleared largely by the burning of existing vegetation, and the traditional assortment of metal tools was supplemented in some cases by mule-drawn wooden plows. The same could be said for the structures of rural property: as three hundred years before, haciendas of varying size occupied the fertile valleys near population centers, and with few exceptions they formed the nucleus of a hyperextensive (as opposed to intensive) cattle sector based on local breeds.

The diffusion and adaptation of new varieties of seeds, sugar mills, metal threshers, or coffee bean dryers depended on the cycles of external demand and on the reduction of internal transportation costs. Since prices were so uncertain, few rural entrepreneurs were willing to use fertilizers, machinery, or methodical pest control (even though locusts periodically ravaged western Colombia from Cauca all the way up to the Caribbean coast). Cold-country haciendas did not even try to compete with smallholders in the production of foodstuffs. In Colombia, as in the rest of Latin America, the interspersing of haciendas, plantations, smallholder parcels, and to a lesser extent indigenous communal properties produced a motley mix of the traditional and the relatively modern, with many regional and local permutations.

World demand deepened the divide between the cold-country regions of longstanding settlement, which produced for internal (mostly local) markets, and the temperate to tropical regions. This is the era par excellence of the Colombian agro-entrepreneur: the coffee grower/merchant of the eastern and central mountains, the cattle baron of the Caribbean coast, and the sugar cane planter of that region and also of the Cauca Valley. The cold-country producers of grains and dairy cattle responded to upticks in internal demand with far less enthusiasm.

The great rural properties of the highlands maintained essentially colonial labor rules, while export agriculture, increasingly penetrated by commercial capital, sought to reinforce them in a new setting. However, the few available statistics permit us to speculate that only a minority of Colombia's rural poor, the so-called *residentes*, actually lived the stereotypical existence of hacienda subalterns. With hacendados who were generally absentees and rural poor who were more mobile than is often assumed, the Colombian countryside did not develop the social, cultural, and legal ties characteristic of European or Japanese high feudalism. A terminology based on any notion of feudalism does not help us to define or understand Colombia's agrarian structures.

During the second half of the nineteenth century many colonial-era haciendas were divided, and 250 hectares was the rough average in such regions as the Sabana de Bogotá, Ubaté, and Sogamoso in the Cundinamarca-Boyacá highlands and Aburrá, Rionegro, and La Ceja in the Antioquian heartland. The great coffee properties of Santander, Cundinamarca, Tolima, and Antioquia usually ranged from 250 to 500 hectares; very few measured over 2,000 hectares. The mills of the great sugar haciendas, at least those that produced for local consumption, consisted of rudimentary wooden parts powered by donkeys or mules, and were very inefficient. Some highland cattle haciendas did introduce new varieties of wheat and potatoes, but productivity remained very low; grain was threshed by the hoofs of pack animals let loose on the harvested stalks. Some mechanical grain mills appeared after 1870, and by the 1890s the Bogotá region had twenty mule-powered mills and one powered by steam.

While the resident and seasonal workers on the highland haciendas were Indians, or at least were considered so by landowners, managers, and townspeople, a considerable proportion of workers on the sugar cane and banana plantations were Afro-Colombian. These tropical plantations began to take off in the 1890s, and differed from haciendas in that they paid their workers cash wages and many were launched by foreign entrepreneurs. Plantations tended to cover larger areas than haciendas — for instance, the Berástegui complex near Cartagena covered 12,000 hectares in 1880. The famous Sincerín plantation, founded twenty years later, covered 14,000 hectares; half of the area was divided into thirty-four plots, which, on the Cuban model, were rented to entrepreneurs who grew the cane and sold it to the plantation's mill at a standard rate. In the Cauca Valley in the southwest, one sugar pioneer bought 1,200 hectares in 1869 and by the end of the century had increased his properties eightfold.

By the late nineteenth century at least some sugar mills, cattle estates, and banana plantations had introduced machinery, new breeds, and other aspects of modern agronomy. But by the First World War neither the cattle nor the sugar sector could compete in the global market. By the early twentieth century, when centrifuge mills for the production of white sugar arrived in the Cauca Valley, they had already been in use in the United States and Cuba for sixty years. And while innovations in cattle raising (new grasses such as pará, the arrival of barbed wire, and the introduction of breeds suitable to the environment) raised capacity from six to eight head of cattle per hectare between 1880 and 1910, the sector could not hope to compete with the United States, whose productivity permitted it to dominate nearby markets such as Cuba and Panama.

Colombia was, above all, a country of independent small producers. The viceregal reports of the late colonial period described them as isolated and individualist mestizos. During the independence era it was almost cliché to note that rural property was highly fragmented throughout the pockets of mountain settlement, from northeastern Cundinamarca to the valleys of Cúcuta and from Antioquia southward into Gran Cauca. Recent historical studies confirm this impression, although it should be noted that the origins of smallholding (defined as less than ten hectares) varied by region. In Santander and Antioquia the independent cultivators, usually poor whites, were the descendants of seventeenth-century land colonizers; in Boyacá, on the other hand, the very small *minifundio* arose largely in tandem with the disappearance of the indigenous *resguardos* in the nineteenth century as a result of racial mixture and geographical redistribution of the population in accordance with ethnic classification. In land transfer documents of some *municipios* in central Boyacá the term *resguardo*, still in common use in the 1860s, slowly disappears until it has ceased to exist by the turn of the century. Population growth and the subdivision of property made *minifundios* even smaller over time. In Cauca, another region of *resguardos*, a higher level of cultural cohesion permitted the indigenous communities to persist, with the aid of a law drawn up to protect them in 1890.

In regions where smallholding predominated, differences in average parcel size were largely a function of population growth: the higher the growth rate, the greater the subdivisions and the smaller the next generation's parcels. An additional factor was that in these largely nonmoney economies, land was the most reliable way to store wealth. The inflation of the late 1800s must have lent this factor greater importance, since we see that during this period many smallholders had parcels in various areas of a given *municipio*, some of them quite large. This phenomenon was especially pronounced in the coffee regions of Antioquia, and later to the south in Caldas.

Artisans and Miners

The symbiosis of agriculture and artisanship that developed in such regions as Santander, Cundinamarca/Boyacá, and parts of Gran Cauca in the eighteenth century continued in force into the nineteenth. In these regions, rural women and children were key elements of the domestic economy, spinning, weaving, and dyeing cotton, straw, or sisal (jute), usually cultivated on the family parcel. The weavings combined pre-Columbian and Hispanic techniques and designs, and continued to rely on the manual spindle and simple wooden looms with sisal cords. These crude products faced stiff competition from the avalanche of English machine-made imports after independence but conserved a precarious place in local markets, thanks to the natural protections afforded by poverty, high transportation costs, and local tastes.

While Santander's rural population in effect annexed the artisanal sector, their peers in Antioquia found a complementary activity in small-scale mining. Later, in the early twentieth century, some areas of central Boyacá and eastern Cundinamarca developed small- and medium-sized coal mining operations, which offered seasonal employment adjusted to the down times of the agrarian calendar.

In the west, gold panning in rivers and streams continued much as in colonial times. Miners used the tools of their ancestors: a small hoe, a long thin iron pole, and a wooden washboard to catch the minute bits of gold. The numbers of these *mazamorreros* (from *mazamorra*, the corn meal that was their staple food) were shrinking, falling from 10 percent to 5 percent of the economically active population of Antioquia between 1870 and 1906. But even salaried miners in large-scale operations did not work year round; they rotated their work between mining and agriculture.

By lumping each of these activities ancillary to agriculture in one of two groups, as either "artisanal" or "mining," the 1870 census offered a distorted picture of the composition of the labor force. It would appear, for example, that a third of the economically active population were artisans: 12 percent of men and 63 percent of women. But if we define the term more narrowly as craft artisans, townspeople who transformed natural products (leather, wood, wool, cotton) into consumer goods, the 1892 survey by the Statistical Office offers a more realistic estimate: around 9 percent of the economically active population, a figure more congruent with the 13 percent shown in the 1912 census.

Land Colonizations

At the start of the 1870s three-quarters of the country, the so-called national territories, were uninhabited or contained only indigenous populations beyond the reach of church or state. The eastern mountains, which had the highest population density, contained 42 percent of the total population. But even some of the most fertile highland areas were underutilized, a situation that could be summed up as "land without people and people without land." The opening of agricultural frontiers came about through the demographic and social dynamics common to rural economies with high population densities. Land colonization was controlled on the economic side by entrepreneurs and politically by local bosses (*gamonales*). Despite these constraints, the process could produce highly fluid societies, with great variation according to ethnic, social, geographical, and ecological conditions. We can distinguish three overall regional forms of land colonization, each with significant internal differentiation.

The colonization associated with the opening of "national lands" tended to combine aspects of violent adventure and commercial enterprise. It was characterized fundamentally by instability, itinerancy, and a strongly masculine ethic. This was the history of the extraction of tagua wood in Chocó and Urabá; quinine in Cauca, Tolima, Caquetá, and Santander; dyewoods on the Atlantic coast; and rubber in Caquetá, Vichada, Putumayo, and on a lesser scale in Tolima. But in demographic terms and for its importance in defining twentieth-century Colombia, the decisive colonization would have to be the coffee-oriented migrations most identified with the smallholder cultivators of the central mountains and the cattle-oriented movements that changed the face of the Caribbean littoral. This lesser-known case deserves a brief aside.

Several factors impeded the takeoff of intensive commercial agriculture on the coast: the climatic cycle, which put much of the region literally underwater for part of the year; the scarcity of labor; and a dispersed population poorly linked by river transportation. The commercial cultivation of tobacco, sugar cane, and bananas and the exploitation of precious woods was carried out in small pockets that were cut off from one another. Cattle raising was the only activity that achieved region-wide importance, and its growth was truly transformative. It spread through all the great river basins, from San Jorge in the west to Cesar in the east, and it linked the ranches to one another and with the interior plains of Corozal. In time it generated important corridors between productive centers and the consumers of the coastal and interior cities, most notably in Antioquia, Caldas, and Santander. The cattle were moved around the region during the course of the year, according to the availability of pastures—from mineral-enriched river shores in the dry season to slightly higher ground during the rainy season.

The three stages in the life cycle of the animals—breeding, raising, and fattening—were managed by three different types of entrepreneurs. As a general rule, breeding was handled by small ranchers while later stages were under the control of larger-scale operators. These were not necessarily large landowners, since the scale of wealth and power, as in other ranching frontiers such as the southwestern United States and Argentina, was a function more of the ownership of cattle than of land. Much of the land was under colonial-era communal titles, as was also the case in the Cauca Valley. The cattle owner would establish a verbal contract, somewhat along sharecropping lines, with one or more members of the communal landholding group. As the commercialization process progressed, these communal lands increasingly fell under individual title and control, and a more complex social structure developed which included genuine cattle *latifundistas*. Each of the three production phases was tied to the next by specialized intermediaries, who according to some accounts received the lion's share of overall profits.

The eastern mountains offered a far different social landscape. The few available statistics suggest that in the second half of the 1800s the purchasing power of wages in the highlands fell by half, at least for such staples as corn, beef, flour, and potatoes. There were many factors behind this deterioration, including demographic pressure, the monopolization of the flattest and most fertile lands, and the dearth of modern technology. The emigration toward the lowlands to the east and west was a matter more of expulsion than of attraction, as the weak economic prospects of these colonization zones were accompanied by the severe health risks (malaria, yellow fever, tropical anemia) associated with newly settled tropical areas.

The flow of land colonizers around the country and the hopes pinned on generous government concessions of mining and land rights to attract foreign investments and loans produced legal reforms to the settlement and titling processes in 1873 and twice more in the subsequent decade. One of the objectives of the legislation was to democratize society by creating small proprietors. Certainly the colonization process accentuated economic individualism and reinforced notions of the inviolability of landed private property, even if the overall result was increased concentrations of landed and mining wealth and of political power. The principal role of the state on the vast agrarian frontier was most often to legalize private land appropriations after the fact. Even so, thousands of families were able to settle on the peripheries, surviving and sometimes even thriving outside of legal processes.

The Civil Code, that wall erected by Napoleon between the power of the state and the rights of individuals to property, was freely interpreted by lawyers (whether credentialed or shyster *tinterillos*) and judges alike. In Colombia, ironically, the Civil Code, which stood as a monument to the end of feudal times, often served to "feudalize" landholding, according to the distinguished Liberal publicist Aníbal Galindo. "Parasites," according to Galindo, managed to appropriate the added value that society and societal progress had brought to previously empty and isolated lands. Nominal contractual liberty, celebrated by liberalism, ended up underwriting feudal obligations. In many rural districts, as late as the 1930s the labor obligations of the rural poor to haciendas were enshrined in civil contracts, complete with threats of punishment supposedly available equally to both parties in the event of the other's noncompliance.

The migrating populations could not escape Colombia's party-political system. The intervention of *gamonales* and parish priests transformed the socioeconomic conflicts around the appropriation of public lands into impassioned partisan rivalries between rural settlements, districts, and *municipios*. The colonizing movements of the post-1850 period reproduced the same processes of conflict and resolution via the political system that were characteristic of regions already settled, but the inevitable issues of initial land titling and the drawing of *municipio* boundaries made the atmosphere even more highly charged. Anyone who wanted to legalize a land claim or settle a boundary dispute needed a political patron. The clientelist party system was thus extended spatially, often (as in the southward movement out of the Antioquian heartland) led by local notables, merchants, and clergy.

Coffee and Colombian Development

Colombia joined the world coffee economy just as coffee consumption was becoming more generalized in Europe and the United States. Despite the rebound of gold and silver mining after 1885, it was coffee that would put Colombia on the international economic map by the end of the century. The product jumped from one-fifth of all Colombian exports by value in the 1870s to one-half in 1898, although the rise of other products pulled that figure back to one-third by 1910. The coffee sector took off and stayed aloft because its product had steady world demand and because it was based on a relative abundance of appropriate land and labor that would otherwise have remained untapped.

Starting with the experience of northern Santander in the 1840s, Colombia's development as a coffee economy followed a series of regional expansions and contractions tied to the cycle of world prices. Until 1906 the global coffee economy had two characteristics that would completely disappear later in the twentieth century: the absolute domination of Brazil and a free market subject to cycles of boom and bust, with price peaks in 1862, 1872, and 1891. But the political economies of Colombia's regions and the roles played by institutional arrangements regarding labor and credit were at least as important. For example, during the downturns large coffee estates were poorly positioned in comparison with small and medium cultivators.

Coffee haciendas anticipated the rise of the coffee era, rather than arose from it. Their initial development and consolidation were made possible by the relative cheapness of land and other setup expenses, such as paying the original land colonizers for their improvements. As the first harvest approached, some four or five years after a coffee plot was sown, hacendados would take out loans from English, French, or U.S. mercantile houses at lower rates of interest than were available locally. They were thus able to finance the purchase and installation of machinery and infrastructure for processing the harvested beans. During the last third of the nineteenth century some six hundred haciendas were established, and their organization varied more over regions than over time. But in all regions, ordinary wage labor was rare.

One common element was the urban and merchant origins of the new hacendados, who could hardly have been more different from their workers, resident or seasonal. In relatively homogeneous regions such as Santander and Antioquia, the semiservile arrangements common in Cundinamarca and Tolima were rare. In these latter regions, resident families on haciendas took on specified obligations in exchange for the use of a piece of land on which to grow food. These obligations were an important factor of differentiation among the rural poor and were a form of intermediation between the haciendas hacendado and rural labor.

Haciendas spread coffee cultivation, but they soon formed islands in a sea of small and medium producers. As in Venezuela after independence, coffee in Santander and later in western Colombia was based on those smaller producers. The coffee economy widened markets for land and labor, and spawned a thicket of new labor and commercial arrangements specified by contract. Whether on haciendas or on smaller properties, coffee maintained the labor and consumption structures of the late colonial period in that the tasks of planting, maintenance, and harvesting of coffee were based on the family unit, which produced its own food.

Locomotives and Progress

Colombia's road network was little improved since before independence, and goods circulated on the backs of horses, mules, donkeys, or even oxen. Time had little economic value, and was measured in days or weeks rather than smaller increments. Poverty also limited mobility, and most people were born, worked, and died within a few square kilometers. Possession of pack animals was as good an indication as any of one's place in the social stratification: in the countryside around Bogotá in the late 1880s, a good riding horse could cost as much as 750 days' wages for a rural worker.

The growing volume of imports convinced the elite that steam transportation had to make the leap from the Magdalena River (where it had existed since the 1820s) to the mountains: without railways to complement steamships, Colombian exports would never achieve comparative advantage. Before, during, and since this period, the tonnage of Colombia's imports has equaled or exceeded its exports (excluding petroleum). But coffee pressured local governments to improve roads and trails, and it created a sustained demand for mules, which in turn created jobs in the establishment and maintenance of pastures and cane fields for the animals' sustenance. Coffee also promised that railroads would have something to carry outbound to ports, rather than just hauling imported goods to the population centers of the interior. This was, however, a slow process: as late as 1930, tonnage for internal markets was a large share of the total carried.

Starting in the 1870s the railroad was widely touted in Colombia as the panacea for national development and as the icon of modernity, although the coming of the motor vehicle in the 1920s would dethrone it to some extent. Even more than the long-established steamships of the Cauca and Magdalena rivers, the railroad was the very image of the new, the potent, and the transformative. When the head of the Cúcuta Railroad reported to Bogotá the successful test of their first locomotive in 1879, his telegram ended with "Long Live Progress!" A few years later, on the brink of the 1884–85 civil war, the first rails fabricated by the steel mill of La Pradera in Cundinamarca were covered with the national flag and paraded down the streets of Bogotá. The pomp was appropriate, given President Rafael Núñez's favorite saying: "Peace and railroads—the rest is quackery." The sentiment could have come from Manuel Murillo Toro or any other politician of the era.

From the 1870s on, the construction of short rail lines down to the Magdalena was the development imperative of all governments. Faced with the shortage of private capital, the state at all levels responded with direct investment in private firms or through development schemes such as the deeding of public lands and the granting of miscellaneous privileges to foreign investors. But governments of all stripes failed to set national priorities for the rail network. The widths of the tracks, the locomotive and carriage types, and overall engineering quality varied from section to section. Colombia's broken geography and difficult soils increased construction and maintenance costs. To these natural elements were added civil unrest and sudden changes in regional and local governments, which led to the suspension or alteration in subsidies, tariffs, and concessions to contractors and entrepreneurs. All of the inputs for railway construction were imported, except for grading stones and the wooden crosspieces for the rails; and at least at the outset, all of the technical personnel were foreigners. Any overall accounting should include the costs of government subsidies to operators, the foreign debt incurred on some projects, and the remittance of profits and interest payments abroad; while on the benefits side the import/export sector received a boost, and land values increased in railway-influenced regions.

The railway era reinforced the importance of the Magdalena River as the national artery, uniting the Andean interior with the Caribbean and thus with the world. On the coast, the longstanding rivalry between Santa Marta and Cartagena for dominance over the Atlantic trade continued, but Barranquilla began to assert its natural advantage as a genuine nexus between the Magdalena and the sea. In 1870 the town overcame the sandbar that obstructed direct access to the sea by building a short railway to Sabanilla, a fishing village that until then had been accessible only by a canal navigable by small canoes. This was enough to displace Santa Marta, which between 1850 and 1871 had handled 80 percent of Colombian imports and exports. Once a second rail line was completed, this time to a deeper port at Puerto Colombia to the west, Barranquilla was assured of an enduring regional hegemony as a transport and commercial hub, consigning the traditional centers to secondary status. Cartagena would need another thirty years to reach the Magdalena by rail line to the river port of Calamar (part of a project to replace the semiabandoned Dique Canal), while Santa Marta never recovered its importance as a national port and functioned mostly as entrepôt for the developing United Fruit Company's banana enclave.

The laying of telegraph lines followed a different logic, in that rather than connecting producing and consuming regions to ports, the lines radiated from the national capital to all regions regardless of economic importance. The first line was inaugurated in 1865, and within ten years three networks extended from Bogotá to Antioquia, Cauca, and the Atlantic coast. As late as 1920, news traveled from one end of the country to the other in minutes while a load of coffee might require as many as ten transfers between its point of production and a seaport, and a traveler might spend two to four weeks traveling from Bogotá to an outlying city such as Medellín, Buenaventura, or Cúcuta.

The State: Taxation without Representation, Representation without Taxation

The republican state had never been able to ensure political stability since the day it was founded. Parties and factions battled to control perennially bankrupt national administrations. Various levels of government sought to gain rights of taxation over a poor and dispersed population. The rural poor, who were the vast majority of Colombians, were with few exceptions immune to the democratic virus (as many conservative critics considered it to be), and their daily lives were ruled by custom, religious belief, and inherited notions of deference and hierarchy.

As during the colonial period, the political struggle took place largely in the urban centers, whose elite was composed of importers, bankers, and merchants. Importers, generally indebted to foreign suppliers, paid their debts in gold, coffee, and quinine. Their position seemed enviable enough: their highly profitable operations were largely insulated from direct social conflict, they served a vital consumer need, and they were major taxpayers to a state with limited ability to extract revenue. Bankers (in the absence of a solid banking system, a better word might be financiers) speculated in government debt paper or bonds supposedly backed by public lands, which the government had used since independence to pay its bills and reward its friends. Merchants frequently were miners, ranchers, urban land speculators, hacendados in the new coffee zones, owners of mule teams, or shareholders in Magdalena steamship companies. Their investments were quite diversified and tightly integrated, given the family character of their business organizations and the small size of the overall capitalist market.

Cities were also home to male artisans (rural craftwork, as noted earlier, being largely a female enterprise within the family unit), many of whom operated small shops and were tied both mentally and materially to the world of property. Their conflicts with importers were not direct, in the manner of workers versus bosses in a workshop, but rather were mediated by the tariff issue, that is, by politics. All of these groups, by the mid-1800s, shared the same political universe of Liberal versus Conservative.

The fragility of public administration can be explained largely by the government's inability to extract taxes from the wealthy, who were able to restrict full citizenship to a narrow range of electors while extending taxation to all Colombians. In early Colombia, as everywhere in Latin America and in much of Europe as well, the principle of "no taxation without representation" was stood on its head: the overwhelming majority of inhabitants saw their political rights cut back even as their taxes supported a state that looked after the interests of the wealthy. It proved impossible to replace the colonial-era system of indirect taxation, although the relative weight of the most important revenue sources, such as import duties and the salt monopoly, did change. Together the taxes produced by these sources exceeded the combined income of all the provinces.

Import duties fell principally upon products of mass consumption, most notably cotton textiles. An official publication of 1888 offered an example of how the system had become even more inequitable since mid-century. The typical textile needs of a lower-class woman might include a few yards of flannel and percale of ordinary quality for dresses and a couple of sheets, with a total cost approaching ten months' wages for a washerwoman, fifteen months' wages for a lowland rural laborer, and two years' income for a vendor of firewood or charcoal in the streets of Bogotá. Of the purchase price, fully half went to taxes of various sorts, mainly duties. Until the reform of 1880, tariffs were figured in general categories and were based on weight rather than value, so that the products favored by the wealthy, such as linens and silks, paid only one-third as much by value as did cruder textiles. Of course, the prevalence of contraband demonstrated the limits of the state's authority in this regard and set practical limits to tariff levels. Many fortunes, both before and after independence, had their origins in this parallel import economy.

The salt monopoly was the second leg of the national state's revenues at mid-century, its share roughly comparable to that of the tariffs. But the growth in foreign trade after mid-century changed that proportion dramatically, and by the coffee boom years of 1885 through 1896 salt revenues accounted for barely 10 percent of the total. The salt monopoly, which was notoriously hard to administer, was the source of frequent disputes between local governments (usually where the salt was produced, whether it came from the sea or was mined) and the national government. Colombia's top administrative tribunal reported in 1889 that since 1823 170 national laws on the salt tax had been issued, and 89 of them were still in effect.

Administrative decentralization, an important aspect of the politically central-ist constitution of 1886, ceded to the departments (successors of the "sovereign states" of the previous federal regime) income from distilled spirits, tobacco, cattle slaughter, road and bridge tolls, and other sources of regional signifi-cance, such as mining in Antioquia and sea salt in Magdalena. The history of the liquor monopoly in Colombia is one of provincial political corruption. It was administered through a direct state production monopoly or by the issuing of production licenses to individuals. Almost all the states, and then depart-ments, eventually chose the license system, which became the basis for extended patronage networks. In practice, the auction system for licenses was a farce, as the bidders agreed beforehand on how the licenses would be allocated. As the system became increasingly important to regional revenues, the government's implicit interest in the growth of consumption encouraged alcoholism.

Post-1886 centralism bore the brunt of the blame for the growing fiscal defi-cit and for the conflicts over how to apportion the national budget. The na-tional state assumed the cost of transportation development and education. It also handled the judicial system, payment of compensation for seized church property under the 1887 Concordat with the Vatican, and foreign debt service. Centralization transferred from the regional to the national level the responsibility for funding security forces, prisons, and the electoral system. The national army, previously a skeletal force, was equipped with modern armaments and its numbers rose to 6,500 in peacetime, rapidly reaching 9,500 at the outbreak of civil war in 1899.

Public finances never broke out of the straitjacket of independence-era debt. Between 1826 and 1844 that debt was in default, and after a renegotiation in 1845 that produced a system of payment in government bonds, Colombia again started to skip payments in the early 1850s. From 1879 to 1896 the country was again in default, and while coffee prosperity permitted a renegotiation that substantially lowered the country's repayment obligations, civil war and a downturn in coffee prices after 1900 led to more late and missed payments. Given this record, Colombia was relegated to marginal status in the burgeoning global capital markets of the last third of the nineteenth century. Only after 1905 would Colombia establish a record—now impressive in the Latin American context—for timely repayment of debts.

Public spending presents a similar picture. After the high costs of debt service, the military, and revenue collection itself, the amounts destined for transportation, education, and the administration of justice were quite small. Investment in transportation modernization was largely British, with a lesser amount from the United States. Only well into the twentieth century can we identify any impact of public spending in overall economic growth and income distribution.

Clientelist Tribulations of the Radicals' Colombia

In the euphoria of fiscal and commercial prosperity at the start of the 1870s, Colombia's Radical Liberal rulers were confident in their access to foreign funding to modernize the country's infrastructure. In this regard their practice of laissez-faire and decentralist doctrines were in obvious contradiction: the task had to be undertaken by the public sector rather than by private enterprise, and it was a matter for the national government rather than local or regional governments. But liberal doctrine was selectively employed, and it could be centralist according to circumstances—especially when it came to favoring the import-export sector. The official plan was to emphasize one rail line, the Ferrocarril del Norte, which would unite Bogotá with Bucaramanga and from there down to the Magdalena. This route favored the strongholds of the Radical faction of the ruling Liberals, and opposing Liberals in other regions (especially Cauca and the Caribbean coast) used it against the Radicals in the hard-fought 1875 election, which marked the beginning of the end of Radical rule.

The presidential elections that year pitted two opposing Liberal candidates against each other, as the Conservatives followed their usual practice of abstention. The Radical (government) candidate, Aquileo Parra, a Santander merchant—frugal, meticulous, and a backer of the Ferrocarril del Norte—faced Rafael Núñez, a politician and intellectual from Cartagena. Núñez was the leader of coastal regionalist opposition to the Santander-dominated "Radical Olympus," and his candidacy was embraced by disaffected Liberals in Cauca and elsewhere in the country. Under the 1863 constitution the president was elected by majority vote of the states; when the elections were annulled in Cauca and deadlock resulted in a draw in Cundinamarca and Panama, however, the Radical majority in the Congress predictably voted for Parra. But the Radicals were fatally weakened, and Núñez consolidated his leadership of the so-called Independent coalition against them.

From the 1860s on, the Radicals had sought to fine-tune electoral legislation to permit manipulation of the results. At the *municipio* level party identity was already integral to local identity, to a feeling of belonging to a shared lineage and community. In some regions party identity had a more identifiably social cast determined by race and class, as with the black and mulatto Liberals of Gran Cauca, Panama, the Caribbean coast, and the Magdalena lowlands. Party and class also converged in the case of Bogotá's artisans, and in some towns of the eastern mountains and Panama. If in the major cities the parties at least sought to define doctrinal differences, in the small towns and countryside the struggle for votes was based on networks of family, friendship, and even godparentage, often in the context of local rivalries that predated the republic.

Voting, it must be noted, had a more precise calendar than civil wars, and a higher level of participation. In Bogotá and its surrounding state of Cundinamarca, genuine political machines were forged by Ramón Gómez (known as El Sapo, "The Frog") and later by Daniel Aldana, based on the saying that "he who counts the votes chooses the winner." They were envied by politicians elsewhere in the country, even as they produced contempt for formal politics among other segments of the elite. The philologist Rufino José Cuervo wrote to the poet Rafael Pombo:

Only once in my life have I voted, back when Aldana was governor of Cundinamarca. They said the box where I put my ballot had a Conservative majority, so the mayor, Garay, came in with four constables, took the box, and dumped it in the creek at the north corner of the cathedral before the vote-counting began. I haven't voted since, but in my conscience and in my circle of friends, and even in my blindness, I will continue to vote as long as I am alive, against violence and the insults of those in power, no matter in what capacity they exercise that power.[1]

Liberals, who earlier (around 1850) were strong supporters of universal male suffrage, came to argue after 1863 that restrictions were needed to avoid manipulation of the votes of the poor by priests and hacendados. In Liberal-dominated states literacy requirements were reinstated, while Conservative-dominated states, ironically, embraced universal male suffrage. Each state enjoyed unlimited autonomy when it came to the electoral calendar, and as noted earlier, each state cast one vote for national president regardless of population: Boyacá had five times the population of Magdalena, but each had the same nominal weight in choosing a president. Presidential voting at the state level took place over a six-month period, further weakening presidential power in a system that established two-year terms with no reelection, and greatly limited the powers of the national government in general.

The expansion of suffrage at mid-century had been a two-edged sword. It offered artisans the chance to mobilize in defense of their interests within the system, and it encouraged them as well as other urban groups—even the elites—to polish their skills of political compromise. On the other hand, it promoted and entrenched clientelism in the countryside. The growing electoral rolls and growing political consciousness, at least for some, were not matched by institutional development. Under such conditions, an increase in political violence was not a surprising outcome. In similar contexts the world over, elections were based not on individuals' rational and voluntary choices but on collective demonstrations of symbolic belonging—rites of identity.

Until well into the twentieth century, in much of Colombia (even in politically peaceful regions such as the Caribbean coast) people would come to the polls on election day in large groups, shouting their *vivas* and *abajos*; insults, threats, and scuffles with knife and machete were part of the local election-day routine when voters from rural districts of opposing partisan identities came into contact. Individuals were subsumed into their respective collectivities, de-

1 Epistolario de Ángel y Rufino José Cuervo con Rafael Pombo, ed. M. G. Romero (Bogotá, 1974), 297.

personalizing themselves and their adversaries, thus increasing the chances of violent conflict. The person you were attacking was not someone you knew by name but simply the *rojo* (Liberal), the *godo* (Conservative), or simply the *forastero* (the outsider, politically defined).

Registering to vote was actually a more contentious process than voting itself. One's ability to read and write or to meet a required level of wealth or income was not a matter that lent itself to calm and objective determination. Collective action had to be used to pressure election boards. Both Liberals and Conservatives pursued strategies to keep adversaries off the electoral rolls, to keep them away from the polls, and to discount their votes once they were cast. From these practices to outright civil war was often just a short step. Almost all the state-level insurrections during the federal period came out of electoral disputes; an alleged vote fraud in Santander triggered the national civil war of 1885, which put an end to federalism altogether. In 1899, the Senate's rejection of an electoral reform law was one of the precipitants of the War of the Thousand Days.

Embryonic forms of democratic representation may have emanated from Bogotá, but many *municipios* were simply petty dictatorships. Throughout the countryside elections and wars alike pitted *municipios*, hamlets, and families against each other. This sectarianism lasted over a century and extended upward into the heavens: the inhabitants of a remote mestizo town in the Sierra Nevada of Santa Marta, interrogated in the 1950s by the anthropologists Gerardo and Alicia Reichel-Dolmatoff, reported that the Virgin Mary, St. Rafael, and St. Anthony were Conservatives, while the Sacred Heart of Jesus and St. Martin of Loba were Liberals.

Wars for the Soul of the Nation

Public lay education was one of the Liberals' most venerated causes. In 1867 they reorganized the National University, giving it the mission of spreading knowledge to the people, developing scientific understanding, and changing traditional teaching methods. Despite the rhetoric, the university ended up training professionals for a tiny market: physicians for the elite, engineers for mining and modern transportation, and lawyers to provide a few judges and counselors to handle the relatively simple cases that Colombian society produced. Perhaps more important was the institution's implicit function, to train the political elite in modern (and imported) discourse, concepts, and methods of understanding Colombian reality.

The Liberals' most important objective was to reform primary and secondary education. The reform law of 1870 established a public education system that was to be "secular, humanitarian, and based on scientific principles." Education was to be the province of the national government, and school attendance would be obligatory for children between the ages of 6 and 14. The teaching of Catholicism was excluded from the curriculum. Teacher training schools were created in each state, directed by German educators (most of them Protestant) brought to Colombia for the purpose, who would give them a modern orientation and provide a large corps of qualified teachers spread throughout the country. In response to the program, Catholic Societies sprang up, determined to prevent the application of the reforms; the bishops of Popayán, Pasto, and Pamplona made opposition to the Liberal educational program a crusade. Whereas the archbishop of Bogotá was willing to accept Aquileo Parra's commitment that Catholic instruction could be provided in public schools outside the official curriculum, most provincial bishops were not. In Antioquia and Cauca the religious struggle joined with regionalist sentiments and agendas to justify recourse to war. For the clergy, the struggle between church and state over the education of young Colombians was a matter of political sovereignty. The education of young Colombians was legitimately the province of the church, not the state. They relied on the *Syllabus* of Pius IX (1864), which condemned liberalism, secularism, religious toleration, freedom of thought, and lay education.

The 1870 reform was thwarted in the end by a combination of socioeconomic and political factors. The former included the geographical dispersion of the population, the lack of funding for school construction and teacher training, and the German teachers' departure when their contracts expired. On the political side, the Radicals thought that the best response to the church's fanatical opposition was an equally rigid anticlericalism—as if in the Colombia of 1870 it would be possible to construct a massive system of public education without the church's agreement. (In the Concordat of 1887, one of the early priorities of the subsequent Regeneration regime, the Vatican accepted public education only after its secular orientation had been scuttled.)

It has been said that the civil war of 1876 had clear religious underpinnings. But in addition to the conflict with the clergy, the Parra government faced a well-organized opposition movement in Cauca and the coast, made up of groups angered by the single-minded push for the Ferrocarril del Norte. Division among Liberals allowed the Conservatives to reenter the political picture, from which they had been marginalized after their defeat in the 1860–63 civil war. But when they sought to recover power in the 1876–77 civil war, even the most bitterly opposed Liberal factions reconciled long enough to defeat them.

This war had characteristics in common with others of the nineteenth century. As in the past, the ability of both sides to recruit, arm, and deploy armies was impressive given Colombian conditions. When the conflict broke out, the national army controlled by the Liberal regime had only 1,255 soldiers, but within three months the government could field 30,000 men. We can assume that this was not a very disciplined army, of course, and such quick action required outlays that exceeded the entire annual national budget. The conflict lasted eleven months and was fought principally in Cauca and Tolima. The clergy of the Cauca towns of Palmira, Cartago, and Tuluá led the antireform campaign that preceded the war, a campaign that was intertwined with social and racial tensions in the region. Liberal troops, predominantly black and mulatto, destroyed property and attacked prominent Conservatives, particularly during the occupation and sacking of Cali on Christmas Eve in 1876.

Regional political situations varied considerably. While in 1877 the Liberal regime in Santander passed anticlerical legislation that led to the exiling of the bishop of Pamplona and the arrest of disaffected parish priests, in the Conservative-run state of Antioquia—whose clergy were among the principal instigators of the conflict—the state government preferred to stand down, even ceding the state presidency to a Radical from outside the state rather than turn its territory into a battleground.

But if the clergy and the Conservatives had to pay a high price for their defeat in 1877, there was also a settling of scores among Liberals. The Radicals' intransigence gave rise to an ever-stronger reaction in the form of Independents, who rallied around the battlefield prestige of the Cauca general Julián Trujillo, elected to the national presidency in 1878. The real winner was Rafael Núñez of Cartagena, and Trujillo worked loyally for him during his two-year term, even attracting some Conservative support. Once Núñez achieved the presidency, as he was bound to do, in 1880, he further infuriated the Radicals by naming Conservatives to important posts, a gesture that opened the door to a more generalized political alliance.

Like most of his fellow politicians, Núñez had entered politics during the high point of liberal effervescence at mid-century. At the age of 30 he was already president of the lower house of Congress, and his bad blood with the Radicals dated to that early period; as a backer of José María Obando, a Liberal impeached by the Radical majority in Congress in 1855, he was passed over for the Rionegro constituent assembly that wrote the 1863 constitution. Instead he went that year to New York, where he could take in the spectacle of the U.S. Civil War, brought about by the conflict between states' and national rights, and he surely noted how Abraham Lincoln was financing the war by issuing paper money over the objections of many bankers and most economic theorists. He then went on to take up the post of consul in Le Havre and later in Liverpool, among the highest-paid jobs in the Colombian consular service (as his enemies noted). He returned in 1874.

During his time in Europe Núñez cultivated his literary side, and refined and tempered his social and political thinking under the influence of Herbert Spencer. His journalistic writings gave him the aura of a deep thinker, and from his return to Colombia until his death in 1894 he was the most influential figure in national politics. Shortly after he became president in 1880, he managed to get what Parra could not: a $3 million loan, which he earmarked for establishing the National Bank and for funding projects that had been postponed when tobacco revenues fell after 1875, with the aim of securing regional support. Since the loan was not enough, he took on substantial internal debt, which by 1882 drove Colombia's budget deficit to new highs.

It is hard to say exactly when Núñez gave up his commitment to secularism. In the early 1880s the Independents still considered the Regeneration, Núñez's government program (promoted in newspaper articles later collected in book form), to be an "inevitable phase" in the maturation of Colombian liberalism. But during the presidencies of Francisco Javier Zaldúa and José Eusebio Otálora (1882–84), Núñez forged ever deeper alliances with leading Conservatives, and the Radicals' not-give-an-inch ideology accelerated the process. He became convinced that liberalism's core beliefs and institutions, such as continued veneration of Jeremy Bentham's utilitarianism and an exhausting deadlock between the executive and the legislature, were responsible for the country's instability. His election to a second term (1884–86) was the final blow to Liberal unity, and culminated in the civil war of 1885.

Like the conflict of 1876–77, this was a short war. The rebels in this case were the Radicals, who first took up arms against the Independent Liberal government in Santander, which they accused of electoral fraud; although they agreed to a compromise after mediation by the central government, it was short-lived and the rebels crossed the border into Boyacá. Hostilities soon broke out in Cundinamarca and on the Magdalena, and in Cartagena and Barranquilla, whose customs revenues were vital to government and rebels alike. By November 1884 the entire country was in rebellion, but Núñez's formal request for Conservative support was still surprising to all sides, given Colombia's partisan history. Within nine months, the new Independent-Conservative alliance crushed the Radical rebellion and left the field clear for Núñez to implement his Regeneration program fully.

Fundamentals of the Regeneration

The Regeneration was a curious and unique program by Latin American standards, combining as it did principles of economic liberalism, state intervention along the lines of the eighteenth-century Bourbon colonial administrations, an antimodernism identified with Pius IX, and Hispanophile cultural nationalism. The economic liberalism was expressed in the opening to foreign investment, the development of mining and railroads, and the assigning of state lands to export agriculture interests. What we might call "Neo-Bourbonism" (a term coined by the historian Frank Safford for Colombian economic thinking of the 1830s) was expressed in measures to raise government revenues, modernize the army, create a central bank with the exclusive power to issue paper money, and protect artisanship within a paternalistic framework.

The Regeneration constitution of 1886, strongly influenced by the constitution of the restored Spanish monarchy of 1876, endured until 1991 — with over fifty revisions, some of them significant. The document reflected not only Núñez's emphases but also those of Miguel Antonio Caro, son of one of the founders of the Conservative party. A grammarian, classicist, teacher, and bookstore owner, Caro entered public life in the 1870s as editor of the Catholic newspaper *El Tradicionista*. He was never a rich man, and he left Bogotá's highland plateau only twice in his life — and then briefly. He considered himself part of a tradition in which belief was worth more than economic success and learning was privileged over material things. Like the hardened realist Núñez, the eccentric Caro had never taken up any weapon other than a pen, and together they conceived of new institutions and a conservative order that they could never manage to establish.

The 1886 constitution was centralist more in its strengthening of the presidency at the expense of the legislature than in its strengthening of the national government at the expense of the regions. It promoted the temporal power of the church and paved the way for a half-century of Conservative regimes of various hues. It restricted individual liberties, and both the size and the iconoclastic vitality of the Colombian press went into decline. The broadsheets and often irresponsible newspapers that flourished during the federal period were supplanted by obtuse religious titles. Núñez and Caro, two men fresh from the "republic of letters," used the idea of a "responsible press" to close avenues of expression to their opponents, with variable success. Authoritarian values replaced liberal ultra-individualism. One orthodoxy took the place of another, but the Regeneration's form of cronyism was more exclusivist and voracious because it enjoyed greater fiscal resources.

The Regeneration project of unifying the state sowed profound discord in the heart of society. Its propagandists glorified Simón Bolívar as the standard-bearer of Colombian nationality and as the inspiration behind the 1886 constitution—the "authoritarian republic," as Caro himself called it. The hero of independence, in this rendering, ended his days disenchanted with the parties he identified with petty factionalism and pining for strongmen at the helm of the new states of Latin America. While the Bolívar cult had a strong bipartisan basis—within the Liberal party Mosquera had always defended him against the attacks of the Gólgotas, precursors of the Radicals—the founding father as reinvented by Núñez and Caro was the strongman of the Bolivian constitution of 1826 and the 1829 dictatorship in New Granada (the future Colombia, Venezuela, and Ecuador), two contentious episodes in a highly varied public life that also had strongly progressive episodes.

The Regeneration vision did succeed in ratifying a historical understanding of Colombia's eras as defined by political leaders: Bolívar in the initial phase, Núñez as the leader for the mature phase. Society was now mature enough to accept and even relish these lay myths. So as not to subvert the Hispanophile cultural focus of the Regeneration, the struggle for independence was presented as a continuation of the Spanish civil war of the 1810s and 1820s, fought on Latin American soil. Núñez revised his own earlier thinking on Colombian history: without writing Bolívar's liberal rival and fellow independence hero Francisco de Paula Santander out of the picture, he depicted a glorified Bolívar as creator of an institutional order thrown into limbo by the liberal experiments of 1850 through 1880. Seen in this light, the Regeneration was merely a return to normal.

The "sovereign states" were turned into departments, with governors named by the president of the republic, and the governors in turn named mayors. Other changes under the 1886 constitution included the extension of the presidential term to six years (later shortened to four) and the establishment of a series of special powers that the legislature could grant to the president apart from the extraordinary powers that accompanied any declaration of a state of siege. The president could make lifetime appointments to the Supreme Court and to the higher regional tribunals from short lists presented by the Court. Transitional provisions, such as the notorious Article K, which established press censorship, became permanent. A law passed in 1888 gave the president wide judicial powers to confront threats to order and property—the "Horse Law," so called because a spate of killings of mules and horses in Palmira, a Cauca town that was the scene of disorders around 1850 and again in the 1870s, was blamed on a Liberal conspiracy.

This new presidential power was exercised in a political and administrative setting in which momentary coalitions were the norm. For example, the appointments of governors depended on the correlation of political factions in the Congress and in departmental assemblies. But even institutions that the Constitution did not envisage as political were treated as such, including the National Bank, a powerful tool used by the national government to neutralize, co-opt, or reduce the opposition of merchant elites in the provinces, and later to defeat armed Liberal uprisings. Congress met only once every two years, and so became even weaker against the permanently operating executive branch.

The Constitution recognized the existence of other religions but embraced Catholicism as the cornerstone of Colombian nationality and social order. Through the Concordat of 1887 as amended in 1892, the church took control of the civil registry, supervision of education, and control of cemeteries; the *fuero eclesiástico*, the separate legal sphere and partial immunity for clergy which existed in the colonial and early republican periods, was reinstated. One immediate effect was the annulment of the legal consequences of prior civil marriages conducted without a corresponding Catholic rite, although the children produced by such marriages were not deemed illegitimate. Many firebrand Radicals of the 1850s and 1860s had no choice but to receive the sacrament of marriage without fanfare. Catholic patriarchy would get its due in the reformed Civil Code, with its distinction between legitimate and illegitimate ("natural") children, the husband's automatic guardianship of children, and the reduction of the wife's legal status to that of a minor in key areas such as control of property, the exercise of a profession, and even choice of residence.

The goal of the new constitution was to establish a disciplinarian state and to strengthen its authority by such measures as capital punishment (which had been abolished under the Liberals), a ban on selling or even carrying arms (a huge cultural change from prior regimes, whatever the party), and restrictions on freedom of the press and other individual liberties. The 1863 and 1885 constitutions were both written by victorious wartime coalitions. The losers were left without a say in the process, and were thus predisposed to turn to resistance—and neither the Radical nor the Regeneration regime had the military force or fiscal resiliency to strengthen its authority. These documents, whether inspired by the example of France, the United States, or Spain, would produce the "republics of air" that Simón Bolívar had predicted.

Paper Money and Political Centralism

Regeneration economic policy was largely a continuation of the previous era's, but both supporters and opponents sought to exaggerate the differences. Some modest foreign investment flowed into the mines, railways, and sugar and banana plantations. There was, to be sure, a renunciation of pure laissez-faire through the issuance of paper money (accompanied by the all-important legal requirement that it be accepted on a par with precious metals—the *curso forzoso* decried by Radicals) and increases in import duties to protect urban artisans. The Regeneration maintained the hectic pace of privatization of public lands, almost half a million hectares a year, 90 percent of which went in large concessions. Radicals and Regenerators contributed equally to the creation of a new *latifundismo*, which in the twentieth century would become a source of social polarization and violence.

For some historians the disagreements between a free-trading internationalist faction and a closed-minded and retrograde elite are mirrored faithfully in the factional alignments of the period. In this interpretation, Radical Liberals and the so-called Historical Conservatives lined up on the progressive side while Independent Liberals and Nationalist Conservatives were the reactionaries. Some also argue that Núñez's protectionism and his emphasis on paper money issued by a national bank planted the seed for industrialization as part of a nationalist development project. But the level of economic interventionism during the Regeneration was modest in comparison with contemporary cases such as Mexico under Porfirio Díaz and Chile under José Balmaceda. This was due in part to the proverbial weakness of the Colombian state and in part to the instability of Colombia's export composition and revenue in the second half of the nineteenth century. The Regeneration's attitude toward foreign capital was one of total openness, and the government made special concessions for investors in mining, railways, and export agriculture. Although Colombian exports were marginal within Latin America's overall picture, with a growth rate far below those of such countries as Argentina, Brazil, Chile, and Mexico, during this period direct foreign investment increased.

In 1887 the state mining code of Antioquia, regarded favorably by British investors, was adopted nationally. It helped to guarantee a modest but constant flow of British technology and capital, which revived silver mining in Tolima and strengthened gold mining in Antioquia. To address foreign firms' worries, in the 1890s President Miguel Antonio Caro changed the mining law by decree in order to move decisions on potentially sensitive matters from the *municipio* to the department level, where governors directly appointed by Bogotá could oversee them. This was also the era of the arrival in Colombia of the precursor of the United Fruit Company; of the creation, with U.S. capital, of the large sugar mills of the Cauca Valley; of the concessions to exploit precious woods on the Caribbean coast; and of the expansion of railways begun in the 1870s. To clean up Colombia's image in the stock and bond markets of London and Paris, the government also renegotiated its foreign debt.

Protectionism was largely about raising government revenues, since by the time of the Regeneration relatively little was left to protect. Duties were not readjusted for inflation, and they did not compensate for the long-term fall in the prices of imported manufactures, especially cotton textiles. The tariff changes of 1880 and 1902 did not prevent the final collapse of Santander's textile sector, but woolen production in Boyacá and Gran Cauca, as well as some types of urban crafts, managed to hold on.

The paper money initiative was to Regeneration politics what education reform was to the Radicals: a tool for increasing the ruling group's power. The debate was not about whether currency should circulate—that was settled around 1880—but rather about a government monopoly (via a national bank) versus unrestricted issuance by private banks. For a quarter-century the debate went on, a mixture of economic theory and party rhetoric. Supporters of the Regeneration saw the currency monopoly and *curso forzoso* as instruments for consolidating political authority and weakening the de facto federalism of a commercial oligarchy based on family networks in Colombia's major regions. They could cite in support of their case the opposition of these clans, especially those in Bogotá, Medellín, Cartagena, Barranquilla, and Cúcuta, whose banks financed and controlled the country's internal and external credit.

In 1887 the limit for paper money put in circulation was set at $12 million, and this became Regeneration dogma to the point where a scandal over "clandestine issuances" over the limit led to the reorganization of the National Bank. During the brief civil war of 1895 and the prolonged war of 1899–1902, the bank was the government's most important instrument for financing the military effort, through the raising of forced loans. Private businesses showed great flexibility in dealing with the new institutional situation, moving money around even during wartime via short-term letters of credit out of reach of the official sector.

It has been suggested that paper money stimulated coffee exports, but there is little evidence to support the idea. Caro believed that there was some connection between paper money and accumulation of wealth by coffee growers, who were largely though by no means exclusively Liberal, and he sought without much success to tax coffee exports to derive some official revenue from that accumulation. But coffee expansion and profits were almost exclusively the products of very high world coffee prices between 1886 and 1896, combined with low wages, which were responsive only to Colombia's permanently depressed labor market.

On the other hand, inflation caused by issues of paper money caused a sharp rise in internal transportation costs. These costs were an important component of the total cost of producing and exporting coffee and more than outweighed any advantages from devaluation. Between 1896 and 1899 the world price of coffee fell by 48 percent from 1889–91 levels, while internal transportation costs (in foreign currency terms) went up by 50 percent. But the central point is a matter of business organization: nobody was solely a coffee exporter. Exporters did business in many areas, and they were almost always importers as well; they did all their business in gold or gold-based currencies and were constantly in debt, so that the exports of one year paid for the following year's imports. Even if they had derived some benefit from the devaluation caused by issues of paper money, those benefits would have been canceled out in the overall picture. By the late 1890s most coffee growers and merchants of both parties were staunchly against Regeneration economics.

The Social Question Is Political

In 1880 it was reported that 3,000 of Medellín's 37,000 inhabitants were wandering the streets without housing or regular meals. This was the crux of the social question, and in the old artisanal centers which lost prominence during the Radical period the situation was especially worrying. Urban voters, except in Antioquia, tended to vote Liberal and were a constant worry to Conservatives. Declining living standards and fear of falling into the ranks of the very poor led some artisans, though by no means all, to consider rebellion along lines vaguely inspired by the struggles of the mid–nineteenth century or the iconography of the French Revolution: liberty, equality, fraternity.

Several towns figured prominently on the map of Colombian political radicalism, among them Bogotá; the Santander towns of Socorro, San Gil, and Bucaramanga; Barranquilla and Cartagena on the Caribbean Coast; and Popayán in the southwest. In these towns between one-fifth and one-fourth of the economically active male population were artisans, and from time to time their liberal vocabulary acquired a life of its own, full of subversive metaphors and allegories. Whatever the electoral system, in the late 1800s artisans voted in large numbers, and in times of civil war they took up arms at higher rates than other social groups. Grouped in artisan-dominated neighborhoods, they created a distinctive style, symbols, and attitudes. Their weekly meetings, as well as newspapers and broadsheets, provided stable leadership, and their electoral weight made them an attractive audience for ambitious politicians and clerics who fought for their favor; Núñez, for instance, was eager to balance the free-trade elite with artisans' votes.

The narrowly sectoral goals of most artisans constrained their utopian political visions. They sought tariff protection to keep them in the local market, targeting specific politicians only when tax or tariff policies identified with those figures threatened their livelihoods. In exercising their suffrage artisans enlarged the ranks of the two existing parties, which set little value on their dreams of a more egalitarian society. The themes and proposals put forward in their newspapers usually were modest and defensive rather than insurrectionary. In short, while they did consider themselves to be a class opposed to the wealthy and powerful and to "oligarchic" politicians, as individuals many aspired to join that realm. Alongside the currents associated with Liberal traditions, during the 1870s many mutual aid societies emerged. These apolitical associations employed a sometimes confused language of "Christian socialism" within a Conservative discursive tradition, and continued as a minority current in the workers' movement through around 1920.

The increasing economic distance between artisans on the one hand and merchants and landowners on the other led to a modified return to colonial-era caste distinctions. As they became wealthier and more cosmopolitan, members of the developing bourgeoisie adopted a more disdainful attitude toward their domestics and other workers. In Bogotá a rise in urban property values led to the first wave of subdivisions of the great colonial mansions in the hitherto multiclass central district, and artisans and small shopkeepers unable to pay the higher rents were displaced to slums on the outskirts.

The traditional upper classes still adhered to the ethos of charity rooted in the theology of eighteenth-century Spain. As a result of the Liberal *desamortización* laws of the 1860s, which stripped the church of much of its wealth and in the process did away with the hospitals and other charitable institutions that depended on church funding, several private associations emerged to fill the void in services to the poor which the Liberal state was both unwilling and unable to provide. These largely Conservative-identified associations offered "charity in a vale of tears" as the Catholic response to the Liberal doctrine of individualism, competition, and nominal equality. The church and its upper-class supporters presented a private alternative to the (almost totally absent) social action of the state, an alternative that became increasingly necessary as the impoverishment and overcrowding that followed from the influx of artisans to the cities produced the predictable effects on "public morality" decried by Conservatives. But private charity underwritten by doctrines of Christian socialism was wholly insufficient to deal with social problems on this scale.

The competing arguments of Miguel Samper and Miguel Antonio Caro offer an example of the dilemmas of the ruling classes in facing up to urban poverty. Samper studied the issue in depth in *La miseria en Bogotá*, a collection of essays published in 1867. Although a leading Liberal, Samper was a practicing Catholic who praised the prudent giving of alms as well as the private organizations that undertook work previously carried out by church institutions. In the absence of official studies, he took one of those organizations, the Sociedad de San Vicente de Paúl, as the source of his statistical information on "misery in Bogotá." For Samper the two basic and interdependent elements of liberalism were economic efficiency and individual freedom. Since the social order was determined by the natural law of supply and demand, anything that went against that law was destructive, including protectionism, centralism, militarism, and bloated official bureaucracy. The economic position of each individual was to be the natural consequence of his or her involvement in the natural order of the market, not of state interference. For Samper the internalizing of morality through education was decisive: the values of hard work, perseverance, frugality, and savings were to be impressed upon everyone to prevent poverty and envy, and education would permit the poor to emulate the virtues of the privileged classes in making rational decisions. Thus would public harmony be guaranteed. For many Liberals of the late nineteenth century this was the vision of an outdated and oligarchic version of their ideology. Although Samper rejected any notion of direct state participation in addressing poverty, he admitted that the privileged classes bore a moral obligation, and he supported private commitments to charity. But by "private" he did not mean "secret," as prescribed by the Gospels — charity was to be out in the open for all to see, or as we would say today, a public relations operation.

Caro's view of Bogotá's poverty and proletarianization was as nightmarish as Samper's, but he considered charity by the elite an insufficient response to the effects of economic individualism. Left to its own devices, capitalism would cause the disintegration of the Christian nation by dissolving family, religion, and community solidarity. Inspired by the encyclical *Rerum novarum* of Pope Leo XIII (1891), Caro warned in 1898 that in Europe individualist capitalism and its liberal ideology "had dissolved the family and subjected millions of workers to a servitude more oppressive than that of the serfs." A vigilant Christian conscience and the positive action of the state (which in 1898 legally recognized the "social sovereignty of Jesus Christ") would, he hoped, be able to restrain the destructive energies of the new industrial society. But Colombia was far from being an industrial society, and the urban-centered concerns of both Samper and Caro ignored vast reaches of Colombia where social tensions were still mediated by political bossism, paternalism, and party polarization.

From Scientific Peace to the Disasters of War

The Regeneration did not succeed in depoliticizing Colombia or in establishing the "scientific peace" that Núñez promised. The centralism of the constitution of 1886 may have been more formal than real, but it caused resentment in the provinces. Colombia's geography and local traditions lent a certain federalist autonomy to local notables and economic elites. Between 1887 and 1890, eighteen departmental laws reorganized internal borders and jurisdictions as local forces adapted to the new conditions, while the national government was unable to create new departments it considered necessary for more efficient administration.

Liberals under the Regeneration, with few exceptions (among them their leader, Rafael Uribe Uribe), were excluded from legislative bodies. Unable to forge a political party of its own, the Caro-Núñez regime was subject to tensions and struggles among Conservative factions. During his 1886–92 presidential term Núñez left government largely to his designates and exercised the presidency on only two brief occasions, in 1887 and 1888; his absence opened the door to Conservative divisions, which were to intensify after his death in 1894. Antioquia's Conservatives, strengthened by the resurgence of mining and their newfound coffee wealth, inclined toward the moderate Historical faction by reason of prudence — prudence being called for in a region whose clergy openly supported the Regeneration.

In the 1891 presidential elections (for the term beginning the following year), the Historicals were not far from the Liberals in many of their positions. When in 1893 Santiago Pérez, former head of the Liberal party, published a manifesto demanding electoral guarantees, freedom of the press, annulment of the Horse Law, and suppression of fiscal monopolies as well as the National Bank, he found support from many Historical Conservatives. The government was unnerved and adopted a hard line, exiling Pérez and three other politicians, thus providing an opportunity for younger Liberals eager to replace the aging party leadership. They went to war against the government in 1895, but their woefully underprepared revolt lasted only three months; it was, however, a political victory. The new party leadership, largely from Santander, won the support of provincial Liberals (under constant harassment from Conservative bosses and fanatical clergy) with their view that only a strategy of arms could return the party to power.

The Nationalists carried the 1897 presidential elections with a ticket of old men: Manuel Antonio Sanclemente and José Manuel Marroquín, 84 and 71 years old respectively. Their age alone created an uncertain political panorama, but the real drama lay in the Liberals' debate over negotiation with the government versus a new revolt. The party's leader, Aquileo Parra, sent envoys to like-minded governments in Guatemala and Nicaragua in search of arms and funds, and even considered approaching Porfirio Díaz in Mexico, the most powerful Latin American liberal of the period. All he received were promises, which at the moment of truth went unfulfilled.

Liberals did have some victories at home, as in 1898, when the Congress (despite having only one Liberal member) threw out the Horse Law and expanded press freedoms. However, the more important electoral reform went nowhere: passed in the Historical-dominated lower house, it was defeated in the Senate, where Nationalists were in charge. Against this backdrop of failure within the system, younger elite Liberals felt free to disregard the nominal party leadership of Parra and then a triumvirate of elderly figures. In the northeast they organized support for Venezuelan Liberals, waging the final offensive that would install them as the ruling party in Caracas. That success excited the zeal of Colombian Liberals, and in October 1899 the uprising began.

The Liberals' call for insurrection on October 18, 1899, launched the most prolonged and bloody civil war since independence. The strictly military history of the war, like that of earlier conflicts, offers less of interest than its cultural and social expressions or its social and political effects. The War of the Thousand Days was the last to try to follow the elite's code of honor. But the armed struggle did have a social leveling effect. From on high Archbishop Herrera interceded on behalf of a Liberal condemned to death in San Juan de Rioseco, Cundinamarca, citing "the consideration due to the family of Señor Don Antonio Suárez Lacroix for the many services they have provided for society, especially for lepers and other invalids." But the request was ignored, perhaps because of pressure exerted from below by Conservatives of less prominent families. When Suárez's family requested a death certificate shortly thereafter, the parish priest dealt with it this way: "The undersigned certifies that fortunately he cannot find in the parish books a death certificate for Antonio Suárez Lacroix, deservedly executed at La Barrigona."[2] Once peace was signed in 1902, execution lost its halo of atavistic honor, and from that point on it would be said that only savage mobs practiced it. In recent years,

2 Quoted in Pedro Escobar, "La Iglesia y la política," in *Estructuras políticas de Colombia* (Bogotá: CIAS, 1969), 2.

of course, it has been commonly applied in the guerrilla/counterguerrilla struggle.

As the first Liberal contingents left Bogotá and the towns of Santander for the battlefield in late 1899, observers noted the marked presence of artisans and the insurgents' lack of military preparedness. The government troops demonstrated the importance of (relatively) modern armament—rifles from the Franco-Prussian War of 1870. The rebels' main arms were flint shotguns and machetes, zealously guarded and employed. Only in Bogotá and the northeastern departments of Boyacá and Santander could they mobilize a respectable force; while Liberals on the Caribbean coast and in the west supported the rebellion, only rarely did they pass from words to actions.

The war changed quickly—in less than eight months—from a relatively conventional conflict (for which the Liberals were hopelessly unprepared) to a guerrilla struggle. During the first stage, in which Liberal armies were led by ambitious and squabbling caudillo generals, their overall strategy was to seize the customs posts of the Caribbean coast and in Cúcuta, on the Venezuelan border. The government was prepared for this strategy and the rebels were repelled. This "war of armies" was an expression of oligarchic values embraced by Rafael Uribe Uribe, who declared guerrillas (defined here as small, mobile, and relatively nonhierarchical fighting groups) to be thugs and outlaws. The formal phase of the war ended in July 1900 at Palonegro, near Bucaramanga, where the Liberals suffered enormous losses and sealed their defeat in an epic two-week battle. From that point on, Liberal offensives were limited to erratic and improvised actions that did not rise to the level of real counterattacks.

In the guerrilla phase of the war the Liberals gained strength in the center of the country, and in 1902 they threatened to dominate Panama. But their principal importance was more long-term, by sowing the seeds of the popular radicalism that would germinate during the first decades of the twentieth century in the marginal regions of the country—the eastern plains, Santander's Magdalena River valley, northern and southern Tolima, and the slopes of the upper Magdalena. All of these regions would become tragically familiar during the Violencia of mid-century.

The Conservative triumph at Palonegro set off a controversy within government circles which reached its apex with the coup of July 1900, in which the Historicals installed Vice President José Manuel Marroquín in the presidency, in the hope that he would negotiate a peace agreement. But they misjudged the new president's inclinations, and with the government unyielding but its army unable to crush the guerrillas, stalemate ensued. After a failed countercoup in October 1900 to put Sanclemente back in the presidency, the Historicals had to accept a Conservative regime with strong Nationalist dominance and the fervent backing of lower-class Conservatives, the church, and the military.

The counterguerrilla operations of 1902 were relatively successful, but the prolonged conflict undermined Conservative civil and military morale. Epidemics both biological (smallpox, yellow fever) and social (corruption, speculation) were rampant, and the government armies were beset by desertions, pillage, and cattle-rustling. The cattle- and mule-trafficking operations of army officers were widely known, and the military's control of navigation on the Magdalena River created a web of corruption between officers and merchants. Marroquín continued to deny the Liberal rebels political status and to demand their unconditional surrender, but by mid-June 1902 his government declared that if the remaining Liberal forces laid down their arms, the government would release all civilian and military prisoners of war and restore all their political rights. After the guerrillas accepted the offer, the three organized Liberal armies that remained after Palonegro did the same. Uribe Uribe's surrender in late 1902, on a banana plantation in Ciénaga, ended the war on the Caribbean coast. Weeks later, Justo Durán surrendered with his Santander forces at Chinácota. That same day, Benjamín Herrera laid down his arms in the name of the entire Liberal party at a meeting with Marroquín's representatives on board the U.S.S. *Wisconsin*, anchored off the coast of Panama (still part of Colombia). Three days later the government declared a general pardon and the size of the military was immediately reduced, first to 50,000 men and then to a mere 15,000 in March 1903.

These three gentlemen's agreements opened the dialogue between moderates of both parties, who saw how military corruption and guerrillas outside the elite's control could threaten the social order. The peace treaty called for elections in 1903, and the new Congress would take up electoral reform, the Panama Canal question, and the still-contentious monetary issue. For Herrera the Panama issue lent force to his celebrated phrase "the country above the parties."

The Legacies of War

Among the winners of the War of the Thousand Days were the big merchants, who had promoted economic liberalism since the mid-1800s. In the postwar period they set up factories, electric plants, banks, and transport firms. On the coffee front, the merchant-hacendado was replaced by the specialized exporter. The west of the country suffered far less from the war, and the Medellín and Cali elites had prospered while it raged: although coffee exports fell, speculators made money by taking out loans in paper money, converting it to gold, and waiting for the next devaluation. Several of the twelve banks founded in Bogotá and Medellín during the war specialized in such operations, but some of them lasted only as long as the war itself. The nominal prices of foodstuffs and real estate rose 250 percent in the largest cities during the war, and the increase in real prices of certain foodstuffs benefited large and small growers alike at the expense of the urban poor, who also bore the brunt of considerable increases in local, departmental, and national taxes.

One of the most important consequences of the war was the reconfiguration of regional hierarchies. Between 1870 and 1890, for example, Santander had generated 80 percent of export income, but this impetus was lost after the war; in fact, it was flagging even earlier, and several parts of the northeast had lost population since the mid-1800s. The slow crisis of the rural artisans in central Santander, the collapse of world prices of quinine in 1882 and then of coffee in 1896, and Liberal political-military defeats in 1885–86 and in the War of the Thousand Days, all exhausted the department. The widespread destruction caused by the war had strangled Santander's transportation system. The importation of machinery to modernize that system would require capital and national political influence, and after the war Santander had neither.

The contrast with Antioquia could not have been more pronounced. Despite its internal geographic fragmentation, the department's elites took common pride in their whiteness and their Catholicism, characteristics they shared with much of the regional population, and they offered to Colombia a new model trumpeting religiosity, respect for social hierarchy, educational development, and material progress based on gold, coffee, cattle, and then (a bit later in the 1900s) factories.

During the 1890s and then the war itself, imports of textiles from the United States supplanted those from Great Britain. One immediate result was an increase in the cost of credit for importers and distributors, which drove up consumer prices. Given these conditions, after 1903 several importers based in Antioquia and on the Caribbean coast decided to embark upon the adventure of starting factories of their own. The magnitude of this investment was on the order of earlier start-ups in river transport or the newer urban electric companies. Using their political influence in Bogotá, they won protective tariffs. This spelled the end for the crude *tejidos bastos* of Santander, which as late as the 1890s still had markets in the towns of Antioquia.

What did Colombian society gain from this series of civil wars? Certainly war reinforced party affiliations and sustained party mythologies. Iconic battles, from Peralonso to Rionegro, deepened antagonisms and suspicions between Colombians even as the elite sought to recast them as heroic episodes that ought to produce a common desire for reconciliation. The victorious Conservatives could say that between 1903 and 1930 they created an unprecedented era of peace and progress, and that they peacefully handed over power after their electoral defeat in 1930, guided by the spirit of their great civilizing opus, the constitution of 1886.

Meanwhile, the postwar Liberals refined the art of courting the popular masses, reading the signs of the times. During the 1920s, Benjamín Herrera's strategy of co-opting the nascent socialist movement drew urban artisans back to the Liberal mystique: the last civil war, in this version, was the lost opportunity of the lower classes to combat a reactionary, "feudal" oligarchy standing in the way of democracy and progress. A half-century later, the heroes of this war would fuel the fervor and imagination of the Liberal guerrillas of the Violencia era. Today the anthem of the Revolutionary Armed Forces of Colombia (FARC), the oldest guerrilla movement in Latin America, commemorates the Tolima Liberal guerrilla Tulio Varón, from the War of the Thousand Days, in one of its verses.

One instant legacy of the war was exaggeration of the number of the dead: 100,000 by common estimate, or one in five males between the ages of 18 and 30. The fact is that strictly military operations were not continuous or nationwide, and the technology commonly employed mitigated the most extreme destruction. Railways, which were such a frequent target of all sides during the Mexican Revolution a decade later, were largely undisturbed. Epidemic diseases and the settling of personal scores under the cover of wartime probably caused more deaths than those caused by warfare.

The pro-war Liberals of the late 1890s, led by Rafael Uribe Uribe, haughtily dismissed the aged party leadership of the 1890s for their commitment to peace and futile attempts at compromise with the government; but after the war, during the authoritarian Conservative regime of Rafael Reyes, Uribe's faction accepted government positions. They claimed as a victory the Reyes "Minorities Law," which guaranteed the Liberals one-third of legislative seats at all levels. Meanwhile, Herrera and Uribe fixed upon the "social question" as an alternative to old-style party sectarianism. Never one to shy away from publicity, Uribe sought to give the Liberals an efficient electoral machine and new doctrinal equipment with which to face the new century. He preached economic interventionism (certainly a radical change in party doctrine) and a more equitable distribution of public lands, and he identified with the economic concerns of the artisans of Bogotá and Medellín. He also emphasized the need to train a new professional class through secular and autonomous public universities.

Uribe was assassinated—by two unemployed artisans, ironically—in Bogotá in 1914. From that moment on, he became the Prometheus who brought the fire of socialism to the people. Even those who doubted the substance of his words saw their potential for gaining urban lower-class support for the Liberals without sacrificing the party's rural strength. This new liberalism, like the old, would venerate the ambition of its charismatic generals.

The Secession of Panama

Another consequence of the War of the Thousand Days was the loss of Panama. On November 3, 1903, the Panamanian elite, goaded by foreign canal-building interests and backed by U.S. naval power, declared the region's independence and dealt the Colombian state the greatest humiliation in its history. Panama's secession underlined the weakness and uncertainty of Colombia's hold on its other far-flung territories, especially in the Amazon and Orinoquia.

Anti-Colombian feeling among the white oligarchy of Panama City dated back to the initial construction of the railway in the 1850s. Successive Colombian governments had to accept their inability to guarantee sovereignty over the isthmus, and they either requested or tolerated a series of interventions by the United States. When it became obvious that the French would abandon their attempts to build a canal between the oceans, the United States stepped in and took control of the project.

The War of the Thousand Days discredited the two parties in the eyes of all classes of Panamanian society. The execution of the popular guerrilla leader Victoriano Lorenzo, even after the amnesty was decreed, confirmed in black and mulatto neighborhoods of Panama City that the Conservatives were evil and the Liberals, who had cultivated their support for decades, were duplicitous. Panama's merchants and political leaders, generally freethinking internationalists, noted with horror the growing abyss between them and the Hispanophile, pro-clerical, and self-absorbed ruling group in Bogotá.

Embroiled in the internal conflict, the Colombian government did not pay attention to the obvious evolution of U.S. diplomacy. In 1901, having expelled Spain from the Caribbean in 1898, the United States negotiated a treaty with Great Britain that guaranteed Washington the exclusive right to build the canal and recognized its dominant status in the hemisphere. Colombian diplomats in Washington sent President Marroquín a consistent message: any rejection or delay of a canal treaty by Colombia would lead to Panama's secession. Eager to resolve the issue, Marroquín approved the Herrán-Hay Treaty in January 1903; while the U.S. Senate quickly approved it on March 17, the Colombian senate rejected it in August of that year because certain provisions, such as the stationing of U.S. troops around the canal, infringed on national sovereignty. A senate commission recommended renegotiation of the treaty to provide for increases in both initial and yearly compensation payments to Colombia. The episode was interpreted in Panama as a strategy to obtain maximum payouts to Colombia without consideration for Panamanian interests, and Washington considered it a breach of Colombia's earlier approval.

On top of the conspiracy between Panamanian separatists and representatives of the French canal company eager to sell their shares to U.S. interests was the famous impatience of Theodore Roosevelt, who called Colombians "contemptible little creatures" and "inefficient bandits," not to mention "a corrupt and pithecoid community" standing in the way of progress. In the name of "universal civilization," the United States was determined to ensure the quick completion of the canal project. Many members of the U.S. Congress were, in fact, even more impatient and arrogant than the president. A few weeks after Colombia rejected the treaty, Panama City erupted in revolt and the rebels wisely paid off the Colombian military to stand down. Meanwhile, the U.S. fleet stationed offshore prevented Colombia from sending fresh troops to quash the revolt. The plotters proclaimed Panama's independence, and their provisional government was recognized by the White House three days later.

Political Values: A Retrospective Vision

Political leaders from the traditionalist Conservative Miguel Antonio Caro to the individualist Liberal Miguel Samper shared a desire to use reason to domesticate a messy Colombian reality permeated to its core by rural values. They saw Colombia from the capital city. But Bogotá, the "Athens of South America," as it was called (although wags changed a single letter to make it "Merely Latin American"), with its barely 100,000 residents in 1900, was still more a village than a modern capitalist metropolis. The occasional iconoclast, such as the poet José Asunción Silva, did not fit in. Pigs, chickens, horses, and cows lived intermingled with families of all classes and conditions. Some physicians wondered whether the city's public hygiene problems could be traced to the stables near the exclusive Catedral neighborhood or the chicken coops in the attics of Las Nieves and Santa Bárbara or the pigs that joined the dogs foraging along the banks of the San Francisco. Bogotá was very much a world of flavors and smells, the senses evoked in the *cuadros de costumbres* (literally, "portraits of customs") written in the mid–nineteenth century. It was a world in which confusion and clarity walked together, as did superstition and faith, arcane ritual and logical deduction. This was the setting, reproduced to varying degrees in other towns, in which the rationalist spirit of republican civilization sought a foothold. Colombians were called upon to replace customs with laws. It was a costly illusion that not even the Regeneration could alter.

The *cuadros de costumbres* and novels of the middle and late 1800s, while not very useful for understanding politics as such, provide insights into the thinking of the urban elite and the changes in the way social actors viewed politics; into the ambiguities of mixed-raced societies based on deference, trapped in a colonial value system; and into the wavering responses of the poor to the pull of traditional habits and customs on the one hand and the modern vocabulary of liberty and constitutionalism on the other. The *costumbrista* writers emphasized these tensions by overstating the gap between the supposed social harmony of the past and the new call for popular participation in politics, which they often portrayed as a form of acute moral degeneration based on shady deals and legalistic tricks. But the genre also depicts the fears of many in the elite who suspected that the arrival of republican ideas and institutions at the local level would sow the seeds of subversion as nominal political equality led to actual social equality.

Two of the most influential *costumbrista* novels of the latter half of the 1800s—
Manuela (1858–59), by Eugenio Díaz, and *Olivos y Aceitunos, todos son unos* (1868),
by José María Vergara y Vergara—combine standard reactionary rejection of
political equality with very cutting and minute critiques of political practices
during the federal period. In *Manuela*, the Gólgota (utopian intellectual) Liberal Demóstenes leaves Bogotá for a lowland town with a copy of the romantic
classic of the moment, *The Mysteries of Paris*, by Eugene Sue, under his arm and a
full dose of romantic republicanism in his head. The town is run by a militarist
and decidedly nonutopian Draconian Liberal boss, Tadeo, who lusts for the
beautiful *mulata* Manuela, who is already betrothed to another man, Dámaso.
Events come to a tragic head on July 20, Independence Day, when Manuela
dies at the hands of the villainous Tadeo. Demóstenes is too obsessed with the
abstract and print-borne passions of political ideology to take note of the personal passions that surround him, and when he returns to Bogotá the town
returns to its usual stupor. Vergara made use of the usual romantic tropes to
depict, in a style as dark as Goya's, the local political life of the thirteen towns
that in 1851 made up the imaginary province of Chrichiquí. (Vergara's fictional
province was closely modeled on the actual province of Chiriquí in Panama.)

But not all political vices were born in the provinces, according to the novel
Blas Gil (1896), by José Manuel Marroquín, the future president. This work finds
the origins of Colombian bossism and thuggery in the strange alchemy of the
capital, which could turn a poor but ambitious university student from the
provinces into a vain dandy. For Marroquín, not surprisingly, the good practice
of Catholicism was the best defense against such a transformation and its dele-
terious effects on political life. The climax of this small-c conservative vein in
Colombian fiction was the 1907 novel *Pax: A Novel of Latin American Customs*, whose
co-authors, Lorenzo Marroquín and José María Rivas Groot, denounced in
great detail the dislocations in the values and customs of a traditional society
produced by political mobilization and a mercantile economy. To Marroquín
and Rivas Groot, Colombia was in a state of moral and material prostration
after the War of the Thousand Days, and now had to tolerate an unscrupulous class of nouveaux riches and opportunistic politicians, two groups with
no breeding.

This pessimistic vision was not shared by those public figures whose practical morality followed the partisan dividing line of Liberals and Conservatives, freethinkers and Catholics. Miguel Antonio Caro and most of the clergy

believed that the "liberal virus" could be contained by bringing Conservative political mobilization and machinery to every part of the country. On the Liberal side things were even clearer: politicians of all factions endorsed, at least nominally, the idea of bringing politics to the people so that they could exercise their rights, raise their voices, be counted, and attain the status of real Colombian citizens.

After the War of the Thousand Days, the elites seemed disoriented. The economic costs of war vindicated the skepticism that fifty years of *costumbrista* literature had expressed in regard to Colombian democracy. Print-driven Reason, instead of bringing to the countryside a culture of tolerance, ended up inciting the most local and vulgar passions. The play of dichotomies — civilization/barbarism, "respectable people"/mob, educated/ignorant — was a slippery slope to outright racism. In repudiating political partisanship, the elite expressed no faith in "Colombian man," whom they now saw as an obstacle to progress and concord. Before extending democracy to the people, the elites would have to build a modern state.

Early in the 1900s, hopes were pinned on attracting white immigrants from Europe: "Italians and Spaniards, and I don't want to hear anything about Chinese coolies," said Rafael Uribe Uribe. Racist attitudes peaked in the decade after 1910, when the biological focus on the "Colombian race" sought to explain the symptoms and signs of "physical degeneration" and "emotionality, suggestibility, impulsiveness, [and] instability" which characterized the average Colombian. This "national pathology" was credited with the "eleven constitutions and sixty-four revolts" of the previous century. It need hardly be said that these judgments were offered in one-off presentations, usually to university students and faculty, rather than as the fruit of systematic studies.

Few Latin American countries have a nineteenth-century electoral history as rich and as continuous as Colombia's. Even so, electoral participation generally did not promote debates that enriched public life, strengthened tolerance, or created an institutional culture able to resolve conflicts. Legalism and the unreflective faith in the intrinsic virtues of the representative system of government coexisted with the common acceptance of violence as a valid method for gaining and holding power. Nothing better illustrates this synthesis of armed force and legalism than the list of generals at the helm of the two parties. The mystique of arms rivaled or exceeded the power of the written and spoken word in bestowing honor, prestige, and authority. There was no space in Colombia for the pure praetorian general, devoid of political talents. But civilian leaders were able to mobilize people to take up weapons, even as they feared crossing a line that might convert their armies into an autonomous means of social mobility. Although after 1902 the elites renounced the appeal to arms, violence and the threat of violence did not disappear from local political life.

With the new dawn of 1903, the Conservative leadership seemed to understand that it was impossible to govern with the total exclusion of the Liberals, as the Liberals came to understand that the government could not be removed by force. With the notion of an internal enemy banished and the loss of Panama standing as testimony to what could go wrong, "Blues" and "Reds" alike understood Colombia's vulnerability.

Chapter 2

LIBERAL ECONOMICS, CONSERVATIVE POLITICS

*T*he ten years that followed the Liberals' surrender in 1902 saw two attempts at political reconciliation: the authoritarian and statist "Quinquenio" of Rafael Reyes (1904–10) and the federalist and economically
liberal Republicanism of Carlos E. Restrepo (1910–14). Both movements
influenced the so-called Conservative Hegemony of 1914–30, a term that
masked the regime's weakness in dealing with the legislature, its complex
relationship with the Catholic church, and its adaptation to the values of liberal capitalism. The administrations of all five presidents, from José Vicente
Concha to Miguel Abadía Méndez, were marked by ferocious internal
struggles.

During the 1902–30 period economic liberalism and political conservatism reached their zenith. The basis of this symbiosis was a peculiar coffee
economy based largely on smallholders in the west of the country and a
population strongly influenced by the clergy and by Conservative electoral
politics. More than ever Colombia's physical infrastructure, use of public
lands, and monetary stability were viewed through the prism of the import-
export economy. The state either took charge of economic planning directly
or delegated it to institutions controlled by business groups. Economic policy
was never far removed from the principal and most problematic question of
the era, Colombia's post-Panama relationship with the United States, which
by now had displaced Great Britain and the other European countries as
the hegemonic power in the Americas.

Economic expansion changed the production map, altering regional balances and the relationships between cities and their regions. New social
actors appeared, such as labor unions in the capitalist enclaves of the frontier. Although they often employed Marxist or anarchist rhetoric, they were
oriented more toward the traditions of nineteenth-century popular liberal-

ism. Toward the end of this period, the Catholic church, despite its huge institutional power, fell into crisis.

Coffee and Socioeconomic Transformations

When peace came in 1902 — "with all its horrors," as one Antioquian landowner and merchant put it — few would have bet on coffee as the star of the new century's economy. Prices recovered from the pre-1900 slump only in 1909–10, and even so, coffee's place in Colombian exports fell from 40 percent by value in 1903 to 30 percent in 1910. In a country accustomed to relatively brief boom-and-bust cycles, many thought it was now the turn of rubber in Putumayo, or bananas around Santa Marta, or perhaps cattle on the plains of Bolívar. Coffee's salvation came through the successive valorization schemes pursued by the Brazilian government in 1906–37, which warehoused or destroyed exportable coffee to keep the price level high. With Brazil doing the work of reining in oversupply, marginal players like Colombia could reap the benefits without incurring any of the economic, fiscal, or political costs. Colombia's businessmen and politicians, protected by Brazil's highly visible hand, renewed their faith in the "invisible hand" of the market.

Figures from 1910–13 suggest that Colombia retained its 1850 status as one of the Western Hemisphere's most economically isolated countries and one of the most backward in economic structure. The country represented only 2 percent of total Latin American exports and received only 1.5 percent of the United States' investments in the region and 0.5 percent of Britain's. Of 305 textile factories in Latin America only 5 were in Colombia, representing less than 1 percent of capacity. Despite the doubling of Colombia's railway network between 1904 and 1910, on a miles-per-inhabitant basis Mexico still had six times more and Argentina had twenty-two times more — although, to be fair, neither country had a river artery to match the Magdalena. Taxes per inhabitant were one-seventh those of Argentina, half those of Peru, and two-thirds those of Venezuela. The human consequence of this economic insularity was provincialism. Relatively few foreign merchants, artisans, or engineers established themselves in Colombia's towns and cities.

Colombia was much more dependent on a single product, coffee, and a single market, the United States, than most Latin American countries. By the mid-1920s, Colombian coffee exports were one-tenth of the world total. Educated Colombians credited coffee with the accumulation of fortunes, the improvement of transportation, the establishment of modern banking and commercial systems, the opening of new cattle and sugar cane lands, and the local production of coffee-processing machines and jute sacks.

The modernization of banking deserves special attention. In 1914 the U.S. government changed the laws to permit its banks to operate abroad without working through foreign banks, usually British or Canadian. Almost immediately a heated battle broke out between New York and London bankers for management of Colombia's foreign debt bonds, which since the 1890s had been in the hands of a small Colombian clique with connections in the Colombian consulate in London. This dispute lasted until the Great Depression, when President Enrique Olaya finally shut down the "fiscal agency" and assumed direct government management of the debt. Colombian businessmen believed that the coffee boom and the establishment of a banking and monetary system as close as possible to the U.S. system overseen by the United States' Federal Reserve Bank would guarantee approval by the U.S. Congress of the Panama Canal Treaty, which in turn would open Colombia to new U.S. loans.

By the start of the First World War in 1914, the United States imported around two-thirds of Colombian coffee exports; by the end of the war its share approached 90 percent. The closing of European markets by the war and their replacement by the United States affected all commercial and credit operations. Pent-up demand for imports was unleashed after the war, and a fivefold increase from 1918 to 1921 clogged Colombia's ports. When coffee prices fell in 1920, imports fell by two-thirds the following year. Not for nothing was the country increasingly known as *Colombia cafetera*, Coffee Colombia.

Until the 1980s coffee took center stage in the economy. Here we should point out four constants that affected cultivators, merchants, and governments alike. All are based on the fundamental reality that the coffee economy depends on a factor beyond its control, the expansion of world demand. That is why no serious consideration was given to improving either labor productivity or technology until the late 1940s, though some attention was paid to increasing domestic consumption of coffee. First among these constants is that coffee is produced exclusively in the tropics, unlike sugar, tobacco, or cotton, which can (with varying efficiency) be produced in temperate zones; it is not a necessity of life, on the order of wheat and petroleum; and it can be stored for long periods. Thus it encourages speculation, which translates into high levels of price instability—year to year, month to month, even day to day. Second, coffee has no economies of scale, and until the "green revolution" reached coffee in the mid-1970s, the only way to increase production was to employ more land and more labor. Third, coffee has little elasticity of supply and demand; that is, it takes a big price swing to make consumers stop drinking it or to make cultivators stop producing it. Fourth, periodic frosts in Brazil play a major role in world prices: the relative shortage in world supply promotes new plantings; inventories build up over the next few years; and despite the efforts of producing countries to let them accumulate, prices inevitably fall.

After the War of the Thousand Days, the smallholder custom of mixing coffee production with yucca, beans, corn, and plantains took on greater importance. With their subsistence attended to, smallholders could sell their coffee for less than larger commercial operators; however low that price was, it was more than they could make from any other commercial crop. The harvesting and processing of coffee on small farms were far less onerous than the dangerous and exhausting dawn-to-dusk labor of cutting and refining sugar cane. Women and children were full participants in the work processes of coffee production. Plenty of uncultivated land was more or less accessible, and thousands of poor families added coffee groves to their farms. By 1920 most smallholders owned a hand-operated machine to extract the coffee beans from the berries, and drying them for transportation and sale was a simple matter of spreading them out on a patio or over some jute sacks on the ground and letting the sun do the job.

The haciendas that survived the financial crisis of the civil war recovered and expanded, but the producers of western Colombia, blessed with more fertile soil, displaced those of Santander and Cundinamarca. In general, the hacienda gave way to the small farm. People with capital found it more profitable and less conflictive to control the market than to exploit peasants in the faraway and hazardous world of the haciendas. Producers, especially smaller ones, were trapped in oligopolist networks that purchased and processed coffee in places well situated for control of a given territory.

The expansion of coffee is the principal reason for Colombia's unprecedented economic growth between the First World War and the Great Depression. Boosted by the positive trend in the terms of trade, the purchasing power of Colombian exports quintupled. U.S. investments in Colombia reached 6 percent of the total for all Latin America, a tripling of the earlier level. Coffee's role as a motor of development was also evident in the financial system, whose assets increased spectacularly in the 1920s, in absolute terms and even in comparison with exports. But the number of banks actually went down, and the remaining ones were concentrated in Bogotá. If coffee was the motor, Brazil's interventionist price policies were the fuel: it has been calculated that without Brazil's valorization program to retain and even destroy excess coffee production, Colombian coffee income from 1920 to 1934 would have been 40 percent less.[1]

Coffee-based economic growth gave the state resources with which to expand the bureaucracy. In 1916 there were 42,700 public employees at all levels, almost ten times the number in 1875. These numbers suggest the importance of patronage appointments in everything from public works to post and telegraph offices to the departments' revenue offices, not to mention scholarships for study at the church's government-subsidized secondary schools and universities. Around the time of the First World War, the emphasis shifted from quantitative expansion within an essentially premodern bureaucracy to foreign technical missions contracted by the state to modernize the republic's infrastructure and financial institutions. Among the results of these missions were the ministries of economic development, the armed forces, education, and public health; a new central bank, the Banco de la República; and new banking legislation. This shift coincided with the emergence of the western coffee zones as a Conservative electoral base under strong clientelist control with the growing economic power of moderate entrepreneurs in that region whose primary concern was Colombia's material development.

The foreign technical missions that came to Colombia in 1920s meshed extremely well with the paternalist ethos of the country's elite. They empowered technocratic groups without formal political responsibility to take the place of political parties and the Congress in officially defining notions of public interest, deploying a technical "rationality" that would soon take on a mysterious and almost sacramental aspect. They were called upon to centralize decision making and to legitimate the redistribution of economic and social power. Whatever the balance of their successes and failures or the internal resistance they faced or their impact on the training of Colombian specialists, by steering clear of political and regional interests the foreign technical missions acquired a reputation for being above suspicion.

The coffee bonanza, the indemnity payments from the United States for the loss of Panama, the sustained rise of banana production, and the promising

---

1   The author thanks Robert Bates of Harvard University for calling his attention to this point, which gives new insight into the "economic miracle" of the 1920s.

takeoff of petroleum, all made Colombia an enticing target of New York investors in their rush to invest money throughout the world. The construction of transportation infrastructure captured nearly half of all foreign credit destined for Colombia in the 1920s. Of the 1,000-odd kilometers of rail lines built during the decade, around 800 served the critical routes of the coffee region. On some railways the improvisation and outright waste were of scandalous proportions. The embryonic technocracy was alarmed: in 1929 the controller of the Ministry of Public Works reported (with some exaggeration) that three-quarters of the money spent on infrastructure between 1923 and 1928 had been wasted. Although these routes did promote the spatial reorganization of the Colombian economy in support of its linkage to the world economy, they also integrated domestic transport corridors to favor seasonal and migratory workers in search of opportunity rather than the first-class passengers they used to serve.

A New Economic Map

Thus was changed the human and economic geography of Colombia. Among the most important changes, not necessarily in order of importance, we can note the revival of the Caribbean coast, the development of the coffee belt in the west, the economic takeoff of the Valle del Cauca, the eclipse of Santander in the northeast, and the economic validation of Bogotá as the nation's capital.

The most active areas of the coast were the hinterlands of Cartagena and Barranquilla and the length of the Santa Marta banana rail line. There was also notable dynamism in the port regions of the Magdalena, Cauca, and Sinú rivers. The expansion of cattle and sugar production in the Cartagena area opened up new and previously isolated regions, a process financed in part by capital from Antioquia and assisted by Medellín's cattle market. To the east of the Magdalena, the United Fruit Company made the Santa Marta banana enclave the hub of its production, transport, and marketing operations, which grew steadily until the mid-1930s, when political and ecological misfortunes sent it into a slow decline. Around 1930 the Santa Marta enclave had been producing twice as many bananas as all of Costa Rica.

As it entered the third decade of the twentieth century, the coastal economy consisted of much more than just old-style cattle ranches. Commercial production of tobacco and sugar, small-scale production of foodstuffs for urban centers, and the multiplier effects of the banana enclave, all generated new regional dynamics. Minor river ports connected local markets and spared them the cycles of foreign trade that were so quickly reflected in the large ports of the Magdalena.

During the late nineteenth century and early in the twentieth, a few of the Syrians, Turks, and Palestinians who immigrated to Latin America, mostly to Chile and Brazil, came to Colombia. They found the most congenial environments in the port towns along the coast and the Magdalena, all the way down to Neiva. These immigrants developed extensive retail trading networks, reaching even the most isolated settlements. Their influence would slowly grow in the worlds of business, the cattle trade, and party politics.

Barranquilla continued to be the base for steamship companies, which in 1918 operated some forty vessels along the Magdalena. By 1910 over 100,000 tons of freight moved along the river annually, and tonnage increased more than threefold by 1916; in that year, around 40,000 people traveled by steam along the river as well. Freight increased to nearly 600,000 tons in 1923 and to an all-time high of 1.5 million tons in 1928, only to fall off with the decline of world trade during the Great Depression. Except for brief price wars between Colombian and foreign shipping companies, river transport generally functioned as an oligopoly.

In the eastern mountains, towns such as Tunja, Pamplona, and San Gil performed their political-administrative roles in an atmosphere of provincial languor and the traditional clientelism with its intrigues and everyday violence. In the Santanders (Santander had been divided into two departments) the political struggle continued within a mosaic of urban centers that vied for supremacy in a geographically isolated region with high transportation costs and declining agriculture and craftwork. Land colonization was its only escape valve, and migrants from the region even crossed into the Venezuelan states of Táchira and Zulia.

Starting in the 1870s the relatively dynamic commercial and manufacturing towns of Bucaramanga, Cúcuta, and Ocaña escaped from the political grip of the old political-administrative centers, but this was no panacea. High transportation costs blocked the takeoff of modern capitalism. Right after the end of the war in 1902, Bucaramanga's merchants threw their efforts into building a rail line to the Magdalena, but the project, actually begun in 1871, came to fruition only in 1931. Other factors also played a negative role. In 1915 Santander was still the principal coffee department and the central and eastern regions still harvested around 60 percent of national production. But during this period Santander's coffee fetched only around 83 percent of the western Colombian coffee price in world markets because of the perception that it was of lower quality. Coffee sales had been in the hands of German firms since the 1860s, and when the United States entered World War I, it blacklisted those firms. This disruption, coupled with frequent closing of the borders and comparatively high production costs, limited coffee's potential as a motor of development in this part of the country.

The Boyacá region limped along, thanks to its strategic location between the Bogotá plateau and the northeast and an economy based on traditional agriculture and craftwork that made it almost self-sufficient, and therefore sheltered it from the booms and busts of international commerce. The region was even able to derive some benefit from prosperity elsewhere, by exporting its surplus production—foodstuffs, textiles, jewelry, even *boyacenses* themselves—to the expanding Bogotá market.

The most important phenomenon of the period was the birth and development of the western Colombian coffee belt to the south of Antioquia. While Antioquia and its migrants played a key role in that process, other regions—Cauca, Boyacá, and Tolima, for instance—also played a part.

The nineteenth century in Antioquia was relatively peaceful and prosperous, thanks to its isolation from civil wars and to its gold mining. Gold experienced far less severe cycles of boom and bust than other export commodities. Perhaps the most important political factor was the early consolidation of Medellín as undisputed capital of the entire region. Its capitalists, allied with a church firmly entrenched in every town, never faced serious rivals for domination of the region. Through the parallel mechanisms of clientelism and the market, they commanded the deference of local merchants and the prominent men of both established towns and colonization zones.

Coffee's social effects in Antioquia were palpable by the 1890s, even though at the start of that decade the value of coffee exported from the region was only 4 percent of that of gold exports. The rapid spread of coffee cultivation starting around 1910 helped to integrate local markets by developing trade in the beans, thus giving impetus to the middle class in the towns. At the same time the system of parties and factions gave this sector control of local resources, and eventually skills and experience in the use of local power. The other side of the coin was their dependence on a purchasing oligopoly of Medellín export houses, always ready to use their power to block potential competitors for the region's coffee output, such as the Tolima firm of Pedro A. Lopez in the years after 1900. The big names of Antioquia's towns became, in a sense, informal employees of the Medellín houses, although the appearance of U.S. processing firms as direct buyers in the 1920s provided some real options.

An idiosyncratic urban culture appeared in Medellín and other cities, whose vitality could be seen in their architecture. The houses of the new rich, often the children of land colonizers, were built of local woods and other materials; they fit into the rugged terrain; they made use of the talents of local artisans; and their doors, roofs, balconies, and windows made unusual use of the modernist European style of the late nineteenth century.

An authentic regional discourse and its material symbols burst forth in all its splendor. Manizales, with its aerial cargo cable down to the Magdalena, its neo-Gothic cathedral, and its overwrought political oratory (jocularly called *greco-quimbayo*: Classical-Indian), crystallized the social triumph of the modest group of land colonizers and mule-pack drivers "of good stock" who founded the town only in the mid–nineteenth century. It became the cultural beacon of the western coffee belt.

In the 1940s the potentates of small coffee towns thought the time had come for them to move to Medellín, Manizales, Pereira, Armenia, or Cali, which offered greater urban comforts and better economic and educational opportunities. The social vacuum left in their home towns was rapidly filled by tavern owners, small truckers, and local bosses more identified with local cultural traditions than with the old habits of deference to the wealthy merchants of Medellín. Parish priests also were increasingly tied to their communities, and they paid more attention to local interests and issues. Here lie the social origins of the Violencia, to an important extent.

Three factors aided the rise of Cali and the Cauca Valley region to national importance in the years after 1900: political peace, the opening of the region with the construction of a route to the Pacific port of Buenaventura (actually a combination of road and short rail links), and the vigor of agricultural investment, principally in tobacco and coffee companies and in sugar operations that perpetuated much of the ethno-social structure of the older cattle or cacao haciendas.

With the opening of the Panama Canal in 1914, coffee could be marketed and transported efficiently from Colombia's Pacific side, and western markets were quick to adapt and grow. Once the Cali–Buenaventura railway was completed in 1915, the river ports of the Magdalena and the Caribbean ports they fed lost much of their trade. In the 1930s Buenaventura displaced Barranquilla as the principal coffee port, though Barranquilla retained its status as leading importer.

Regions and Cities in an Era of Expansion

The development of export agriculture had several effects on the relations between cities and their regions, but two are of special importance. The first was the creation of new urban hierarchies and the emergence of new oligarchies that linked arrivistes with the old families. This phenomenon could be seen in Bogotá, which in the 1920s consolidated its position as national financial hub, but also in Medellín and even Cúcuta. The Caribbean port cities were more cosmopolitan, their elites taking in members from abroad and becoming more familiar with the customs and styles of Panama City and Havana; they even adopted some of the trappings of the "American way of life," albeit more New Orleans than, say, Boston.

The second effect was the weakening of links between the regional ruling classes and the "notables" of smaller towns. While departments are constitutional creations, *municipios* offer their inhabitants the natural and historical setting for collective identity, even if the *municipio* is of recent vintage. This was also the stage for the parish priest, a figure of immense importance in Conservative towns and in many Liberal ones as well. As the regional elites increasingly looked outward to other regions and to foreign markets and norms, many towns fell further into cultural isolation under the leadership of traditionalist and often sectarian local figures.

Just as during the colonial era and the postindependence nineteenth century, the cities of the twentieth century were centers of power, wealth, and culture. But now urbanization consisted almost exclusively of the expansion in area and density of existing centers rather than the creation of new ones. The first signs of the extreme segregation that would come to characterize late-twentieth-century Colombian cities were already visible.

Between 1870 and 1938 the population of Colombia's twenty largest cities

TABLE 1

Indices of Urbanization, 1870–1951 (Percent)

Number of Inhabitants	1870	1918	1935	1951
<10,000	89	75	52	34
10,000–19,999	8	8	7	8
20,000–100,000	3	14	19	20
>100,000	—	3	22	38

Source: Population censuses.

increased 50 percent faster than the national average. While the overall distribution of population from smaller to larger towns and cities was very substantial (see Table 1), Colombia's urbanization actually lagged behind that of many other Latin American countries.

The cities themselves were still subject to the rhythms, values, and limitations of rural life. According to the census of 1918, even the larger cities (including Bogotá, Medellín, and Cali) had at least as many rural proprietors as urban ones, according to the census takers' assessments. In 1938 only 14 percent of nominally urban buildings had all three of the basic public services: running water, electricity, and connection to a sewer.

The scanty available information about literacy, school attendance, and vaccination rates during the early twentieth century all show the country advancing steadily if slowly, but with increasing gaps in living conditions between regions, between classes, and between cities and the countryside. Certainly cities began to look different, thanks to streetcars, new building materials, and the slow introduction of cars. The gradually increasing demand for electricity, largely limited to the wealthy and to public street lighting, was supplied in Bogotá and Medellín by family firms and in the Cauca Valley and on the Caribbean coast by foreign capitalists, at least until the wave of pubic takeovers in the 1920s.

Between the lower class *pueblo* and the upper class *gente de bien* were the artisans. In Bogotá, for instance, around one-quarter of the economically active population was composed of artisans, stratified according to the years required to learn their trade, the complexity of their work, and the fees they could command. The word "artisan," like "merchant" and "cultivator" (*agricultor*), was still ambiguous. While some trades, such as tailoring and shoemaking, lent themselves to piecework done by a single worker at home, others such as carpentry and baking tended to gather several workers together in a workshop. In that case owners and employees alike considered themselves artisans, even if they owned their own stores to sell their products.

While this artisan class was characterized by low technical levels and even lower capitalization, out of it came an entrepreneurial group that would establish medium-sized factories and large retail establishments, and in time — the third or fourth generation — would flow into the new middle classes and the liberal professions such as law and medicine.

We know little about the social transformations experienced by new arrivals to the cities, and about how they interacted with established residents. Illiteracy and lack of training were not barriers to entry to the construction trades, or to workshops or the few factories; or to "women's work" — washing, sewing, and ironing clothes, domestic service, and of course prostitution, which was stratified into several categories of brothels and streetwalkers. The urban masses were in fact a constellation of all these groups, plus others from shopkeepers to transporters to family dependents. With local variations, this would be the norm for the first half of the twentieth century.

The organizers and foot soldiers of the 1912 census faced classification issues that were symptomatic of the changes in the nation's workforce. The preexisting broad categories were continued, and new jobs were wedged into them: electricians and stenographers found themselves among the "liberal professions," while photographers, typographers, and piano tuners ended up under the "fine arts," and the already catchall category of "arts, trades, and manufactures" now included nurses, guitarists of all sorts, sacristans, and bullfighters. Bar owners joined currency traders and capitalists under "commerce," while the agents of shipping lines, mule drivers, and oarsmen were part of the "transportation industry." If we reclassify this gamut of jobs according to modern notions of the primary, secondary, and tertiary sectors, we see in Table 2 that the last category — services, broadly defined — grew notably over the first half of the century. The details may be debatable but the trend is clear.

Movement from one occupational category to another was not a function of training but rather of the cheapness of labor in general, so that rising sec-

TABLE 2

Composition of Economically Active Population, 1912–51, by Sector (Percent)

Sector	1912	1938	1951
Primary[a]	75	62	55
Secondary[b]	13	17	16
Tertiary[c]	12	21	29

Source: Population censuses.
[a] Agricultural and mining activities.
[b] All manufacturing (artisanal and factory) and construction activities
[c] All other activities.

tors, such as manufacturing, coffee production, and urban construction, could easily attract labor from stagnant ones. The overall average national level of schooling remained relatively stable at around two years of formal education from 1915 to 1945.

By any measure of population or economic role, Bogotá in 1900 was hardly at the level of Havana, Lima, or Santiago, much less the metropolis of Buenos Aires or Mexico City. Still, the Colombian capital set the standard that other urban centers sought to emulate, as their capacities, climates, and regional cultures allowed. In the 1890s the city of mixed-class neighborhoods began to disappear as the poor began to move to the new slums on the outskirts—the movement of better-off residents to new and more comfortable neighborhoods came later. Around a third of Bogotá's residents in 1890 paid rent for what was known as a *tienda*, a single room without windows and usually with a dirt floor, which served as bedroom, kitchen, and perhaps workshop. Renting out these rooms was so profitable that landowners began to build new ones beyond the city's water and sewer lines, where typhus, dysentery, pneumonia, and tuberculosis would run rampant.

An official report of 1916 counted sixty-two factories, almost all of them in Bogotá, Medellín, Cartagena, and Barranquilla. Several of them would grow into the most important in the country by the industrial census of 1945, and some came to dominate the economic scene in their respective cities. While some factories had begun as workshops, most workshops had no future as factories. With electricity unreliable or nonexistent, factories often had to be built near waterfalls, away from established centers. In those sectors where modern processes and techniques were the norm, such as railroad and steamship repair or the processing of precious metals, the encounter of foreign and Colombian talent led to the establishment of factories to produce agricultural tools, machines to extract coffee beans from their berries, mills for processing sugar cane, pickaxes for small-scale mining—and shotguns for Liberals and Conservatives.

The tariff reforms of 1905, 1913, and 1931 stimulated the local production of manufactured goods otherwise imported from the United States and Europe —what economists call import substitution. The influence of manufacturing interests can also be seen in the 1927 passage of an "emergency law" that reduced tariffs on such staples as rice, corn, and sugar to calm urban protests against high inflation; this law, in turn, provoked a lobbying effort by agricultural interests to repeal it. But Colombian industry as a whole was still quite weak, whether measured in political clout or in actual production. Even the vanguard textile industry met only one-fifth of internal demand in 1928, and the 52,000 spindles installed in the whole country amounted to a single mid-sized factory in England's textile heartland of Lancashire—itself already facing more modern competitors in Japan, the United States, and Germany.

The Imperative of National Reconciliation

As Rafael Reyes assumed the presidency in 1904, political leaders had already agreed to remove fiscal and monetary policy from the realm of electoral politics, a significant moment for Colombia's twentieth-century history. The most pressing economic issue in late 1902, when the treaties that put a formal end to the War of the Thousand Days were signed, was the convertibility of paper currency issued before and during the war (eventually at hyperinflationary levels) and the status of civil and commercial contracts denominated in paper money. The end of military operations put an end to new issues of paper, but the Treasury found itself unable to pay public employees. Congress, which had not met since 1898, reconvened to approve the adoption of the gold peso as the monetary unit, its valued tied to the U.S. dollar and convertible from the paper peso at the prevailing rate of 100 to 1.

Reyes was an exception to the Colombian political rule: he was neither a lawyer nor a poet, but rather a failed businessman who had roamed half of Colombia in search of fortune and eventually found it in his personal charisma and political talent. During the first months of his government Reyes enjoyed strong support among businessmen, who saw him as the best hope for stability. Although coffee prices remained depressed throughout his presidency, exports of gold, hides, and even live cattle from the Caribbean coast increased.

According to Reyes, the two most important obstacles to economic development were Colombia's primitive transportation system and the lack of a modern banking structure. To tackle the first obstacle Reyes proposed a program of road and rail construction, complemented by port improvements and the dredging of the Magdalena River. For the latter project he created a central bank, which to many Congressmen looked like a return to Regeneration fiscal policy, and the measure was defeated. In response to this and other legislative defeats, Reyes convened a handpicked National Assembly in 1905, most notable for its decision to guarantee the minority party — the Liberals, since Reyes was a prominent Conservative despite his nonpartisan charisma — one-third of the seats in all legislative bodies.

In the hope of obtaining fresh foreign loans, the Reyes administration renegotiated the foreign debt in 1905. But the continuing coffee slump and Colombia's very modest overall level of exports were clear cautionary signs for the international financial markets. When a fall-off in imports and therefore of customs revenues threatened to plunge the government into a nineteenth-century-style budget crisis, Reyes opted to appropriate the departments' principal lines of revenue — liquor, cattle slaughter, tobacco, and sea salt. He also established a fiscal monopoly on animal hides and nationalized the railroads owned by the departments, a move that was particularly offensive to Antioquian interests and turned Medellín into the center of anti-Reyes agitation.

By 1908 Reyes managed to neutralize his growing unpopularity, but the next year he made the mistake of insisting on approval of the so-called Tripartite Treaty between Colombia, the United States, and Panama. There was a widely held view that the treaty's indemnity payments to Colombia for the loss of Panama would end up in the pockets of Reyes and his cronies, and even relatively efficient institutions such as the Banco Central were attacked as corrupt. A bipartisan coalition claimed that the Assembly was not authorized by the Constitution to ratify international treaties, and the debate soon overflowed the legislative chambers, the salons of high society, and the halls of academia. Bogotá's students and artisans took to the streets to pressure the government to reconvene Congress. A chastened Reyes reversed the centralization of departmental revenues and railroads, and during a trip to the coastal banana zone he slipped aboard a United Fruit Company boat and sailed off into exile. Jorge Holguín was named acting president, and Congress eventually named the Conservative war hero Ramón González Valencia to serve until the following year.

The five-year regime of Rafael Reyes—the *Quinquenio*—sought to create a climate of political cooperation in the interests of economic development and to attract foreign capital, largely from the United States. Its negative consequences included authoritarianism, cultural provincialism, and the uncharacteristically visible corruption of a circle of favorites and political allies who made no distinction between the public treasury and the private trough. As soon as Reyes left, press freedom was reestablished and the Banco Central became just another bank.

The collapse of the Reyes regime was an opportunity for the Republican movement, a coalition founded in Medellín and Bogotá in 1909 to press for a constitutional restriction of presidential powers and the strengthening of Congress and the departments. Its leadership, based in Bogotá's city council, won enough support among the elites of other cities to force the vacillating González Valencia to call a new National Assembly to reform the 1886 Constitution and elect a president for the new term.

The new Assembly pared the Regeneration's centralism to the benefit of regional elites and emerging economic groups. The former resented excessive centralism in general; the latter were narrowly concerned with eliminating the president's powers to manipulate the currency and the budget deficit. The Assembly's reforms included reduction of the presidential term from six to four years; direct election of the president, albeit with suffrage limited to men, and then only to those who could meet literacy and income or property requirements; replacement of the vice president with a designate whose only function was to replace the president; and a return of responsibility for official acts to the president rather than the cabinet. The president lost the power to nominate Supreme Court justices, who were limited to five-year terms; however, the court's powers to review and invalidate laws were expanded. In addition the death penalty was abolished; sessions of Congress were made annual rather than biennial; and, in a statement of monetary orthodoxy that in practice turned out to be symbolic, any new issue of paper money without the backing of precious metal was "absolutely" prohibited.

Departments recovered their lines of revenue and eventually acquired new ones, such as lotteries, beer taxes, railway receipts, and for favorably situated departments even a modest share of oil and mineral royalties. The *municipios* enjoyed substantial autonomy in levying local taxes, especially on property, and received a share of the department's liquor revenues. The 1910 reform opened the way to the creation of new departments. The large "historical" region of Cauca was split into (from north to south) Valle del Cauca, Cauca, and Nariño. Antioquia gained the northern province of Urabá with its lumber wealth but lost Caldas in the south, which joined with Quindío, formerly in Cauca, to create the new department of Caldas; Santander was divided into two departments, north and south; Huila was separated from Tolima; and Barranquilla finally won complete autonomy from Cartagena with the creation of the department of Atlántico.

The system of *intendencias* and *comisarías* to administer Colombia's sparsely populated peripheral regions, established in the 1886 constitution, continued until 1943. These regions were placed under the political and economic tutelage of neighboring departments: Chocó was subject to Antioquia, Casanare to Boyacá, Putumayo to Nariño, and Caquetá to Huila. In the latter two cases, however, state authority in general was constrained by powerful missions operated by Catholic missionary orders.

The constitutional reform of 1910 produced two long-term consequences. First, direct election ended up strengthening the president against the rest of the political insiders, putting him in closer contact with the electorate. Second, the direct or indirect designation of judges by the legislature resulted in even greater politicization of the judicial branch and turned a judgeship into just one more article of party plunder.

The National Assembly, with a nominal Conservative majority that was divided into factions, chose as president for the 1910–14 term a young Antioquian lawyer named Carlos E. Restrepo, one of the leaders of the Republican movement that drove Reyes from power. With the support of the Liberal leader Benjamín Herrera, he narrowly defeated the mainstream Conservative (and future president) José Vicente Concha within the Assembly. This defeat hardened the opposition of many Conservatives to bipartisanship.

Although Restrepo was convinced of the merits of fiscal decentralization, free enterprise, and the separation of powers, he lacked the political skills to deal effectively with Congress, which already resented him because he was elected by the parallel National Assembly. In addition, Restrepo seemed not to understand or value the urban middle class—often of the "poor but respectable" sort—that relied on political patronage for sustenance and upward mobility. This group was the nursery, in effect, for many town councilmen, departmental deputies, and national congressmen, not to mention priests, notaries, schoolteachers, and a miscellany of public posts "from ministers to doormen." In addition, Restrepo was aghast that populous backward regions such as Boyacá, Cauca, and much of the Caribbean coast had an effective veto on legislation by virtue of their representation in Congress.

These tensions stymied the government and weakened the Republican movement at the national, departmental, and local levels. Restrepo's proposal for electoral reform was conceived, presented, and received as a frontal attack on the members of Congress. The president thought the electoral system was rotten and the source of violence, and since the judiciary was unable or unwilling to correct its faults, his bill sought to establish a new autonomous branch of government dedicated exclusively to the electoral process. In addition the reform bill stripped priests, police, and soldiers of the vote; the hierarchies of those institutions, openly Conservative, went over to the opposition. Political leaders of both parties turned their backs on the reform effort, which ended up as debate fodder for lawyers and scribblers in Bogotá and Medellín.

Around 1910 foreign trade picked up, and the government could face up to returning to the departments the income that Reyes had taken from them. But at the same time, business leaders asked for an increase in public spending on infrastructure, while politicians at all levels demanded more public-sector jobs to satisfy their clienteles, all of which put new strains on the budget.

Restrepo was selective in applying liberalism to economic affairs. In 1913 he signed a new tariff schedule that, without changing the major thrust of the 1905 tariff, reinforced protection for the nascent textile industry, even raising levies on ready-to-wear clothing and household sewing machines in order to build the market. The same measure quintupled tariffs on wheat, wheat flour, and rice. At the end of his administration Restrepo railed against "state socialism," complaining that "salaries, benefits, pensions, and contracts are parasitic perks and the great enemies of production, the Treasury, and honest government." But this was a hollow complaint, given the extent to which "producers" in Restrepo's Antioquia, despite their claims of heroic accomplishment, relied upon protectionist tariffs, sales of public lands and mining rights on favorable terms, and access to liquor monopoly revenues.

On foreign policy, which during this period meant the Panama Canal, Restrepo sought to build a consensus. The rocky road to final ratification of the treaty illustrates some key aspects of Colombia's entrance into the twentieth-century world. After Panama became independent, some Colombians, Rafael Reyes among them, vainly hoped to persuade Washington to return to the status quo ante by signing the Hay-Herrán Treaty, which the Colombian Senate had rejected. Other options were international arbitration and a plebiscite of the Panamanians, both rejected by the United States. Eventually it was understood that the only solution was a direct treaty with Washington that accepted Panama's independence.

The fall of Reyes in 1909 put the Panama issue into limbo, and in March 1911 the arbitration idea was briefly revived after the former president Theodore Roosevelt admitted that his actions in 1903 were illegal: "I took the Isthmus, started the canal, and then left Congress not to debate the canal, but to debate me. . . . While the debate goes on, the canal does too." But it was Woodrow Wilson who realized the need for some final agreement, given Colombia's proximity to the canal and the country's new importance as a source of oil. Henry Cabot Lodge, Roosevelt's powerful ally in the Senate, put a straitjacket on U.S. negotiators by declaring the 1903 events a question of "national honor" not subject to debate or apology; but the countries were able to come to terms on a treaty that granted Colombia an indemnity of $25 million, recognized special rights for Colombian civilian and military ships in the canal, and expressed the United States' "sincere regret" for past events. Panamanians were skeptical that the Colombian Senate would ratify the treaty, given the Hay-Herrán experience, but the Conservative majority passed it with enthusiasm.

There is little doubt that outright corruption played a part in getting the treaty through, especially given the growing importance of oil, but the treaty's contents and its passage had more to do with the limitations and weaknesses of the Colombian state, the diplomatic inexperience of its leaders, and above all the domestic struggle to gain control of the long-awaited indemnity money. The treaty, whatever its defects, would boost public finances and reinforce electoral patronage. The business class, recognizing an opportunity to modernize Colombia's physical and financial infrastructure, strongly supported the treaty. Merchants, especially on the Caribbean coast, were eager to have the treaty signed before the canal officially opened in order to make Cartagena and Barranquilla viable transit ports for interocean trade. Ironically, the outbreak of World War I tied up the treaty in the U.S. Senate for seven more years.

On February 9, 1914, some 380,000 voters went to the polls in the first direct popular election for the presidency since Mariano Ospina's victory in 1856. The Conservative José Vicente Concha, supported by the Liberal leader Rafael Uribe Uribe—famous proponent of the "state socialism" derided by Restrepo—defeated the Republican candidate by an 8-to-1 margin. Concha continued the Reyes and Republican practice of "mixed cabinets," but without Republican participation so that he could better serve the Conservative party machinery and the church, whose influence was especially overt and pervasive during this period. Within a month of Concha's inauguration Uribe Uribe was assassinated, and the president lost an important ally and spokesman among the loyal opposition.

The Concha regime became the model for the image of "Conservative hegemony" cogently advanced by Enrique Santos, the most perceptive and feisty Liberal journalist of the period. Santos attacked the government for its "dishonesty, intolerance, and corruption," and revived the nineteenth-century Liberal rhetoric of the "two Colombias": one that was urban and urbane, cultured and tolerant, its inhabitants respectful participants in democratic politics, and another whose inhabitants were essentially cave dwellers, exploited in the overpopulated and destitute countryside by fanatical priests and sectarian Conservative bosses. Still, Colombia had entered its second decade of relative political peace, until that point the longest continuous period of peace since independence. It was a peace based on the idea that rigged elections were preferable to a good war.

The regimes of Concha and his successor, Marco Fidel Suárez, faced the economic and fiscal contraction brought on by World War I, aggravated in 1917 by the United States' entry into the war and the tabling of the Panama Canal treaty, which hobbled U.S. investment and bilateral trade and roiled the political scene. The dislocation caused by the war led to an alarming budget crisis as revenues fell in 1914 and 1915, recovered the following year, but then fell precipitously in 1917 and 1918. The closing of European markets and their partial replacement by the United States had an impact on all credit and mer-

cantile operations. According to the market opinions collected in the Finance
Ministry's annual report for 1916, this rapid rise of the United States as trading
partner would have been unimaginable without the special circumstances of
war, given that "the habit of buying English goods dates to the colonial era,
when smuggling compensated for the abuses of Spanish commercial policies."

The war softened the dogmas of liberal economics and forced government
and businessmen into a closer relationship. Exporters, merchants, and industrialists all needed state intervention to control the costs of rail and river transportation, the prices of imported and domestic goods by regulating tariffs, and
bank rates. An additional problem was the continued lack of a single currency:
as late as 1918, 42 percent of money in circulation was still Regeneration bank-
notes (to be sure, freshly printed in England and the United States), and another 40 percent was silver coinage (still popular near the borders of Venezuela
and Ecuador, since those countries were on the silver standard), U.S. dollars,
or pounds sterling. Often public employees were the only ones paid in official
coinage, and they lost money when they had to exchange it for silver-based
currency at a discount.

The happy and expansive 1920s began very badly. The value of imports doubled
in 1919 from the previous year and quintupled in 1920, and the government was
unable to cope with congestion in the ports and popular agitation against inflation in the country at large. In 1921 foreign trade fell back by two-thirds, dealing
a devastating blow to merchants and contributing to general deflation. The
government lacked mechanisms to regulate the money supply, but a series of
ad hoc measures such as issuance of treasury vouchers, acceptance of mortgage
certificates in payment of taxes, and wider use of pounds sterling in everyday
circulation were reasonably effective in maintaining the money supply. The fiscal deficit was addressed by cost-cutting: firing some employees and delaying
salary payments to others, even in the armed forces.

This preview of the crisis of the 1930s had its political fallout. Suárez was
forced to resign a year before the completion of his term in 1922, and the three-
way Conservative contest to succeed him was especially bitter.

The New Conservatism

Marco Fidel Suárez represented a new doctrine of Conservative realism for the
twentieth century. In his vision, the United States was the North Star, leader

of the hemisphere and Colombia's natural ally. Suárez was the illegitimate son of a washerwoman from Antioquia, and his rise, aided by the enthusiastic support of the church and genuine popularity within his party, represented the Conservative ideal of social mobility based on embrace of traditional values. As a member of the cultured elite he assumed that Europe's spiritual torch would continue to light the way to civilization, although his lifelong scholarly interest in Colombian Spanish as distinct from its peninsular roots has burnished his image as a nationalist.

To Suárez, Colombia's dilemma was whether or not to industrialize. The new society would surely be forged on the basis of the natural sciences, private initiative, and charity of the traditional conservative sort, but the relative weight of each component was yet to be determined. Put another way, Colombia had to combine the materialism of the North Star with the pontifical doctrines of the *Rerum novarum*. Technology and the instruments of capitalism were welcome and necessary, but they could not be allowed to affect the Catholic peasant soul of a Colombia the Conservatives and the church feared to lose. This recipe of Catholic social doctrine and Yankee progress would put its stamp on "progressive conservatism" for the rest of the century.

The practical impact of the North Star doctrine was quite limited. Successive governments tried to use commercial, financial, and oil rivalries between Europe and the United States to their advantage, and the legislature's power to approve or reject treaties undermined the president's leadership in foreign policy. Colombia remained neutral throughout World War I, and the "abnormalities" of its foreign trade were plainly exposed: the United States was the principal purchaser of Colombia's coffee, but Europe was the principal supplier of its imports. This situation evened out over time, but not without diplomatic friction.

The United States' participation in the war obliged Wilson to redouble military protection of the canal, which in turn meant guaranteeing that neutral countries such as Colombia did not succumb to German influence. With this argument Wilson brought the canal treaty before the U.S. Senate and won its passage, but only with important modifications: the "sincere regret" line was dropped; Colombia was to give the United States a 100-year option on opening an alternative canal through the Atrato region; it would lease to the United States, also for 100 years, the Caribbean islands of San Andrés and Providencia (whose possession was disputed by Nicaragua, especially since the Liberal José

Santos Zelaya came to power there in 1893); and it would agree to receive the indemnity payment in installments rather than all at once. In 1918 Colombia accepted the first and fourth changes and rejected the second and third, and all seemed set for a final agreement.

However, the separate peace signed by the Bolsheviks with Germany in May 1918 threw a last-minute and wholly unexpected obstacle in the way of the treaty. Russia was a major supplier of platinum to the United States' war industry, and with its new status of neutral, its supplies were no longer available. Colombia, which in 1913 supplied only 9 percent of the United States' needs, by 1918 supplied over half, and the U.S. government demanded that Colombia increase its platinum production rather than use platinum along with gold to shore up its domestic money supply. The State Department warned Colombia of severe trade reprisals if it failed to cooperate, and despite Concha's efforts to satisfy the United States' demand, Washington sharply reduced imports of leather, Colombia's second-largest export line at the time. Cattlemen on the Caribbean coast and in Antioquia felt a severe pinch, and they lobbied the Colombian Congress to place export tariffs on precious metals, escalating the conflict. Fortunately, the war ended the next month, and the urgency on the United States side quickly evaporated.

A year later, in August 1919, the treaty was once more on the verge of ratification in the U.S. Senate when a new obstacle appeared: a Colombian government decree reaffirming the longstanding principle that subsoil rights to Colombia's oil were vested in the state. Members of the Senate Foreign Relations Committee were concerned that Colombian legislation might set a precedent for Mexico and other countries in the region at a time when the United States depended on imports for 90 percent of its oil. Washington demanded Colombian guarantees for existing U.S. claims, and Suárez instructed his ambassador to assure the United States that the decree was in no way confiscatory, that "acquired rights" would be respected, and that in any event the decree was suspended. Privately the Colombian government hoped that the Supreme Court would annul the decree and make the issue moot.

While many Colombians thought the decree represented a dangerous expansion of state power against property rights, Suárez's explanatory telegram was denounced as shameful, unworthy, even traitorous. To a great extent the range of opinions about the decree and the telegram reflected the range of opinion about the government in general rather than the specific issue. When Washington proposed to amend the treaty to include guarantees of the vested rights of U.S. oil companies, much as Suárez's telegram offered, opposition in Colombia was fierce and the idea got nowhere. In November 1919 the Supreme Court did indeed strike down the decree, as the government had hoped, but the State Department wanted to be sure that the new legislation conformed to the president's promises, and only when it was satisfied on that score did the U.S. Senate finally approve the treaty, in April 1921.

The Suárez regime was exhausted by successive crises: the economy, urban unrest, and the treaty debate. By 1921 the next presidential campaign was at the forefront, joined now by the question of control of the indemnity money. These were, in fact, a single issue: regional and political interests fighting for the $25 million threw themselves into the struggle for the presidential succession. Suárez had to cede all of his leverage by giving the United States a new decree acceptable to the oil companies and promising Conservative leaders that he would leave decisions about the indemnity to the next government. In October 1921 the Colombian Senate ratified the amended treaty, and one month later Suárez was forced to resign, accused of collusion with foreign interests.

A broader explanation of Suárez's fall is that he deviated from well-established official dogma on the government's actions in regard to the export sector by questioning the priority of physical infrastructure designed to complement Colombia's comparative advantage in the world economy. Suárez wanted the indemnity spent first on primary education; then on teachers' training schools and vocational schools offering training in the natural sciences, agriculture, and mining; transportation and ports came in third. That program spurred a coalition of bankers and speculators (led by the future Liberal president Alfonso López Pumarejo) and ambitious politicians (led by the future Conservative president Laureano Gómez) to orchestrate the campaign that led to Suárez's resignation.

In March 1922 the United States and Colombia exchanged diplomatic notes completing the treaty process, and Colombia finally received the first installment on the indemnity, some $10 million. Ironically, Colombia's oil and precious-metals wealth had delayed rather than facilitated the country's passage into the post-Panama era.

One Church, Many Clergies

Economic growth and the slow but noticeable crisis of rural society represented a threat to the social and political values of the Conservative regime, as traditional institutions beginning with the church found themselves competing with new ones, such as labor unions.

The church's intimate relationship with the 1914–30 regimes was at the heart of the "Conservative Hegemony." The papal nuncio, archbishops, bishops, and parish priests had their say in the selection of Conservative candidates for the presidency and the whole chain of public offices. The church hierarchy itself could not have been more stable, under the leadership of Bogotá's archbishops Bernardo Herrera Restrepo (1891–1928) and Ismael Perdomo (1929–50): until 1901 the Bogotá archdiocese covered the whole of Colombia, and when new archdioceses were created in Popayán and Cartagena (1901) and then Medellín (1903), the archbishop of Bogotá received the title of primate to denote his continued national leadership.

Herrera doubled the number of dioceses from eight to sixteen and increased the number of religious communities (banned by the Liberals and reinstated by the Regeneration in the 1880s) to thirty-one women's orders and fifteen for men by 1929. He created four "apostolic vicariates" and six prefectures covering the sparsely populated "national territories" on Colombia's margins, within which seven missionary communities enjoyed wide powers recognized by the government. During Herrera's tenure Colombia's ecclesiastical geography changed radically, after Colombia's population shift from traditional highland areas (Bogotá, Tunja, Popayán, Pasto) to more dynamic regions such as Antioquia. By 1930 almost all members of religious orders were Colombian-born, the products of the seminaries and convents that reappeared during the Regeneration era of the late nineteenth century. They were educated by priests who were themselves refugees from the anticlerical liberal regimes of Ecuador and Central America, or from the losing side of Italian, French, and Spanish struggles between ultramontane Catholicism and liberal laicism.

But the church was no monolith, and the clearest division was the same as during the colonial era: between the diocesan clergy, who owed obedience to the bishop, and the clergy of religious congregations, who followed the rules of their orders. The former attended to the Catholic population as parish priests, while the latter devoted themselves—in accordance with the 1887 Concordat between the Vatican and the Colombian state—to education, charity, and frontier missions. Canon law gave bishops wide autonomy in running their dioceses, and during the first half of the twentieth century Bishops Rafael Afanador in Popayán, Manuel González Arbeláez in Pamplona, and Miguel Ángel Builes in Santa Rosa de Osos (Antioquia) were notorious for their incendiary antiliberalism. Despite occasional reprimands from the upper reaches of the church hierarchy, they were effective promoters of political violence.

The attitudes and priorities of the clergy often corresponded closely with regional agendas and disputes. In 1902, for example, the bishop of Medellín urged cultivators in his region to sow crops for local industries. In the 1910s the bishop of Cartagena went so far as to excommunicate members of the local elite as part of an escalating conflict over control of education. In Bogotá, with its new proletariat, a Jesuit founded a Catholic workers' association in 1911, then two years later a savings bank, and then the first planned neighborhood for working-class families.

In the closing years of the nineteenth century the papal dictum that liberalism was sinful took on new relevance in a Latin America mostly under the grip of liberal regimes, even in unlikely places like Ecuador. In 1898 Pope Leo XIII brought the Latin American bishops to Rome for a council, and Colombian church leaders returned with orders to subject all primary and secondary teachers to an oath of obedience to the principles of the Council of Trent, the (first) Vatican Council, the just-completed council in Rome, and the *Syllabus of Errors*, which rejected liberalism, naturalism, socialism, and rationalism. In July 1902 Liberal Party members who wished to return to the Catholic fold had to condemn, "without reservation and with fullness of heart, any and all political or religious liberalism and all false liberties that threaten our Catholic faith."

From the high perch of Monsignor Rafael María Carrasquilla in Bogotá's elite Colegio del Rosario to the pulpits of the most far-flung parishes, priests were guided by *The Teachings of the Church on Liberalism*, a text that explained the sinful nature of the phenomenon and how to combat it. The bishop of Pasto, as popular as he was radical in his hatred of liberalism, made his last will and testament of 1905 a public display of his fervor:

> Liberalism has made unspeakable gains, and this horrible reality is sadly proclaimed by the failure of all efforts to reconcile those who love the altar and those who despise it: between Catholics (that is to say, Conservatives) and Liberals (that is, atheists). Once more I testify that LIBERALISM IS SIN, fatal enemy of the Church and of the kingdom of Jesus Christ, ruin of peoples and of nations; and desiring to teach this even after my death, I request that in the hall where my body is displayed, and even in church during the funeral, a large sign should be displayed which says: LIBERALISM IS SIN.

The indefatigable Rafael Uribe Uribe replied several years later with a pamphlet titled *On How Colombian Political Liberalism Is Not a Sin*, which was of course roundly condemned by the hierarchy.

The church's charity work raised few objections but its missions became the object of criticism by the second decade of the twentieth century. The church took the place of the state in the so-called national territories as their links to Bogotá became more tenuous during the Regeneration, until by 1900 the state was represented there by only a few public employees dependent on the sufferance of the local society and a few Spanish, French, and Italian missionaries who were subject to their hierarchies rather than to the nominal state authority. In 1922 the intendant of Meta, a Conservative colonel, complained that the resident French Marist priest had turned the region into "an ecclesiastical colony where civil power is not respected." Missionaries saw the problems of their profoundly impoverished and marginalized regions in narrow terms, as when the apostolic prefect of Chocó listed his most urgent problem as the increase in prostitution among young women, a consequence of the arrival of British and U.S. platinum mining companies.

The evangelization effort in the Putumayo rain forest deserves special mention, as it would eventually reveal the weakness of the Colombian state on two fronts: the demarcation of its international borders and its treatment of indigenous peoples. Under the 1887 Concordat and a special missions agreement signed in 1902, the government put the Capuchins in charge of evangelizing Putumayo's indigenous population. The order established its base in the Sibundoy Valley and with impressive efficiency established a theocratic ministate encompassing the various "tribes of savage Indians," in whom the government showed so little interest that they were not counted in the national censuses of 1912 and 1918. But when the friars became aware of the hideous abuses of the Huitotos by the Peruvian firm Casa Arana during the full frenzy of the rubber boom, they did nothing. Their attitude changed only when the papal encyclical *Lacrimabili statu* of Pius X (1912) joined the chorus of international condemnation of Casa Arana's forced-labor practices.

As the clergy was well aware, the moral indicators of the urban poor were all pointing downward. At the turn of the century over half of all births in Bogotá were illegitimate, and that in a city with a higher density of priests, both secular and regular, than anywhere else in the country. To protect working-class families from the threats of liberalism and socialism, but also from the social consequences of pauperization (delinquency, alcoholism, prostitution), brought on by unemployment, Conservative governments, with the church's support, developed three responses: vocational training, a campaign against alcoholism, and a timid labor law.

The church's crusade against alcohol could not be reconciled with the fact that revenues from the liquor monopoly were the bulwark of the departments' budgets, especially in the Conservative west of the country. Still, between 1890 and 1924 liquor production in Antioquia declined by 75 percent, from 2.4 liters per person per year to only 0.63, if statistics are to be believed. Meanwhile on the plains around Bogotá a half-century of estimates (1890–1939) suggest that rural workers consumed corn liquor in stable and enormous amounts, enough to supply half of their daily calorie intake.

Labor legislation, rooted in Catholic social doctrine, developed slowly but steadily. In public enterprises such as the railroads, most of them owned by the national or departmental governments, politicians mediated between workers and management and brought about some important institutional reforms. On the legislative level the principal innovations were coverage of work-related accidents (1915 and 1927); decriminalization of peaceful work stoppages—in effect a recognition of the right to strike, although employers were free to use scab labor (1921); obligatory group insurance for blue- and white-collar workers (1921); a special labor law covering public employees (1923); establishment of safety standards in the workplace and the creation of an inspection system (1925); the requirement of Sundays off (1926); and regulation of child labor (1929). During the 1920s the first steps were taken to establish institutions to deal constructively with labor disputes, and the National Labor Office (1923) intervened in both rural and urban workplaces. The Liberal regimes of the 1930s would extend and broaden all these measures, but they were Conservative creations.

The Church and Education

The church's political activism by way of the education system exacerbated the party conflict, and Liberals returned to their nineteenth-century argument that the church's pedagogical function was merely indoctrination rather than education in any modern sense.

At least in the cities, one's life chances did improve with schooling. But the labor market was just one facet of a more profound social change. Since the nineteenth century the urban working classes, most notably the artisans, had accepted the idea that education was the path to dignity and social emancipation. In 1870 nine out of ten Colombians were illiterate and barely 9 percent of school-age children attended school at all, if only for a year; around 1915 one-third of Colombians reported that they could read and write, and a third of children attended school.

The census of 1918 illustrates the relationship between regional educational attainment and the finances of *municipios* and departments, an inequality that would persist throughout the century. The gap between urban and rural education was overwhelming in all regions: the rate of school attendance for children between 5 and 14 was two to five times higher in departmental capitals than in other towns. More children dropped out in the rural areas than in the seats of *municipios* and the cities because their labor was needed on the farms and because of the distance between home and school.

The fundamental factor in the low demand for education in the rural areas was poverty. In a society where people lived at the subsistence level with minimal technology, people could hardly place much value on reading and writing. A newspaper could easily cost more than a day's wage for a rural laborer—and in any event, newspapers had small press runs and circulated almost exclusively in the cities. It is worth noting as counterpoint that in the small and remote black Protestant community on the islands of San Andrés and Providencia in the Caribbean, one of Colombia's "national territories," the level of literacy—in English—was twice the national average and higher than in Colombia's largest cities. Possible explanations for this phenomenon may lie in the islands' high population density and the Protestant emphasis on reading the Bible.

The so-called women's revolution was already visible in turn-of-the-century Colombian education. Female literacy rates slightly exceeded male rates in Antioquia and Caldas, and even in departments where this was not the case, such as Boyacá, Nariño, and Cauca, in artisan-heavy districts more women than men were literate. If we are to believe the information gathered by Medellín textile factories, whose labor force consisted largely of young single women, literacy rates ranged from 60 to 90 percent.

Religious communities competed with one another and responded to the market created by local elites, who wanted to get the most out of what the communities offered: high-quality, inexpensive, and officially sanctioned education. Boys' secondary schools operated by the church offered the title of

"Bachelor of Philosophy and Letters," an automatic passport into university studies. Girls' secondary schools inculcated morality and good manners and granted the "Diploma of Sufficient Education." During this era the church had no interest in establishing its own universities, since it had substantial say in the faculties and curricula of public universities. Direct control of teachers and textbooks in primary and secondary schools would do. In the late 1880s only 20 percent of Bogotá's secondary students attended a church-run school (the remainder going to state or private schools), but twenty years later than figure stood at 80 percent.

The educational institutions deepened the cultural chasm between the elites and the masses. The prevalent model was French-influenced (most of the principal religious communities, with the notable exceptions of the Jesuits and Dominicans, were French), unattached to the Hispanic legacy and to popular traditions of *mestizaje*, and were frankly hostile to the indigenous and African elements of Colombian national culture.

In 1903 the government centralized the supervision of education and many Conservative politicians began to argue for compulsory primary education, an idea denounced by the church. The church fought the notion of the "teaching state," but Carlos E. Restrepo considered primary education one of the state's foremost responsibilities. Some religious publications warned that educating everyone would create a dangerous "intellectual proletariat," as allegedly occurred in France. But the introduction of compulsory military service for men put a new twist on the question: how could military service be required, but not schooling?

Vocational and technical education also had a certain tradition in Colombia, although its results were depressingly sparse. In a largely agricultural country, the few schools oriented toward practical training were located in the main cities, trained students for urban jobs, and were very costly operations. Between 1890 and 1930 the Salesian community led the way by establishing four centers offering training for work in industry, agriculture, and the trades. Next to their elite secondary schools the Jesuits built "annex schools" for poor children. But business leaders showed little interest in these experiments, and artisans, most of whom were Liberals, considered them a form of unfair competition.

Education was, above all, a matter of power. Sectors of the church hierarchy insisted that the power to educate was the sole province of the clergy, as an expression of its political sovereignty. Others, less absolutist on the issue, were merely distrustful of state control and feared the undermining of traditional church authority by the large-scale expansion of public education. There was also disagreement on the question of overall supervision. Did the church have the right to inspect private institutions that received no state support? Archbishop Herrera argued that all education, by definition, belonged to the public realm and that the church therefore had the right and obligation to inspect even private institutions such as the Universidad Republicana, operated by adherents of Restrepo's fleeting Republican movement. Conservative political leaders interpreted the Concordat more restrictively: church inspection applied only to state schools.

In Colombia, as in other parts of the Catholic world, the church was also divided on the question of what should be taught as "truth." The Jesuits, for instance, condemned the Christian Brothers' curriculum for its emphasis on abstract reasoning and relativism; although these ideas were taught only in the context of solving scientific and mathematical problems, the Jesuits feared that they would open a Pandora's box. The basis of all instruction, in Jesuit thinking, was Latin and neo-Thomist formal logic.

All of these conflicts between factions of the church and government came out during the educational reform process of the mid-1920s. The government brought in a German education mission (1924–26) that proposed a series of reforms that were criticized by Liberal and extremist Catholic educators alike, and were initially rejected by Congress. The intensity of the ideological and doctrinal struggles was a preview of what would come under Liberal regimes in the 1930s. Despite the controversy, the Germans' report did persuade Congress to adopt the principle of parents' responsibility for the basic education of their children, including the freedom to choose their school. This move brought Colombia one step closer to compulsory primary education.

The church could no longer hope for a monopoly in education. Business schools offering courses in stenography, typing, and bookkeeping proliferated in response to a growing demand for specialized workers in the banking and commercial sectors. The public universities again became politicized and students could now learn about the ideas and intellectual currents of the times, from the Bolshevik and Mexican revolutions to the new Italian criminology of Cesare Lombroso and Enrico Ferri. In their struggle against conservative authoritarianism Colombian student leaders were inspired by the Argentine student movement's Córdoba Manifesto (1918), which made "university autonomy" everlasting dogma throughout Latin America. The Liberals made it a plank of their party platform in the 1920s, posing academic freedom against church interference in the battle for the conscience of the nation. The archbishop of Bogotá would later call it "autonomy of error," but the students carried the day: academic freedom was reflected in the ideal of the "roundtable student," iconoclastic, freethinking, and above all, a budding politician.

Labor Radicalism on the Peripheries

Colombia's working classes differed markedly in makeup from those of Argentina, Uruguay, and southern Brazil, where European immigrants played major roles. But just as in those countries, workers' mobilization and protests took off between 1918 and 1929. Colombia, in other words, also was buffeted by what the Peruvian Marxist theorist José Carlos Mariátegui called the "rough seas" of the postwar period, composed of "messianic hopes, revolutionary sentiments, [and] mystical passions."

Leaving aside the peasants, the working class of the 1910s could be divided between those who worked in the cities and those who were involved in infrastructure: in the big modern mining complexes; in railroads, ports, and highway construction; and in the operations of modern sugar and banana plantations. Compared to the artisans and petty merchants who formed the bulk of the urban population, this proletariat in the making was mobile, dispersed, and isolated. We know little about their origins, but presumably they retained close ties to their native villages and rotated between agricultural labor and their new jobs.

Petitions for improved wages and working conditions led to collective protests, which in turn often led to violent repression. This was the case with miners in Antioquia, stevedores on the Magdalena River, oil workers in Barrancabermeja, and most famously the banana workers of Santa Marta. Even artisans at the heart of official Colombia were vulnerable. In March 1919 a demonstration in front of the Presidential Palace by tailors protesting the importation of military uniforms degenerated into rock-throwing as the president himself was addressing the protestors. The army fired into the crowd, killing nine people and wounding eleven; three years later, a court-martial acquitted the general who gave the order to fire.

This resort to repression in support of liberal economics was only strengthened in the late 1920s. Officials were eager to invent a subversive enemy that could be repressed through draconian antivagrancy laws (1926) and the so-called Heroic Law of 1928, which fought "communist plots" by outlawing freedom of association and unionization. But this legislative offensive was opposed even by members of the ruling Conservatives, and added one more element to the growing split in the party.

Repression was accompanied by vilification. The clerical and conservative press of the 1910s depicted workers as lazy and caught in a vicious circle of vice and libertinism: card-playing, drunkenness, blasphemy, sensuous dancing, promiscuity, brothels. Many priests thought that economic progress brought only sinfulness. In fact, the economic geography of the "new Colombia" did coincide with the incidence of venereal disease. On the other side of the political spectrum, the left saw prostitution as a form of capitalist exploitation. In 1919 one of the many socialist parties of the period called for the "regulation of prostitution, so that this social cancer may be eradicated scientifically."

Public participation was more peaceful, by and large, among urban workers. Unions were organized in transport and utilities enterprises, construction, some breweries and soft-drink factories, and elsewhere. While company-run unions were the norm in Medellín's textile industry until the 1940s, Barranquilla's were influenced from the start by the radical transport workers of the Magdalena River. But overall, the proportion of the working-class population that was unionized was very small.

The factory proletariat, just a fragment of the overall urban working class, was segmented, and not just by geography and local idiosyncrasies. There were considerable sociocultural differences even among workers in the same city. For instance, the female workers of the Medellín textile plants showed little solidarity with the (also female) coffee-processing workers across town, and vice versa. Both groups were paid on a piecework basis and their conditions of employment were equally tenuous, but they were separated by civil status (textile workers were always young single women, while coffee workers were generally widows and single mothers), years of formal education, and social networks (a recommendation from the parish priest was often required for employment in a textile plant).

At least in Colombia's factories, Marx's predictions fell flat. Workers' demonstrations, when they occurred, depended not on a homogeneous structural situation or the commodification of labor under capitalism, but on one's family situation, gender, and religiosity, the life of one's neighborhood, and the company's hiring policies.

The party loyalties of artisans, in a sense the original Colombian working class, were not easy to pinpoint. After the short-lived artisan-backed dictatorship of José María Melo was deposed by an alliance of Liberal and Conservative elites in late 1854, artisans had no choice but to adapt to successive party-based regimes. But in critical situations the sectors tied to the Liberal tradition embraced radicalism, which in the 1920s took the form of identification with the revolution in Russia. During World War I Colombia's frontier proletariat was suddenly exposed to Spanish and Italian anarchism, and then to Marxism and its Bolshevik variant. But the spirit of rebellion was also fed by the novels of Victor Hugo — friend of the barricades and enemy of capital punishment — and by the pamphlets of the exiled Colombian firebrand José María Vargas Vila, who spared no rhetorical device in his thrashing of clerics, Yankees, and Conservatives.

Although socialists and anarchists were stirring things up in the cities, they had better results in the mining and oil enclaves and on the banana plantations, where traditional institutions were at their weakest. Company rules imposed rigid spatial, labor, and economic segregation, with separate living quarters, commissaries, and pay scales according to nationality and job description. A further important ingredient of radicalization was the essentially fraudulent labor contracting system that brought workers to enclaves: most were hired through subcontractors, so that the actual employer was relieved of any contractual obligations in regard to work conditions, pay, or job security.

Given the precariousness of legal mechanisms for resolution of social conflict, especially but not exclusively in the enclaves, the common recourse was to force. The obvious chasm between foreign-owned enterprises and local workers in the enclaves fed an intense nationalism that extended to the regions surrounding the enclaves. By the late 1920s rebellion also took the form of boycotting elections, which further marginalized enclave regions politically, since politicians sought votes in cities and long-settled rural areas where the marginal cost of each vote, in time and money, was far lower.

The principal centers of discontent coincided with the activities of the three most prominent revolutionary agitators of the 1920s, Raúl Eduardo Mahecha, Ignacio Torres Giraldo, and María Cano. Mahecha worked with stevedores and laborers on the Magdalena River, and from 1923 to 1927 with the oil workers of Barrancabermeja. From there he left for the coast and organized banana workers, until the strike that culminated in the infamous massacre of December 1928, after which he was court-martialed and imprisoned. Torres Giraldo was at the center of activism by workers of the Pacific Railway, a diversified company that built the port in Buenaventura and the department capitol in Cali, and also mined coal, so the strikes he organized covered a relatively wide range of workers.

Torres Giraldo was a key figure in the Socialist Revolutionary Party (PSR), founded in 1926, and in the Communist Party, which succeeded it in 1930. In 1926 he joined up with María Cano, one of Medellín's "flowers of labor" — young female activists who came from the local elite. She had begun her political career the previous year as a defender of "social and political prisoners" and as an opponent of capital punishment, a polarizing issue of the moment. Cano's travels from 1925 to 1927 faithfully followed Colombia's new labor geography, from mining and railway camps to coffee-processing plants. In Girardot she agitated among river workers, and in Barrancabermeja she took up social discrimination in the oil enclave and the loss of national sovereignty, but she also traveled to traditional highland Boyacá to highlight the miserable conditions of the rural poor.

Their revolutionary instincts also brought the socialist organizers of the 1920s to the struggle of the indigenous peoples of Cauca, which went beyond economic protest to pose a singular cultural and political challenge to the "white man's republic" that was Colombia. The second decade of the twentieth century saw an escalation of the longstanding indigenous mobilization in defense of communal lands, against the pretensions of Popayán's white landowners (now negligible figures on the national scene but still lords of their region), and against outside land colonizers. Both of those groups claimed that indigenous lands were legally vacant, the same claim that underpinned the land grabs during the quinine and rubber booms.

Around 1910, Manuel Quintín Lame became leader of the native peoples of Tierradentro. In 1914 he burst onto the national scene as organizer of a protest against obligatory service on haciendas and in defense of the indigenous institutions of communal landholding and self-government through the town council. A legalist in the best colonial tradition, Quintín Lame knew the political world and was in fact a lifelong Conservative; he used his authority in the indigenous world and his knowledge of wider Colombian society to bring his protest to indigenous communities throughout the southwest and beyond. In 1917 the government declared his movement illegal, and its leaders were imprisoned until 1921. After his release Quintín Lame organized the indigenous communities in southern Tolima, under siege by Liberal hacendados. Even during the ideological fervor of the late 1920s he rejected revolutionary socialism, and he had no faith in the indigenous "soviets" that sprang up in southern Tolima in 1931.

In the Santa Marta banana enclave on the Caribbean coast, strikes broke out in 1918 and 1924, but the third and greatest was in late 1928. Some 25,000 workers, mostly seasonal subcontracted laborers from Santander, Antioquia, and the coast itself, stopped all activities after their union, under the guidance of the PSR, failed to win concessions from the United Fruit Company (UFCO). The company was faced with stiff international competition, and its Colombian operations were already some 20 percent less productive than similar operations in Central America and the Antilles, while the greater distance raised the cost of transporting bananas to the United States.

The workers, whose chief demand was an end to subcontracting, appealed to nationalism: "The slogan of this crusade is 'For the Worker and for Colombia.'" The UFCO had in fact earned the enmity of many people in the region. Its practices made it the only wholesale buyer of bananas in the region, and Colombian planters were always eager to find competing purchasers; small cultivators detested the UFCO's meddling foremen; and local merchants were squeezed out by the company's commissaries, which garnered most of the workers' pay, since workers were paid in scrip that was good nowhere else. The position of local politicians was ambiguous: they recognized that the region's prosperity was tied to the company's activities, but starting in 1910 they launched a legal battle to transfer control of the railway servicing the banana enclave from the company to the department.

The strike ended in a bloodbath when between 2,000 and 4,000 workers gathered in the plaza of Ciénaga, intending to march to Santa Marta. A state of siege and a curfew were imposed on the region, and soldiers were dispatched to Ciénaga with orders to disperse the strikers. The ensuing massacre shook the political conscience of the working class and nascent middle class, and revived nationalist and anti–United States sentiments latent since the secession of Panama. As usual with such tragedies, the numbers are unreliable: the general in charge counted 47 dead in the Ciénaga plaza and along the rail line, while the U.S. consul in Santa Marta estimated the death toll at 1,000 and Alberto Castrillón, one of the strike leaders, claimed 1,500 dead.

The PSR argued that the problems of the working class came from capitalism itself, as practiced by an insufficiently nationalist Conservative regime. They joined Liberals in criticizing the restrictions on electoral competition, and they even joined Liberal veterans of the last civil war in plotting insurrections against Conservative rule. Two such insurrections actually broke out in 1928, one in the coffee town of Líbano (Tolima) and one in the railroad settlement of La Gómez (Santander). Despite draconian "public order" laws, political proselytizing through meetings, demonstrations, and the publication of broadsheets and pamphlets was less closely policed than union organizing within companies. Workers could be mobilized more effectively in the street than in the workplace. Apart from the repressive atmosphere in most workplaces, this strange political ecology was largely a function of Colombian society of the 1920s. The future president Alberto Lleras Camargo called Colombia a "country in flood": the constant geographical and social mobility created fluid and unforeseen situations that required programmatic and tactical flexibility of its leaders.

Liberals and revolutionary agitators agreed on this point, and both groups appealed to nationalist and populist feelings. Their methods were well suited to the plasticity of the situation, though none of them came close to the acute analytical skills of their Peruvian contemporary Mariátegui. During the late 1920s young "ex-communist" intellectuals happily swam in Liberal currents, which enabled them to embrace and express, at least rhetorically, the repressed radicalism of hundreds of thousands of Colombians struggling through what sociologists would call "social transition." Socialists could not displace the urban Liberal tradition, but were absorbed by it. In 1921 Liberal slates did poorly in Bogotá and other cities while Socialists did surprisingly well, and the Liberal leader Benjamín Herrera wasted no time in co-opting Socialist leaders and courting "Los Nuevos," a group of café intellectuals and pamphleteers who flirted with Marxism-Leninism. For the old civil war general Herrera their attraction lay in their uninhibited self-confidence, in contrast to the provincial pomposity of the regime's leadership. On the Conservative side, an extreme rightist group of young intellectuals known as Los Leopardos railed against Anglo-Saxon industrialization and its accompanying proletarianization, which they were sure would corrupt the working class, destroy rural values, and undermine the foundations of Colombian identity.

The Liberal press, ever more influential in the major cities (except for Conservative-dominated Medellín), identified with the causes of artisans and workers; it condemned violent strikes but supported peaceful ones. The Liberal Party's incipient organization, which was slowly supplanting the ad hoc leadership of civil war veterans, filtered out the revolutionary rudiments of the union movement in its electoral machinery. This task was made easier by the middle-class origins of many union leaders and the nonexistence of a stable proletariat. In 1922 Herrera defined the "popular classes" as "the very basis of the Liberal Party, blood of its blood," and he went on to lament that in Colombia "they find themselves in a state of obvious inferiority and hardly know the names of reforms and institutions that in more fortunate societies already grant the worker effective guarantees."

Several additional factors helped to deflate radical tendencies: the nationalist rhetoric the government spouted during its disputes with foreign oil companies; the repression of strikes by the military and the Liberals' co-optation of the radicals' grievances (most famously by Jorge Eliécer Gaitán, who denounced the Ciénaga massacre in Congress); the fall of the Conservative regime in 1930 and the reforms introduced by the Liberals. This was what in 1960 the Colombian Communist Party, recalling its series of failures, would call "the socialist shipwreck on the high seas of ascendant Liberalism." After 1930 a few enclaves of radical subculture would remain: the ports of the Magdalena, the indigenous south of Tolima, the oilfields of Barrancabermeja, and the coffee haciendas of Viotá (Cundinamarca). But on the whole, the 1930s were the culmination of an era in which Liberals took from socialism a sense of the future — one that would bring an end to the social and political inequality that followed from the unequal distribution of wealth.

Oil and the Dance of the Millions

The political and business elites that defended Colombia's neutrality during World War I were fully aware that the postwar balance of power had shifted in favor of the United States. Progress in dealings with the United States depended on two central issues, the legal framework for oil exploitation and the so-called dance of the millions.

In 1918 a British diplomat commented that oil was becoming a pillar of Colombian development, but that control would stay in the hands of the United States. By 1926, after a round of intrigues, bribes, and legal skirmishes between the companies, two ended up with oil exploration concessions: the Tropical Oil Company, a subsidiary of Standard Oil of New Jersey (eventually Exxon), and the Colombia Petroleum Company, a subsidiary of South American Gulf Oil. The Troco, as the first was known, was the only one to enter into operation in the 1920s, with pumping and refinery activities in Barrancabermeja; another subsidiary transported the refined oil by pipeline to Cartagena, whence it was shipped to the United States. The Colombian, as the second company was known, controlled the Barco concession in the Catatumbo region, adjacent to Venezuela (where its parent company had considerable interests), but it kept the concession untapped in expectation of a future frontier-crossing operation to drill for, refine, and transport oil which never developed.

In 1926, the last year of Pedro Nel Ospina's administration, the government declared the expiration of the Barco concession, and by extension the Colombian's rights there, but the declaration (upheld by the following administration of Miguel Abadía Méndez) had little practical effect. The Conservative regime also passed decrees increasing the share of oil revenues collected by the state, under pressure from New York banks to strengthen its ability to repay recent loans. Congress, seized with patriotic fervor, launched an investigation of the Tropical Oil Company and concluded that its original concession, dating back to 1905, was unconstitutional; but the matter ended there, and the government received legislative authorization to revive the concession.

In 1923 Colombia's oil production was a mere 318,000 barrels of crude, or 0.04 percent of world production. By 1930 the amount had reached 20.3 million barrels, or 1.4 percent. Between 1925 and 1927 production increased fifteenfold. The international context shows the importance of this growth. Mexico, still recovering from its revolution, saw its production fall from 157 million barrels in 1920 to 64 million in 1927. Venezuela, under the iron grip of the dictator Juan Vicente Gómez, was able to fill the gap: its production soared from 457,000 barrels in 1920 to 64 million in 1927. In the late 1920s Colombia was seen, both at home and abroad, as a key player in the current and future world oil economy, perhaps equal to Mexico and Venezuela.

In 1929 the world oil market began to show signs of overproduction, which strengthened the negotiating position of the oil companies. Colombia, whose oil was expensive to produce and bring to port, remained behind Venezuela. This fact, recognized in new oil legislation drafted by a group of international experts, did nothing to dispel the dream of Colombia as an oil powerhouse. Now it was said that the oil companies had decided to leave Colombia as a reserve, much as the Colombian Oil Company had treated the Barco concession.

The Antioquian president Pedro Nel Ospina made modernization the keynote of the 1920s by implementing projects the nineteenth-century progressives dreamed of: he built railroads, founded the Bank of the Republic as a central reserve bank, and created a modern national accounting office. With prosperity came inflation, a dreaded word after Colombia's experience late in the War of the Thousand Days. But as was also said at the time, Colombia had acquired the habit of thinking in millions, thanks to the growth of coffee income and foreign financing. Until 1925 all eyes were fixed on the Panama indemnity money — $25 million — but the access to foreign funding opened up by this sum and by high coffee prices was more significant in the longer term. In the thirty months from 1926 through the first half of 1928, the public debt soared to $180 million, almost as much as the country's exports during that period.

The central government was responsible for only 27 percent of foreign loans, an unusually low figure for 1920s Latin America. Most activity came from *municipios* and departments in the western coffee region, where borrowing was encouraged by private bankers and by a central government eager to secure their political support. Of every $10 disbursed in foreign loans to authorities below the national level, $7 went to Antioquia, Caldas, and the city of Medellín. In 1928 the central government, at the urging of the U.S. government, tried to control the situation; right around that time, the flow of foreign funding abruptly dried up. Political conflict soon erupted between Conservatives in regions that had been left out of the bonanza, including departments that represented large political constituencies such as Boyacá, and the political middlemen of regions that had most benefited.

Competitive Elections and the Conservatives' Undoing

Colombia was the only South American country besides Uruguay not to experience the rise of a third political force to contest the domination of the two postindependence parties. Just as we cannot understand the economy of the first half of the twentieth century without looking at the rise of coffee, we cannot understand politics during this period without looking at the expansion of the electorate. Voters as a percentage of the overall population soared from 7 percent in the 1914 presidential elections to 23 percent in the legislative elections of 1949. Was the political system prepared to accommodate the consequences of this expansion peacefully, and to take account of the sociological changes in the electorate?

The direct election of the president and the growth of towns obliged politicians to develop new electoral strategies. This task fell mainly on the Liberals, who were at a disadvantage because the countryside was a Conservative stronghold. The increase in voters, from 331,000 in 1914 to 670,000 in 1922 and 824,000 in 1930, posed a challenge to local party committees: to organize these new politically active citizens as stable party resources, would they have to welcome them into their respectable midst? In the cities, new "people's juntas" and "civic" or "workers' circles" sprang up. Some urban politicians tried to establish stable followings by the conventional methods (access to scholarships, jobs, legal favors), but they soon found that public utilities were of greatest interest to the greatest number: a politician who could claim credit for their smooth functioning would enjoy success.

In the Bogotá of 1912 the percentage of men over 21 who could read and write and therefore were qualified to vote varied from 90 percent in the relatively exclusive neighborhood around the cathedral to 79–86 percent in artisan neighborhoods near the center to 30 percent in the more rural areas within the city limits. These statistics suggest that the Liberals of the early twentieth century were reaping what their radical precursors of the mid–nineteenth century had sowed: an urban electorate that leaned strongly in their favor. The Conservatives had to look elsewhere for votes, to the countryside and to towns with a more traditional orientation.

The presidential election of 1922, which pitted Liberals against Conservatives without the "third force" of the Republicans (who had dissolved the previous year), was won by Pedro Nel Ospina with 62 percent against 38 percent for the Liberal candidate, Benjamín Herrera. Liberals were convinced that their crushing defeat had to be due to fraud, and their frenzied accusations raised fears of a new civil war. The assassination of the Liberal civil war caudillo Justo Durán in 1924 moved Herrera to send Ospina a "political testament" from his deathbed, in which he demanded electoral guarantees and listed forty-one *municipios* throughout the country (mostly in Tolima, Cundinamarca, Antioquia, Boyacá, and the two Santanders) where since 1913 Liberals had been persecuted and sometimes killed with the complicity of Conservative authorities. With very few exceptions, the *municipios* on Herrera's list would figure prominently in the wave of selective killings in the early 1930s, and later during the Violencia of 1946–53.

The Conservative regime, for all its limitations, did encourage Liberals to trust more in the electoral process than in an eventual return to civil war — and most Liberals did prefer ballots to bullets. In 1916 the so-called incomplete-vote law reinforced the Reyes-era guarantee of one-third representation to the minority party in all legislative bodies. Two other important changes came in 1929: a form of proportional representation through a system of limited quotas (expanded in 1932), and the requirement of voting a straight party ticket. The quota was determined by dividing the number of valid votes by the number of seats to be filled. The party slates could be changed up to a few days before the election. Until then, candidacies had been strictly individual, and there was no control over whether a candidate's stated party affiliation was genuine. The basis of the national electoral system was not departments but ad hoc districts that could be made and unmade by the president. The manipulation of these election districts and the movement toward a proportional representation system enabled national-level politicians to control and undermine local party bosses.

Political stability had encouraged economic growth and an increased role for the state in the economy and society. Although the Conservatives of the 1920s were economic liberals, the mounting debt of privately and departmentally owned railways and utilities turned them into reluctant nationalizers. Given the politicization of everything state-owned, these enterprises were operating at a loss, with the costs now borne by the national treasury. Worse, even the nationalization of public utilities called all property rights into question, making the large landowners nervous and fanning protests by land colonizers and lessees. It was a situation the Liberals could capitalize on in the 1930s.

What would happen if the Conservatives lost the presidential election? Until the end of 1929 this was hardly a serious question, but by that time there were some ominous signs. The split within the party now spread to the church. While the clergy, from parish priest up to velvet-robed bishop, were united in their struggle for the nation's soul, many of them wanted their own say in elections. Both of the short-listed candidates, Alfredo Vázquez Cobo of the Nationalist faction and Guillermo Valencia of the Historical wing, had substantial support within the party and the church. Despite last-minute efforts by the Vatican to bring the clergy to heel, they remained divided, and their division split the Conservative electorate.

Further complicating the political scene, a new student-led protest campaign developed at midyear over the government's repression of the banana workers' movement in Magdalena. This "June 8th Movement" was reminiscent of the 1909 unrest that contributed to the fall of Rafael Reyes, and President Abadía was quick to sacrifice two cabinet ministers and the director of the police to satisfy the protesters' demands. The more general demands of the movement — civil rights for women, reform of the civil and criminal codes, action against official corruption — represented the rise of an urban middle-class agenda newly embraced by the Liberal party. Artisans and socialists, prominent actors earlier in the decade, were now in full retreat.

The Conservative party no longer represented to friend and foe alike the majestic principle of authority; now it was just a free-for-all. Vázquez's supporters in Congress obstructed legislation, for which they were denounced by the chambers of commerce and by a middle class increasingly dependent on the government for jobs. The two Conservative candidates, the incumbent president, the newly installed archbishop, and the Vatican's representative were embroiled in an increasingly public and acrimonious controversy; the recent deaths of such figures as Ramón González Valencia, José Vicente Concha, and especially Archbishop Herrera Restrepo marked the end of deference and consensus as lynchpins of Conservative national politics.

In 1929, in contrast to 1922, the Liberals hardly seemed a credible alternative. They were the minority party in the legislature, they lacked a recognized national leader, and they also lacked a platform capable of energizing an apathetic electorate, as the most recent elections demonstrated. Given this state of affairs, the party's launching of the presidential candidacy of Enrique Olaya Herrera, Colombia's ambassador to Washington, just two months before the February 1930 elections was highly unexpected. Olaya was from a small town in Boyacá but he had aristocratic roots, which he effectively conveyed through a somewhat haughty demeanor and unusual appearance: he was tall and blond, characteristics not typical of a *boyacense*. He won some notice as a student leader in 1909 and opposed the Liberals' more partisan leadership when he took a cabinet position in the Republican administration of Carlos E. Restrepo, and again in 1921 when he joined the frankly Conservative cabinet of Marco Fidel Suárez in order to defend the Panama treaty in Congress.

Olaya declined the Liberals' first offer of the presidential nomination, saying that no single-party government could constructively govern Colombia. He insisted on a nominally bipartisan "National Convergence" (*Concentración Nacional*), which the Liberals were forced to adopt, since the alternative was no candidacy at all. Olaya's emphasis on bipartisanship was heaven-sent for the Liberals, since it defused any impulse among the Conservatives to force a last-minute agreement between their rival candidates. The continuing internal split and the Abadía regime's relative sympathy for Olaya made his victory by a plurality of votes possible and smoothed the long transition period between the elections in February 1930 and his inauguration in August. During that period Olaya was practically a co-president, successfully delaying a special session of Congress to deal with oil legislation and fiscal oversight and remaking the cabinet to include members of both parties.

During the first half of 1930 Colombia's national accounts were hit hard by falling coffee prices and a deterioration in the overall terms of trade. The positive capital flows of the 1920s suddenly turned negative, and sharply reduced government revenues left 30,000 public works laborers unemployed—though the layoff of a smaller number of white-collar employees was of far greater political concern. Private investment plummeted in industry, mining, electricity production, and urban construction. In these circumstances, Olaya's most important action during the transition period was to return to the United States to plead the case of Colombia as a good destination for investment before private bankers and the State Department. He shared the view, still widely held in mid-1930, that the capitalist world was suffering only a "panic" of the sort previously experienced and quickly overcome, rather than a profound crisis; and he knew from experience that Colombia's most effective tool was a good word from Edwin Kemmerer, the "money doctor of the Andes," whose program of banking and finance reforms was embraced by Conservative regimes in the 1920s, to the delight of Wall Street. Kemmerer obliged, and Olaya received a friendly hearing.

But it was not just Kemmerer's influence—Olaya went to the United States willing to relax investment controls, and it was that willingness that permitted him to return to Colombia with a fresh loan of $20 million, almost unheard of for Latin America at the time. Several decades later Guillermo León Valencia, son of one of the defeated Conservative candidates of 1930 and himself a president in the 1960s, told Charles de Gaulle that this was the moment—rather than, for instance, the approval of the Panama treaty several years earlier—when Colombia fell into the "natural orbit" of the United States.

Chapter 3

FROM THE EXPANSION OF CITIZENSHIP TO THE PLUTOCRATIC ELITE

*T*he 1920s left a legacy of aspirations. More Colombians wanted to vote freely and defend their labor rights; they wanted a good job, a higher level of education, and a right to the land they worked. The Great Depression threw the import-export economy into crisis and forced the state to rethink its role in the economy. The changes on the international scene were greater still, calling both political and economic liberalism into question.

In the conventional version of the years from 1930 to 1958, the period had two distinct phases: the Liberal republic of 1930–46 and the decade that began in a state of siege and ended in outright dictatorship (1946–58). This periodization is certainly valid, but the period is best understood in its entirety, against the backdrop of the consolidation of the modern national economy and of the interest groups behind that new economy.

The party-political currents of the period were defined with reference to individual leaders: lopismo, olayismo, santismo, and gaitanismo on the Liberal side, ospinismo, gomecismo, and alzatismo for the Conservatives. Factionalism on the Conservative side was of particular significance, because the party boycotted elections more than once and turned to obstructionist tactics in the legislatures, opening the door to direct action and thus to violence.

Politics may be more than just leaders, but much of the historical interest of Colombian politics during this period resides in the conflict between figures representing distinct visions. This divide, which can be summarized as ideologues/mobilizers ("extremists") versus administrators ("moderates"), cut across the partisan schism. The first group called for remaking the nature and goals of the state and of political action, while the latter group sought primarily to modernize the institutions of government. The extremists of *both parties shared the goal of preventing the strengthening of the political center, and in pursuit of that goal they invoked both traditional sectarianism and the new realities of Colombia and the world. The moderates sought to strengthen links between state institutions and the regional and national economic interests that were taking shape.*

Political crisis took the form of violence, but also of institutional breakdown: every regime change from 1945 through 1958 occurred in emergency or extraconstitutional circumstances. The military coup of 1953, born of the profound division of the Conservative Party and instigated by one of its factions, marked the emergence of the military as supreme arbiter of Colombian politics. In this chapter we examine the socioeconomic origins and context of the national crisis that gripped Colombia from the mid-1940s on; the political aspects will be examined in the following chapter.

Depression and Presidentialism: Oilmen and Bankers

Compared to the happy 1920s, the Liberal years were austere. Between 1930 and 1945, annual growth of GDP slowed from 3.8 percent to 1.6 percent. Colombia, along with the rest of Latin America, responded to the external shocks of the Great Depression and the Second World War by reorienting its economy toward the domestic market. Industrial production as a share of GDP increased from 7.1 percent in the late 1920s to 14.4 percent in the late 1940s.

The Liberal project of modernizing the economy by modernizing the state had three central elements, which got under way at different times: the use of macroeconomic policies in support of economic development (1931), the overhauling of the tax structure (1935), and the creation of state-owned industrial firms (1940s). Each element represented a different mix of two factors that are often confused—responses to the economic and fiscal crisis wrought by the Depression and the arrival of a supposedly novel spirit of "modern interventionism." Even the latter factor by itself is sometimes misunderstood, insofar as state intervention in the economy had a long history in Colombia and the world by the 1930s.

The Depression was somewhat less traumatic and long lasting in Colombia than elsewhere in the region, and its worst effects were countered relatively quickly. Although the price of coffee, which accounted for two-thirds of Colombia's exports, did fall significantly, Colombia benefited from Brazil's aggressive policy of destroying warehoused coffee in order to drive up the world price. In the end the price of coffee fell less far and rebounded more quickly than that of copper, sugar, or bananas. The low costs of most Colombian coffee production by peasant households enabled them to weather price drops by adjusting the supply and to tolerate the consequent redistribution of income to the marketers and financiers. The United States' upward adjustment of the price of gold revived Colombian production, and exports of oil and even bananas rose.

Although there is truth to the idea that the Depression wrecked the old dogmas of unfettered free trade and hard money, by the 1920s the Colombian state had already shown little commitment to them. The last few presidents of the Conservative Hegemony increasingly centralized economic matters in the hands of the national government and of the presidency itself, with resources that a would-be centralizer like Rafael Núñez never even dreamed of. So there was only a change of degree rather than of kind when Enrique Olaya personally renegotiated the foreign debt in the months before he took office in 1930, and when he sought and found new sources of financing. But in his initial commitment to maintaining the gold standard and parity of the peso with the dollar and in his slashing of government spending to the point of deflation, unemployment, and political unrest, Olaya showed a lingering loyalty to traditional notions of how to cope with economic crisis.

In September 1931 the Bank of England abandoned the gold standard, and Colombia was forced to suspend free trade and exports of gold in favor of exchange and import controls. Olaya increased taxes under special authority granted to him by Congress, and the central bank expanded domestic credit to permit public works and the state bureaucracy to continue functioning; future revenues were pledged to secure short-term funding. The government's last stand of fiscal orthodoxy was to continue paying interest on the foreign debt, and it required bankrupt departments and *municipios* to do the same, if only with promissory notes. But in May 1933, faced with an accumulated peso devaluation of 40 percent, which made continuing servicing of foreign-currency debts impossible, Olaya finally declared a moratorium.

The administration of Miguel Abadía in the late 1920s had been mildly nationalist on oil issues but unreservedly internationalist on financial issues; Olaya, under the changed circumstances of the 1930s, was the opposite. A revised oil law issued in 1931 prohibited the granting of concessions to companies owned by foreign states, a provision that had the effect of favoring U.S. firms over British ones. The legal ambiguities surrounding public lands continued to thwart competitors of Tropical Oil, whose titles to its properties were more solid. Moreover, Olaya reversed his predecessor's hostility to the Barco Concession of 1923, which ceded oil rights over a large territory to U.S. firms. Olaya's oil policies, which joined extreme right-wing Conservatives and Communists in street protests under the banner of anti-imperialism, were designed at least in part to persuade the U.S. State Department to lean on private banks to get credit flowing to Colombia again. The success of this quid pro quo was minimal. The bankers imposed ever tougher conditions, which eventually included budget controls and the complete privatization of Colombia's railroads.

The Depression and Regional Interests

Early in the Olaya administration the country's most powerful agricultural organizations were given their own seats on the central bank's board of directors, thus beginning the institutionalization of links between government and economic interest groups which would characterize modern Colombia's political economy. In 1931 the coffee growers' federation, FEDECAFÉ, sponsored the creation of the Caja de Crédito Agrario, a rural bank that at first operated only in coffee-producing regions. The state assisted the recovery and expansion of sugar production through exchange controls and also through the promotion of a domestic cartel, the Socieded de Crédito Azucarero, which purchased the output of the country's top ten sugar mills and coordinated pricing with tariffs on imported sugar.

By adopting protectionist tariffs the government won the support of industrialists hurt by the Depression. The domestic production of import-substituting manufactured goods, which started in the 1880s and grew modestly into the 1920s, speeded up in the 1930s as Colombia lost some of its import capacity. Domestic agricultural inputs for manufacturing also expanded: cotton for textiles, hops for beer, tobacco for cigarettes, and a variety of products for processed food and drinks. The economic isolation imposed by World War II strengthened this process, and by the war's end Colombia had an industrial capacity deemed worthy of continued support through government policy.

Colombia was still an economic mosaic; some regional elites were openly hostile to protectionism while others could not thrive without it. By and large the governments of the Liberal Republic sided with the protectionists, led by Medellín textile producers, against the free-traders, led by coastal landed interests. In political terms the coast was stymied by its own internal mosaic—differing agendas and cultures among the strictly coastal towns such as Cartagena, Barranquilla, and Santa Marta and between those towns and the inland centers of Sincelejo, Montería, and Valledupar—and by the reluctance of the elites to mobilize the black and mulatto majorities of the region in defense of coastal interests. In the end the coastal elite had to tolerate not only protectionism but a stereotype of their rural economy as backward, invented in Medellín.

The Depression and War with Peru

In September 1932 Peruvian forces occupied the Colombian Amazon port of Leticia, in a move instigated by the ubiquitous rubber magnate Julio César Arana and supported by the oligarchy of the Peruvian province of Loreto, which had never accepted a 1922 border settlement between the two countries. The subsequent war with Peru gave the Colombian government a perfect opportunity to accelerate the move to state involvement in the economy which it had already initiated. Under the exigencies of war the government increased the public debt and spent freely on civil and military infrastructure, thus creating employment and reducing social and political unrest. By late 1933 the deflationary phase had ended and with it the roughest patch of the Depression.

The army came out of the brief conflict better equipped, better trained, and with a professional ethos it lacked earlier. With a new emphasis on defending Colombia's previously tranquil borders, the military was no longer seen primarily as a tool for suppressing domestic disturbances; that would eventually be the function of a national police force. While the new-model military served as a further guarantee against the outbreak of civil war, it could never be entirely marginalized from party politics. Politicians of both parties tried to influence the appointment and promotion of officers, and officers were far more closely linked to their parties than their Prussian field manuals advised. Episodes such as the coup attempt of 1944, the army's decisive role in crushing the popular uprising in Bogotá and other cities in April 1948, and its complex participation in the violence and dictatorship of the 1950s, all underlined the ambiguity of civil-military relations even before they were further colored by Cold War ideology.

The long-term impact of the war on the society was less apparent. The military imperative of reinforcing the state's presence on the frontiers promoted road construction, which in turn promoted flows of migrants from the interior to frontiers such as Putumayo in the south. The growth of these frontier regions, propelled not by a consistent economic motor like coffee but by boom-and-bust products from rubber to coca, would eventually change established political balances.

The Rise of the Coffee Growers

Coffee's place in Colombian exports rose, first to 68 percent by value in the late 1920s and then to 72 percent in the 1940s, and the interests of coffee growers came to be identified with the national interest. Production increased at an ever faster pace, while world coffee consumption declined; but Brazil consistently made painful adjustments while Colombia enjoyed a free ride. The 1932 coffee census revealed that three-quarters of Colombia's production came from small properties, which represented 98 percent of all coffee properties; studies in the mid-1950s suggest that these proportions changed little in the intervening years. Around 40 percent of growers could not survive solely on the coffee they produced.

During the Depression coffee interests filled the vacuum left by an archaic and incompetent state administration. Moderate Conservative growers in Antioquia and Caldas were behind the early development of FEDECAFÉ and transformed it from an advocacy group into an economic force that controlled a national purchasing system, penetrated international markets (especially in Europe), promoted domestic coffee consumption, and slowly drove U.S. coffee roasting firms out of Colombia. The organization was also a model of bipartisanship as moderates of both parties studiously kept it out of political disputes.

FEDECAFÉ used the results of the 1932 coffee census to argue that Colombia, instead of joining a producer's alliance as Brazil had been suggesting, should compete openly on the basis of the lower costs of its smallholder-based model of production. In any price war, Colombia's more desirable *suave* coffee would benefit if its traditional price differential over Brazil's harsher *robusto* product were reduced. Acting within or outside of government according to the situation, FEDECAFÉ lobbied for the reduction of differential exchange rates, which were a de facto tax on coffee exports, and for the renegotiation of mortgage debts. Such was their influence that the government ceded on the latter question, intervening in private contracts to reduce the repayment obligations of large coffee estates.

But the government necessarily took a wider view of the national interest, and in 1936 it decided to join forces with Brazil in defense of stable world coffee prices. President López imposed a new leadership on FEDECAFÉ that was willing to go along with the alliance, but it lasted only a few months because the government could not persuade the business sector to finance a policy of withholding or destroying coffee stocks. Even with the coffee growers' organization under nominal state control, the growers themselves could still effectively oppose government policies.

Moderation Above, Sectarianism Below

During the Liberal Republic, as during the latter years of the Conservative Hegemony, political legitimacy emanated from the electoral process—but everyone was convinced that elections were fraudulent. Enrique Olaya, at the start of his campaign in 1929–30, reminded his ally Carlos E. Restrepo (who as a former president did not need the reminder) that "among us, it's not votes that are calculated but tricks."

The election statistics of the period reveal such great departmental and local variations from the national averages that we can ask whether there really was a national politics in the 1930s and 1940s, or just the sum total of regional and local situations. In the presidential elections of 1934, 1938, and 1942, the Conservatives alleged a lack of electoral guarantees and declared their abstention; in the first two elections there was only one candidate, and in 1942 Conservatives supported a dissident Liberal candidacy. Throughout the period only the elections of 1930 and 1946 were genuinely competitive, and in both instances the governing party was hopelessly divided, thus offering the opposition (Liberal in 1930, Conservative in 1946) the chance to offer a "moderate" alternative.

The Conservatives were initially convinced that they would return to the presidency in 1934, because they controlled 80 percent of town councils, all departmental assemblies, and the Congress. They held a 2-to-1 majority in the judiciary, and in some court circuits they held all the judgeships. But Olaya, true to his Republican principles, insisted on parity in his cabinet and in his ministries, and he required the governors to do the same. Governors had to choose principal secretaries (*secretarios de gobierno*) from the opposing party, and mayors—who under the 1886 Constitution were appointed by the governors, who were strongly influenced by the president—had to be from the locally dominant party. This scheme required executives at all levels to have the same gift for negotiation that Olaya possessed, and much the same resources for dealing with interest groups. With Liberals and Conservatives at each other's throat, there was a disconnect between elected town councils and mayors appointed from above, especially since it was the council that appointed other town functionaries, including the judge. In some towns the council appointed the local police force. There was little a mayor could do if even the police belonged to the other party.

The church-state dispute, which had been reduced to purely tactical issues under the Conservative Hegemony, resurfaced as an ideological cleavage during Liberal rule. The clergy were distrustful of Olaya and began to skirmish over the previously settled education issue. In many parishes in the highlands of Nariño, Boyacá, and the Santanders, as well as in eastern Antioquia and much of the Caldas coffee zone, priests worked with local Conservative administrators to sow partisan discord, especially when town councils shifted to Liberal control and there was a politically motivated turnover of teachers.

The 1931 congressional elections unleashed a wave of partisan violence in central Boyacá and in the Pamplona and García Rovira regions of Santander. For the first time in half a century, Liberals obtained a majority of votes nationally, but the peculiar system of electoral districting kept them from parlaying that into a congressional majority. In 1933 they amassed nearly twice as many votes as the Conservatives and won in all but three departments. From then until 1949 they controlled both houses of Congress, nearly all departmental assemblies, and between 60 and 70 percent of the several hundred town councils.

The Liberals' vote totals did not increase under Olaya solely because of the party's increased capacity for coercion and fraud now that it was in power; they also attempted to enlarge their base through policy changes. For example, Olaya began to move the state toward a new way of perceiving and dealing with labor strife. His labor law guaranteed basic worker rights and promoted collective bargaining, thus obviating direct confrontation and lessening police repression. The official encouragement of labor negotiation, the establishment of the eight-hour day and the forty-eight-hour week, and the specifying of employers' obligations to workers won over the urban working class. Under Olaya's successor, Alfonso López Pumarejo, this reform agenda would be strengthened and accelerated. (Table 3 shows the makeup of both houses of Congress from 1927 through 1949.)

Ideology and the Creation of Mass Politics

Demoralized and divided after their devastating losses in the 1933 legislative elections, the Conservatives decided to abstain from the 1934 presidential elec-

TABLE 3
Party Composition of the Colombian Congress, 1927–49

	Senate		Chamber of Representatives		
	Liberal	Conservative	Liberal	Conservative	Communist
1927	15	33			
1929			42	71	0
1931	25	31			
1935	56	Abstained	118	Abstained	0
1937			118	Abstained	0
1939	37	19	76	42	0
1941			81	50	0
1943	43	20	86	44	1
1945			82	47	2
1947	34	29	72	58	1
1949			69	62	0

tions. López, who declared himself more Liberal than Olaya (in the sense that he was not part of a bipartisan agreement) and more nationalist on economic issues, won the presidency almost by default and his party occupied all the seats in Congress after the Conservatives sat out the elections. The inauguration of López brought the true beginning of what has been called the Liberal Republic, which in Liberal historiography represents the birth of modernity in Colombia. The era and the leader were ripe for mythmaking: the return of the Liberals to power after a half-century, at a time when the old political and economic dogmas had failed so disastrously, had an element of historical drama, and López had the audacity and eloquence to set forth new ends for the state and the party, while the rest of the party leadership seemed content merely to modernize the means.

New political formulas were circulating around the world: totalitarianisms of the right and left and liberal reformism. Even the latter, exemplified by Franklin Roosevelt's New Deal, was based on the inability of free-enterprise capitalism to handle the crisis without substantial intervention by the state and the establishment of a coalition of capitalists and workers. As we have seen, capitalism at least in Colombia had never operated without state intervention, but what was new about López's version of intervention was its explicit social content.

It was impossible to avoid the question of the purpose of the state, especially when the two parties increasingly saw their historical polarization in the distorting mirror of Spanish politics. In Colombia, to be sure, the social content of the partisan divide was far weaker and less distinct than in Spain. But the growing confrontation between the Republicans and Nationalists in Spain, which exploded into the Civil War of 1936–39, did offer a similar cultural paradigm, and many Colombian intellectuals of the Conservative right, including clerics at all levels, saw in the Spanish Falange a rejuvenated version of Miguel Antonio Caro's vision of the Catholic family and the peasantry as the nuclei of a hierarchical social order, founded on unchanging values. As under Caro, it was less clear how these concepts would relate to capitalist development. When the Conservatives finally came to power in 1950 and had to confront these problems, the extremist faction looked to Francisco Franco in Spain and to Juan Perón in Argentina for rhetoric if not for concrete models.

Other isms threw more fuel on the fire. Leftist Liberals admired the centralism and statism of the Mexican Revolution—which the Catholic clergy cursed as heartily as they did the Spanish Republic—and they also looked to Peru's Aprista movement for its novel synthesis of Marxism, nationalism, and indigenism, a combination with great potential for mobilizing the very diverse sectors of the Colombian population.

Technological change was transforming the style and practice of politics. Air travel, radio, and modern graphic design all enabled politicians to present themselves to a wider range of publics. During this period no important politician, either in Bogotá or in the provinces, passed up a chance to start a newspaper or magazine. The number of radio stations and sets grew rapidly, with broadcasting based on the U.S. model of programming financed by commercial announcements. Textile, beer, and soft drink manufacturers also purchased stations directly, and by the late 1930s radio signals were within reach of most of the seats of Colombia's several hundred *municipios*. By the end of the decade very few of them were without a power plant, however modest.

Radio had only a marginal role in the 1930 election, but its power to mobilize was already apparent during the war with Peru in 1932, and López established a "newspaper of the air" to defend his administration; Laureano Gómez, the Conservative leader, went him one better by buying one of the country's most powerful stations, the Voice of Colombia. In the constant war for listeners, radio stations promoted new and ever more secular popular tastes. Even in traditionally devout Antioquia, the death of the Argentine tango legend Carlos Gardel in an air crash in Medellín was a bigger event of 1935 than the Eucharistic Congress held there — an inversion of traditional priorities that would have been unthinkable but for radio.

Olaya had left the presidency with immense popularity, and his successor seemed destined to live in his shadow. But López had extensive local political connections and was the man who engineered Olaya's rise to power. By Colombian standards he was a man of the world, having spent part of his youth in London, and he had also been tutored by the arch-Conservative Miguel Antonio Caro, a master of political rhetoric. He had a unique ability to deploy complex words in a popular style and to fuse the sectarian Liberal tradition to modern expectations of social reform. He was of the same generation as Olaya and Eduardo Santos, but unlike them, he had always detested the Republican spirit of elite nonpartisanship; that movement's founder, Carlos E. Restrepo, detested him in return as a mere banker, "the Colbert of the López family."

During and shortly after World War I his father, Pedro López, controlled the most important commercial bank in the country and the largest coffee export house, although the bank failed in 1923. Alfonso's business experience was more as an employee of foreign firms; he ran the Colombian operation of New York's American Mercantile Bank. In the early 1920s he decided to give up his lucrative banking career for politics, and since he did not give up his lavish lifestyle, the rumors began to fly. British diplomatic cables alleged that he was on the secret payroll of a cement factory, while their U.S. counterparts said he was paid by two oil companies. Members of the López family have long been representatives of U.S. oil firms.

The Spirit of the "Revolution on the March"

With no Conservatives in the cabinet for the first time in over half a century, López could govern in a frankly partisan fashion. He even ended most of his speeches with "Viva el Partido Liberal!" three times over. But the first few months of the López administration were largely a continuation of the Olaya regime, with continuing issues such as the peace treaty with Peru, a new commercial agreement with the United States, and electoral and agrarian reforms. He broke with his predecessor on economic policy. His scathing criticism of the high inflation that he inherited from Olaya won him substantial popular support, while he promised business leaders that his social reforms would require no new taxes. In fact the reforms required very little actual spending, and López was able to balance the budget in each of his four years in office.

His tax reform of 1935, modeled on FDR's New Deal and on Lloyd George's hiking of taxes on income and land in Great Britain (1910), represented a great leap forward in fiscal modernization and centralization. Government revenues grew from 6 percent of GDP in 1935 to 10 percent in 1950, even as the share of import and export taxes in total revenues fell from 46 percent in 1930 to less than 20 percent in 1950. He shifted the load to make direct taxes more progressive. Direct taxes as a share of overall revenues grew from 8 percent in 1935 to 24 percent in 1940, 33 percent in 1945, and 46 percent in 1950.

López's program of government, known as the *Revolución en marcha* (Revolution on the March), had only a modest nationalist component. He supported a strike against the United Fruit Company's banana operations in 1934 and invoked memories of the 1929 massacre in the Santa Marta banana zone in his campaign to transfer the company's holdings to Colombian hands, although his attempt to seize the company in 1938 on legal technicalities was quashed by the judiciary. (Ironically, it was Olaya who managed to get the best of United Fruit when he forced the company to turn over the Magdalena Railroad.) As in the past, the oil sector received special treatment, and although López announced the establishment of a state oil refinery, nothing came of it; what did come was new and even more generous legislation on foreign oil concessions and the repatriation of profits. After 1936 he even withdrew his support for the oil workers' union.

Above all López was a realist, especially on trade issues. To secure passage of the 1935 trade treaty with the United States, which he considered vital to protecting Colombia's export markets, he faced down powerful opposition from Medellín textile manufacturers and unions alike. In 1935 he revived a trade agreement with Germany despite the Liberals' contempt for fascism, and the Third Reich soon imported enough Colombian coffee to become Colombia's second most important export market after the United States, displacing Great Britain.

The government dealt skillfully with strikes in the transport and oil sectors, in several Bogotá factories, and in Caldas coffee-processing plants. In this atmosphere of heightened expectations, the nation's attention was focused on the great haciendas of Cundinamarca and Tolima, which were being occupied by land-hungry peasants, and on rural unrest elsewhere in the country.

Although Lopez's ideal of a modernized Colombia clashed with the traditional clientelist interests, he was generally willing to defer to local practices that were less than democratic, especially if the practitioners were Liberals. In Armenia (Caldas) the notorious "Colonel" Carlos Barrera Uribe presided over a fiefdom based on coercion and such rampant fraud that many local Conservatives abandoned all hope for democracy and turned toward fascism. In June 1935 Barrera fatally shot the department's comptroller, a young Conservative from an elite family, after the official accused him of embezzlement. Local Liberal judges buried the case and the party's national leaders sent Barrera telegrams of support; after four years, during which time Barrera was out on bail, he was sentenced to a mere thirty months in prison, reduced to ten for good behavior. During his brief incarceration Barrera was shuttled to various prisons around the country, which he managed to leave from time to time to "do politics."

The Agrarian Question

Colombia in the 1930s was still very much an agrarian society, one of the poorest in Latin America. Life expectancy toward the end of the decade was only 40 years for men and 44 for women. Although the urban population rose steadily, 70 percent of the population was still rural.

The government's plan to widen the scope of effective citizenship called for a new official tone in dealing with the upper classes, especially the rural elite. When in September 1934 a group of landowners wrote to López requesting official protection against the growing wave of peasant mobilization, he pointedly and publicly told them that property was not an absolute right. His reply, while surprising to the recipients, did not come entirely out of the blue, since dealing with rural unrest had been on the agenda for a full decade by that point. In 1926 the solidly Conservative Supreme Court ruled that the mere registration of a property in notary and registry offices was not sufficient proof of legal tenure, implying that other considerations could come into play. French legal-philosophical ideas about the social function of property had made their way into Colombian thinking, and the examples of Mexico's 1917 Constitution and the Spanish Republic's 1932 agrarian survey were known and invoked. It was Olaya who had called for a rethinking of the legal basis of property rights, although he was motivated less by agrarian issues than by the needs of the developing oil industry for iron-clad legal guarantees.

In the 1930s the rural Colombia whose future was debated in Bogotá was a complex blend of continuity and change. The profitability of the agricultural sector was increasing as the transportation network and internal demand progressed; plenty of rural labor was available, although many rural people chose to migrate to colonization zones or to cities. While productivity was improving, the technical bases of rural production were still quite primitive, and social relations continued to rest on a tripod of traditional haciendas, commercial plantations, and peasant holdings. In the seats of rural *municipios*, the 1930s was the decade when we can begin to see the rural Colombia of today: long-distance buses brought cities within easier reach, and beer and liquor from modern factories began to displace *chicha* (corn beer) and *guarapo* (made from fermented sugar cane).

In the early 1930s an official report from Cundinamarca explained the interaction of local power, exercised from *municipio* seats, and outlying districts and haciendas. The rural poor, said the report, "were out of touch with civilization." Their relations with the local hacienda had changed little since colonial days. They received a tiny cash wage and a place to live that they paid for in labor, and were assigned an area to clear or plant or harvest. Their relationship with the state was always negative: "For the tenant the government is (a) the mayor who throws him in jail for violating a law he didn't know about; (b) the authority who throws him in jail for making or drinking contraband liquor; (c) the authority that charges road and bridge tolls; and (d) the authority who is quick to evict him whenever the landowner requests it."

In this atmosphere of generalized rural discontent, the Supreme Court decision on the limits of property and Olaya's draft property reforms fed the proprietors' sense of insecurity and the peasants' expectations. The initial version established a legal presumption of state ownership of uncultivated lands, in the absence of properly documented private ownership; moreover, these uncultivated lands were to be given only to those who would work them. Somewhere along the line these principles were inverted, and in the 1936 land law there was a strong presumption in favor of the validity of private land titles over uncultivated land. There was, to be sure, a provision that such lands might revert to the state if they were not exploited within ten years of the law's enactment.

The legal status of the great estates was thus ensured, although land colonizers who showed a good-faith belief that they owned their parcels were given an opportunity to make their case in court, buttressed by evidence of value added to the property by the improvements they had made. But there was always a shortage of specialized "land judges" to hear these cases, and their activities were not defined until a year after passage of the law that established them. Thus estate owners had plenty of time to drive tenants and colonizers out before they could prepare their case.

Rural agitation during this period consisted more of isolated outbreaks than a continuous and consistent campaign. It was concentrated in the southwest of Cundinamarca, and to a lesser extent in certain coffee-growing areas of Tolima, the Vélez region of southwestern Santander, the Sinú Valley in the modern departments of Córdoba and Sucre (then part of Antioquia), and the modern department of Quindío (then part of Caldas). In the early and mid-1930s, when the Communist Party supported the Olaya and López governments under instructions from the Comintern to support progressive regimes, most unrest was easily neutralized by the officially mandated or independent breaking up of properties that were under assault, with the resulting small properties allotted on a case-by-case basis.

But rural life did not revolve entirely around property issues. Political clientelism was responsible for the myriad unwritten rules that governed rural labor relations, and the López administration was ignorant of those rules. Moreover, during his second term in the 1940s López gave legal standing to informal sharecropping contracts that often contained onerous provisions for the sharecropper, and he postponed by five years (from 1946 to 1951) the reversion of unexploited lands to the state. Liberals, even many reformist ones, had no interest in meddling with the nominally contractual relationships of rural labor and property or in refereeing matters of costs, labor discipline, and distribution of agricultural production.

On the whole, the Liberal Republic left the social structure of the Colombian countryside more or less intact, but it did unloose sporadic rural protests here and there and it did embrace the idea that "land is for the one who works it"—but in a formulation that included the entrepreneur as well as the direct cultivator. The economic effect of this view in the long term has been considerable. In the twenty years following the nominal deadline (1951) for lands to be brought into production or returned to the state, Colombian agriculture experienced the greatest sustained rise in productivity in its history.

God, Women, and Education

Conservatives, the church, businessmen, and even some Liberals saw nothing but danger and subversion at every turn in the 1930s. The conflict became more intense in 1936, when the government introduced a constitutional amendment that stripped references to God from the preamble. The religious conflict, long submerged under the Conservative Hegemony and then under Olaya, burst forth again. According to Colombia's primate, the idea of authority emanating from the people rather than from God would destroy the country's structure of values and beliefs, and the government's endorsement of such a change was sufficient proof of its illegitimacy. This view soon extended to all government initiatives—land, fiscal, and labor reforms, even the reorganization of the National University—as the clergy and Conservative leadership joined forces against López's entire reformist program.

As in the nineteenth century, the doctrinal polarization of the two parties revolved around issues of education and the family. The Liberals of the 1930s, however, were more cautious than the Radicals of the last century. They recognized, for example, the unpopularity of divorce on demand, and they left intact a 1924 law that required Catholics (some 98 percent of the population) to renounce their faith in order to obtain a civil marriage. Nor were they interested in extending political rights to women, who were still not eligible to vote or to hold public sector jobs that involved political authority.

The Liberals of the 1930s did try to address through legal reforms the dependent status of women in family and society, an issue that was first raised in the 1920s. The Conservative regime had passed legislation on day-care centers and a few other matters, and the Civil Code was reformed in 1932 to improve the status of married women with regard to selling their own property and choosing their own professions, although the reform did maintain the father's absolute authority over his legitimate minor children, regardless of their best interests.

The new Penal Code of 1936, put into effect in 1938, addressed some remaining issues of gender inequality which were perhaps less important in themselves than for what they said about dominant social conceptions and practices. For instance, the reform eliminated differential punishments for men and women caught in adultery or cohabitation, offenses that were rarely if ever prosecuted by the 1930s. As for an offense that did occur with some regularity, the killing of wives by jealous husbands, the reform eliminated the doctrine that the husband was innocent if he killed his wife during a "carnal or dishonorable act" with another man. However, it reduced the punishment on the presumption of "ire and intense pain," and until the 1950s jealous husbands went on killing their wives with impunity.

The education debate during the López years displayed little change from the last go-around in the nineteenth century. The church questioned the state's sovereign right to educate its young, and Liberals invoked the "freedom to teach" while paying little attention to increasing school attendance. There was no substantial change in access to schooling during this decade, and strong local and regional inequalities continued on the principle that the state funded universities and some model secondary schools, while most secondary and all primary schools were left to departments and *municipios*.

In the longstanding competition between Liberals and the church to train new members of the cultural and power elite, the Liberal Republic revived the "national high schools" that originated during the Santander administration in the 1830s; still, in 1938 there were two students in church-run secondary schools for every student in a state-run school. That year saw the creation of the Confederation of Catholic Secondary Schools, which until recently defended two central values: confessionalism, the notion that only Catholic teaching could transmit "the truth," and elitism, the notion that the purpose of secondary education was to train the ruling class. The widening of access to secondary education since around 1960 diminished the social prestige of the title *bachiller* (high school graduate). The elite title was now *licenciado*, or university graduate, and the preferred universities were the private ones, which are generally very similar in organization and ethos to private secondary schools.

An official report of 1936 found that 90 percent of the 10,000 state (mostly primary) schools failed to meet even basic hygiene standards, and that around half of the teaching staff were incompetent. Even so, two out of three children were not in school at all. The average Colombian primary student—barefoot, poorly dressed, undernourished—received only modest returns on the heroic efforts that attendance entailed: the child could hope to learn to read and write; to add, subtract, multiply, and divide; to acquire smatterings of history, geography, and civics; and, ironically, to be drilled in the sixteenth-century catechism of Gaspar Astete, long a staple of church schooling. Despite the central place of mass public education in the Liberal discourse of equality and secularism, there was a huge gap between the 1936 constitutional reform's requirement of "free primary education in state schools, obligatory to the extent defined by law," and the poorly funded reality.

Despite the general low level of public education, girls were catching up with boys in school attendance. Literacy rates for children between 7 and 15 years of age were the same for boys and girls. A 1935 law opening public universities to female students paid important long-term dividends: while only 54 enrolled that year, by the mid-1950s the number exceeded 4,000.

In his continuing effort to woo Colombia's emerging middle class, López reorganized the National University, granted it academic freedom, and gave it a splendid campus in Bogotá. He also founded the Escuela Normal Superior, a national teacher-training college. Although public universities were still marginal to Colombia's intellectual life and operated in a politicized and often hostile environment, they did spawn some centers of modern social research during this period. Outside the universities, intellectuals began to go beyond unstructured essays to studies that employed the methods and theories of the social sciences, as exemplified by the works of Alejandro López on economics, Antonio García on economic geography, and Gregorio Hernández de Alba on the society and culture of the indigenous people of Guajira.

The distinctively public and secular intellectual realm developed in the midst of the old doctrinal rivalries. Liberal anticlericalism was invigorated, and the church and its allies revived the dictum that "liberalism is sin." The Jesuits opened the Universidad Javeriana in Bogotá in 1931, and the Archdiocese of Medellín founded the Pontificia Universidad Bolivariana in 1936. The recruitment and training of future leaders became a top priority for the church, and many future Conservative politicians came of age in this fevered environment.

López, Communists, and Unionists

In contrast to the Olaya and Santos administrations, López's government passed few labor laws and little social legislation in general. However, under its auspices the Liberal-affiliated union movement was reorganized into the

Colombian Workers' Federation (CTC). New unions swelled their enrollments. Arbitration of labor disputes became more consistent and productive: between 1935 and 1939 fully 70 percent of disputes between unionized workers and employers were resolved by government intervention. López's young governing team wanted to formalize the state's guiding role in the union movement, and they had no qualms about competing with the Communist Party or with leftist intellectuals; but at the same time they were willing to establish alliances on the left even at the cost of provoking the Conservatives and the church.

The government's strategy effectively curtailed the influence of the Communists, who were already hobbled by Stalinist clichés and by their increasingly obsolete artisan roots. But the Communists were not entirely an exotic presence: their organizational model of tight control over the "masses" was a faithful expression of the elitism of Colombian political culture, and their leadership has proved more durable than any archbishop, coffee federation director, or Liberal or Conservative kingpin. Stalin's rise to undisputed power in the Soviet Union by 1929 transformed the Comintern into an appendage of Soviet foreign policy, whose constituent parties were instructed to adopt a monolithic model that isolated them from the workers they claimed to represent and viewed all issues through the prism of class conflict.

This was soon evident in three instances. In the conflict with Peru the party took a pacifist stance (as did the Peruvian Communists) in the name of proletarian internationalism, which was offensive to popular patriotic sentiments. Next, they implemented the Comintern's directive to organize their fellow workers in the factories, ignoring the tradition of agitating and organizing outside the workplace, a tactic that was probably better suited to the heterogeneity of the Colombian working class. Third, their rote adoption of Stalin's "class struggle in the countryside" led them to label as odious "kulaks" the modest *arrendatarios* (tenant farmers) of the large coffee estates of Cundinamarca and Tolima. Ironically, this was a social group in which the party had had some influence before this misstep.

After 1930 no amount of Marxist theory or Bolshevik conspiratorial mystique could seduce the brightest and most ambitious young Liberals and freethinkers, who were on their way to positions of influence in government and the Liberal press. The Liberal Party monopolized reformism, as demonstrated by the experience of Jorge Eliécer Gaitán, the most intrepid politician of his era. Disenchanted with the pace of reform under Olaya, in 1934 Gaitán founded the National Leftist Revolutionary Union (UNIR), only to see it lose support and credibility as López's "Revolution on the March" captured the public imagination. After a poor electoral showing in 1935, Gaitán returned to the Liberal fold and never left it again.

The young radicals of the 1930s had both organizational and ideological aspirations. They dreamed of taking control of the Liberal Party, but without imposing a Leninist "democratic centralism." Ideologically, they were influenced by the Spanish philosopher José Ortega y Gasset's *The Rebellion of the Masses* (1926), which was widely read by Colombian intellectuals; Ortega warned of the "leaning toward dictatorship" among modern Europeans, who were the products of universal education and the collective passions typical of politics and modern war. The era of the individual, according to Ortega, was giving way to a flood of the masses into every corner of civilized life. Although Colombia was still far from the modernity described by Ortega, it was still subject to the dangers of mass eruptions, which according to the radicals could be prevented through intelligent reformism.

The Communists changed course in 1935 to become "fellow travelers" of López's revolution. This tactical move implied a profound shift in the party's class analysis of Colombian reality, now led by a putative "progressive national bourgeoisie" captained by López. The tactic of the "popular front," devised by the Comintern to address the threat of fascism, which supplanted social democracy as the Communists' greatest enemy, called for renewed interest in elections and in the grassroots organizing that elections required. Alliance with the Liberals was seen as a way of jump-starting the Communists' electoral efforts; meanwhile, López was immersed in an ever more strident dispute with the church and the Conservatives on the issue of constitutional reform, and when in April 1936 the church hierarchy issued a direct threat to the government, López retaliated by appearing on the presidential balcony for May Day with top union and Communist leaders, who duly attacked the bishops in their speeches.

That joint appearance and the campaign later that month to establish a popular front in Colombia became a cause célèbre for both left and right. For the right, López was at best a Colombian Kerensky, the "useful idiot" of revolutionary Marxism. But the outbreak of the Spanish Civil War in July 1936 and the rapid turn of the Republican movement there toward the extreme left put

López on the defensive. He downplayed Colombia's nascent popular front as mere wordplay — and he was right, because it was just a loose coalition of Communists, a few intellectuals and Liberals, "vanguard socialists" without any real organization, and elements of several labor unions, most notably teachers.

Meanwhile the Conservatives were also becoming radical, beginning with language. In their 1937 convention delegates approved a motion by Gilberto Alzate Avendaño to define the party as being "of the right." The next year Alzate founded the Popular Nationalist Alliance in Manizales, and the party's national leader, Laureano Gómez, moved toward an endorsement of corporatism on the Portuguese and Spanish Nationalist model.

The marriage of convenience between Liberals and the unions was especially noxious to the Conservatives. They viewed unions as a new means to distribute favors and garner votes, but they were not sure how to neutralize it. The church tried to set up "Catholic Worker Youth" organizations as a foil to unions, but Liberal legislation against "parallel unionism" doomed these efforts to failure. The church hierarchy and its Conservative allies in the Medellín business community lacked the experience and credibility to establish full-fledged Catholic labor unions led by "worker priests" on the Belgian model.

Examination of the relationship between the Liberals and the unions from the era of Benjamín Herrera and Rafael Uribe Uribe around 1910 through the split that lasted from 1945 to 1953 throws light on both sides and yields a key to understanding how the backwardness of the Colombian social structure permitted the parties' continuity. Three factors in particular are noteworthy. First, the relationship between the unions and the Liberal Party was very much a one-way street: while workers were denied any political expression outside the party, unions had no meaningful influence on its policies or personnel. Second, the low rates of union membership, the precariousness of workers' organizations, and the continued pattern of strikes followed by apathy, all were proof that a proletariat of the sort dreamed of by leftist intellectuals and Communists simply did not exist in Colombia. Third, even the most readily identifiable working class was immersed in a heterogeneous lower-class world still dominated by artisan sensibilities, and those sensibilities were effectively addressed by López and later by Gaitán. Its most radical wing came to rest in the pettybourgeois heart of the Communist Party, where it lost all relevance to national political life.

The Second World War and the
Hegemony of the United States

The rise of anticommunism after mid-1936 weakened López's position in the party at the expense of Olaya's supporters. Even in the all-Liberal Congress the government could not win majority support for minimum-wage legislation because of the opposition of legislators from agricultural regions. When Darío Echandía, a leftist favorite of López, lost to the moderate Eduardo Santos in the legislative elections that functioned as a de facto presidential primary, López decreed a moratorium on the reform agenda. It was still in effect when his term ended.

Santos was the political heir of Olaya, who died prematurely in 1937. He won the presidency the following year without opposition, since the Conservatives continued to abstain from electoral politics and the Communists lent him their support. He was very much a centrist but was agile enough to co-opt a good number of radical intellectuals. Santos was conciliatory by nature, and while he was basically an intellectual himself, he could also be pragmatic—a combination that served him well as owner and director of the most influential newspaper in the country, *El Tiempo*. He saw no reason to court the radical left, since he was convinced that the liberalism of Santander and Murillo Toro was an inexhaustible fount of timeless doctrinal wisdom. He had a strong Francophile streak that could be traced to his early education, and he trusted more in the orderly workings of institutions than in the unpredictability of "great men." Santander was his hero, and he embraced the motto "less politics and more administration," which joined him ideologically to Nuñez's Regeneration before it became beholden to Nationalist Conservatism, and politically to the modernizing Conservative regimes of Carlos E. Restrepo, Marco Fidel Suárez, and Pedro Nel Ospina.

Santos strongly objected to the presence of López's ministers at union congresses; he had no interest in mobilizing a tiny portion of the population (less than 100,000 unionized workers) at the risk of polarizing public life. He distanced the government from the CTC, but early in his administration he settled a strike by the Communist-dominated FEDENAL union, representing the railroad workers, in favor of the union. As usual, the settlement was paid out of the national treasury. Soon thereafter Santos called in the favor, insisting on the railroad workers' support for moderate positions in the CTC.

Santos strengthened the Liberal party's machinery and cultivated the middle sectors. He persuaded the Conservatives to take part in the 1939 local elections, which the Liberals won handily (650 of the 800-odd town councils). However, during the campaign the killing of ten Conservatives by the Liberal local police in Gachetá (northeast of Bogotá) was grist for Laureano Gómez's incendiary brand of Conservatism.

On education the Santos regime continued Lopez's policy of secularization first, new schools second. A government proposal to bring all primary schooling under the inspection and funding of the national government was defeated by church and Conservative opposition despite the negligible Conservative presence in Congress. Santos, again following López's lead, tried to direct the steady trickle of European refugee intellectuals toward the National University. One exception was the distinguished French anthropologist Paul Rivet, who was invited to the new Escuela Normal Superior; under his leadership a generation of social scientists was trained and the National Ethnological Institute was founded. The goal was a Colombian national identity founded on rationalism, humanism, and liberalism, rather than the existing parallel identities of Liberal and Conservative. The tutelary figure of this unified identity was to be the founding Liberal, Francisco de Paula Santander, for his role in constructing the rule of law as vice president in the 1820s and as president in the 1830s. The centenary of Santander's death in 1940 was the apex of a government-led civic cult that began with Olaya, but it also was the start of a counter-offensive by Gómez and the Conservatives, who embraced the figure of Simón Bólivar—first Santander's mentor, later his mortal enemy.

The Second World War interrupted Colombia's steady recovery from the Great Depression, prolonged the fiscal austerity imposed by Olaya and sustained by López, and reinforced the diplomatic alliance with the United States. For the first time two U.S. military missions came to Colombia as advisers to the navy and the air force. Colombia, however, was not interested in taking part in Washington's lend-lease program to strengthen Latin American militaries against possible Axis aggression. Colombian Liberals tended to be antimilitarist and Santos was even more so. This stance was applauded in much of Latin America and even influenced Costa Rica's National Liberation Party when it wrote the 1949 constitution, which famously abolished the army.

Nevertheless, Colombia was one of Washington's most solid allies in the hemisphere. It was the first country in South America to break off diplomatic relations with the Axis powers after Pearl Harbor, and Santos personally assured the United States of access to Colombian territory in the event of an attack on the Panama Canal. He also worked with the United States to intern German, Italian, and Japanese nationals who were resident in Colombia; but he ignored Washington's requests to collaborate with its "black list" against Axis properties, preferring instead to sequester those properties under Colombian government control. Among the affected companies were a German bank in Medellín and a French-Italian bank in Bogotá, several important chemical and pharmaceutical companies, and SCADTA, the principal civil aviation company. Colombia's leading brewery was Dutch-owned, and was sequestered when Germany overran Holland; the transfer of its shares to Colombian ownership in 1943–44 was one of the twentieth century's biggest political scandals, involving family members of Alfonso López Pumarejo, then in his second term (1942–45).

The United States' strategy to secure Latin American support in World War II had three important manifestations in Colombia:

1. The closing of European markets in 1939 came at the worst possible time for Colombia, because there were substantial world inventories, and also because Brazil had suspended its policy of destroying surplus stocks. Despite FEDECAFÉ's predictions (which were borne out earlier in the decade), Colombia was no longer winning the price war. The government had to step in to subsidize producers in the interests of social and economic stability. To stave off an eventual reduction in coffee supplies in response to falling prices, the United States agreed to a Pan-American coffee pact based on national quotas. The effects were dramatic: prices doubled in the twelve months after the signing of the pact in October 1940, and Colombia was able to boost its U.S. market share above the designated quota because of the difficulties in transporting coffee from Brazil.

2. The U.S. government took a similarly proactive role in settling the impasse over Colombia's foreign debt, 80 percent of which was owed to U.S. creditors. With the debt moratorium lifted, U.S. investors could make use of the new Export-Import Bank to finance investments they were eager to make in Colombia, especially in manufacturing and in oil exploration and refining.

3. As part of the plan to safeguard the Panama Canal against Axis attack, SCADTA was "denazified." After tangled diplomatic maneuvers, the U.S.

Treasury issued an indemnity of $1 million to Pan Am, which by 1940 owned far more of the airline than the Germans did, and Avianca was born. The new airline was owned by Colombian businessmen, and it grew into a successful operation: it had a monopoly on airmail service, a dominant share of the domestic passenger market, and control over foreign carriers' landing rights in the country.

Every hint of cooperation between Colombia and the United States that reached the public ear was fiercely attacked by the Conservative right, which sympathized with the fascist powers and detested the "Anglo-Saxons."

The Santos administration rivaled that of Pedro Nel Ospina in the 1920s in the creation of key economic institutions. The experiences of the 1930s and the early stages of World War II crystallized into new economic thinking, which privileged direct state investment in key industries. The Industrial Development Institute (IFI, founded in 1941), the Colombian version of Chile's pioneering CORFO (1939), was to be the linchpin of the new industrial strategy. IFI would make investments in sectors where risk, slow returns, or the initial capital required made private financing unlikely: steel, basic chemicals, fertilizers, pesticides. Companies would be sold off once they became attractive to private investors. Other public enterprises created in the early 1940s were devoted to social or regional goals, such as affordable housing, electrification, and water and sewer systems for smaller towns.

This statist initiative gave rise to a new group of functionaries who melded liberal principles with Keynesian interventionism—the use of fiscal policy to boost aggregate demand. The leading figure among this new generation of modernizers, Carlos Lleras Restrepo, was finance minister in 1942 when he summed up the new position: the budget deficit was not the nightmare that most people imagined but the perfect instrument for "revving up business." Lleras was not trying to shrug off a sudden fall in revenues, which actually doubled between 1940 and 1945. The government also made use of internal credit and external public loans (the Export-Import Bank was key here as well) to diversify agriculture and ranching and to speed up highway construction.

Of all the institutions founded under Santos, the most important and longlasting was the National Coffee Fund (FNC). Created as a result of the 1940 coffee pact, the FNC was a nominally private entity that administered an account in the national treasury from which it set the internal price of coffee to keep growers' income steady, bought the entire national harvest, and controlled exports according to the pact's national quotas. For the first time the coffee market was a truly national one with uniform payments to growers, warehouses, and processors. The FNC's success strengthened the marriage between the government and the coffee growers' FEDECAFÉ, and it also preserved the working alliance between moderates of both parties during an era of increasingly bitter partisanship.

The Predicaments of the Liberal Republic

In 1940–41 the transport workers' unions split along political lines: the railroad and drivers' unions supported leaders allied with Santos while the port and maritime workers of FEDENAL remained in Communist hands. FEDENAL held a congress in Barranquilla which formalized the moderate–radical division of the recently created CTC. Once Hitler invaded the USSR in mid-1941, the Communists were quick to revive the popular front, and they even deferred to Liberals in the visible leadership of the temporarily reunited CTC. Although the CTC was a loose organization with little funding and little control over its member unions, it did coordinate union support for Alfonso López in his campaign to return to the presidency in 1942. López soundly defeated his right-wing Liberal rival, Carlos Arango Vélez, most of whose support came from the Conservatives, who once more were without a candidate of their own because the party chose not to field one.

The second López administration was one of the most traumatic of the twentieth century, and not just because of the attempted military coup of July 10, 1944. Businessmen and landowners felt stirrings of insecurity, although López had been president of SAC, the landowners' lobby, in 1941. Unionized labor, which was feeling the pinch of inflation, and the rural poor, who were still fighting for title to the lands they worked, added fuel to expectations of social justice. The church, the Conservatives, and rightist Liberals were determined to prevent a return to the reformism of 1936. In the first months of his second administration López, who had rebuilt the Liberal mystique on the basis of social reformism, abandoned that stance and lost popular support without gaining the confidence of the right. He adopted a dictatorial line against the unions, and when workers in the foreign-owned Frontino Gold Mines, the railroads, and the Magdalena ports went on strike, they were shocked to find that the government, far from supporting them, threatened to send in the troops.

To Gómez, whose leadership of the Conservatives had been weakened by the conciliatory posture of Santos, López appeared like manna from heaven. The "Masonic, atheist, Communist" regime was the ideal target for Gómez's overwrought verbiage and his well-honed confrontational tactics. But López gave up the mobilizing tactics of his first administration and embarked on a balancing act between the multifarious groups of an ever more complex power elite. His cabinets were a mix of Bogotá bankers, Medellín textile magnates, Caldas coffee growers, and coastal merchants and cotton growers.

Under López the state's economic power grew weightier, in part because of the exigencies of the war. He tightened monetary controls and increased direct taxation, and in an effort to control the inflationary effects of rising foreign currency reserves, in 1943 the government proposed a sophisticated package of price controls, forced savings and bond purchases, and froze gold stocks held in New York. There were war-related shortages of gasoline, tires, and spare parts—and of steel, which affected the construction industry during a period of rapid urbanization and infrastructure expansion. Inflation, hoarding, and even food shortages all contributed to widespread unrest.

In this atmosphere of high expectations among the common people and exaggerated fears among the elites, Gómez capitalized on two opportunities to portray López as tempestuous and untrustworthy. The first was the new concordat with the Vatican, which Santos had negotiated and submitted for congressional approval. It restricted the clergy's role in public education, guaranteed that bishops serving Colombia would be citizens of the country, returned cemeteries to state administration, ordered civil registration of church weddings, and recognized civil jurisdiction over the separation of married couples. Gómez saw in these provisions the hidden hand of Freemasonry, which he claimed was behind the Liberal Republic in general, and he accused the papal nuncio of misinforming the pope about the real situation of Colombian Catholics. A pastoral letter from the archbishop of Bogotá censured Gómez for making such claims, but the Conservative leader was more interested in attracting the support of the lower clergy and the rural faithful, and in that he succeeded. The second incident revealed one of the government's key weaknesses, its worsening relations with the army. The arrest and firing of the secretary general of the War Ministry, a career officer accused of conspiracy, was poorly received in the corps; it was rumored that López wanted to subordinate the armed forces to the police.

After that dispute died down, Gómez's newspaper, *El Siglo*, began a fierce campaign against official corruption, focusing on the roles of the president's brother and two sons in the handling of sequestered German assets. In the newspaper's rendering, Colombia was ruled by an insatiable family that was getting rich by colluding with unscrupulous corporations. The use and abuse of these incidents damaged López without especially benefiting Gómez; overall confidence in Colombian democracy was the loser, as evidenced by the decline in the number of votes cast in the congressional elections of 1943 and 1945 from those of 1941. In mid-1943 there were transport workers' strikes in Barranquilla, the Magdalena River ports, Bogotá, Santander, and Caldas. With no clear support from his party at a critical moment, López made his first attempt to resign the presidency in late 1943; the various Liberal factions united in support of his continuation in office, but the accusations and problems kept coming. In November 1943 he left the presidency in the hands of his faithful lieutenant Darío Echandía while he traveled to the United States, but he returned in May 1944 after Congress rejected his second letter of resignation.

On July 10 López flew to Pasto, in the extreme southwest of the country, to witness military exercises, and was taken prisoner by a group of army officers. Their leader, a colonel, announced that he was taking power. Although the attempt attracted some sympathy among the officer corps, it was quickly isolated and thwarted. The labor unions and urban masses came out in support of the government, and in the brief afterglow of López's return to Bogotá the Liberals united behind him. The court-martial of the participants in the coup found that it had been a strictly military conspiracy without civilian accomplices, but Gómez went into exile after he was briefly detained and his newspaper shuttered.

To improve relations with the army López broke with tradition and appointed a general as minister of war; a month later, he approved a new military penal code that exempted the armed forces from civilian courts. But he also insisted on strengthening the police, who were subject to local and departmental control, and he asked the United States for lend-lease support for equipping them. The request was denied, but it did hurt his standing with the military high command, which was already unhappy with López's personal handling of the vital military relationship with Washington.

Between July and November 1944 the government declared a state of siege and legislated by decree, and it also imposed strict censorship of the press, which was especially resented by Santos (who was a newspaper editor before he was a politician) and his wing of the Liberal party. Among the decrees (later ratified by Congress) was a package on union and labor rights that included provisions covering vacations, layoffs, work accidents, a minimum wage, and night work; it also prohibited the use of strikebreakers and granted some protections to union leaders. This was seen as the government's reward to labor for its support during the attempted coup. At the same time, the new laws prohibited strikes while the country was under a state of siege and gave priority to company-level unions over labor confederations.

In 1945 López won support for a constitutional reform that instituted direct popular election of senators (until then elected by departmental assemblies) and strengthened the executive's power to intervene in the economy. But Gómez, returned from his brief exile, was once more attacking the government's legitimacy, and Liberal leaders were more concerned with the race to succeed López than with his fate in office. When López once more submitted his resignation in July 1945, Congress accepted it and chose as his replacement Alberto Lleras Camargo, minister of the interior, who pledged to remain neutral in the party's internal conflicts. Lleras established a government of national unity and appointed three Conservative cabinet ministers. This approach pulled the ideological rug from under the partisan divide.

If 1945 was a fruitful year in the consolidation of a state interventionist in economics and liberal in politics, it was at the expense of social reforms that could bring the benefits of citizenship to everyone. The CTC, the labor confederation born of López's Revolution on the March, illustrated the shifting course of the Liberals' social concerns. Cast adrift by Santos and then by López and Lleras, it could not voice the diverse concerns of its affiliates. This was largely a structural issue: the CTC was weak in the industrial sector, covering only 100 of the 8,000 firms that appeared in the 1945 industrial census. In the industrial center of Medellín CTC-affiliated unions were outnumbered by Catholic and company unions. The emphasis on craft skills in the large majority of manufacturing and mining workplaces and the demographic pressure of unskilled labor made it difficult for a strong union movement to develop. The unions in state enterprises, scattered as they were throughout the country, were manipulated by local political machines.

The most effective and radical labor union was FEDENAL, which represented the Magdalena River workers. In 1937 it became the first and only union to win a closed shop, but after 1942 it fell prey to wrangling among the Communist factions that dominated its leadership. In 1945 the union launched an ill-advised strike that the Lleras regime declared illegal, and with the loss of its legal status, the union fell apart. Within two days the shipping companies brought in replacement workers, and the CTC fell in line with the government against FEDENAL. Lleras famously declared that there could not be two governments in Colombia, one in Bogotá and another on the Magdalena River—a truism that signaled a definitive shift in the Liberals' position on unionism.

The fate of FEDENAL was also proof that unions lacked the resources, both financial and organizational, to exert any meaningful pressure without the government's recognition and support. Recognizing this, the CTC and its largely Communist leadership decided to throw their support to the official Liberal candidate in 1946, Gabriel Turbay. The dissident Liberal candidate, Jorge Eliécer Gaitán, was more popular among the labor rank and file, but his idea of establishing a rival union confederation made him anathema to the leadership.

The Lleras regime's relations with the other end of the bargaining table, Colombia's increasingly well-organized industrialists, were even more ambiguous. Businessmen, whom the Conservative candidate, Mariano Ospina Pérez, pointedly called "working men," were nervous about the 1946 presidential campaign. They were less concerned about the state's growing powers to intervene in the economy, enshrined in the 1945 constitutional reform, than about the specific path future interventions might take. A reopening of old debates between protectionists and free traders, or between manufacturers and coffee growers or importers, was something to be dreaded.

Industrialists, Transportation, and Power

As early as 1941 the Allies had declared that the postwar period would require a new international political and economic order. The International Monetary Fund (IMF) and the World Bank, founded in 1944, were the cornerstones of that new ideal. The United Nations would be assigned the role of promoting economic and social development in the world, encouraging trade liberalization, and generally pulling down the economic walls that were thought to have contributed to the rise of fascism. The General Agreement on Tariffs and Trade (GATT, 1947) was the institutional expression of this thrust. While it was initially conceived in truly international terms, very soon the Cold War and then decolonization in Asia and Africa opened an era of growing ideological polarization.

Worried that the "less developed" parts of the world might be as ripe for Communist revolution as the Soviet Union was claiming, in 1949 the Truman administration designed the Point Four program, which paved the way for the World Bank and later the Inter-American Development Bank (IADB) to take the lead in accelerating economic growth. At the same time, U.S. private capital was interested in Latin America as a market for industrial goods, in addition to its longstanding role as supplier of raw materials.

In Colombia, continuing development of the transportation grid made the idea of an industrial economy seem quite reasonable. The wild spending on railroad construction in the 1920s and the pressure of New York creditors in 1930–31 led to a rethinking of the transportation system along more systematic lines, with increasing emphasis on highways. Between 1930 and 1950 an average of 850 kilometers of roads were built annually, in accordance with a plan of national trunk roads approved by Congress. By mid-century, some 21,000 kilometers of highways tied the country together.

Low gasoline prices and unrestricted importation of motor vehicles favored the new highway-centered vision, but travelers still faced great obstacles. The secondary grid was still highly uneven—quite developed around Bogotá, much less so around Medellín and Cali—and the total number of vehicles was still low. Transportation costs were high, and a range of factors from unstable geology to poor engineering (or corrupt contractors) made for uncertain travel. Meanwhile, on the established railroad system the rolling stock was largely obsolete and labor costs were higher than revenues could support.

The decline of the Magdalena River as a major transportation artery was steep and irreversible. The most dynamic coffee-producing regions sent their harvests to the Pacific coast via three rail lines that by 1935 carried more tonnage per kilometer than all other Colombian lines put together. In 1910 the three main ports of the Caribbean coast, which used the Magdalena as their main route inland, handled 83 percent of imports and 79 percent of exports (measured by value), but by 1945 these figures dropped to 57 percent and 51 percent respectively. During the same period the Pacific port of Buenaventura increased its share from 7 percent of imports and 6 percent of exports to 32 percent and 47 percent respectively.

There were many other factors behind the eclipse of the Magdalena artery. Some were natural, such as the shifting sandbars near the river's Caribbean terminus, which required ever more costly countermeasures; and the natural river cycles of drought and flood that made transportation unreliable. Other factors were human, such as the system by which cargo was loaded and unloaded in strict order of arrival, rather than according to technical or economic criteria. In competitive terms, FEDENAL's closed shop between 1937 and 1945 was a further negative factor.

Around mid-century Colombians were humming a popular song:

> The alligator's going,
> The alligator's going,
> He's going to Barranquilla.

The alligators were indeed disappearing from the Magdalena, and Barranquilla turned a page of its economic and social history. For centuries much of Colombia had made use of the river in a multitude of ways, and they assumed it would always be there. Much of Colombia's progress since the colonial era had depended on it. But Colombians never gave anything back to the Magdalena, and deforestation eventually wreaked havoc on its watershed. Millions of cubic meters of woods were taken from the subtropical forest with no restriction or replanting, to be used as fuel for household cooking or for steam engines, in construction, or in mine shafts (despite a farsighted ban on this practice in the 1890 mining code). Oil largely replaced wood as industrial and steamship fuel by the 1920s, but the damage was already done.

As the flora and fauna that so impressed travelers and scientists from the Botanical Expedition of the 1780s to Alfred Hettner in the 1890s receded into memory, the cumulative deterioration of the Magdalena ecosystem made travel on the river increasingly unreliable. From December to April there were impassable stretches between La Dorada and Calamar as the river dried up; from May to November the river was navigable but its banks near the coast were flooded. As early as 1860 merchants began to notice that the river was in trouble, and its condition shocked President José Manuel Marroquín in 1898; Mariano Ospina Pérez is said to have requested a daily report on river levels during his presidency in the late 1940s.

If nothing else, the battered Magdalena was witness and proof of the substantial economic change than had occurred between the late nineteenth century and the mid-twentieth. Colombia had, in the words of the optimists, "jumped from the mule to the airplane." Aviation was, in fact, taking its place among the country's main modes of transportation: in 1950 planes carried as much cargo as steamships had carried only thirty years earlier, and 800,000 passenger tickets were sold.

Like the coffee census of 1932, the industrial census of 1945 helped to spread a new image of the Colombian economy. The growing importance of manufacturing was suddenly apparent, but there were clear signs of excessive concentration and technological backwardness. One-half of 1 percent of industrial firms controlled fully one-third of total capital and assets; the highest levels of concentration were found in Medellín, Manizales, and Barranquilla, and in the industries of petroleum and its derivatives, beer, and textiles. Around half of total manufacturing took place in the west of the country, a little over a third in the central and eastern regions, dominated by Bogotá, and around 14 percent on the Caribbean coast.

Within a few months in 1944–45 two important trade associations were founded: the National Industrialists' Association (ANDI) and the National Merchants' Federation (FENALCO), which joined the bankers' association and FEDECAFÉ at the cusp of Colombian capitalism. From that point on, the state control required by the new economic model would entail constant tension and negotiation between regional and corporate interests, under the supervision of poorly trained and sometimes corrupt administrators. There was some continuity with the previous model, since FEDECAFÉ, a public-private entity, continued to be the axis of the mixed economy. The business elite rotated from cabinet posts to governing boards in state and private enterprises, and the public had very little access to their deliberations and decisions.

ANDI's incorporation into the power structure, in particular its encounters with the competing interests represented by FENALCO and FEDECAFÉ and with the two parties, provides a key to understanding the political, institutional, and ideological context of the late 1940s and the 1950s. The formative period of the new lobby groups also reflects the state and society that emerged in postwar Colombia. ANDI's power, for instance, was derived not from the thousands of industrial firms enumerated in the 1945 industrial census, but by the initiative shown by a small clique in taking on the representation and leadership of an entire sector. In its early years ANDI was largely the tool of a small group of family-owned textile manufacturers in Antioquia, and its early conflicts with FENALCO reflected their running conflict with textile merchants based in Cali.

The industrialists depended on support from politicians who controlled the selection of officials in charge of setting interest rates and currency exchange rates, issuing import licenses, and classifying merchandise for tariff purposes. From the outset ANDI specialized in direct lobbying of key figures and in swaying public opinion. FENALCO adopted similar methods but its objectives were diametrically opposed: in the name of defending the consumer, it advocated undoing recent economic regulations and price floors and opening the economy to imports. For over a decade these two lobbies fought each other on multiple fronts, and for the first time in decades one could at least hazily perceive a difference between the parties on economic issues: ANDI had Conservative proclivities, while FENALCO leaned more toward the Liberals.

At the close of the 1940s ANDI chalked up two decisive victories: Colombia's early termination of the 1935 trade treaty with the United States and its rejection of GATT. But in the 1950s and thereafter, as the industrial sector became more complex, ANDI adopted a more generic discourse to suit its more varied membership. In the 1960s more specialized lobbies were organized, usually more interested than the long-established and locally financed textile manufacturers in free importation of capital and intermediate goods.

The Political Bases of the Plutocratic Elite

Mid-century Colombia suffered from high mortality rates, low life expectancy, and still low levels of urbanization. The economy was still dominated by agriculture, principal fount of wealth and employment, but its productivity was low and production techniques remained mired in the past. Even so, the cumulative effects of economic growth and sociocultural change presaged an era of dislocations and conflicts. To face down these challenges, the Colombian political system, like many in Latin America and southern Europe, had to resort to dictatorial methods.

The tragic collapse of Jorge Eliécer Gaitán's populist Liberal movement in 1948 (detailed in Chapter 4) had several important consequences in this regard. First, it lent credence to the idea that Colombia was not sufficiently mature for democracy, because its political and social movements tended to emphasize income redistribution. This was especially unpalatable to the elite at a time when high coffee prices were launching the country into a sustained period of high capital investment, which would be derailed by redistributive politics and policies. Second, the violence of *gaitanismo*'s collapse precipitated a turn to authoritarianism by the Conservative government of Mariano Ospina Pérez. Third, the perceived dangers of the moment brought together the disparate capitalist interests that had been at cross-purposes for much of the previous decade: manufacturers, bankers, coffee growers, ranchers, real estate developers, and importers. They forged a basic consensus on subsidies, tax exemptions, and miscellaneous policies to guarantee high returns on "modern" economic activities. This new plutocracy thought no more highly of social reforms than the old elites did. Social justice was reduced to a matter of minor public spending, rather than the all-permeating issue it represented for Latin American populism.

With coffee export revenues relatively abundant throughout the Conservative dictatorship and the first part of the military regime (1949–56), the government was able to pursue a variety of modernization initiatives with relatively little controversy. While industrial development (including capital-intensive and high-risk projects, through the IFI created by Santos) was first on the list of priorities, others included road and airport construction, electricity and telecommunications infrastructure, and the mechanization of commercial agriculture. The tools created in the 1930s and 1940s were sufficient to weather the short-term ups and downs of coffee prices. Of course, not all was harmony within the new plutocracy; in particular, large coffee growers (especially in Caldas) decried the use of any coffee revenues for other purposes as a form of expropriation.

FEDECAFÉ reached new heights of influence and financial power and even built its own merchant fleet, the Flota Mercante Grancolombiana, whose operations further strengthened the links between FEDECAFÉ and the state. (The federation was so concerned about avoiding partisan conflict that it went for ten years [1946–56] without holding a national congress.) As the Grancolombiana name implied, the Flota was a trinational entity with representation by Venezuela and Ecuador; however, FEDECAFÉ controlled its operations and supplied much of its cargo. Eventually it came to handle 45 percent of Colombia's coffee exports. In a further example of diversification to advance its mission, FEDECAFÉ designed and administered a barter system with European countries suffering from a scarcity of foreign currency, and in 1953 it started a bank, the Banco Cafetero, guaranteed by the National Coffee Fund.

In 1950, when the country entered its most accelerated phase of urbanization, occupational diversification, and industrial expansion, Colombia still had ten students in primary schooling for each student who reached the secondary stage. Only one primary student in one hundred reached the university, and over 70 percent of students did not make it to third grade. With numbers like these, the shortage of trained personnel for economic growth was no surprise. In the 1930s and 1940s universities graduated a nucleus of trained administrators for the public and private sectors and engineers in various specialties who were highly responsive to the needs of industry. The picture was different on the agricultural side; it was still rare to find a trained agronomist or veterinarian.

Ospina continued his predecessors' policy of growth at the expense of inflation, and the consumer price index rose by 15 percent in 1947 and then by 20 percent in 1950. At least initially, this was partly the result of the opening of the world's markets to meet the pent-up demand for foreign goods after World War II. Fierce competition among industrialists, coffee exporters, and importers drove up rates and eventually prices. The peso's value against the dollar, which had remained largely stable since 1938, fell in 1948 and a parallel unregulated market developed. All of this stimulated speculative ventures, distorted the norms of productive investment, and further concentrated wealth and income. The profits of commercial banks, insurance companies, and urban real estate grew more rapidly than those of large commercial, industrial, or agricultural firms, which in turn grew more rapidly than the incomes of unionized workers. The unorganized majority of the urban and rural working class benefited still less, with the exception of coffee workers in the west. Meanwhile, Colombians' certainty of rampant official corruption came complete with popular slang, such as the *serrucho* (hacksaw). The Finance Ministry lacked trained personnel to review the tax returns of large companies, and it was commonly held that customs offices in port cities were political piggy banks.

ANDI and FENALCO: Protection versus Free Trade

Despite ANDI's public relations and direct lobbying efforts, the government associated tariff protection with high prices. The Ospina administration's policy was "integral protection," which it defined as: (1) preferential exchange rates for imports of equipment and import quotas for everything else, (2) a more protectionist tariff schedule, with implementation delayed until 1950, and (3) the creation of an Institute for Cotton Promotion to coordinate the interests of cotton growers and textile manufacturers. The U.S. ambassador strongly objected to the first policy as a violation of bilateral trade agreements, and FEDECAFÉ objected because it preferred overall currency devaluation. While wages and working conditions were excluded from the definition of "integral protection"—in other words, it was an economic development doctrine—there were some controls on consumer prices, which would be strengthened during the military regime.

The state's pact with the industrialists was sealed in 1949 with Colombia's abrogation of the 1935 trade treaty with the United States and by its rejection of membership in GATT and then by the 1950 tariff revision. The banking reform of 1951 continued along this path, inspired (ironically enough) by the populist Liberal Jorge Eliécer Gaitán's 1947 plan to expand industry's access to long-term bank credit. Laureano Gómez's willingness to implement these industry-friendly policies helped to dissipate the entrepreneurs' misgivings about his incendiary and polarizing rhetoric.

The Liberals attacked high tariffs in the name of free trade, while the Conservatives played the protectionist card. ANDI moved closer to identification with the Conservatives, and in 1950 FENALCO's national congress refused to send the customary message of congratulation to President-elect Gómez. Until the military coup of 1953, the Liberals' complaint was that the Conservative regimes subordinated everything to "stock market fluctuations and the wishes of industrial capital." At the 1951 Liberal convention the tariff reform was condemned as "ignominious" and the following year's party manifesto reinforced the charge. The Liberal press, especially the newspapers identified with Alfonso López, attacked the new industrial oligarchy—which it called "the oligarchy of the 175," referring not to their number but to the preferential exchange rate of 1.75 pesos to the U.S. dollar enjoyed by industrialists under Ospina, while the rate for everyone else was 3.00 to the dollar. But under the military regime, around 1955, the Liberal leaders Alberto Lleras Camargo and Carlos Lleras Restrepo reversed course on the issue: Alberto Lleras, after all, had been a key figure in the Santos regime, which placed great emphasis on the promotion of industrialization, though through different policies, and Carlos Lleras had become familiar with the industrialization experiences of other Latin American countries when he served as secretary general of the Organization of American States (OAS). Besides, by the mid-1950s the industrialists were an established power bloc, with a good public image and the resources to finance political campaigns.

Gómez was always careful to separate "economic government" from "political government." He surrounded himself with good economic advisers, and his government was blessed with high coffee prices, ready access to loans, and an overall sound budgetary situation. His successor by military coup, Gustavo Rojas Pinilla, was far more erratic in his choice of advisers (some were anti-communist socialists) and had to face one of the deepest coffee price plunges of the second half of the twentieth century.

Despite his hatred of Liberal rule, Gómez embraced the institutions created under Santos in the early 1940s and incorporated them in his overall social and economic development plan. No amount of separation of economics and politics, however, could keep the state's direct role, through IFI and state-owned companies, from becoming immersed in partisan and regional conflicts. In an attempt to maintain some balance among the regions, IFI distributed its investments among Bogotá, Medellín, Cali, and Barranquilla, but the potential riches of the new state oil company, ECOPETROL; the new state steel company, Acerías Paz del Río; and the coffee growers' Flota Mercante were constant magnets for individual and collective ambitions.

In a message to the Bucaramanga newspaper *Vanguardia Liberal* in mid-1950, Alfonso López spoke of a "government of marked regional profiles": subsidized exchange rates, strong tariff protections, and overrepresentation in government for Antioquia and the west, while eastern Colombia got only "high prices, official violence to clear out Liberal peasants before election time, [and] a pair of shoes and overalls twice a year," that last item a reference to a provision of the 1950 labor law. He dismissed the new state-owned steelworks as "lifeless, or at best precarious," and ECOPETROL as a "historic and decisive advance" not for Colombia as a whole, but for "an industrial group" in its campaign to dominate the nation's economic life.

The state oil company had emerged from Congress after the defeat of a competing Liberal proposal for a company jointly held by the state and a consortium of U.S. firms. The chief sponsor of that bill, Alfonso López's brother Eduardo López Pumarejo, had a long history of advocacy on behalf of foreign oil firms. ANDI also wanted a mixed public-private company, but it envisioned a dominant role for Colombian capital, especially Antioquian. The interest of that region's elite in the oil industry dated back to Olaya, when a Medellín group formed the Unión Colombiana de Petróleo and worked for the passage of Olaya's oil-friendly legislation. In the 1950 debates they presented an explosive list of demands: control of ECOPETROL, elimination of labor unions, liquidation of employees' pension funds, and expulsion of peasants who had settled on the company's landholdings. As for the U.S. firms engaged in Colombia, they had little interest in any model that ceded control to Colombians, and were content with a ten-year extension of their monopoly over refining for Colombian domestic use.

Gómez went his own way on this key issue for Colombian development: he wanted an oil industry composed of large producers, as in the Medellín textile industry, but he did not think the Antioquians were equipped for the job. While Gómez was not an economic nationalist in the mold of Mexico's Lázaro Cárdenas, who expropriated foreign oil interests in the late 1930s, he believed that only the state could properly develop Colombia's oil resources, and he insisted on 100 percent state ownership of ECOPETROL. This model did not exclude a substantial foreign role, because the actual tasks of the new company— exploration, drilling, refining—would require more capital and expertise than Colombians could muster, at least in the short term.

With the creation of the state steelworks at Paz del Río in 1948, Colombian industrial policy gained a new standard-bearer. Located in a backward corner of the backward department of Boyacá, the steelworks employed French technology and local raw materials, with financing coming from taxes and obligatory bond purchases. The United States opposed the project because it was state-owned, and the World Bank wondered if the benefits to Boyacá would justify the costs to the rest of the country, since the scale of the initial operation did not permit cost-effective production, while any substantial expansion would outstrip Colombia's demand for steel. The bank preferred the construction of two smaller plants in Medellín and Barranquilla, but eventually agreed to help finance a single plant in Boyacá if its size were reduced. The government refused to budge, in part to show that Liberal opposition was demagoguery but also to placate Boyacá's Conservatives, who were enormously influential in an era of highly contested elections. The initial government plan won out, and in 1954 Gustavo Rojas inaugurated the first foundry.

The Conservative regime did not ignore the unions, and given the Cold War atmosphere, its positions were not too far removed from the Liberals' mounting anticommunist zeal. It was the Liberals who purged the CTC, probably with some technical assistance from the FBI, after a failed strike in 1947. In 1949 the Conservative regime eliminated the ban on "parallel unionism" to clear a path for the Unión de Trabajadores de Colombia (UTC), founded in 1946 under the aegis of the Jesuits and paternalist Medellín employers. Now backed by Conservative networks of power, the UTC entered a period of growth while the CTC, though duly purged of radicals, was still on the wrong end of the sectarian divide. But the weakening of Liberal unionism did not leave urban workers totally at the mercy of the labor market. The diplomatic currents of the Cold War, which brought in U.S. labor experts from the AFL-CIO and experts from the International Labor Organization, along with the government's own political agenda of extending patronage networks among urban workers, made a wholly laissez-faire approach inadvisable. Toward the end of his administration Ospina brought in minimum-wage legislation and a new labor law, and while his government promoted the UTC at the expense of the CTC, the latter was not actively suppressed. Ospina even joined several other Latin American countries in rolling out a modest Social Security Institute (ICSS), nominally along U.S. and European lines. This initiative managed to unite ANDI and FENALCO in opposition, though by the mid-1950s they seemed to grow more tolerant of the idea.

The labor conditions of rural workers, whatever their category (wage laborers, tenants, or sharecroppers), were of as little interest to the Conservative regime as they were to the Liberals. The rural labor market was still dominated by custom and by patronage arrangements. The government's rural bank, the Caja de Crédito Agrario, based its loans on the notion of the peasant household kitchen garden that harked back to the 1932 coffee census. The López government's plan to put idle and underutilized lands into production, which the World Bank endorsed (even proposing a land tax based on what the land could produce rather than on its current value), was filed away along with any possibility of expropriation. The production of most food, except for sugar and rice, remained in the inefficient hands of small producers, while Colombian agriculture on the whole began to mimic the dualism of manufacturing, with substantial external financing for mechanization and technological innovation in small pockets of commercial agriculture.

The Impossible Populism of Rojas

The military dictatorship of Gustavo Rojas Pinilla (1953–57) is frequently characterized as populist. If by "populist" we mean an unstable coalition of industrialists, factory workers, and popular masses, both rural and urban, under the leadership of a charismatic figure who supplanted the old alliance of landowners, merchants, and bankers, then the policies of Ospina and Gómez, made possible by high coffee prices, canceled that possibility from the start. Industrialists were already part of the power structure.

Rojas came to power in June 1953 and his first economic measures were announced later that year: he loosened import restrictions and introduced taxes on stock dividends (decried as "double taxation" because the companies were already paying taxes on assets and profits). These provisions were in keeping with the Liberals' ideas of tax justice and opposition to monopoly, but as astute observers noted, Rojas was too much under Ospina's tutelage to take on the oligarchy. Rather, the main obsession of Rojas and his team was economic planning and big projects. Even David Lilienthal, "father of the Tennessee Valley Authority," who came to Colombia in 1954 to lay the groundwork for a similarly multifaceted development corporation for the Cali region, the Corporación del Valle del Cauca or cvc, was surprised by the enthusiasm for planning among Rojas's advisers.

Another obstacle to Rojas-as-populist was the crisis and collapse of Juan Domingo Perón's unambiguously populist regime in Argentina. Rojas's lukewarm identification with Perón, which peaked in late 1954, could not have come at a less opportune moment: the Argentine president was at the end of his political and economic rope, and the idea of Colombia as the next Argentina met a hostile reception by the church, the U.S. government and press, and international financial agencies. But Rojas did have a more sustainable political agenda: to build mass support for his government without the need for the traditional parties. From 1953 to 1956 real wages rose rapidly by twentieth-century standards, and the government spent heavily on public education, low-cost housing, health centers, and even the importation of toys for poor children. Road construction was accelerated in backward regions, victims of the Violencia were given titles to public lands, and the pacification of the eastern plains was given massive national publicity as the centerpiece of the government's concern for Colombians' well-being. As noted earlier, Rojas inherited an excellent fiscal situation built on high coffee prices; the collapse of those prices in 1955 unleashed a budgetary and currency crisis that was made worse by inept management and contributed to his downfall in 1957.

Despite his populist forays, Rojas was still very much in line with Colombian economic policy as it had existed since 1931; after all, those forays were financed largely by current revenues. Colombia's lack of restraint in importing goods the industrialists and urban middle class were clamoring for led inevitably to an imbalance of payments that could not be ignored. By late 1954 Rojas had so much riding on the satisfaction of the industrialists and the middle class that he could not follow the International Monetary Fund's recommendation that import controls be restored. When coffee prices collapsed and remained low, foreign currency reserves were quickly depleted and a recession soon followed.

The opposition, both Liberal and (increasingly) Conservative, were quick to pin the blame for the economic crisis on the government's wasteful and sometimes corrupt spending and on Rojas's bad relations with the U.S. ambassador. He also alienated international agencies, as when in October 1956 he rejected the World Bank's objections to a vast aqueduct plan with French financing, because "the people want water." The differential exchange rate produced a black market in dollars and encouraged trade in contraband coffee and false pricing of imports and exports, a gimmick that left spare dollars to speculate with or to keep in foreign bank accounts. The tariff structure encouraged corruption, since so much depended on the classification of imported goods. There was nothing new in any of this, however.

At the end of 1956 the IMF, seconded by Colombia's central bank, asked the government to devalue the peso, increase import controls, and cut back drastically on public spending and bank credit. Rojas refused to implement measures that he said would harm the national interest and the pocketbooks of the poor; his more radical advisers even presented him with an improvised go-it-alone economic scheme that included nationalization of the banks. But his regime fell before he could do anything, and within a matter of weeks the caretaker military regime went ahead with the devaluation; the corresponding rise in consumer prices was partially compensated by moderate pay raises by decree. By 1958 the World Bank resumed its lending to Colombia.

The fall of Rojas marked the close of a chapter that began in 1930: while it promised an expansion in citizens' rights, its ending demonstrated that the real beneficiaries were those members of the oligarchy who were able to modernize.

Chapter 4

IN THE SHADOW OF THE VIOLENCIA

*C*apitalist modernization came accompanied by the Violencia. And the Violencia justified a permanent state of siege, the constitutional weapon used by the state to neutralize the mobilization of the urban masses, whom the Liberals had made their base.

The basic images that govern and order our thinking about the Violencia were designed during the early years of the National Front, the bipartisan agreement that governed Colombia between 1958 and 1974. In this rendering, the Violencia was a popular and largely peasant convulsion rather than an authentic national tragedy that never really went away. As its details became known, public opinion viewed it as a regression from human history to natural history, and during the military regime of 1953 to 1957 it was impossible even to bring up its causes and contexts, much less subject it to judicial investigation, because of the regime's ties to the Conservatives.

A political description of the Violencia starts with its periodization into four phases: (1) traditional sectarianism, 1945–49; (2) from the Liberals' decision not to field a candidate in late 1949 to the installation of the military government in 1953; (3) the rise of the pájaros or Conservative assassins from 1954 to 1958; and (4) the residual violence that lasted through 1964, as the death squads sought to thrust themselves back into Colombian civic life on their own terms.

Each of these phases had a dominant geographical center. The first was centered in rural regions of high population density, and, as in the partisan violence of the early 1930s, entailed the export of violence from some municipios to others, egged on by the electoral struggle and by the clergy. The second phase is associated more with frontier regions, the ideal setting for an irregular war between guerrillas and counterguerrillas: the plains of Meta

*and Casanare, the coffee-growing north of Tolima, Sumapaz in Cundinamarca, Urrao
in western Antioquia, Muzo in western Boyacá, and the entire Magdalena Medio lowland area of eastern Antioquia and western Santander. The third phase was centered in
the coffee zone of Quindío, and if one takes the long view can be seen as an extension of
the endemic violence of southward land colonizations from Antioquia dating back to the
nineteenth century.*

*We will probably never know the true count of the dead, the dispossessed, and the exiled.
The figure of 300,000 dead has been widely accepted in Colombia, but in many communities the dividing line between common criminality and the Violencia was too blurred
to permit an accurate accounting.*

In Search of the Violencia

Although the "May generation" whose protests helped to bring down the military regime in 1957 was largely young and without ties to the traditional parties,
all of the National Front's senior political personnel were from the same Liberal and Conservative machinery active in earlier years. They wanted to stay
silent about past responsibilities, reserving their eloquence for the tasks of the
present and the future. Peace was more important than truth or justice. The
Violencia was seen as a sociological means to plumb the depths of society.
especially peasant society, but not the depths of the party system, the state, or
the church—as if those bodies existed apart from society.

This line of thinking was opposed by some writers of the late 1950s and
early 1960s, especially in the pages of *Mito*, a magazine headed by the poet Jorge
Gaitán Durán, and in *La Calle*, a weekly published by a leftist dissident faction of Liberals that opposed aspects of the National Front. Gaitán Durán
wanted to know why the armed forces were so prone to "implacable repression
of the peasantry" during the Violencia years, but the Liberals had become so
"conservatized" that they kept silent, and even sought to silence those who
would ask.

The Violencia was an ever-present background of Colombian life and culture. Its interpretation and symbolism ran through all musings about the past
and the present. As oral tradition the episodes of 1945–64 appeared as a more
or less trustworthy collection of firsthand testimonials, transformed into frag-
mentary legends through constant retelling by a series of narrators. In the
1950s they already provided the raw material for essays, novels, theatrical works,
movies (a bit later), and works of visual art.

The Violencia even lurked in Colombian poetry, with its themes of sickness of all sorts, desperation, and death. In 1959–60 writers debated whether a "novel of the Violencia" was helpful in efforts to comprehend the phenomenon. In 1962 Alejandro Obregón won the national painting prize for his canvas titled simply *Violencia*, which depicted a pregnant woman lying dead: her breasts and womb, open in a red-violet gash, suggested the desolation that spilled through the flanks of the Colombian Andes. That same year, the new Faculty of Sociology of the National University published *La Violencia en Colombia*, a controversial book by Msgr. Germán Guzmán, Orlando Fals Borda, and Eduardo Umaña Luna, which would mold the literate middle classes' understanding of the phenomenon, and in some later interpretations would help to justify the armed movements of the left which developed later in the decade. Camilo Torres, the priest-sociologist who joined the guerrillas of the National Liberation Army (ELN) in 1965 and was killed shortly thereafter, was said to have seen it in this light. These early artistic and intellectual efforts were largely a collage of ambiguous opinions, funereal poses, feelings of guilt, and pessimistic ontologies that have barely begun to give way before the force of new research and analysis.

The key characteristic of the Violencia, and the key obstacle to its study, is that relatively few deaths were the result of armed contacts between guerrillas or other unofficial forces on one side and military, police, or other state forces on the other. One or another armed group, legal or illegal, would take over a territory and impose its control on the population. Deaths were caused less by acts of war, however unconventional, than by atrocities and vengeances. These acts left no witnesses among the victims, or the victims fell mute; some might remember later on, but how did they reconstruct their memories?

There are, to be sure, descriptions of the "body of evidence": some 80 percent of the corpses were male, including children and teenagers. The vast majority were unarmed civilians, rural rather than urban, poor rather than rich. They were shot point-blank, stabbed, or slashed by machete; sometimes quartered, decapitated, or burned. They were killed in or near their dwellings, or they were found floating in nearby rivers. Around one-fifth of victims were female, and there are few accounts of female perpetrators. Massacres of entire families were frequent, accompanied by rape, the burning of homes, theft of cattle and coffee, and the destruction of harvests.

The fragility of state institutions, the recomposition of some regional political leaderships during the turbulent elections of the 1940s, and the spread of capitalist values to agrarian society, which broke down the old hierarchies and patterns of deference, all served to create more offenses, but they also provided openings for some local and regional figures to rise in power and prestige. In this regard the Violencia's social impact was not unlike that of the civil wars of the nineteenth century. Anchored as it was in the life of rural districts and small towns, the Violencia developed interwoven forms of peasant resistance, nomadic banditry, profitable entrepreneurship, and political patronage. Violence sank more roots and acquired more autonomy in agrarian frontier regions removed from the market economy than in long-settled peasant regions. Finally, and over the much longer term, the Violencia debased the incipient development of judicial and police apparatuses, as well as the moral foundations of political action.

The Violencia spread in a manner even more labyrinthine than the multiple amnesties, demobilizations, surrenders of weaponry, and government-sponsored "rehabilitations" that sought to put an end to it. Only two large-scale pacification efforts were clearly successful: the military government's amnesty on the eastern plains, Boyacá, and the Santanders in 1953 and the National Front's 1959–63 campaign in Tolima.

Although the Violencia has often been called a civil war and perhaps can be included among the many Third World conflicts conceived in the heat of the Cold War, let us keep to the specifics of this Colombian catastrophe. "Violencia," capitalized, refers to some twenty years of crime and impunity facilitated by political sectarianism (1945–65), which dislocated the lives of tens of thousands of families and communities. It is estimated that some 40 percent of the population of the Andean regions and the eastern plains suffered its effects directly or indirectly. On the Caribbean coast it had barely marginal impact in a few districts of Magdalena, Córdoba, and Cesar. The reasons are still unclear, but we do know that since the War of the Thousand Days election campaigns were far less aggressive on the coast than in the interior. (The exception may well prove the rule: the 1931 campaign was highly contentious, and there were violent incidents in Cartagena, Lorica, Cereté, and Montería, where twenty-eight people were killed in one of the most deadly outbreaks of electoral violence in Colombian history.) Another factor in the small role played by the coast in the history of the Violencia may reside in human geography.

The coast was quite isolated from the interior now that the Magdalena River was no longer a major artery and travel by road and rail was still precarious.

Sectarian Violence and Popular Mobilization

In 1946 Mariano Ospina Pérez won the presidency with 41 percent of the vote, thanks to divisions among the Liberals, and he recognized that a strictly Conservative government would be impossible. Liberals controlled both houses of Congress, the judicial branch, and nearly all department and *municipio* police forces. Business groups felt a great affinity for the "national union" concept of power-sharing, and Ospina came from their ranks: he had been an efficient leader of FEDECAFÉ in the 1930s, and in the 1940s he was a speculator in suburban land. He was a pragmatist like his grandfather Mariano Ospina Rodríguez (president 1857–61) and his uncle Pedro Nel Ospina (president 1922–26), but unlike them, he had little pull with the Conservative Party machinery and was an unknown quantity to the party's rural voters in the center and east of the country. He did, however, move like a fish in the clientelist waters of the western coffee belt. His selection as Conservative candidate in 1946 was a tactical victory for Laureano Gómez, who saw him as uniquely suited to lead the Conservatives back to power.

On the Liberal side the dissident Jorge Eliécer Gaitán won 26 percent of the votes, but he was left in control of the party after his officially endorsed opponent, Gabriel Turbay, retired from politics and left the country. Gaitán defeated both of his opponents in a majority of department capitals, although in Medellín and the capitals of the coffee belt his tallies were minuscule. After the 1946 elections he fine-tuned his discourse against "the unacceptable marriage of politics and business." He drew clear connections between growing social inequality and the rise of the new plutocracy, and he concluded that just as the hunger of the poor knew no party, neither did the interests of the oligarchs. In 1947 his congressional candidates defeated those pledged to the former president Eduardo Santos, and he was officially designated "sole leader" (*jefe único*) of the party. He was now the arbiter of the Liberals' participation in the National Union government, the party's relations with the union movement, and its support of Liberals in the provinces, who were now subject to persecution in many places.

During the last three years of his life (1945–48) Gaitán was the most influential politician in Colombia and the first to make methodical use of modern techniques of mass mobilization. His oratory was rooted in a popular Liberal tradition associated with past caudillos and their quasi-mythical qualities and exploits. His socialist-inspired language helped to revitalize an election system characterized by high rates of nonvoting. Gaitán was a strong believer in willpower, both individual and collective, and he was a peerless salesman of illusions. With his slogan "The nation is better than its leaders," he opened the political system to thousands of Colombians: participation in congressional elections had declined from 45 percent in 1941 to 38 percent in 1945, but under Gaitán it rose to 56 percent in 1947 and to 63 percent in 1949, in the aftermath of his assassination.

Gaitán understood better than most politicians that urban voters were still wedded to the individualist peasant values of their home regions—the eastern highlands for Bogotá, the coffee belt for Medellín, Manizales, and other western cities. In the 1938 census, there were as many respondents in the craft industries classified as "owners or managers" as there were "workers and peons," and in some activities the bosses outnumbered the workers. This was the characteristic that led Alejandro López, one of the keenest social commentators of the era, to speak of a battle between craft production and what he called "factoryism." In López's thinking, artisans joined small merchants, professionals, and small landowners to form the middle class that "is the backbone of all societies, and especially of ours." The factories were certainly winning: in 1925–30 there were roughly 100,000 factory workers and 200,000 artisans, and in 1948–53 there were 250,000 factory workers and 330,000 artisans. In other words, artisans were still more numerous, but their growth rate was far lower. More important, the aggregate value of their production was less than one-third that of factory workers.

For all their periodic eruptions, artisans had been a bulwark of stability. They now suffered inevitable decline within a dualist manufacturing sector, as the mechanization and electrification so widely embraced as a national priority in the 1930s displaced and proletarianized many artisans, or left them at the margins of modern life with only the poorest consumers as their clients. The urban masses, who struggled every day to maintain and perhaps improve their precarious standard of living, instantly grasped the moral content of Gaitán's discourse as he tore into the excesses of unrestrained capitalism and the links between private fortunes and state power. People's hopes for advancement, dignity, and social integration fitted better with Gaitán's vision, which was in tune with their cultural orientation, than with Marxist socialism. The ecology of urban poverty and the dynamics of urban population growth also help us to understand the strength of *gaitanismo*: Bogotá's population grew fivefold between 1918 and 1951, and cities such as Cali grew even more rapidly.

The political system could not digest the new levels of political participation that Gaitán had wrought. Liberal leaders, perhaps frightened by the demands of a populace that they had helped to mobilize, opted for the old model of party bosses, local notables, and up-and-comers. As the Conservatives set out to recover their bases in the *municipios* after they won the presidency, sectarian violence rapidly worsened. In fact it was already substantial by the time of the 1946 elections, meriting a special mention by Alberto Lleras Camargo in his 1946 presidential message. In many towns the party in power protected common criminals and let them operate with impunity. Juries in criminal trials and judges in both criminal and civil cases favored members of their own party, while at the cusp of the system Congress was overtaken by partisan conflict and by wrangling among the Liberals. Overall the pendulum had swung to the Conservatives, as the October 1947 congressional elections showed.

Most Colombian voters still lived in the countryside or in small towns, and it was in these settings that the presidential changeover had the most significant short-term electoral effects. The Liberals lost one-fourth of the *municipio* councils they had controlled. The Conservatives' campaign to intimidate voters by murdering Liberal politicians and burning party offices and newspapers began in strategic cities such as Pasto, Palmira, Tuluá, Armenia, Ibagué, Rionegro, Miraflores, and Socorro, but soon spread to adjoining *municipios*, which were "cleansed" of Liberal voters. By late 1947 the Liberals had established safe houses in many cities, and the politically displaced were commonly referred to as refugees. The worst expressions of sectarian violence occurred in the poorest *municipios*: of the fifty-seven locations cited by Gaitán in his famous appeal to President Ospina shortly before his death in April 1948, some 90 percent were among the poorest in the country.

The Assassination of Gaitán and Its Consequences

On April 9, 1948, Jorge Eliécer Gaitán was fatally shot in the center of Bogotá, while the city was hosting the Ninth Inter-American Conference. He was at the height of his popularity. On many occasions he had told his followers, "If they kill me, avenge me!"—and just minutes after his death a wave of popular fury was unleashed in the capital, already seething after months of water and electricity rationing because of a prolonged drought. Liberals were also irritated because Laureano Gómez, who was foreign minister, left Gaitán off the Colombian delegation even though it was supposed to be bipartisan, and Gaitán was the titular head of the Liberals.

The agitated and (eventually) inebriated crowds that would later be known as the *nueveabrileños* or "April Ninthers" burned churches, trams, and public buildings; they forced open the prisons and sacked warehouses and hardware stores. This was the *bogotazo*, and before it was over thousands of people, overwhelmingly civilians, were dead, mostly in Bogotá but also in other key cities and more than one hundred other towns. The role of intellectuals and university students was limited to the seizure of some Bogotá radio stations, from which they issued calls to insurrection.

By the night of April 9 the Liberal leadership had made its way to the presidential palace. As the negotiations with Ospina dragged through the night, the president managed to strengthen his position by securing the absolute allegiance of the army; a steady rain helped to snuff out the flames that threatened to destroy Bogotá as the army retook the city. Ospina was thus able to dismiss the Liberals' suggestion that he step aside in favor of Eduardo Santos, the designated substitute, and the two sides eventually worked out a bipartisan cabinet under Ospina's continued leadership. Notably absent from the negotiations was Gómez, who wanted to hand over power to the military.

Liberals of all stripes, including *gaitanistas* and near-communists, blamed the *bogotazo* on "criminals who distorted the authentic grief of the people." This interpretation was itself a distortion, and permitted elites of both parties to speak in the most extravagant and racist terms about the impossibility of civilizing the Colombian masses: such phrases as "incompetent rabble" and "country of savages" became common currency. Conservative interpretations of that bloody Friday were largely variations on a pastoral letter from the extremist bishop of Santa Rosa de Osos (Antioquia), Miguel Ángel Builes, who wrote that the bloodletting was inspired by international communism but carried out by Colombian Liberalism.

The government was actually strengthened by the events of April 1948, and Ospina won a measure of authority among the party faithful that he had never enjoyed before. He denounced the *bogotazo* as a Communist plot and broke off relations with the Soviet Union. Ospina's election in 1946 had been greeted with strikes and riots in Bogotá, Cali, and other cities. In the oil-refining town of Barrancabermeja, protesters demanded the nationalization of the industry. On April 9 they seized the refinery, and they held the port for several days. Their fifty-day strike, along with a forty-day strike in the main exploration zone, the Concesión Barco, cut Colombian oil production in 1948. While the Soviet connection was shaky at best, Ospina may have been on more solid ground in accusing Venezuela's Acción Democrática regime of working with some Colombian Liberals to foment labor unrest.

Like many other Latin American leaders, Ospina hoped that the Inter-American Conference would encourage the United States to commit itself to support the region's agenda for economic development, industrialization, and peaceful social change, in exchange for Latin America's acceptance of the Truman administration's containment policy. But the United States offered little in the way of commitments, and it took another revolution scare a decade later, the Cuban revolution of 1959, to spur such innovations as the Inter-American Development Bank (IADB).

There was a brief political honeymoon after the April 10 agreement between Ospina and the Liberal leadership. Certainly it was a marriage of convenience rather than a genuine long-term commitment, but among the immediate legislative results were a comprehensive amnesty for participants in the *bogotazo* and the failed Pasto coup against Alfonso López in 1944, and an electoral reform that eliminated municipal juries, mandated the issuance of new identity cards (thereby addressing a longstanding complaint of both parties, each of which accused the other of building its majorities by issuing fraudulent identity cards), and created an independent election commission. The next presidential elections were postponed until June 1950 to permit the implementation of the reforms, and the state of siege was lifted in December 1948.

By 1949, however, Colombian politicians were in a sectarian and confrontational mood, as the April 10 pact collapsed under the weight of the tensions that produced April 9. Conservative mayors rebelled against the requirement of Liberal representation in their local councils, and the Conservative governor of Antioquia openly defied Ospina on the issue. In May 1949 the Liberals pulled out of the Ospina government, confident of victory in the upcoming presidential elections despite their continuing factional divisions.

In the late 1940s it was common for family, friends, and neighbors to gather together around the radio. Dramatic series and comedies were popular, but for sheer emotion the live broadcasts of congressional debates were without peer. The 1949 sessions that opened on July 20 brought something new for listeners: Laureano Gómez's son Álvaro led a furious chorus of toy whistles whenever Liberal legislators rose to speak. By September whistles gave way to bullets. More than a hundred shots were exchanged in the House of Representatives, killing two members.

The Liberal majority in Congress sought to provoke Ospina by proposing direct popular election of mayors and governors and the confirmation of cabinet ministers by the legislature. They even tried to bring the recently nationalized police force under direct congressional control. More menacingly, because they were able to do it, the Liberals moved the date of the upcoming presidential election back to November 1949 from June 1950, which meant that the old identity cards issued under Liberal rule would still be used. Ospina vetoed the bill but Congress passed it a second time, overriding the veto; the Liberal majority on the Supreme Court rebuffed Ospina's claims that the change was unconstitutional.

In the first half of October 1949 the two parties named their presidential candidates: Darío Echandía for the Liberals and Laureano Gómez for the Conservatives. As sectarian violence spread from town to town, party leaders met behind closed doors at Echandía's request to pursue a bipartisan formula along the lines of April 1948, or perhaps Olaya's National Concentration of 1930. But all hopes for an agreement vanished on October 21, when the Casa Liberal in Cali was attacked by police under the command of Conservative local authorities, leaving twenty-four dead and sixty wounded. Two days later the Liberal official in charge of identity cards and electoral administration, Eduardo Caballero Calderón, resigned, charging that flagrant intimidation by Conservative officials in 126 *municipios* promised to make the upcoming elections a "bloody farce." (Three years later Caballero wrote *El Cristo de espaldas*, one of the first novels of the Violencia, and a classic depiction of political bossism in the highlands of Boyacá.) Ospina asked the consultative State Council if he could declare a state of siege, but the Liberal-dominated body replied that he had no legal basis to do so because the government itself was responsible for the deterioration in public order.

Ospina then presented his own plan for a bipartisan solution, with support from business leaders. He proposed to postpone the presidential election for four years—a full term, in effect—during which time executive power would be vested in a four-member junta equally divided between the two parties. The Supreme Court, the State Council, and the Electoral Court would be evenly divided, and while congressional elections would proceed freely, a two-thirds majority would be required to pass legislation. Ospina must have known that his proposal would be rejected as too little and too late; even conciliatory Liberal leaders such as Alfonso López Pumarejo and Alberto Lleras Camargo rejected the plan as thinly disguised dictatorship, while Gómez and the Conservatives saw it as an obstacle to outright victory. (Readers with some knowledge of later events will recognize Ospina's proposal as a close precursor of the National Front agreement that governed Colombia between 1958 and 1974.)

On October 28 the Liberal party's director, Carlos Lleras Restrepo, announced in the Senate a new and extreme policy of noncooperation with the Conservatives. Liberals were instructed to withdraw not only from official bodies except for Congress (for instance, the two Liberal ex-presidents quit the Electoral Court) but from all personal contact with Conservatives. As Lleras famously declared, "For Conservatives, not even a greeting." That same day, the Liberal Party's offices in Medellín were attacked, and a flood of rumors sent thousands of Colombians to pull their money out of the banks.

Events moved rapidly after that: in characteristically peremptory language Gómez reaffirmed that his goal was outright electoral victory rather than a negotiated settlement. In response the Liberals withdrew from the elections. The head of Colombia's Catholic bishops made an energetic if belated appeal for political peace on November 6, noteworthy insofar as it did not contain the usual condemnation of one of the two parties. Three days later, the Liberal leadership of both houses of Congress informed Ospina that they planned to begin impeachment proceedings against him; the president immediately imposed a state of siege throughout the country (notwithstanding the earlier statement of the State Council), deployed soldiers to guard the presidential palace, and dissolved both the Congress and all departmental assemblies. He also changed the voting process of the Supreme Court to prevent any judicial challenge and imposed censorship of the press and radio.

Ospina's *autogolpe* took the Liberals by surprise, despite what in retrospect seems a natural climax of events. Alberto Lleras, from his post as secretary general of the OAS, condemned it but could do nothing more; the U.S. government took a hands-off approach, and its ambassador in Bogotá told Washington that both parties were to blame and that Ospina's reaction was understandable. The Liberal leadership did send a manifesto to Ospina protesting that the party "was kept from the polls by an unprecedented official coalition" of the government and the Conservative Party, which jointly imposed "a reign of terror unknown in Colombia since the era of the Spaniard Pablo Morillo," who executed patriots during the Wars of Independence. The manifesto called attention to the thousands of families who had been uprooted by political violence, many of whom had sought refuge in Venezuela. As for Ospina's state of siege, the Liberal leadership considered it a "totalitarian dictatorship."

While organized Liberal resistance to the state of siege was scattered and ineffective for the most part, two violent episodes were harbingers of provincial Liberals' willingness to repay cruelty with cruelty. In the eastern plains department of Meta, Eliseo Vázquez and a band of Liberals attacked the town of Puerto López and its environs, leaving a trail of dead Conservative police and civilians, including entire families. While the killing was new, Vázquez was no stranger to Puerto López—he had thrown the Conservative authorities out of town in April 1948, in a provincial reprise of the *bogotazo*. Significantly, some party leaders in Bogotá embraced Vázquez as a resistance figure despite his murderous foray. Meanwhile in Santander, Rafael Rangel—another Liberal with April 1948 credentials—returned to San Vicente de Chucurí, where he had been police commander under Liberal rule, and massacred two hundred Conservative civilians.

Laureano Gómez: The Revolution of Order

Laureano Gómez took over the presidency in August 1950, under the state of siege. The new president was, by a wide margin, the most popular and the most controversial Conservative leader of the twentieth century. For his admirers, he embodied all the qualities that Colombia needed in a leader; to his enemies, he was simply "the monster"—the personification of resentment, as a Liberal psychoanalyst famously wrote. Gómez was the consummate professional politician with a highly developed ability to reverse course. He attacked the United States with such ferocity in 1939–42 that his sympathies for the Axis were taken for granted, but as president he sent a battalion to fight alongside U.S. troops in Korea. In 1952 he proposed a constitutional reform along Spanish Falangist lines, but only five years later he defended the bipartisan National Front plan in almost exactly the same terms.

The Gómez of 1950 wanted a "revolution of order," and he looked to the Regeneration as the obvious Colombian model; he wanted a return to the era's civic-religious cult of "Christ and Bolívar." Francisco Franco's Spain and Antonio Salazar's Portugal also inspired Gómez; he attacked political vices in terms reminiscent of the 1920s Spanish dictator (and precursor to Franco) Miguel Primo de Rivera. At the same time Gómez relied on those vices, particularly local bossism, to consolidate Conservative domination of the countryside as a counterweight to the Liberals' strength in the cities. It was axiomatic to Gómez that popular mobilization led to anarchy, and while the class-conscious popular organizations and institutions had been largely dismantled even before the state of siege, the grassroots Conservative mobilization on behalf of his candidacy had the perverse effect of unleashing the anarchy that was already known as the Violencia. Ideally, the church, the military, and the state, duly equipped with a new ethic through a sort of ideological shock therapy, would organize the masses rather than the local bosses of one or the other political party.

Gómez sought to secure the church's support by raising its educational profile and weakening its secular adversaries. The Jesuits and Christian Brothers recovered a level of influence not enjoyed since the Regeneration, and a slew of new male and female religious orders arrived from postwar Europe. Bogotá's two public institutions of higher learning, the National University and the relatively new Escuela Normal Superior, were purged of radicals and modern social scientists. A wide range of clerical and lay organizations were given control of public secondary institutions, while parish priests and local Conservative Party organizations won similar control over primary schooling. Genuine secular education was relegated to marginal status at all levels of the education system.

Despite his eagerness to please on a key church issue, the hierarchy had reasons to distrust Gómez. As a young legislator he had led the campaign that drove the church's pious protégé Marco Fidel Suárez from the presidency in the early 1920s, and more recently he attacked the papal nuncio as part of his assault on the Liberals' renegotiation of the Concordat. His uncompromising position on the party conflict was increasingly troubling. For the subject of his pastoral letter in 1950 the archbishop of Bogotá chose "Thou shalt not kill," and he decried the "social breakdown" that came from widespread loss of respect for human life. The following year, Colombian bishops jointly declared their partisan neutrality—a novel position not really shared by all of them—

and pointedly left responsibility for political violence "to the judgment of history." In 1952 several bishops, including the archbishop of Bogotá, directly asked parish priests to help restore political peace among their parishioners.

While there were radical rightists in the clergy who looked to Franco's Spain as the only relevant model of the day, they lost influence in the early 1950s; the presence of many Basques in the religious orders, who were as nationalist as they were culturally conservative, may also have taken the luster off the Franco model. Starting in the late 1940s and throughout the following decade, new forms of "pastoral care" spread among parish priests of the Andean highlands, with emphasis on the daily needs of the rural poor, starting with literacy and housing. The most famous example was Acción Cultural Popular, founded by a young priest in Sutatenza (Boyacá), who in 1948 founded an educational radio station and distributed 5,000 radios among his parishioners. The initiative spread rapidly and became a major force for progressive change in the Colombian church.

The overall vitality of the church in the early 1950s did not match its nominal influence. There was wide variation in the number of inhabitants per parish priest: from 2,000 in the diocese of Santa Rosa de Osos to 4,000 in Socorro (Santander) and 11,000 in Montería (Córdoba). The national figure had declined somewhat since 1912, in part because seminaries now had to compete against more effective educational routes to social mobility, thanks to the rise of public secondary schools and universities in the 1930s and 1940s. New cultural influences—movies, radio, and, since 1954, television—and the rise of a new and relatively cosmopolitan middle class presented additional challenges.

The few attempts at dialogue between the government and the Liberal Party and the guerrillas went nowhere and further divided the Conservatives. With the Liberals sitting out the congressional elections in September 1951, the dispute was entirely between Conservative factions, among them a new generation of extreme sectarians. The most important were the *alzatistas*, led by Gilberto Alzate Avendaño, whom many people dismissed as the Conservative version of *gaitanismo*. When Gómez took a leave of absence from the presidency in late October 1951, the party's division broke out into the open: the *alzatistas* went so far as to seek an alliance with the persecuted Liberals, but within a few months they were forced out of all their offices by the official Conservative machinery.

Gómez may have ceded the presidency to the designated substitute Roberto

Urdaneta, but he still tried to run everything in the Conservative Party and government by remote control. In 1952 he proposed a constitutional reform to unite the party and "regenerate" the country. Although the military coup of 1953 put an end to the initiative, its key aspects are worth examination. The Congress would lose much of its authority, especially over security issues, and the executive would rely on a "moral elite" to formulate laws. The church would recoup in toto the privileges accorded it by the 1887 Concordat, and at least 15 percent of the national budget would be devoted to education. Press censorship would be made permanent, and criticism of the government by Colombians in the foreign press — precisely what Liberals had been doing so effectively — would be prosecuted as treason. On the economic front, the state would be given wide powers of intervention "to coordinate diverse economic interests and to guarantee national security." Special stimulus would be given to "corporations and firms that distribute profits to their workers."

The only aspect of the proposed reform that provoked widespread debate among Conservatives was woman suffrage. The officially sanctioned veneration of the Virgin Mary, which was explicitly a veneration of woman's traditional roles as mother, daughter, and wife, provided an opening for women's groups, among them some Liberal women, to petition the government's constitutional commission and take their case to the press. Years of participation in Catholic Action and other traditional organizations had given many middle- and upper-class women the leadership and political skills to influence the nominally all-male deliberations. After spirited debate the commission decided to recommend woman suffrage in town council elections, leaving the rest of the question for future consideration.

The mechanism Gómez chose to implement his proposed reform, an elected constituent assembly (ANAC), deepened Conservative rivalries and guaranteed Liberal nonparticipation. Ironically, Gómez was unable to field a unified slate of his own, while the former president Ospina cautiously began to assemble a coalition of such economic groups as the SAC and even made political tours of the Conservative west. In April 1952 Ospina declared his intention to run for president in 1954, and Gómez responded in his usual intemperate style. The split between the party's two main figures was now irreparable. A few months later, the Liberal leaders, Alfonso López and Carlos Lleras, went into exile after Conservative crowds destroyed Bogotá's two Liberal newspapers. Almost unnoticed in the continuing turmoil, General Gustavo Rojas Pinilla, commander of the armed forces, returned to Colombia after a lengthy official visit to the United States.

Military Coup and Dictatorship

Gómez did not understand that the limits to his authoritarian rule had, in effect, been set beforehand by the privileged groups that backed his regime. Among them were the armed forces, whose leadership increasingly doubted his sympathy for military concerns and feared his politicization of the national police. Rojas returned to Colombia at a time when the guerrilla war on the eastern plains was heating up once more. He enjoyed being in the public eye, and Gómez's dislike for him was widely known; many observers were surprised that Gómez had not replaced him as commander while he was out of the country.

On the night of June 13, 1953, with support from Ospina and much of the Conservative Party, Rojas announced a coup d'état. The church, leading economic groups, and the whole political spectrum except for the Communists and the Gómez faction of the Conservatives supported the coup: it was certainly one of the most peaceful and widely acclaimed regime changes in Colombian history.

There were reasons for rejoicing, especially among the Liberals. The new military regime's first measures included a pardon and amnesty for political prisoners and for guerrillas in the field, and the restoration of freedom of the press. Newspapers of both parties, duly briefed by the government on the meaning of "responsible" press freedom, even started to preach the virtues of reconciliation between the parties. Rojas benefited from the happy circumstance that Gómez's ANAC was in session at the time of the coup, and was able to legitimize it by declaring him president through the end of the current presidential term. The assembly promptly went into recess, its constitutional reform agenda buried forever.

The commonly held assumption that Rojas was a political novice by virtue of his military career could not be more misleading. Success in the upper reaches of the officer corps required skillful relations with politicians and with one's fellow officers. In this regard Rojas enjoyed an advantage as a native of Boyacá, a region that provided many officers to the army and police. His career path in the army, mostly in engineering and construction positions, enabled him to cultivate alliances in different parts of the country. He also was an active cattle rancher and land speculator. Politically he was an *ospinista*, in part out of gratitude to the former president for naming him minister of communications toward the end of his administration.

During his first year in power Rojas traveled widely throughout Colombia, looking very much like a presidential candidate. His goal was to restore equilibrium between the parties without alienating his Conservative base of support; some key ministries and department governorships were given to military officers, but most other appointments continued to go to Conservatives. His balancing act was largely successful: there was a bipartisan consensus in favor of peace, and the successful amnesty on the eastern plains proved the government's good faith to most Liberals. Violencia deaths fell from 22,000 in 1952–53 to only 1,900 in 1954–55. In late 1953 Rojas turned his attention to the judiciary, purging many local loyalists under the guise of a campaign against corruption. He remade the Supreme Court with equal numbers of Liberals and Conservatives, and named the Liberals' most prominent judge-politician, Darío Echandía, to that body. The Supreme Court was supposed to reform the entire judiciary, but it never tried.

The Rojas regime was not a military one in the conventional sense. He did govern in the name of the armed forces and with the support of all three services, despite his opponents' efforts toward the end to label him a "usurper" of the military's authority. The initial legitimacy of his regime relied on the military's credibility as guarantor of pacification and national reconciliation. But from the outset he relied on support from the Ospina and Alzate Conservative factions, from the church, and more ambiguously from the Liberals. While military spending did increase more than other parts of the national budget, this policy was in keeping with trends since the 1948 *bogotazo*. It is interesting to note that his regime did not grow harsher over time, in typical praetorian fashion. Until its dissolution in March 1957, the ANAC gave the regime an appearance of legislative legitimacy; a few Gómez loyalists among its members consistently opposed Rojas, and toward the end he enjoyed only a narrow majority.

Toward a "Third Force"

Rojas reported to the ANAC in April 1954 that the country was not ready for presidential elections, and that he would remain in power until the conditions for lasting democracy were restored. He won approval for woman suffrage, the banning of the Communist Party (something that never happened under

Gómez), and the replacement of town councils and department assemblies by nonelected administrative bodies.

The Liberals decided to cultivate the goodwill of the "Supreme Chief" to gain breathing room for the reorganization of their electoral machinery. They were especially eager to gain Liberal representation on the ANAC, and its membership was still in Rojas's hands. The party's decision to support the regime was soon tested. On June 9, 1954, a student demonstration to protest a police raid of the National University ended in bloodshed: thirteen students were killed and many wounded by the Colombia Battalion, an army unit that had only recently returned from service with United Nations forces in Korea. Liberal leaders, including a former rector of the university, went to the Presidential Palace to show their support. The government ordered a "special investigation," which came to nothing.

The pacification of the eastern plains, high coffee prices, monetary stability, and a steady flow of foreign loans were assets too formidable to be put at risk by a presidential election. In August 1954 ANAC extended Rojas's term through 1958, and Rojas started to entertain more ambitious thoughts about his longer-term political role. Only at this point did some Liberals begin to see him as a continuation of the Conservative dictatorship. In his 1955 New Year's message Rojas announced that the state of siege would continue. Bogotá's two Liberal newspapers, *El Tiempo* and *El Espectador*, openly challenged him for the first time. The government tightened press censorship and closed them down, but he let them reappear almost immediately under new names.

Rojas's interior minister took the lead in creating the National Action Movement (MAN), a personal movement for the general, tied to a new National Workers' Confederation (CNT) that would be Colombia's affiliate of the Peronist Association of Latin American Workers (ATLAS). The church hierarchy, which was close to Rojas from the start of his regime, was quick to condemn the CNT because of its links to the increasingly anticlerical Argentine regime, just as it had condemned the Liberals' CTC for alleged communist tendencies. The church had invested its organizational efforts in the competing UTC, and was especially concerned not to lose the allegiance of Medellín's workers.

To placate the bishops Rojas hardened the official line on Protestant evangelizing and launched a thorough anticommunist campaign; with their party already outlawed, the Communists were now driven out of the unions and back to their old niches among the tradesmen, which were better suited to clandestine activity. But Rojas was unable to develop an authentic popular base for the regime, and his efforts to duplicate Gaitán's mobilizational success came to nothing. The government's manipulation of the media and phantom *rojista* organizations served only to alarm the people they were intended to win over.

The government's political ineptitude rose to new heights in 1956. Early that year, the crowd at Bogotá's main bullring gave a standing ovation to the Liberal leader, Carlos Lleras, but refused to cheer the government. When they booed Rojas's daughter, María Eugenia, who had imitated Eva Perón by installing herself as director of the government's social welfare agency, SENDAS, plainclothes police fired on the crowd, killing eight people. On the third anniversary of the coup in June, Rojas presided over a bizarre ceremony to baptize his "Third Force" political movement. Thousands of supporters marched past the Supreme Chief, resplendent in his military decorations, swearing their loyalty to the *binomio pueblo–fuerzas armadas*, the unity of the people and the armed forces. The archbishop of Bogotá told Rojas in an open letter that the use of the liturgical oath to sanctify Rojas's movement was unacceptable, and he condemned the Third Force itself in terms reminiscent of earlier church attacks on the CNT.

The Origins of the National Front

In February 1956 the Liberals held their party convention in Medellín, and by that point they assumed that Rojas would seek to remain in power indefinitely. To break his alliance with the Conservatives, they proposed to endorse a Conservative "national unity" candidate in the next presidential election. They also named a new leader, Alberto Lleras Camargo, who had a track record of cooperation with the Conservatives (especially as acting president in 1945–46, when he transferred power to the victorious Ospina) and could credibly argue that Liberals and Conservatives were a better *binomio* than the people and the armed forces. Although the *ospinistas* and *alvaristas* were willing to talk by mid-1956, they were reluctant to sign on to a full-fledged power-sharing agreement, especially if Gómez was poised to attack it from his exile in Spain.

But perhaps the old caudillo might be willing to accept a bipartisan solution. Armed with a mandate from his party's convention, Lleras visited Gómez in the Mediterranean resort town of Benidorm, and on July 24, 1956, the two signed a statement calling for a return to civilian rule under a bipartisan power-sharing arrangement. Meanwhile Rojas's Third Force was getting nowhere, and he asked the ANAC to authorize the addition of twenty-five handpicked new members, presumably to guarantee an extension of his mandate without a popular vote. This move persuaded Ospina and his supporters to join the Lleras-Gómez "civil front," and as Rojas saw his influence in the ANAC dwindle with the loss of the *ospinistas*, he proposed to replace it with a new body whose membership would be more firmly in his pocket. He also turned his political discourse from populism to socialism in an effort to appeal directly to the people.

In April 1957 the bipartisan opposition chose as their presidential candidate the Conservative Guillermo León Valencia, son of one of the two Conservative candidates in 1930 whose recalcitrance paved the way for Olaya's election. The church hierarchy warned Rojas that his proposed new assembly would be illegitimate, and so would his reelection. Even the military's senior officers wondered why Rojas had adopted the most confrontational path to reelection, especially given the regime's growing unpopularity.

Rojas fell for essentially the same reason that brought an end to Laureano Gómez's regime four years earlier: he lost touch with the powerful interests that initially backed him. When banking and industrial leaders told their workers to stay home (at full pay) as part of a businessmen's strike, and even the students of Catholic universities organized noisy demonstrations against his rule, Rojas knew his situation was untenable even though most of the population remained apathetic. On the morning of May 10, 1957, Colombians awoke to the news that Rojas had resigned and left executive power in the hands of five generals with Conservative sympathies.

Transition to the Bipartisan Coalition

Rojas's departure was negotiated and calm, as befitted a regime that had always been mild by the standards of contemporary Latin American and Caribbean dictatorships. The unrest that helped to force him out was largely a peaceful mobilization by what observers called "modern Colombia," based in Bogotá, Medellín, and Cali: banks, industries, universities. There was some street violence, but, except in Cali, where social unrest and close proximity to some of the most active hotbeds of Violencia were both reflected in antiregime protests, the outbreaks were less bloody than expected. On the Caribbean coast and in the east the crash of the Rojas regime was hardly heard at all. These contrasts provide some insight into the continuing heterogeneity and ambiguity that the emerging bipartisan coalition would have to face.

The first months of the post-Rojas military junta faced the usual issues of democratic transition: how to reconstruct legitimacy and how to settle accounts with the previous regime. Alberto Lleras waited a full ten days before giving his support to the junta as a legitimate transitional government. Both Lleras and the junta were interested in narrowing the focus of mounting anti-military sentiment to the figure of Rojas himself, rather than the generals who had kept him in power. A few weeks after his departure a National Investigative Commission was created to look into the possible criminal activities of "high government officials in recent times," but Rojas was the commission's only target.

The unity and loyalty of the military were by no means certain, and there were rumors of *rojista* plots even after his closest allies were forced into retirement by the junta. The Conservatives were also divided, and Gómez was determined to make his rivals pay for their "treason" in 1953 and even earlier. But there was consensus across most of the military and most of the leaders of both parties on the merits of what Lleras and Gómez hammered out during Lleras's return visit to Spain in July 1957. The Sitges Declaration called for a "very simple and concrete referendum," without precedent in Colombian history, in which voters would approve the broad outlines of long-term bipartisan cooperation and a timetable for democratic elections. When the junta agreed to the Sitges terms, the "civil front" became the National Front: the military would be a guarantor of the new order.

The plebiscite of December 1, 1957, asked voters to approve, as a single proposition, a number of significant reforms, including full political equality for women, the allocation of at least 10 percent of the national budget for education, and the restoration of the phrase "God, supreme source of all authority" to the Constitution, from which it was removed in 1936. But the key provisions, of course, were for bipartisan government: equal representation of Liberals and Conservatives in all official bodies (starting with, but not limited to, legislatures at the national, departmental, and even *municipio* levels), and the requirement of a two-thirds majority to pass important legislation. Judicial and administrative positions would be filled through an apolitical civil service, and judges of the Supreme Court and State Council could not be removed during their terms of office. The mandate of the military junta would be legitimized until

August 1958, when a civilian government would be installed. Lastly, further constitutional reforms would have to proceed via the mechanism established by the Constitution itself, rather than by plebiscites or constituent assemblies, neither of which had any basis in the existing 1886 document.

The plebiscite was approved by 95 percent of voters, though there were substantial pockets of opposition in Rojas's home department of Boyacá (22 percent) and in Santander (28 percent), where hostility between the parties was especially strong. Both parties threw their efforts into the March 1958 congressional elections—efforts that could be entirely factional, because the parity provision of the National Front meant that only the internal composition of each party's 50 percent share of seats was in question. In fact, the Liberals won 58 percent of the national vote, and since that time it has been a given that they are the majority party. Gómez's supporters won a majority of the Conservative seats, which was the former president's intention when he asked that legislative elections be held well before the vote for president: he wanted the Conservative caucus to veto Guillermo León Valencia's candidacy, which they promptly did.

Only one month before the presidential election there was still no official bipartisan candidate, although there was consensus on the idea of alternating the presidency between the two parties and limiting the president's power to declare a state of siege. The junta even made plans to turn power over to a caretaker president on August 7, rather than outstay its welcome. Having sunk the Valencia candidacy, Gómez now did the unthinkable: he proposed the Liberal Albert Lleras Camargo as bipartisan candidate. Many Conservatives were furious and even Liberals (starting with Lleras himself) were wary, but after last-minute discussions the major faction leaders agreed to alternate the presidency for four terms (a total of sixteen years), so that if the first president were Liberal, the all-important last president would be Conservative. By the time Lleras was inaugurated, the Conservative Party, which had governed directly or indirectly since 1946, was split six ways: the leaders of three factions supported the National Front (Laureano Gómez, Mariano Ospina, and Guillermo León Valencia), while three opposed it (Jorge Leyva, Gilberto Alzate, and Rojas, who was not without his supporters, civilian as well as military).

The outgoing junta and incoming civilian politicians agreed on two things. First, they wanted to shield the military, as individuals and as an institution, from any legal responsibility for past events, in part to defuse continuing plots by Rojas's supporters. Second, they insisted that the Violencia was still going on, albeit at a lower level than during the Gómez regime, and they wanted the state of siege to continue. By 1958 the Violencia had taken on an almost fetishistic place in Colombia's language: it was not just a descriptor but an autonomous phenomenon capable of doing, destroying, killing. But what, exactly, was it?

The Violencia of the 1950s

The electoral struggle at the *municipio* level, already extremely violent in several parts of the country, was aggravated by Gaitán's assassination in April 1948. Over 43,000 political killings were reported that year. After a brief lull in the second half of 1949, violence reached new highs, especially in rural Boyacá and the Santanders in the east and Caldas in the west. Once the Conservatives won control throughout the country under Ospina's state of siege and then under Gómez, the level of violence decreased somewhat in those regions and in Nariño. There is some statistical evidence to support the thesis, advanced in the 1970s by Paul Oquist, that the Violencia—at least in the late 1940s and early 1950s—correlated with increasing success in mobilizing the vote over the course of the 1940s, as Table 4 shows.

The Violencia was the outgrowth of hostility between Liberals and Conservatives, but it did nothing to unify either of the parties. In 1950 the Liberals were divided into *gaitanistas* (predictably weakened since the death of their leader), *santistas*, and *lopistas*. Eduardo Santos sought party unity with an ambiguous statement of solidarity with persecuted Liberals around the country: "Public liberties and republican institutions—nothing more, nothing less. And to bring them about, two things are indispensable: faith and dignity."

For Alfonso López, who had just quit his post as Colombia's delegate to the United Nations, Santos had it all wrong: he was being too soft on the Conservative regime for its "atrocious official abuses" of Liberals, but at the same time he was ignoring the lesson of recent Colombian history, that "neither party can govern well without the help of the other, because there are not enough capable people." To the *santistas* this sounded like surrender, but López, despite his highly partisan first administration in the 1930s, or perhaps because of its crises and reverses, had been toying with a structured system of bipartisan rule for several years. In April 1950 his son Alfonso López Michelsen and the historian Indalecio Liévano proposed in the Liberal press a constituent assembly with even representation of the two parties.

TABLE 4
Electoral Participation and the Violencia, 1939–57

Department	Homicides per 100,000 population, 1946–1957	Electoral participation (%) 1939[a]	Electoral participation (%) 1949[b]	Growth in electoral participation, 1939–47 (%)
Meta[c]	9,736	24	62	158
Norte de Santander	5,496	58	101	74
Tolima	4,353	47	78	66
Caldas	4,175	46	65	41
National average	1,562	49	63	29

Sources: Paul Oquist, *Violence, Conflict, and Politics in Colombia* (New York, 1980); Departamento Administrativo Nacional de Estadística, *Colombia Política. Estadísticas, 1935–1970* (Bogotá, 1972).
[a]Legislative elections.
[b]Presidential elections.
[c]Meta was not made a department until 1960; these figures apply to the *municipios* it was to comprise.

Santos's *El Tiempo* responded that any change in the existing situation would only serve Conservative interests, and that Liberals should demand the full and fair implementation of the Constitution. The dispute continued throughout the Gómez/Urdaneta regime but the Santos line prevailed, with the party abstaining from legislative elections in 1951 and 1953 and ignoring Gómez's constitutional commission and ANAC.

The Conservatives were divided between *laureanistas*, *ospinistas*, and *alzatistas*, a division that to some extent (and far more than on the Liberal side) mirrored their social origins. The *laureanistas* of Medellín's *La Defensa* were a young and sometimes provincial group who kept up a steady stream of invective directed at the *ospinista* patriciate represented by *El Colombiano*; small bombs often went off at both newspapers. In July 1950 *El Colombiano* carried an article about Urrao in western Antioquia, detailing the widespread recourse to the *aplanchada* (steamrollering), a particularly grotesque technique used by Conservatives in attacks on the region's Liberal peasantry. The newspaper pointedly asked whether the Conservatives' departmental directorate, dominated by *laureanistas*, approved of such practices. There were similar conflicts in Manizales between the oligarchy represented by the newspaper *La Patria* and the Alzate faction (whom the oligarchy called *aplanchadores*, in the dual sense of steamrollering their Conservative opponents at the polls and massacring Liberals) and in Cali, where the oligarchy's voice was *El País* while the *laureanista* up-and-comers used the *Diario del Pacífico* to voice their support for Conservative death squads in northern Valle del Cauca.

Ospina's state of siege and the Liberals' boycott of the elections in late 1949 marked the start of what we have called the second stage of the Violencia, the one that came closest to becoming a full-fledged civil war. But this never happened: while over 50,000 Colombians died in political violence in 1950, the peak year of the Violencia, most lost their lives in outbreaks of local bloodletting. The armed forces' firm loyalty to the government made any Liberal declaration of war along nineteenth-century lines completely unfeasible.

The military was viewed favorably by *gaitanista* Liberals, and the other two factions saw it as essentially neutral in the partisan struggle. The Liberals directed their ire at the national police force, which was formally established after a long gestation on January 1, 1950. Although there were compelling arguments to be made in favor of a centralized national force to replace the mosaic of *municipio* and department forces, many of which had swung to the Liberals during López's second administration, the new force that answered to the Ministry of the Interior soon became a powerful tool for the bureaucratization of political persecution. Many towns with Liberal majorities, especially in Tolima, Valle del Cauca, and Caldas, were in effect invaded by police detachments whose members were recruited in solidly Conservative towns in Boyacá, Nariño, and Santander. They brought crime instead of security, and the armed Liberal response—against them and against neighboring Conservative districts—was not long in coming. The governors of Antioquia and Tolima, themselves Conservatives, often complained about them, and the army thought they made the job of pacification more difficult.

Starting in 1951–52 and throughout the rest of the 1950s, Tolima suffered like no other part of Colombia. A hurricane of cruelty roared into the central part of the department and then forked: toward the north, where agrarian capitalism and competing waves of peasant migrations from Antioquia and Boyacá had created a tense and volatile atmosphere in an area with 1920s antecedents of revolutionary unrest, and toward the south, a frontier area that had seen successive waves of commercial agriculture (quinine, rubber, coffee) and politicized ethnic conflict dating back to the 1910s. In the south there was a strong collective memory of extreme electoral violence, including the killing of thirty-one indigenous residents of the Llanogrande community on the orders of Liberal landowners in 1931, after the community voted Conservative. During the 1952–54 period most of the violence in the south had little to do with Conservatives: it was a war between Liberal and Communist peasants, *limpios* and *comunes*, as they called themselves.

Besides Tolima the principal foci of Violencia in 1950–53 were the eastern plains (*llanos*), whose agricultural potential had recently attracted Bogotá investors, especially in the transitional piedmont zone; Urrao in western Antioquia and the mining northeast of the department, regions of majority Afro-Colombian populations that were largely ignored by the white Medellín elite; the extremely poor Yacopí–La Palma region in northwestern Cundinamarca, bordering the emerald-producing Muzo region of Boyacá; and the Carare-Opón region of southwestern Santander, an old frontier area that bordered a strategic railway.

The principal actors during this period were the army, police, and Conservative paramilitaries: the "peace guerrillas" of the eastern plains, the *contrachusma* ("counterscum") of Antioquia, and the "rural police" of northwestern Cundinamarca, supposedly facing down Liberal guerrillas who were aided by the local population. These paramilitary groups generally had from ten to fifty men under arms, connected by a network of logistical support; some groups numbered as many as five hundred, Around mid-century about two hundred of these base-level groups operated in the country.

Despite their lack of formal organization and direction from above, the Liberal guerrillas created hierarchies and legitimating symbols. The earliest Tolima groups were based on groups of relatives, ritual kin (*compadres*), and friends; on the plains, eleven of the seventeen groups operating in 1953 were based on a nucleus of brothers or cousins. Later additions to the group, such as rural day laborers in the region, were incorporated as if they were poor relations, receiving protection in exchange for loyalty. Army deserters and escaped prisoners were welcomed according to what they could provide in the way of expertise.

Like the traditional political bosses, the guerrilla bands were successful insofar as they reinforced their links with the communities whose territories and beliefs they defended. The guerrillas of Rovira (Tolima) defended the Protestant faith of the peasants of Riomanso, while Juan de la Cruz Varela in Sumapaz (Cundinamarca) and Jacobo Prías in southern Tolima embraced communism, at least notionally, as an expression of their regions' agrarian struggles. While all guerrillas and paramilitaries were initially Liberal or Conservative, in many areas these labels had lost their relevance as early as 1953.

The Liberal leadership's majority preference for peaceful resistance, combined with the vacuum left by the flight of many prominent Liberals from small towns to the relative safety of the cities, meant that some guerrilla groups were entirely on their own, an experience that radicalized them. But other groups were secretly supported by prominent local Liberals, and the guerrillas of the eastern plains came the closest to attracting the sympathy and implicit support of the national Liberal leadership.

The plains and the cowboy *llanero* embodied the origin myth of the Colombian state: they were the bearers of liberty in 1819. As José Eustasio Rivera depicted them in his classic novel *La vorágine* (1924), they represented the possibility of conquering the nation's vast frontier. For these legendary figures to take up arms in the name of the Liberal Party was like a grenade thrown into the heart of the Conservative regime, which responded with both military force and a public relations campaign. In his 1951 message to Congress, Gómez pointedly referred to the "typical banditry" prevalent in "Antioquia, Tolima, and the eastern mountains of Boyacá"—a euphemism for, or more accurately a diversion from, the evocative reality of warfare on the plains.

In mid-1951, in preparation for possible negotiation with the Conservatives on the disarmament of guerrillas, the Liberal leadership distinguished between four types of armed rebels: "(a) innocents harassed by persecution [i.e., who take up arms in self-defense]; (b) those who have joined the guerrillas for political reasons and have no incentive to leave them; (c) those who have committed crimes during the guerrilla struggle but have no confidence in the judicial system; and (d) war criminals who, under cover of political violence or official repression, are responsible for atrocious crimes." The right vocabulary was the key to legitimizing the guerrillas, at least the bulk of them. Meanwhile the Conservatives were equally keen to use the power of language for their own ends: for the government, the guerrillas were "bandits without political labels," grist for the army and police. Not surprisingly, one of the insurgents' first and most common demands was that they be recognized as guerrillas.

Gómez's government did send an emissary to speak with the plains guerrillas, and even asked Alfonso López, a major landowner in the region, to serve as mediator. On October 6, 1951, Colombians were surprised to read of a bipartisan agreement to seek peace, based on a Liberal Party proposal. The Liberals would persuade the guerrillas to lay down their arms, and the Conservative regime would lift the state of siege. The plains were to be the first experiment in pacification, and there was in fact a notable reduction in violence there after the announcement.

The initiative was, however, subject to the dynamics of factionalism within the ruling party. In September 1951 the *alzatista* faction scored important victories in the (Conservative-only) legislative elections. Although Gilberto Alzate was strongly implicated in political violence in Caldas, he now demanded an end to the state of siege and the lifting of press censorship. With Alzate now joining Ospina against him, Gómez canceled the peace initiative as a way to snub the Conservative dissidents who had spoken out in favor of it and appeal to grassroots Conservatives who supported his regime.

Peace initiatives developed at the departmental level as well, most notably in Antioquia. In April 1952 the two parties' directorates in Medellín, along with departmental units of ANDI and the ranchers' association, formed a "pro-peace committee" to put an end to the Violencia on their territory. They asked landowners of both parties to stop supporting armed groups—to some extent a disingenuous request, since rural labor markets operated in a clientelist world in which the "bandits" were well integrated after several years of activity.

In the second half of 1952, after the failure of high-level interparty discussions, the Violencia again heated up. On July 26 the army lost ninety-six soldiers in a single ambush by the plains guerrilla leader Guadalupe Salcedo. On September 6, after the funeral of six police officers who were massacred in Rovira (Tolima), Conservative crowds, aided by police and intelligence agents, destroyed the two Liberal newspapers in Bogotá and the homes of Alfonso López and Carlos Lleras Restrepo. López may have seen it coming: only days before, he asked Ospina and the archbishop of Bogotá to appeal to the government for peace. The two Liberal leaders went abroad, and the government clamped down on the press.

In late 1952 and early 1953 the plains were the setting for a large-scale conventional counteroffensive by the military, including the air force. The United States declined a request for 1,000 napalm bombs for use in the operation. The guerrillas redeployed their forces easily, and launched attacks and ambushes along a wide front. The civilian population had to leave everything behind, including their cattle, but the guerrillas only gained in popularity with their resistance. Their activities began to take on a marked social slant, as when they destroyed the installations and machinery of agribusiness companies recently established around Villavicencio.

Even so, the *llaneros* were the bearers of traditional political values. Their objective was to bring down the government of Laureano Gómez, not the social order and the state that represented it. But the intransigence of the government, which insisted that "the plains cannot be turned over to bandits," hardened their determination and led them to expand their areas of operations; they also started to forge contacts with other guerrillas, such as the Communist Juan de la Cruz Varela. After meeting with them in December 1951 and January 1952, López was convinced that "behind the guerrillas comes social revolution," and recent historical studies have confirmed his premonition.

In August 1952 there were clear signs of radicalization. A delegation from the plains guerrillas attended a conference of insurgents in Viotá (Cundinamarca), a center of Communist Party influence since the 1920s. On June 18, 1953, immediately after the Rojas coup, the *llaneros* formally united behind the charismatic Guadalupe Salcedo as their commander; they also issued a basic legal code known as the "Second Law of the Plains" which combined rough-and-ready justice with egalitarian provisions on land and labor.

A few weeks later Rojas's government issued its generous amnesty plan for the plains, and by September 12 urban Colombians could read a reassuring article in *El Tiempo* under the large-print headline "Return to Normal on the Plains." An accompanying photograph was captioned "With the mountains in the distance and the immensity of the region all around them, the guerrillas walk single-file to the military base of Tauramena to surrender their arms and return to civilian life." The government's press office emphasized that the fighters came in small groups, on foot (rather than on horseback, as per the heroic *llanero* image), and that their leaders recognized the futility of continued warfare: the victor was Rojas, "the second Liberator of Colombia," second only to Simón Bolívar. It was reported that 3,220 guerrillas surrendered in six weeks. That figure included a small Conservative counterguerrilla force. Modest loans from the Agrarian Bank would help them return to their usual rural activities.

When the Liberal guerrillas turned in their arms, the initiative passed to the Communists, who won the allegiance of peasant groups who chose not to accept the government's offer. Their new strategy was "self-defense," rather than the overthrow of a government that had wide popular support. Juan de la Cruz Varela pioneered the strategy in Sumapaz in late 1953: his group turned over a token number of arms and pledged support for the government's pacification scheme, and then retreated to the most remote corners of their home region to resume the struggle on behalf of settlers' and sharecroppers' rights in the coffee *municipios* of Cunday, Villarica, and Icononzo. Varela led an agrarian movement with roots in the peasant agitation of the 1920s and 1930s. Since shortly after the *bogotazo*, the region's absentee landowners sought to throw the settlers off their lands, and the government sought to plant Conservative migrants from elsewhere to challenge the "Red" peasants.

In 1954 landowners complained of extortion, "taxation," and restrictions on the coffee trade by the Sumapaz guerrillas. The military, armed with now counterinsurgency strategies learned in the Korean War, took up positions in the area and launched a conventional campaign that sent large numbers of peasant refugees toward the city of Ibagué. Other "invisible" refugees hid in nearby forests and expected to return as soon as the military pressure lifted, but eventually they formed part of the larger-scale exodus of Violencia peasant refugees toward the Ariari region in Meta, Guayabero, and Riochiquito in southern Tolima and other colonization zones that would become early bastions of the communist FARC guerrillas of the 1960s.

The Violencia flared in the mid-1950s in some parts of western Colombia, thanks to the military's complicity with local Conservative bosses in the sponsorship and tolerance of *pájaros*, the political assassins who had been active in the region as early as 1947. They were initially the agents of marginalized but ambitious Conservative operatives of the *alzatista* sort in the small and midsized towns where they operated, but by the mid-1950s the strings were pulled from the *laureanista* Conservative directorate in Cali.

The greater Caldas region, Quindío in particular, was depicted as a region where rural society had a uniquely middle-class cast, but the truth was that the best lands and the bulk of political power were in the hands of a small oligarchy. In 1932, when the national coffee census forged the myth of coffee-based social democracy, 60 percent of peasant families in Caldas did own the land they worked, although that figure declined somewhat by the 1950s. The region suffered the highest incidence of tropical diseases in Andean Colombia (in other words, not counting regions that actually were tropical), and even in years of decent coffee prices such as 1950, a small producer made no more from the sale of his harvest than a wage laborer could make in a year's work on a nearby rice plantation. In short, the visible prosperity of the towns of the coffee belt was not a fair indicator of the conditions of the rural population.

This was the backdrop for the process by which strictly political violence, including early *pájaro* killings and the *aplanchadora* massacres of the *alzatistas*, spiraled into what was called "the business of violence." Under Rojas there were no elections and no direct reasons to kill for electoral gain, but hacienda foremen, bar owners, and local politicians took advantage of institutional disorder to take over key parts of the regional economy through murder or the threat of it: they manipulated the local labor market, took control of the coffee and cattle trades, and threw farmers off their land. The emblematic figure of this phenomenon was León María Lozano, alias "The Condor," an active *laureanista* Conservative from Tuluá in northern Valle del Cauca, who became the military's chief confidant in their "pacification" of the region in the mid-1950s. He appeared in a famous photo with Rojas, and enjoyed the protection of the president. Liberal landowners in Quindío turned to the remaining Liberal guerrillas of northern Tolima, on the other side of the mountain range, for protection and retaliation. While the Bogotá press rightly held the Rojas government responsible for the new wave of violence, it could not fully grasp the intricate network of small-town tensions and complicities, mostly revolving around property and wealth, that was really behind the killings.

These years left a deep mark on the region's social structure. Far more than in other parts of Colombia, smaller proprietors ("family farms" in the classic 1932 sense) were replaced with a new breed of rural bourgeoisie who would take advantage of the National Front years to bury their pasts and legitimate their modest fortunes. The dispossessed of the 1950s either left for cities or colonization zones or stayed on as day laborers.

The military junta recognized its inability to crush the guerrillas and miscellaneous killers who continued to plague parts of the country by 1958. In the early years of the National Front the surviving armed groups of the central mountains met a variety of fates. Some managed to rejoin civilian life, thanks to the patronage networks of the official Liberal party. Others rejoined society more ambiguously, through the dissident Movimiento Revolucionario Liberal (MRL), which did not fully endorse the bipartisan agreement that brought a return to nominal peace. Many simply demobilized without official mediation, and as individuals they joined the migratory flows to any number of colonization zones throughout the country. But some had committed so many egregious crimes that they had no one to protect them and could not give up the fight without being killed themselves; concentrated in Quindío and northern Tolima, they reverted to an atavistic spirit of killing for the sake of killing.

By 1964 the army had managed to destroy most of these groups through improved intelligence and counterinsurgency methods, and also through "civil-military action brigades" that won over local populations by offering basic medical and infrastructure services. This strategy was, in a sense, derived from the strategy of the most successful guerrilla groups, whatever their ideology: win the confidence of the local population, gain intimate knowledge of local geography and society, wage war with small groups (as opposed to large conventional forces, as was the military's preference in the 1950s), and practice psychological warfare. Between 1960 and 1963 some fifty-seven armed bands were liquidated, and another twenty were defeated over the following two years. By 1965 it was reported that only twenty-seven remained, most of them on their last legs.

Social Parameters of the Violencia

The Violencia of the 1950s gathered up the loose strands of frontier colonization. In all the years since then the agrarian frontier has been the theatre par excellence of guerrillas and counterguerrillas, both sides made up of young men (many just adolescents), unemployed or underemployed, in search of opportunity. The life and miracles of the settler took on a new dimension as violence filled the longstanding vacuum of official authority. Hobbes wrote that we enjoy a kind of equality when any of us can kill anyone else, and that is the terrifying but in some sense leveling reality of Colombia's frontiers.

Like the Bogotá and Antioquian merchants who won title to public lands a century earlier, the guerrillas of the 1950s and beyond sought to establish order. We can superimpose a map of the 1950s guerrilla hot spots of the Opón, the plains, and Sumapaz onto a contemporary map of FARC or ELN fronts, or onto a late-nineteenth-century map of public land concessions, and find substantial continuity through the three eras. But the guerrillas also recruited from more recent colonization zones, such as the Guaviare and Vaupés in the far reaches of Orinoquia, or the remote tropical forests of Santander that attracted the attention of oil companies in the 1940s.

Since the nineteenth century, poverty has expelled peasants from their *patrias chicas*, their ancestral regions. They gamble on success where they think their chances are best: in the temperate coffee zones, on the plains, or in the rain forests. In the Amazon and Orinoquia they contribute to the physical and cultural destruction of the native inhabitants, but everywhere they are subject to the control of storekeepers and middlemen, political bosses and land speculators. In an insecure environment, they seek protection by joining networks of godparentage and clientelism, which take the place of absent state institutions. This is the peasant migrant—settler today, construction peon tomorrow—who sometimes found in the Violencia a new if perverse option.

His labor in incorporating the frontier into the national economy is one of the most important hidden sources of capitalization, and his poverty is the hidden face of Colombian progress. His tribulations and generalized insecurity are the price of free competition for land in a profoundly unjust and viscerally independent society. On the agrarian frontier the state has always been waiting in the wings, and there it waits still: the weak have no laws to free them from the freedom of the strong.

Not all peasants joined the colonizations. Starting in the 1920s, the "dance of the millions" era of large-scale investment, many joined road construction crews or worked in river ports, refineries, and mines. The labor union was their method of economic self-defense, community expression, and political participation. When they faced persecution starting in the late 1940s, they found protection by joining the Liberal guerrillas.

There is very little research about refugees, the small and medium proprietors or day laborers who fled with their families, with the hope of returning later to their properties and memories. They have been examined as a factor of urbanization, but this approach avoids the issue: urban slums would have developed even without the Violencia, although in many cities refugees were important contributors. The exodus left unanswered the question of how local societies would face up to their recent histories (given that the official basis for pacification was a return to normal, starting with the homestead) and how the cities would incorporate hundreds of thousands of Colombians whose recent traumas were ignored by their neighbors and employers. We simply do not know how their behaviors and attitudes affected urban society, which in the late twentieth century increasingly was Colombian society.

The Violencia respected old lines of deference and social class. Very few large landowners or high-ranking military officers lost their lives. It was a rural phenomenon of poor rural people; they were the killed and the killers. In the cities the terror was more psychological, as in the case of Liberals who stopped wearing red neckties in order to avoid being beaten by the police. Urban repression during the Violencia has received little attention. We do know that there were tortures and political killings, but on the whole Liberals in the larger cities lived under the shadow of arbitrary abuse rather than a centralized and bureaucratized repression. The detention and trial of a handful of well-connected Bogotá Liberals in 1951, accused of starting a clandestine radio station in nearby Fusagasugá, attracted wide attention precisely because it was so unusual.

The Violencia is best seen as an expression of the chronic deficit of state authority, rather than as a manifestation of the state's collapse. In fact, the state during this period was powerful enough to facilitate an unprecedented accumulation of capital: the plutocracy served itself with a big spoon throughout the 1950s, even as the socioeconomic gap widened. The state measured its legitimacy by the results of its macroeconomic policies, and even then it ignored key factors such as the transparency and efficiency of state subsidies, the improvement of industrial competitiveness, the waste and underutilization of the best agricultural lands, the excessive concentration of income, growing social and regional inequalities, the housing shortage, and the chaotic growth of cities.

The self-styled "working men" did not grasp and would not have believed that the Violencia was part of a generalized contempt for law, a contempt they shared insofar as they evaded taxes, trafficked in import licenses, and made use of the parallel currency market. This mentality was reinforced during the coffee bonanza of 1945–54, with its strong economic fluctuations that called for agile and not always legal responses. The fact that more than half the population considered the Conservative regime illegitimate was also a factor, although many in the Liberal elite agreed that some temporary dismantling of the machinery to mobilize voters was necessary in order to restore the old civility.

The armed forces became involved in the civil conflict at a time when the Cold War was beginning to propagate the notion of the "internal enemy," a notion that eventually proved harmful to the construction of democratic institutions and the effectiveness of the military. This was evident in the laws and practices of paramilitary organizations after 1965, most of which soon escaped official control. The police, an institutional pillar of any modern state, were implicated in crimes both big and small, and earned a reputation for brutality and inefficiency which they did not even begin to overcome until the 1990s.

The judicial system, marked by corruption and venality, came out of the Violencia even more subservient to the executive branch. The Ministry of Justice was established only in 1945, after a half-century in which justice was organizationally subordinated to politics in the Interior Ministry. The sectarian tidal wave that came after 1946 prevented the development of an independent and trusted judiciary. Precisely at the time when society needed dependable enforcement of the law, the two state institutions most responsible for that enforcement were deeply suspect. The effects of this failure are still felt today in Colombia's high crime rates and in the corruption of its police and courts.

Chapter 5

AN ELUSIVE LEGITIMACY

*T*he National Front (FN) and the regimes that followed it have sought to reconcile the institutional principles of the Liberal Republic (1930–46) with the matrix of state and business ideologies and interests forged during the state of siege (1948–58).

The FN, despite pessimistic forecasts, did complete its itinerary. Four presidents, alternating Liberals and Conservatives, were elected by popular vote: Alberto Lleras Camargo (1958–62), Guillermo León Valencia (1962–66), Carlos Lleras Restrepo (1966–70), and Misael Pastrana (1970–74). The FN was an institutional project conceived and shepherded by the political and business elites and the Catholic Church hierarchy to overcome by measured steps the authoritarianism and violence of the preceding period. The establishment of a peaceful, participative, and pluralist civic culture required the abandonment of confrontational styles of politics, the restoration of representative institutions, and the development of a modern public sector. Bringing the state and its citizens together would require the reconstruction of the judicial and police apparatuses, but also the honoring of commitments ranging from union rights and agrarian reform to the widening of access to education and urban housing. Such a wide-ranging scheme required some degree of sacrifice by the same capitalist sector which took credit for removing the Rojas dictatorship, and which was arguably the strongest social base for the new experiment.

Because of its defining characteristic of bipartisanship (to the exclusion of other groups) and of the Cold War context in which it existed, the FN repressed political dissidence and sought to co-opt and control both the poor and the emerging middle classes by widening their patronage networks. It created a cynical alternative to the promised reconstruction of the world of citizenship.

The FN strengthened relations between the state and the business elite, although these relations would change in style and substance by the 1980s. Meanwhile the new middle classes of the postwar period were promoted, while the unions, already beginning to cut their ties to the party machines since the Violencia, completed their divorce from them. FN governments erratically promoted programs of agrarian reform and subsidized urban housing to favor the poor, while they promoted such mechanisms as local grassroots committees (Juntas de Acción Comunal, JAC) which ended up administering poverty rather than attacking its root causes.

While the presidency was strengthened, aided by a technocracy of economists who were increasingly set on securing jobs in international financial agencies headquartered in Washington, the legislative branch lost credibility. The judiciary failed to gain the independence and technical basis necessary to rescue the public's confidence in the concept of equality before the law. The church and the military continued to play starring public roles: while the church adapted to the new social setting—even to state-sponsored birth control—the military held onto its privileges and even was able to expand the scope of its autonomy under the umbrella of anticommunism and the fight against guerrilla movements. Colombia may have been under a state of siege for much of the second half of the twentieth century, but in not experiencing a military coup since 1953 it occupied an exceptional place among Latin American countries.

The constitutional pact produced greater apathy and disinterest in voting, and in the absence of ideological controversy or viable opposition, it refined the most vulgar mechanisms of politics. Outright corruption played its part in the exhaustion of the FN system, a process that lasted from 1974, when the two parties ceased to alternate in the presidency, to the unrestricted competition of 1991. A crisis of legitimacy came over the political system in the 1970s, which in the following decade was aggravated by financial scandals, the emergence of drug trafficking, and the strengthening of the guerrillas. Throughout the dismantling of the FN and afterward, the Liberals maintained their majorities, and six of the eight postalternation presidents have come from that party: Alfonso López Michelsen (1974–78), Julio César Turbay (1978–82), Virgilio Barco (1986–90), César Gaviria (1990–94), Ernesto Samper (1994–98), and Álvaro Uribe (elected in 2002). The two Conservatives, Belisario Betancur (1982–86) and Andrés Pastrana (1998–2002), won the presidency in large part because of divisions among the Liberals.

Capitalism, Economic Institutions, and the Cold War

The FN was the golden age of gentlemen's agreements between the leadership of the state and the quasi-corporative trade associations such as ANDI (industrialists), FENALCO (merchants), ASOBANCARIA (banks), and SAC (large landowners).

The influence of regional business elites was exercised through development corporations such as the cvc in the Cauca Valley and the car in the Bogotá region, or by the cattlemen's fedegan in Antioquia, to cite the most prominent examples. These pacts and influences lent a certain oligarchic air to the National Front regimes, and sometimes pacts were not even necessary because state and capitalists were embodied by the same person—for instance, Carlos Lleras was not only the most visionary and creative modernizer of Colombia's twentieth-century institutions during his public life, but also a tax attorney who bragged to the newspaper *El Espectador* in 1960 that his clients included the country's most prominent companies.

Overall economic growth left a more complex business structure, from the point of view of region and specialization. Within the industrialists' andi the textile producers of Medellín now had to share leadership with Bogotá businessmen, and the appearance of other trade associations contributed to the segmentation of the sector as a corporative group. With or without gentlemen's agreements, ranchers managed to take the teeth out of the agrarian reform debated in the congress, and the industrialists who worked closely with government on tax and tariff reforms in 1959 and 1964 simply bought the votes required to gain additional concessions. But with the modernization of economic institutions and the rise of a technocracy armed with graduate degrees from the United States, the axis of power was shifting to the state.

The Cold War played a fundamental role in the push for capitalist modernization. Already in 1950 Colombia figured among the principal beneficiaries of the policies of the World Bank and the Export-Import Bank. A decade later, faced with the challenge of the Cuban Revolution, the United States revised its policies to address Latin America's longstanding demands for economic assistance. The Inter-American Development Bank, a promised outcome of the 1948 Inter-American Conference in Bogotá, finally began operations in 1962. With the same Cold War motivations the United States supported the creation of the International Coffee Organization (oic). To support the packet of economic and social reforms enshrined in the Punta del Este agreement of 1961, President Kennedy proposed the Alliance for Progress, for which Colombia was to be a showcase. Under the aegis of the Alliance and with the assistance of a mission from the U.N.'s Economic Commission on Latin America (ecla), the National Planning Office prepared a ten-year development plan and a four-year investment plan. What with the U.N. and its specialized agencies, the imf and other multilateral credit organizations, and the U.S. government, Colombia's government operations had ever more numerous foreign advisers on all fronts.

The continuity of economic policy was not absolute, but rather was affected by the styles and varying levels of efficiency of successive governments. Each president baptized his own development plan to underline one or another contrast with his predecessor. But all have learned that their scope of action is very limited. Until the late 1980s coffee income was the key variable. The periodic "adjustments" in fiscal, monetary, and exchange policies which followed the ups and downs of coffee were a cross that all governments had to bear in their efforts to keep inflation and the budget deficit at favorable levels by the prevailing Latin American standard.

These adjustments would have been more traumatic if not for the moderating action of the OIC on world coffee markets, via four multilateral pacts (1963, 1968, 1976, and 1983) which stabilized and even raised prices in a context of global overproduction. This gave Colombia some predictability in macroeconomic policy making and strengthened the National Coffee Growers' Federation (FEDECAFÉ) in its role as custodian of the national coffee stabilization fund. This power was in decline since the late 1960s, but when the OIC, subjected to pressure by the United States, failed to agree on a new pact in 1988, it suffered a severe blow.

The fundamental economic strategy of the National Front was to deepen Colombian industrialization through import substitution. Even though coffee prices fell sharply between 1957 and 1963, the economy managed to grow robustly because of industrial development. During the 1950–64 period industry created 10,000 jobs each year, to which should be added a significant (though difficult to determine) number of indirect jobs, particularly in the production of raw materials, transport of finished goods, and finance and distribution networks.

From the mid-1960s on Colombian industrialization faced three types of problems. First, it became evident that new industries—metallurgy, paper, chemicals and plastics, transport and electrical equipment—could neither expand nor increase productivity without a substantial increase in imported machinery and technology. Second, the long chapter of labor-intensive industrialization, where Colombia as a country with abundant low-cost labor enjoyed an advantage, was coming to an end. Third, and related to the second problem, the very low purchasing power of most Colombians meant that the market for industrial products was still quite small.

In response to these problems, import controls were redefined in order to secure the rapid development of intermediate industries and those producing capital goods (categories that registered annual increases of over 10 percent from 1958 through 1974), and policies were developed to encourage the manufacture of goods for export. Although the U.S. market has been important to this strategy, between 1970 and 1990 around 60 percent of Colombia's manufactured exports went to Latin America. Initially the regional focus was based on the Latin American Free Trade Area (ALALC) of 1960, but as that initiative failed to develop adequately, Colombia looked to subregional agreements, most notably the Cartagena Accord of 1969, signed by Colombia, Ecuador, Chile, Peru, and Bolivia, which became known as the Andean Pact.

The Andean Pact called for the adoption of a common external tariff, the control of foreign capital flows, industrial planning, the creation of multinational Andean companies, and the coordination of macroeconomic policies. The different levels of industrialization among the member states, with Chile and Colombia in the lead and Bolivia and Ecuador farther back, were behind differences of opinion on key policies: Chile and Colombia were more interested in commercial liberalization (access to regional markets), while Bolivia and Ecuador were more interested in "industrial harmonization" (preference in the establishment of new factories). The gap in national perceptions, between highly visible short-term costs and hazy long-term benefits, grew over time, and in 1973 the agreement went through a series of predicaments from which it has not recovered.

The Imperceptible Development of a Bureaucratic Elite

The growth and complexity of the state's economic functions provided an opening for the economist-administrator, known as the "young economist," a new prophet who discreetly displaced the earlier emblematic figure, the "politician-lawyer," in public economic institutions. Insofar as the Colombian economy could be modeled mathematically, the economist was the representative of this supposed ideological neutrality, which was especially important to a regime such as the FN, which had banished controversy. To the collective imagination of the 1960s, young economists were the bearers of modernity.

The country required their professional expertise, and both politicians and the press took an indulgent view of their diagnoses and recommendations. The politician, that traditional Colombian type, was now seen as a representative of tradition rather than of solutions and modernity. During the 1960s technocrats and politicians learned to live and benefit together, albeit with the conflicts to be expected in any cohabitation.

The genealogy of these social engineers can be traced to the Regeneration era, with its motto "Less politics and more administration." This leitmotiv of modernization, liberal or conservative, privileged a rationalist style of thought, according to which passion and will could be understood and channeled through the use of reason—legal reason especially—as opposed to mere tradition and customs. The constitutional order was a form of reason, authoritarian for the dominant group in 1886, democratic for the dominant group of 1936. As noted earlier, the 1936 reform under Alfonso López Pumarejo defined a modern country as one in which social conflict could be understood and solved through the rational use of the state, its laws, and its modern public administration.

During the 1960s economics seemed to be the key discipline, the master trope for confronting the conflicts inherent in a new society and a new state. The National Front leaders of the 1960s, particularly on the Liberal side, were determined to cement a new political, administrative, and institutional rationality. The middle classes, educated to a worshipful view of the power of intellect and of "orderly politics," would be the principal source of support for this conception of modernity, and more concretely they would provide the expertise needed by the public and private sectors to make it happen.

The economist, not the lawyer, was now the key figure in the functioning of the state machinery. But while the lawyer worked within a distinctively Colombian legal system and within a broader legalism that was itself Colombian (and usually identified with Francisco de Paula Santander, thus the *santanderista* label for such thinking), the economist was effectively transnational, often rotating between multilateral bureaucracies in Washington or elsewhere and service in Colombia. He adopted the focus, language, techniques, and norms of the wider world. More important, in a state and society resting on an underdeveloped economic base and therefore subject to constant uncertainty, the economist enjoyed privileged access to pertinent information, almost always from foreign sources or via foreign techniques.

This was the master key to an invisible power, reinforced by the "conditionality" clauses in balance-of-payments loans from the IMF and by more subtle means in loans from the World Bank and IADB, such as the "pari pasu" provisions that dictated the spending pace and priorities of loan disbursements. These requirements took debates on public spending and investment out of the realm of the Congress and beyond the reach of pressure groups, whether corporate or "popular."

These constraints were most evident in Bogotá, Medellín, and Cali, the three principal cities and the three biggest clients—after the national state— of multilateral lenders. Their relatively gigantic public utilities expanded at a rate of 10 percent annually between 1960 and 1990, entering into a closed loop controlled by Colombian bankers and transnational technocrats, principally in the World Bank, who determined expansion strategies, equipment purchases, utility rates, and overall management. Today the marginalization of mayors and city councils is even more apparent with regard to public services, despite the move to popular election of mayors in the 1980s.

With the expansion of a more complex capitalism and the onward march of urbanization, the economic role of the state grew and some of its functions became more specialized. The participation of the public sector as a whole in aggregate demand (consumption plus gross investment) increased from 10 percent of GDP in the 1950s to 20 percent in the 1990s. State-owned companies developed with less vigor than in advanced capitalist countries or the so-called Asian tigers or even the more prosperous countries of Latin America. They were concentrated in utilities and other infrastructure services: electricity production and distribution, telecommunications, water, gas, railroads, and ports.

The state's role, however, had been dominated by regionalist or corporatist interests. A classic example of the former are the *municipio* and regional electric companies and the national distribution network whose establishment and operation have provoked rivalries between the political center and the regions and between regions. As for the latter, a prime example is the determining role of labor unions in the ports and railways, at least until the 1990s.

If in the 1920s and 1930s the bureaucratic elite was composed of lawyers with a vaguely and indirectly French orientation, their counterparts of the FN period were, as noted earlier, economists of a clearly "Anglo-Saxon" bent. In the constitutional context of a "state of rights" (*estado de derecho*) inspired by continental

Europe, a model that emphasizes the responsibilities of the state, economic policies derived from a market-based model were bound to be a tough sell. This conflict can be seen in the way economic legislation has been treated by the Council of State, the highest administrative tribunal, both before and after the rights-oriented 1991 constitution.

In the last quarter-century the Colombian state has paid its vast bureaucracy (which grew from 100,000 employees in 1950 to almost one million in 1990) around a quarter of the country's total payroll. The government's discretionary control over this enormous spending has given it ample room to freeze the pay of public employees or keep them below the inflation rate. Since public-sector salaries set the standard for those in the private sector, where labor unions are generally fragmented and weak, and even those in the informal sector, Colombia differs from most Latin American countries in not suffering salary-based inflation. The political weakness of the popular sectors also permits the government to hold back on spending for education, health, and housing. Another basic function of any modern state, public safety and security, received substantially less funding than it required, a deficit that is only now being addressed.

But while the Colombian state has been relatively strong when it comes to restraining spending, at least on salaries and public goods, the same cannot be said about taxation. It has proved unable to stem the flight of capital abroad, and has resorted to tax amnesties that end up laundering ill-gotten gains. It has also failed to bring in equitable contributions from the wealthy and powerful in Colombian society. In the late 1980s only one-third of national revenues came from taxes approved by Congress, and since the 1960s the share of total taxation represented by direct income taxes has fallen while the share of indirect taxes, which fall heavily on the poor, has increased.

The technocracy administers an ever-wider range of complex and opaque financial operations, including a peculiar tax regime for the coffee sector, and more recently for the oil and natural gas sector; the internal debt; social security funds; and Colombia's foreign debt, which in the 1970s was still exceptionally low by Latin American standards.

The need to increase public investment, the volatility and unpredictability of government revenue (especially customs receipts and other income related to foreign trade), and the demands of the electoral cycle all led to a mounting budget deficit and to its inevitable inflationary financing. Before elections, fiscal and monetary discipline flagged; afterward the screws were tightened once more.

The liberalization of foreign trade after 1988 laid bare Colombia's crumbling infrastructure. The parlous state of transportation, ports, and telecommunications sapped the competitiveness of the country's exports. Business leaders, politicians, and the general public all look to the state to be a key agent in these investments. But the economic Achilles' heel of the Colombian state is its very limited fiscal capacity. Other factors—the size of the public sector, the inefficiency of many public enterprises, and the cyclical nature of such exports as coffee—are certainly significant, but they have been controlled effectively within the political process whereas the inability to raise significant revenues is a long-term structural problem that the increase in income from petroleum exports in the early 1990s cannot adequately address.

Weak and Atomized Labor Unions

Changes in the labor force (increased educational attainment, growing participation of women, decline in manual labor, excess labor supply with the stagnation of labor-intensive industrialization, and increasing fragmentation of the labor force because of specialization), all combined to weaken blue-collar unionism. Meanwhile white-collar unions appeared, most strongly among public employees, whose numbers increased eightfold between 1960 and 1990. The sociological and regional diversity of blue-collar *obreros* and white-collar *empleados* and the lack of interest shown in them by the political class explain the weak and erratic trajectory of the union movement throughout the period. Blue- and white-collar government workers could hardly help becoming radicalized, perhaps less under the influence of leftist ideology than in response to the government's easy resort to keeping public salaries low as a means to fight inflation.

The FN was greeted with a wave of labor agitation, much of which came from middle-class *empleados*. Teachers marched from the provinces to Bogotá to demand back pay, since many departmental treasuries were so poor that teachers were paid in crates of liquor from corrupt departmental liquor monopolies. There were strikes in sugar mills, cement plants, construction, and foreign-owned factories, which sometimes were repressed by force. The 1963 strike at

ECOPETROL, the state oil company, was one of the most radical and it grew to include the population of the refinery town of Barrancabermeja, the surrounding rural population, and the developing university student movement in the main cities.

According to statistics, union membership grew from 250,000 to 700,000 between 1959 and 1965, and from 5.5 percent to 13.4 percent of the economically active population, which would prove to be a historical peak. As inflation rose and unions were ignored or abandoned by their previous patrons in the church and the parties, strikes reached epidemic proportions by mid-decade. The administration of Carlos Lleras (1966–70) changed the labor laws to encourage company unions rather than trade unions and made arbitration mandatory. These measures, combined with organizational fatigue in the two main labor confederations, weakened the power of unions and the strike weapon by the 1970s. The main tool of protest against a new and more damaging wave of inflation in that decade was the general strike, which united poor and middle-class Colombians as aggrieved consumers rather than as workers.

From a mobilization perspective, the vacuum left by the decline of the labor confederations of the early FN era was filled by public sector unions, especially the teachers' union, FECODE. New labor federations arose within existing structures, some based on region (principally in the three key regions of Bogotá, Antioquia, and the Valle del Cauca), others on industry (such as the petroleum workers' USO). Most of these unions were under strong leftist influence and control, from old-line Communists in the urban unions and from more exotic radical sects in the others. They all burst forth in 1974 and subsequent years, only to enter a rapid decline during the 1980s, in part due to the influence of guerrilla groups among some of them.

The Co-optation of the Middle Classes

One of the FN's favorite social groups was the middle class, which had been burgeoning in Colombia's cities since the late 1940s. In the larger metropolitan areas that group was ever more clearly segmented into upper and lower, according to occupation, education level, consumption standards, and residence. In the cities of the western coffee belt, the middle-class figure par excellence was the well-off coffee grower whose business dealings afforded him an independent way of life. In the four largest urban centers, the middle-class standard was defined more by formal education, a liberal profession, and a position in a public or private bureaucracy. As in other Latin American societies, the middle classes were also to be found in the officer corps of the military and in parallel positions in the clergy, judiciary, journalism, and teaching. From this varied middle sector there emerged the leaders—of politics, unions, guerrillas, and drug trafficking—who in varying degrees and settings would challenge the status quo.

The governments of the FN cultivated the middle class with special care. The state tried to respond to their expectations of advancement, respect, and well-being (often summed up as "*casa, carro, y beca*": house, car, and scholarship) with a bundle of policies that subsidized access to higher education, advanced health care, decent housing, and conspicuous consumption. For instance, the university population grew from barely 19,000 in 1958 to over 543,000 in 1992, although it must be noted that over half of today's students are in cut-rate programs at private "garage" universities whose facilities differ hardly at all from the average high school. In any event, the state did devote more resources to education as the clergy's historical fears of secular education dissipated.

Like other middle-sector groups in the countryside and in the cities, urban professionals were geographically and sociologically segmented but were quite compact and coherent when it came to defending their interest in social, political, and price stability. They balanced the electoral map and fended off the ideological extremes, especially of the left. Their ascendancy can be traced in the slow transformation in styles of political rhetoric and literary expression popularized from the 1940s on in magazines such as *Semana* and in Sunday literary supplements of such newspapers as *El Tiempo*, *El Espectador*, and *La República* in Bogotá, *El Colombiano* in Medellín, *El País* in Cali, *El Heraldo* in Barranquilla, and *Vanguardia Liberal* in Bucaramanga.

Change and Continuity in the Catholic Church

Like all the other traditional institutions, the Catholic Church was swamped by urbanization and secularization. The number of Colombians per priest increased from 3,846 in 1950 to 4,678 in 1980. As in past eras, the nominally unified church was composed of multiple subgroups. Newly ordained priests and nuns of the early 1960s embraced the "spirit of service" of Pope John XXIII, whose tolerance of leftist ideology and renunciation of church interference in Italian politics resonated strongly in Colombia. John XXIII's emphases on social justice and the integration of the poor into the sociopolitical order (in his encyclical *Mater et magistra*, 1961), the need for the church to adapt to the realities of the modern pluralistic world (in his opening of the Second Vatican Council, 1962), and the need to substitute international cooperation for Cold War confrontation (*Pacem in terris*, 1963) were at least as much of a sea-change in Colombia, whose most visible clergy had long been extremely conservative if not ultramontane, as elsewhere in the Catholic world.

When these new emphases were not embraced by church hierarchies throughout the world (especially after John XXIII's death in 1963), younger clergy showed their displeasure. The frankly leftist "liberation theology" that took hold in 1960s Brazil did not have as great an impact in Colombia, but when the dashing Bogotá priest Camilo Torres joined the Castroite guerrillas of the National Liberation Army in 1965 and died shortly thereafter in his first armed action, his example resonated throughout Latin America. Colombia was also the seat of the "rebel priests" behind the Golconda Declaration of 1968, one of the clearest and most polemical expressions of liberation theology.

Pope Paul VI's visit to Colombia in 1968 did not settle disputes among the local clergy, although the new Conference of Latin American Bishops (CELAM), founded in Medellín in 1968, did attempt to bridge the gap between the traditionalism of the hierarchy and the radicalism of many young priests. Meanwhile, by the early 1970s several "ecclesiastical base communities" were started in Colombia's most desperate urban slums; these organizations were practical vehicles of liberation theology, interpreting the Gospels from the perspective of the suffering and hope of the dispossessed. They denounced the disconnect between the consumerist values preached in the media and the everyday misery of the poor, and they decried the contempt with which people in positions of power looked at the majority of Colombians. Needless to say, such sermons only deepened the conflict between liberation theology priests and most bishops.

However, this new "church of the poor" was met largely by indifference among the poor. The residents of the slums were for the most part preoccupied with the daily exigencies of survival; they had no time or energy for utopian visions of change, especially those that implied confrontation with the government. Later in the 1970s the Catholic identity of the urban poor would be further challenged by the coming of evangelical Protestants, whose superior funding and organizational techniques were accompanied by a utilitarian approach that many poor people found more comforting than any ideology.

The church did show pragmatism on one big issue, population growth. Although the hierarchy never really saw the issue as urgent, they gave tacit approval to a government strategy based largely on family planning, including birth control pills. By the time Paul VI issued an explicit condemnation of birth control, in the encyclical *Humanae vitae* (1968), the infrastructure was already in place and irreversible throughout Colombia. Today 70 percent of Colombian couples practice contraception, thanks to one of the most dynamic family planning organizations on the continent, and average family size has dropped from six (1970) to five (1990). Family size, it turned out, was tied more to educational and labor conditions than to the position of the church: the highest rates of fertility, birth, and death are found on the Atlantic coast, a generally poor region where the church has held relatively little sway, the rate of female participation in the formal labor force is low, and the illiteracy rate is high; the lowest fertility rates, similar to those of urban areas, are found in the prosperous coffee belt, a region of strong church influence.

The Limits of Change: The Example of Agrarian Reform

Land reform in the 1960s Colombian countryside was no small matter, entailing as it did a redistribution of wealth, income, and power. While it was largely a strategy of political control through co-optation, it was the purely economic argument that often took the lead. Statistics in hand, reformist bureaucrats demonstrated that while small *minifundios* were quite efficient (at least in land use, if not in labor use), the largest properties were often underexploited or simply unattended. Both very small and very large landholdings were obstacles to capital accumulation, agricultural productivity, and rising living standards. Large-scale and chaotic migration from the countryside to the cities was also part of the problem. An effective agrarian reform would stimulate food production and thus preserve rural employment while keeping urban food prices under control.

In late 1961, after two years of squabbling among political factions and economic interest groups and after rejecting a far more ambitious plan offered by the World Bank consultant Laughlin Currie, Congress approved a modest law designed to give land to the rural poor and increase irrigation infrastructure. From the outset, the government agency created to administer the reform (INCORA) was submerged in legalistic quicksand that made expropriations almost impossible; the Ministry of Agriculture, which largely represented the interests of the largest landholders, retained great latitude in deciding which lands would be off limits for redistribution. Regional associations and the coffee growers' lobby, FEDECAFÉ, successfully appealed for criteria that kept their lands out of the reform as well.

By 1971 only around 1 percent of the land originally targeted in the reform had actually been expropriated. The greatest success came in the titling of public lands, but even here the precariousness of the titles and the needless complexity of the process produced endless legal disputes and prevented landholders from obtaining bank credit. Irrigation projects, often poorly planned and far too expensive to build and maintain, benefited large landholders on the Caribbean coast, who managed to keep their region almost totally untouched by redistribution programs.

The political history of agrarian reform is inevitably tied to the expansion of patronage relationships. But by the late 1960s this phenomenon produced a strong response in the form of grassroots peasant mobilization, which was repressed and co-opted by the state. As early as 1960 the Movimiento Revolucionario Liberal (MRL), a leftist Liberal faction that opposed aspects of the National Front, denounced agrarian reform as "a political and electoral enterprise . . . meant to convince the Liberal masses that they can enjoy the benefits of reform only if they resign themselves to voting for a Conservative in the next presidential election." On the Conservative side, the faction identified with Mariano Ospina Pérez supported the reform while the Laureano Gómez faction, whose electoral support was concentrated in longstanding smallholder regions with nothing to gain from redistribution, decided to couch its opposition in ideological terms.

Just as the first redistribution programs were about to start in 1962, the presidency passed to Guillermo León Valencia, a Conservative who had no interest in reform. Valencia was a political tactician almost to the exclusion of other considerations, and in his quest for the two-thirds majority in Congress required for important legislation he willingly gave in to the Gómez faction's opposition to reform. Although the following president was one of the reform's principal architects, the Liberal Carlos Lleras Restrepo (1966–70), by that point the adversaries of redistribution were well entrenched.

In 1968 Lleras laid the legislative groundwork for ANUC, a national peasants' association (covering a wide range of tenure relationships, from smallholding to sharecropping to squatting) that he hoped would strengthen the Liberals' electoral fortunes in the countryside in time for the post-FN era of open party competition. The strongest opposition came from the overwhelmingly Liberal Caribbean coast, where the new organization was blocked at every turn by landed interests working through local henchmen. Even where elite opposition was not so overtly fierce, ANUC was unable to achieve its stated goal of peasant organization; it was born of state initiative and quickly split into pro-government and radical factions, named for the cities where they were launched, Armenia and Sincelejo respectively.

In 1971 the Sincelejo faction organized a vast movement of marches and land occupations on traditional haciendas, cattle ranches, and public lands claimed by well-off entrepreneurs. The movement was strongest on the coast, but it began to peter out in 1972 and disappeared shortly thereafter. The collapse of ANUC-Sincelejo was largely a function of official repression joined to landowner violence, which claimed the lives of many organizers. But it was also brought about by the byzantine politics of the Colombian left. The Communist weekly *Voz Proletaria* pontificated on the failure of a last-gasp 1974 conference, calling it a consequence of "extreme sectarianism" in a movement dominated by "Maoists, Trotskyites, *camilistas* [sympathizers of the late guerrilla priest Camilo Torres and of the ELN], and leftists of other extreme views who can never agree on anything." The reality was that the Communist Party and its FARC guerrilla allies had failed in their own attempts to take over the Sincelejo faction and were equally guilty of the factionalism they decried.

In 1971 the administration of Misael Pastrana suspended land redistribution, and the following year Liberal and Conservative leaders agreed, in the Chicoral Pact, to end the program entirely. They offered in its place the promise of rural development and tax reforms. When he reached the presidency in 1974, Alfonso López Michelsen, whose MRL had expressed skepticism about the motives behind agrarian reform from the outset, proposed taxing rural properties on the basis of potential income, a policy the World Bank had recommended a quarter-century earlier to encourage the development of idle or underutilized properties. The initiative was well received by the public and was accepted by some rural producers as a lesser evil than continued agitation in favor of redistribution, but it faced insurmountable technical obstacles, starting with the absence of a trustworthy registry of rural properties. In 1979 Congress reversed the López reform, leaving only a weak program of "Integrated Rural Development" (DRI) after nearly two decades of agrarian reform.

The Political Mechanics of the National Front

Under the FN party politics continued to revolve around political families, in the dual sense of actual ties of blood and marriage and also of loyalties built over a lifetime of political activity. There was a set and predictable system of confrontations, truces, and alliances between the two main political families on the Liberal side, Lleras and López, and on the Conservative side, Gómez and Ospina. It is hard to characterize them as modernizers or traditionalists, although certainly the Liberal families were more comfortable identifying themselves with institutional innovations. They were all defined more by styles, talents, and vocabularies than by ideologies.

With its accumulated experience dating back to the 1930s, somewhat greater party unity, more affiliates on the ground, and dominance of the country's main media outlets, the Liberals managed to place their party leaders in the presidency during the FN: Alberto Lleras (1958–62) and Carlos Lleras (1966–70). (Although they were usually called cousins, Carlos Lleras was actually Alberto's nephew, although he was only six years younger.) They felt less constrained than their Conservative counterparts, Guillermo León Valencia (1962–66) and Misael Pastrana (1970–74), when it came to proposing agrarian or constitutional reforms, since Valencia and Pastrana were compromise candidates rather than Conservative leaders in their own right.

The most durable state-directed mobilization initiative of the FN era, the Juntas de Acción Comunal (Community Action Boards, or JACS), created in 1958, were a Liberal initiative. JACS were organized by rural subdivision or urban neighborhood and were assigned funds by the state for specific development goals such as the construction of schools, clinics, and roads, or the extension of water and sewer lines. In return the communities provided volunteer labor and some funding, although the latter often came from aid organizations. But there was also substantial participation by politicians, who used their special legislative allocations ("parliamentary assistance") to assist projects. The program was a great success and reached into the far corners of the country; by 1974 there were 18,000 local boards. In the long run the program served to buy votes.

Because the Liberals were more unified than the Conservatives during the 1960s, they were the legislative backbone of the FN at the national level, especially after the MRL returned to the official fold in the mid-1960s. The Lib-

TABLE 5

Party/Faction Composition of the Colombian Congress under the National Front, 1958–70

	Liberal			Conservative			
	Official	MRL	ANAPO	Gómez	Ospina	ANAPO	Other
Senate							
1958	40	0	NA	28	10	NA	2
1962	37	12	0	16	31	2	0
1966	47	7	0	14	20	18	1
1970	37	NA	12	5	18	26	9
Chamber of Representatives							
1958	74	0	NA	19	19	NA	6
1960	58	18	0	38	37	0	1
1962	59	33	0	36	50	6	0
1964	60	31	1	24	40	26	2
1966	69	21	4	24	35	33	2
1968	94	2	4	17	47	30	6
1970	60	NA	28	13	30	43	19

Sources: Registraduría Nacional del Estado Civil, *Organización y estadísticas electorales* (Bogotá, 1968); *Gaceta del Congreso*, July 1970.

Note: Because factional identities are not official and may vary, these figures represent best estimates based on contemporary accounts. Because all candidates were nominally Liberal or Conservative under the FN, ANAPO candidates could be inscribed under either party.
NA: Not applicable (because the faction did not exist at the time).

erals used their unity to prevent the Conservatives from placing their "natural leaders" in the presidency for their two allotted terms. The task was made easier by the factionalism among the Conservatives, as can be seen in Table 5. The Conservative electorate watched in surprise as the congressional factions loyal to Laureano Gómez and Mariano Ospina preferred tactical alliances with the Liberals to their own party's unity. This disenchantment fueled the rise of the Popular Nationalist Alliance (ANAPO) movement of the former military ruler Gustavo Rojas Pinilla, which built a grassroots electoral machine in the face of strong FN opposition: working within the legal straitjacket of the FN's requirement that all candidates be identified as Liberal or Conservative, ANAPO managed to grow from 3.7 percent of votes in Congress in 1962 to around 35 percent in 1970.

By 1960 the Conservatives' division was already creating serious problems for the FN. By mid-decade three key aspects of the arrangement were up for reform. First, the constitutional requirement of a two-thirds majority (designed to require bipartisanship) had largely paralyzed the Congress, departmental assemblies, and even town councils. Opposition by either *ospinistas* or *laureanistas* could block key initiatives and appointments at all levels. Second, the electoral system itself permitted the consolidation of rotten boroughs (to use the nineteenth-century British term, which was adopted in Colombia), districts that had far smaller populations than others but the same voting power, and so provided safe seats for a given faction or for an incumbent. Third, the power of factions and even individual legislators to demand quotas in the government's bureaucracy for their followers outstripped the executive's capacity to accommodate those demands.

Carlos Lleras, a bitter critic of clientelism and factionalism, proposed a constitutional reform that would turn things in the direction of increased authority for the president and technocrats. First proposed in 1966, the reform was blocked by Liberal legislators from the Caribbean coast who were more upset by Lleras's sympathies for agrarian reform than by his swipe at legislative power. Two years later, backed by a concerted campaign in the media to mobilize middle-class opinion in his favor, the Lleras reform was passed.

The 1968 reform limited the size of Congress and eliminated rotten boroughs through a revision of the proportional representation system at the departmental level. Save for a narrow range of subjects touching on the operation of the parties themselves, the two-thirds requirement for passage of legislation was eliminated. Although the reform stripped Congress of much of its power to make economic policy, its members were given increased allotments of "parliamentary aid" to help them grease patronage networks and guarantee their reelection. Economic planning was elevated to a constitutional precept and concentrated in the executive branch, which was charged with formulating periodic development plans. The executive was now able, in addition, to intervene in the central bank's policy making and to decree a state of "economic emergency" in order to set policy by decree without resort to a full-fledged state of siege. The legal attributes of departments and *municipios* were redefined to promote a more rational transfer of national funds to the poorest jurisdictions.

The FN successfully faced down its most significant political challengers, the MRL and later ANAPO. This success was made possible by the support of business leaders, who coordinated wage policy with the state, helped expand coverage of basic public services, and at least intermittently adopted reformist attitudes. But an even more basic factor was the monopoly structure of the FN itself, which fatally weakened would-be challengers.

From the beginning of the FN in 1958, López focused his attacks on the mandated alternation of the presidency, which he considered undemocratic, although he did accept party parity in legislative bodies as a necessary evil, given Colombia's recent history. He gathered a group of modernizers around him in the Bogotá newspaper *La Calle*, and his MRL quickly became a de facto socialist movement within the Liberal Party; while it included many Marxists and idealistic students, it also attracted highly sectarian Liberal politicians of no particular ideology but who were strongly opposed to any arrangement founded on a pact with the Conservatives. For a time López even enjoyed the tacit support of the Moscow-line Communist Party. His objective was to win so many votes in the 1962 presidential elections — which he could freely contest as a Liberal but was legally barred from winning, according to the odd logic of FN democracy — that he could become a major player in Liberal politics. His 600,000 votes achieved that objective, and he quickly swung back from the left to the Liberal center with an energetically anticommunist speech in Ibagué in late 1962 that drove most leftists from the faction. The MRL, much diminished by López's progressive return to the Liberal fold, was finally wound up in 1967 when its leader was named the first governor of the newly created department of Cesar. From there he would set the strategy that carried him to the presidency in 1974, when the enforced alternation provision of the FN expired.

ANAPO was initially created as a vehicle for restoring the public honor of General Rojas after his trial and conviction by the Senate in 1958–59. The movement appeared in 1962 and took off after the Supreme Court annulled the Senate trial and restored Rojas's political rights; he threw his efforts into the movement when he realized that the military had made peace with civilian politicians and had no inclination to return him to power through a coup. He appealed for support in speeches that highlighted the polarization of oligarchy and *pueblo*, punctuated by jabs at the high cost of living. He concentrated power in the hands of a small circle of acolytes led by his daughter, "the people's captain."

ANAPO's improving electoral fortunes over the 1960s can be traced to several factors. It was the only political group to endorse the Vatican's stance against artificial birth control, expressed in Pope Paul VI's 1968 encyclical *Humanae vitae*. This position made Rojas a favorite of many rural priests and won him the sympathy of anti-imperialist radicals, who saw birth control as another manifestation of the United States' domination of Latin America. The increase in urban unemployment over the decade was an additional issue that Rojas exploited in ANAPO's favor, and he was able to tap into the anger of some bosses of both parties who were marginalized by the Lleras constitutional reform of 1968. He also benefited from timing: whereas López's presidential candidacy in 1962 was strictly for show, because of the FN's allocation of the presidency that year to a Conservative, Rojas actually was a Conservative and would have been entitled to assume the presidency in 1970 with a plurality of votes.

Indeed, the night of April 19, 1970, seemed to augur a decisive Rojas victory, but the Lleras regime suddenly ordered a stop to the live transmission of incoming vote tallies; when Colombians awoke the next morning, they were told that an influx of rural votes in favor of the official FN Conservative candidate, Misael Pastrana, had given him the victory over Rojas. Lleras himself ratified the result and declared a curfew to forestall unrest in the cities. Several days later, Rojas quietly accepted the outcome despite widespread belief that it was fraudulent.

Pastrana's style proved decisive in defusing the tense situation brought about by Rojas and his populist challenge to the FN. He recouped Conservative votes lost to ANAPO by manipulating budgetary support for ANAPO-controlled town councils, either cutting them off or co-opting them. He made effective use of the Agricultural Marketing Institute (IDEMA) and its distribution of subsidized foodstuffs by targeting pro-Rojas neighborhoods and towns for massive "people's markets," which were gratefully received. He employed a social-Christian language which offered a modernized Conservative ideology, a turn that was predictably and strongly opposed by the old Gómez faction, now led by Laureano's son Álvaro.

In 1971, with the FN scheduled to be dismantled over the next several years,

Rojas formally launched ANAPO as a third party at a mass rally in his home province of Boyacá. But the experiment could not withstand Pastrana's mastery of carrot-and-stick politics, Rojas's poor health, and the transfer of leadership to the erratic María Eugenia. Even before the general's death in 1974 ANAPO was fast disappearing from the electoral map. However, a splinter group known as Socialist ANAPO, working with dissidents from the FARC guerrillas, decided to take up the banner of the "stolen" elections of 1970 by founding a new armed group, the April 19th Movement, known as M-19.

The Guerrillas of the Left

The Cuban Revolution of 1959 gave a continental dimension to the guerrilla operations in Colombia and new prospects for the Colombian military as it continued to hone its post-*bogotazo* role of guaranteeing "internal public order." With its 1960s program of Civic-Military Action, the military took on economic and social development functions alongside an aggressive armed response to insurgency. The use of paramilitary forces, an especially destructive aspect of the Violencia era, was expanded in 1961 and enshrined in law in 1965 and again in 1968. One of the advantages of using not-quite-official counterinsurgency forces, of course, was that they could carry out "dirty war" operations without directly tarnishing the state or its armed forces.

On the guerrilla side, the successful Cuban insurgency influenced the formation of several armed groups, of which two significant ones still survive, the FARC and ELN. The revolutionary guerrillas of the 1960s were several things at once: the continuation of the most radicalized Liberal fighting spirit of the high Violencia, the response of part of the Colombian left to the Liberal-Conservative oligarchy's monopoly of legal politics under the National Front, and an opportunity to bring the Colombian peasantry into a socialist project from which they had been excluded.

The dominant revolutionary theory of the era was emphatic on this last point: Che Guevara and the French theorist Régis Debray declared that the *foco*, or rural zone controlled by the guerrillas, could create and accelerate the conditions for national revolution identified by Lenin. They agreed with Franz Fanon, theorist of the Algerian independence struggle, that cities represented bastions of imperialist domination and would corrupt active revolutionaries. Liberation would come from the countryside. Support for this notion also came from China, where Maoist theory, derived from the experience of the 1930s and 1940s, predicted that the countryside would "engulf the city," just as Asia, Africa, and Latin America would engulf Western capitalism. This rejection of Leninist theory with its reliance on an urban working class was reinforced by the student protest movements of the 1960s, whether in Berkeley, Paris, or Mexico City, where the leftist fringe of protestors embraced (however psychedelically) Mao's "Little Red Book," the Vietnamese revolutionary leader Ho Chi Minh, and Che Guevara rather than Leninist methods and Stalinist outcomes.

In Colombia Guevara's style of revolutionary voluntarism made some minor inroads among university students, who in the 1960s accounted for only 3 percent of the population aged 18 to 24. Of the student leaders of the era who were identified with revolutionary politics, many were spiritually or physically immolated on the altar of the armed guerrilla war, which lost its romantic aura only with the disastrous seizure of the Palace of Justice by M-19 in November 1985.

By the early 1960s the guerrillas had already established some *focos*, "liberated" by the MOEC (which soon disappeared), the Castroite ELN, and the Maoist EPL. The ELN set up operations in a jungle area of western Santander, near Barrancabermeja and San Vicente de Chucurí, and not far from the departmental capital, Bucaramanga. This region had a noteworthy if erratic tradition of popular mobilization and peasant land colonization; San Vicente in particular was associated with Liberal guerrillas in the War of the Thousand Days and with those of Rafael Rangel during the Violencia, and it was briefly held by Liberal insurrectionists in April 1948. The area adjacent to the Barrancabermeja–Bucaramanga railway line was the site of a "Bolshevik" uprising led by the Socialist Revolutionary Party (PSR) in 1928. More recently, the oil workers of Barrancabermeja and the students of Bucaramanga's public university were known for their militancy.

This promising revolutionary base was represented in the first group of would-be guerrillas who slipped off to Cuba for military training in 1963–64: they included peasants, university students, and oil workers. This military leadership, which quickly took control of the ELN, never moved beyond a purely tactical notion of the *foco* to consider how to transform the region socially and politically. The local population came to hold them in the same low regard as the peasants of Bolivia held Che Guevara during his disastrous campaign of 1967—an outcome he had predicted from a theoretical perspective in his 1960 book on guerrilla warfare.

The incorporation of student leaders in the guerrilla movement would end in tragedy. According to Jaime Arenas, a prominent student militant who was assassinated by the ELN in 1972 in Bogotá, the group's guerrilla camps were hotbeds of hostility to the "petty bourgeoisie of the city." Many of the student leaders were killed by their guerrilla comrades, sentenced to death for one or another deviation. Others were killed on wildly dangerous missions whose alleged purpose was to temper them for combat, the most famous case being Camilo Torres Restrepo, the "revolutionary priest" who died in his first armed encounter with the army, only weeks after joining the ELN.

Disconnected as it was from the people in whose name it operated, the ELN survived on Cuban assistance in the form of money, arms, and military training; later its tactics of kidnapping for ransom and extortion of cattle ranches were so successful that it needed no outside assistance. When victory over the Colombian state proved more elusive than its leadership had optimistically projected, in view of Castro's three years in the mountains before he took Havana, the ELN started to look more and more like a private caudillo army, its activities confined to marginal colonization zones. In the early 1970s the group attempted to cross the Magdalena River into the gold mining region of northeastern Antioquia, but was almost totally wiped out by the military. For the rest of the decade the ELN was largely a memory, but in the early 1980s it rose again like a phoenix, particularly in Arauca, along the Venezuelan border, newly flush with extortable wealth from oil exploration.

The EPL was the fruit of the Sino-Soviet split in the world communist movement, and in following Chinese revolutionary strategy the group eventually took a different road from that of the ELN. The EPL did initially seek to develop *focos*, but it turned to Mao's "Yenan path" and embraced his vision of "prolonged popular war," with guerrillas striving to be "fish in the water" of large regions rather than the lords of small regions. This ideal took several years to realize, but ultimately the vast Urabá region of Antioquia, with its mixed underclass of land colonizers and wage-earning banana plantation workers, became the EPL's principal setting for the prolonged war it envisioned.

Unlike these two organizations, the FARC came out of the Violencia, and (more indirectly) out of the agrarian and indigenous mobilizations of the 1920s and 1930s. It emerged without any mediation by university-trained intellectuals, although until the 1980s it was tied to the Communist Party with all of the intellectual baggage that entailed. Its commander, Manuel Marulanda (Tirofijo, or Sure Shot), is Latin America's longest-active guerrilla leader by a wide margin. When the ban on the Communist Party (imposed by the Rojas dictatorship rather than by the rabidly anticommunist Laureano Gómez) was lifted with the establishment of the National Front, the party started to rebuild its never fully inactive organizations within the student and union movements. For the countryside, its slogan and organizational reality was "mass self-defense," and it even achieved the election of the longstanding Communist peasant guerrilla Juan de la Cruz Varela to Congress. He was elected on López's MRL slate because of the FN's exclusion of explicit third-party representation; at this early moment in the MRL's trajectory, López had not yet broken with the radical left.

President Valencia, subjected to constant browbeating by the *alvarista* (formerly *laureanista*) faction of his own Conservative Party for the existence of "sixteen independent republics" on Colombian territory, all of them at the service of "international communism," decided in 1964 on a large-scale military offensive against Marquetalia in southern Tolima. This was Marulanda's home base, and the attack was carefully planned in accordance with U.S. counterinsurgency doctrines formulated in response to the Cuban Revolution. The military campaign against Marquetalia and several other such "republics" was successful, but the guerrillas were never captured or killed in significant numbers; instead they formed an "armed colonization" in other areas and adopted mobile tactics. This was, in a sense, the birth of the FARC as a national organization of dispersed and shifting regional "fronts," which today number over forty. Their collective level of organization, discipline, and cultivation of local support networks far exceeded anything the Colombian military had seen in its successful extermination of Liberal and Conservative guerrilla holdouts from the Violencia. With the growth of the FARC the Communist Party won some degree of prestige or at least notoriety at home and abroad, as its "armed wing" was both stronger and more peasant-dominated than any of its rivals at home or comrade organizations in the region.

The Dismantling of the National Front and the Crisis of the Liberal Machine

The scheduled return to fully competitive politics, and the decrepitude (physical and political) of many FN leaders, predictably increased competition among politicians at the regional and national levels. The 1968 constitutional reform permitted parties to register multiple electoral lists as their own, in deference to the party factionalism of the era, and politicians developed the strategy of running on multiple lists in order to take advantage of the peculiarities of proportional representation Colombian style. This new generation of savvy operators, known as departmental "barons," largely displaced the more localized bosses of the Violencia era. They were useful to the state, in that they preserved its legitimacy without the need for consistent or expensive social policies.

There was also transformation in the relations between the business leadership and the political families. During Carlos Lleras's presidency public disputes already arose between the government and industrialists or landowners, whose interests were increasingly specific and fragmented. Under Pastrana there were disputes about the government's creation of a new financial sector in support of housing construction. The previously dominant industrialists' association (ANDI) lost ground to more specialized entities covering the metallurgical, chemical, and plastics sectors, while there was a similar fragmentation on the agricultural side with the rise of trade associations devoted to the interests of cotton, rice, and African palm cultivators.

Without true opposition parties, the political class under the FN lost touch with national interests while it worried about the mechanics of distributing favors at the local level. In rural areas it preferred the easier work of seeking financial support from landowners and businessmen to the mobilization of peasants who had been promised agrarian reform. The middle classes and urban working class were increasingly marginalized by these practices. In general, the distance between ordinary people and political institutions widened during and immediately after the FN period, especially after the collapse of ANUC and the stagnation of the labor movement. In this setting of generalized discontent, which reached its zenith in the late 1970s, many Colombians saw little difference between opposing a discredited state and condoning or even applauding acts of political violence; in short, there was a serious problem of political legitimacy.

López's alliance with Liberal political barons led by Julio César Turbay Ayala led to eight years of *turbolopismo* (1974–82), limited only by the residual bipartisan demands of the FN. (Until 1991 the opposition party enjoyed the right of "equitable participation" in the Cabinet, under Article 120.) Despite his noisy break with the Communists in the early 1960s, one of López's earliest presidential acts was to legalize the union confederation they dominated, the CSTC. At the same time he surrounded himself with foreign-trained economists committed to what would later be known as neoliberalism. To take the sting out of the failure and abandonment of agrarian reform, these technocrats adopted the World Bank's advice (and took its financing) to launch programs in integrated rural development (DRI) and in nutrition (PAN). These programs were focused on smallholder regions, especially those close to guerrilla *focos*, and had some success in stabilizing rural society through the strengthening of a middle peasantry.

The twilight of the FN coincided with a transnational sea-change in economic and social policy under the aegis of the World Bank, which urged a "rethinking and reformulation of the state." The import-substitution industrialization model led by Argentina, Brazil, Mexico, and Chile entered a period of profound crisis, which the oil shock of the 1970s and rising interest rates would further propel into a massive debt crisis requiring severe fiscal adjustments. In Colombia, the bottlenecks of the industrialization process were already apparent by the late 1960s, and in the 1970s there was a modest shift toward import liberalization, exemplified by the country's accession to the General Agreement on Tariffs and Trade (GATT) in 1975 and again in 1980. The more prescriptive aspects of state economic planning and direct state investment in industry were abandoned during this period.

According to the new global orthodoxy, the "populist state" had been the cause of economic stagnation and deterioration and the supreme source of corruption and inefficiency. The solution was to give free reign to markets through the liberalization of foreign trade and the financial sector, the privatization of state enterprises (including banks) and public services, and overall fiscal decentralization. López believed that embracing these principles would make Colombia "the Japan of South America"—not by following that country's model of intensive industrialization, but by "rescuing Colombia's agricultural and mining vocation." In this spirit the government began to question the economic and social costs of industrialization, over the bitter opposition of ANDI, and concluded that the process had harmed Colombia's economic efficiency and competitiveness.

In the end the López regime had little to show for its talk of trade liberalization. Although it did reduce tariffs, a new coffee export bonanza once again saved the captains of Colombia's protected industries: flush with coffee-related revenues, the government could not invoke the need to curtail spending by reducing subsidies to manufacturers. Without that rationale, there was little possibility of successful liberalization, given the continuing political weight of the industrialists.

The government had pledged that the benefits of the coffee bonanza of 1976 would flow to the cultivators, but fulfillment of this promise had significant consequences. In order to control the inflationary pressure produced by this massive inflow of income, the government cut the salaries of public employees and postponed the disbursement of foreign credits it had already received for expanding the electricity grid.

In the financial sector López did proceed with effective liberalization. Real interest rates were increased, and the government implemented "Decision 24" of the Andean Pact to put foreign-owned banks in the hands of local owners. This benefited a handful of individuals and financial groups, most notoriously Jaime Michelsen Uribe and his Grupo Gran Colombiano, without achieving the government's goal of redeploying the financial sector's resources in the national interest.

Like his father, Alfonso López Pumarejo, during his second administration (1942–45), López faced accusations of corruption and considered resigning the presidency. Unlike his father, López completed his term, although the scandals clouded public reception of the genuinely novel parts of his program—the introduction of civil divorce, renegotiation of the Concordat with the Vatican, and judicial reform.

In this atmosphere of widespread distrust of government, M-19's vague ideology and theatrical armed actions captured public attention. In 1974 the group stole Simón Bolívar's sword from a downtown Bogotá museum, declaring that it would be returned when Colombia was "free." Far less popular were its "people's prisons," where kidnap victims were held for ransom, and its murder of José Raquel Mercado, an old-line pro-government union official whom the group accused of betraying the working class.

Although the urban poor almost never resorted to organized violence, the government was unable to prevent their participation in general strikes under a variety of banners—some demanding improved public services, others in sympathy with the strikes of doctors or teachers, still others in support of land invasions organized by a weakened but still active ANUC. The most serious of these general strikes, in September 1977, was endorsed by all three union confederations, even the two usually closer to the government. The root cause of the unrest was inflation, which that year reached 33 percent. Apparently the government took more seriously than union leaders the idea of the general strike as prelude to the collapse of bourgeois authority, promoted earlier in the century by the French theorist Georges Sorel, because it prepared a forceful, even violent response. The number of deaths caused by military repression of the strikers is still a matter of speculation, but the regime's unpopularity reached new highs.

López, however, pointedly rejected new legislation demanded by the top thirty-three military leaders in the aftermath of the strike. Their petition represented a Colombian version of the "national security" orientation imposed by the dictatorships in Chile, Argentina, Uruguay, and several years earlier in Brazil. The president replied that changes on that scale would require a constituent assembly, and he did win legislative approval for convoking one; but when the Supreme Court declared the idea unconstitutional, he let the matter rest.

In the 1978 elections Julio César Turbay, representative par excellence of the Liberal political class, narrowly defeated the Conservative candidate, Belisario Betancur. Turbay, less inhibited than his predecessor on security questions, revived the generals' petition in the form of the Security Statute of 1978, the most extensive collection of restrictions on civil liberties since the fall of the Rojas dictatorship. The statute created new offenses and increased the penalties for existing ones; it also subjected civilians to military courts-martial and established censorship over radio and television coverage of armed conflicts. The changes were positively received by business groups, most politicians, and much of the church hierarchy, and were applied so zealously that over 60,000 people were detained in the first year. In the media, apart from Communist publications, only the magazine *Alternativa* systematically criticized human rights abuses. Although nominally directed toward all forms of organized crime, the statute was employed only against the left—and not just the guerrilla left—rather than against drug traffickers or kidnapping networks.

The drug trade ushered in a new phase of criminality. It melded with a preexisting illegal trade in emeralds, which made the Muzo region of western Boyacá one of the most violent in the country, and the development of marihuana cultivation between Barranquilla and Maicao on the Caribbean coast brought unprecedented violence to that region as well. The west of the country, with its long history of contraband trade, was the incubator of cocaine mafias, which would achieve international prominence over the next decade.

During his campaign Turbay had emphasized the importance of suppressing drug trafficking, and in 1979 he negotiated an extradition treaty with the United States. Several years later the Supreme Court, perhaps cowed by the traffickers' terror campaign, struck down the treaty on procedural grounds. Drug money entered the country freely, through the no-questions-asked "sinister window" in the central bank and through unregulated currency exchange businesses. The cash inflow was stimulated by periodic tax amnesties, and the money was laundered in rural and urban real estate, the service sector, and contraband imports. Some fraction of it ended up in the increasingly costly campaigns of Colombian politicians.

There was substantial continuity in economic policy between López and Turbay, especially regarding trade liberalization. Turbay's acceleration of financial deregulation proved costly to the official Liberal coalition in electoral terms, but his government's much-maligned social programs (collectively known as the National Integration Plan, or PIN) were the most effective and redistributive of the entire period—surpassing the institutionally and rhetorically more ambitious plans of Belisario Betancur (1982–86) and Virgilio Barco (1986–90), for example.

The guerrilla left stepped up its campaign of killings and kidnappings, and the Colombian military was increasingly dismissive of human rights concerns. A report by Amnesty International in April 1980 detailed thirty-three military detention centers where some fifty forms of torture were administered, and in another report later that year AI documented six hundred individual cases of military abuses.

Two spectacular actions by M-19 demonstrated that for wide sectors of the Colombian population there was not much distinction between the government's unpopularity and the state's basic illegitimacy. The theft of 5,000 rifles from a military depot in Bogotá over the 1979 Christmas vacation (thanks to the patient construction of a tunnel from an adjacent private house) and the seizure of the Dominican Republic's embassy during a reception attended by fifty-seven foreign diplomats, including the U.S. ambassador and the papal nuncio, were unprecedented coups for their audacity and propaganda value. While the military did recover most of the rifles in subsequent searches, after arduous negotiations Turbay agreed to permit the guerrilla detachment that seized the embassy to depart for Cuba—most likely with a ransom payment.

The clearest sign of the government's growing international image problem came later in Turbay's presidency, when the government broke off relations with Cuba after discovering that a group of 160 guerrillas in the Pacific coastal region of Tumaco had received military training by the Castro regime. Colombia requested an urgent meeting of the Organization of American States to discuss Cuba's role, but the request was buried in an avalanche of headlines when the novelist Gabriel García Márquez, far and away Colombia's most famous cultural figure, left the country under Mexican diplomatic protection. He accused the Colombian government of planning to imprison him for alleged sympathies with M-19. The allegation may or may not have been true, but it was enough to nullify any sympathy the government hoped to win by playing the Cuban card.

With its string of public successes, M-19 ("La Eme," as it was popularly called) turned its attention to urban organizing, especially among young people in the slums and "pirate neighborhoods" of Bogotá and Cali. Meanwhile the more traditional guerrilla groups looked to rural areas, especially recently settled colonization zones. Flush with resources from extortion and contraband, the guerrillas could offer rural young people better prospects than the labor market could, as well as the sense of adventure and crude empowerment that came from carrying a rifle. There was no colonization frontier without a guerrilla front, and some guerrillas were themselves active in expanding the colonizations.

The Security Statute notwithstanding, every group in Colombia with even a modicum of organization seemed to take the law into its own hands during the Turbay years. When a young woman from a drug trafficking family was kidnapped for ransom by M-19, her family recruited others to join them in establishing Colombia's first modern paramilitary group, Death to Kidnappers (MAS), in Medellín. Organized crime, in effect, became the preferred way to solve any conflict. Rural political action was caught in a free-fire zone, as in the case of the Regional Indigenous Council of Cauca (CIRC), the organizational legacy of the great indigenous leader Manuel Quintín Lame earlier in the twentieth century: local landowners pursued a campaign of assassination against its leaders, and the guerrillas made offers of protection which could be refused only at the organization's peril. In the colonization zones affected by drug trafficking, the situation was practically Hobbesian.

Buoyed by his successful negotiation of a peaceful end to the embassy stand-off, Turbay sought to press his peace credentials by amnestying imprisoned guerrillas, but they rejected his conditions and nothing came of the gesture. This failure lent credibility to López's belief, expressed during the previous presidential campaign, that the guerrillas would negotiate for peace only if they were on the verge of military defeat, as was the case with Venezuela's leftist guerrillas in the 1960s.

Nineteen-eighty was the year of financial scandals, especially in Jaime Michel-sen's Grupo Gran Colombiano, which offered a valuable glimpse into the back-room deals that characterized the *turbolopista* political and economic elite. Mi-chelsen created a holding company in which he and his son were the principal shareholders. The Grupo eventually controlled some 168 firms, a mix of re-spected and long-established companies such as the Banco de Colombia and others of recent creation which turned out to be spurious, created for the sole purpose of moving funds around and consolidating liabilities in firms where outside investors carried the risk. Industrial firms caught in the Grupo's web were looted to buy still more firms. Eventually the entire operation fell like the proverbial house of cards, and newspaper revelations of the extent of the government's facilitation of the Grupo's operations deepened divisions within the Liberal Party and permitted the electoral triumph of the Conservative Belisario Betancur in 1982.

Betancur's Propaganda for Peace

The new president was a stereotypical early-rising Antioquian with a varied political past. He began his public life as an unconditional follower of Lau-reano Gómez in the late 1940s, and as such he opposed the Rojas dictatorship; he was a founding participant in the National Front, but in 1962 he started to cast off his allegiances—starting with Gómez himself—to become more of a free agent unencumbered by a political machine. He knew how to take advan-tage of disputes among his rivals, and while his campaigns of 1970 and 1982 fell short of victory, in 1982 the chasm between the official Liberal candidacy of the former president Alfonso López Michelsen and the dissident candidacy of Luis Carlos Galán (backed by another former president, Carlos Lleras Restrepo) provided him with a unique opportunity. Apart from the split in the Liberal vote, many urban voters not identified with the Conservatives were fed up with the cronyism and scandals of the López and Turbay years and alarmed by the prospect of López's return to the presidency.

Elected under the banner of a "National Movement," Betancur quickly sent to the Liberal-majority Congress a proposal for an amnesty and pardon more generous than any of its modern predecessors with the exception of the Rojas amnesty of 1953. But he never formulated a clear strategy for achieving peace, defined as a cease-fire and the reincorporation of the guerrillas to civilian life and peaceful politics. That question was referred to a new bipartisan "peace commission," which was hobbled by the lack of military participation and the standoffish attitude of the political class. This was but one instance when it could be said that Betancur's chief political asset, his lack of a political machine and independence from the main political families, was also his chief liability. Many members of the political class were instinctively hostile to him, reserving for him their most poisonous epithet: they called him a populist. They were ready to pounce on any evidence that Betancur might use the state's resources for political mobilization outside of the patronage systems they controlled.

During this period the United States focused increasingly on drug control and pressured Betancur to apply the extradition treaty. When Ronald Reagan visited Bogotá in December 1982 he hardly mentioned anything else. This elevation of drugs and extradition to the top of the United States' agenda complicated the peace process and Betancur's wider agenda of a "democratic opening" after the repressive Turbay years. Inasmuch as the supply created the demand, the war on drugs could not be won short of an essentially military-led strategy to suppress production.

The national press, business leaders, the political class, and (less publicly) the military all attacked the president's peace agenda, accusing him of being soft on communism; he was accused, in effect, of embracing M-19's criticism of Colombian democracy. His interest in attaching Colombia to the Nonaligned Movement, which many saw as a surrogate for Soviet interests, and to the Contadora peace process for Central America, in association with Venezuela and Panama, added to this hostility. Betancur had hoped that these foreign policy moves would show the guerrillas that Colombia was leaving behind a Cold War orientation and adopting a more nationalist and regionalist political identity.

The approval of the amnesty plan freed around a thousand prisoners, mostly affiliated with M-19, whose capture and trial under Turbay had been very costly to the image of the military and judicial system. Shortly afterward, the attorney general's office accused over fifty army officers of belonging to the MAS organization in the Magdalena Medio region of Santander and Antioquia, a colonization zone with predictable FARC presence. The military's growing anger at these events must be understood within a specifically Colombian context. Despite the armed conflict, Colombia consistently had one of the lowest military budgets per capita in Latin America, and the country had avoided the 1970s wave of harsh military dictatorships in the region. But the military did enjoy considerable autonomy in taking measures in defense of public order, and the National Front pact of 1958 came about in large part because of the military's acquiescence; so Betancur's innovations were seen to some extent as the breaking of an agreement.

The Betancur government had to face a budget deficit, waning foreign financing, and increasing interest rates on the foreign debt, and its lack of a legislative majority led the president to invoke López's invention, the "economic emergency" by decree. This was struck down by the Supreme Court, whose Liberal majority did not go unnoticed. With this route closed, Betancur staved off direct intervention by the IMF by agreeing to its "monitoring" of Colombian fiscal policy. He demonstrated to the private sector and to the political right that he was no economic populist: to continue his political reforms he gave up the social justice card and turned macroeconomic policy over to technocrats. The devaluation of the peso in 1985, accompanied by a drastic reduction in the budget deficit (achieved by freezing public-sector salaries and cutting education and housing programs) became an example in international circles of how to devalue without provoking inflation or deep recession. Although the "fiscal adjustment" of 1985 had severe effects on social spending and further impoverished the poorest Colombians, there was no general strike as in 1977; an attempt to organize one, led by the three labor confederations and the combative teachers' union, FECODE, failed and led to the downfall of several longtime labor leaders.

From this failure came the Unified Labor Confederation (CUT), which was founded in 1986 and soon claimed 80 percent of Colombia's union membership, including the public employees' union, FENALTRASE. Despite this unity, the CUT suffered from a split between blue-collar and white-collar members, leadership disputes, and financial and organizational problems. These limitations weakened the CUT's ability to contest the labor reforms of the Gaviria administration in the early 1990s, which did away with many labor laws after labeling them vestiges of economic populism that prevented the free market from functioning efficiently.

Betancur's government also had to face the consequences of Turbay's liberalization of the financial sector. One of the stated motives of his declaration of economic emergency was "the need to reestablish the confidence of the public and of the international financial sector in Colombian financial institutions." Between 1982 and 1985 five private banks were nationalized, in what observers considered a clear case of "socializing losses." Jaime Michelsen's collapsed empire entered the labyrinth of the judicial system, while the banker himself fled to Panama (where he advised General Manuel Noriega); he later returned to Colombia, was imprisoned briefly, and fled again.

Meanwhile the rural guerrilla groups had turned the peace process into a formidable propaganda weapon. Barred from attacking the guerrillas while peace talks were proceeding, the army worked with landowners to organize paramilitary groups that effectively cleansed entire regions of guerrilla sympathizers. The geographical reach of the paramilitaries extended from the Magdalena Medio to Caquetá in the south and to Urabá and Córdoba in the northwest.

As for the predominantly urban M-19, Betancur met with their leadership during a visit to Madrid in late 1983—a gesture that led the group to believe, mistakenly, that they were stronger than ever, and therefore needed to stage even more spectacular armed assaults. A wild and costly attack on Florencia (Caquetá) in April 1984, the first guerrilla attack on a departmental capital in modern times, was reported live on Colombia's private radio networks and threw the entire peace process into disarray. Surprisingly, only a few days later the Peace Commission reached a draft cease-fire with the FARC, known as the La Uribe Agreements. A few months later, the EPL and M-19 joined the cease-fire. By late 1984 only the ELN remained outside the process.

The Rise of the *Narco*, or the Challenge of the Pariah Capitalists

The political dimensions of the drug trade, a problem that had been brewing since the late 1970s, came to the fore in the early 1980s. The question was now widely posed: How could the "emerging bourgeoisie" wrought by the cocaine economy be brought into the mainstream, now that that their income exceeded that of their counterparts in coffee and oil? What political effects would such an integration bring—not to mention moral effects? There were reasons to hope for a positive outcome. There was a Colombian tradition of fortunes based on contraband and tax evasion making the transition to respectability. Also, there was no shortage of Colombian industries that could make good and productive use of hot money as investment capital. Lastly, there were recent institutional antecedents, including the tax amnesty of 1983 and Lopez's "sinister window" for turning foreign currency into pesos at the central bank.

But although these were all necessary conditions, they were not sufficient. They may have given false hope to drug barons who saw themselves not only as respectable businessmen but as political manipulators. The varying goals and techniques of the drug barons in their quest for legitimacy were behind the rise of the famous cartels of Medellín and Cali. While the Cali group was exclusively interested in business legitimacy and largely shunned the public eye, the Medellín group threw itself into party politics and civic movements. Pablo Escobar founded the Civics in Action faction of the Liberal Party in Medellín and won election as an alternate member of Congress in 1982. In the coffee department of Quindío, Carlos Lehder organized the Latin National Movement, whose ideology was a hodgepodge of Nazism, populism, and anti-imperialism; he even founded a daily newspaper to propound his views.

The two emerging cartels did not have a monopoly on Colombia's drug trade during this period; there was instead a regional mosaic of actors. The border regions—Bucaramanga and Cúcuta in the northeast, Nariño in the southwest, and the vast Amazon region from Villavicencio to Leticia—had their own cartels, and the coffee zone between Medellín and Cali had barons such as Lehder, who were even more aggressive than the Medellín group in entering the public realm in the region's principal cities.

The reaction of Colombia's national political leadership to this phenomenon was not uniform, either nationally or in individual regions. While many politicians were content to adopt a permissive attitude toward the drug barons' money and influence in politics during the cocaine bonanza years, which peaked in 1979–82, others such as Luis Carlos Galán categorically rejected their presence from the outset. Still others, while not embracing figures such as Lehder and Escobar, did seem willing to recognize their enormous spending in support of social projects ranging from low-cost housing to parks, even if that spending was intended in large part to garner votes.

Although the possible acceptance of these pariah capitalists was a Colombian issue, there was strong foreign interest and intervention in the debate. In the early 1980s the U.S. government stepped up pressure for the effective application of the 1979 extradition treaty. In response, the drug barons turned to bribery, nationalist rhetoric, and support of the paramilitary group MAS in its campaign of assassination against leftist leaders and rural people considered sympathetic to the guerrillas. The motivation here was to garner the support of the military and of the landowning elite — not to mention the fact that drug barons were now a substantial part of that elite in many regions.

The year 1984 opened a new phase in their campaign. Rodrigo Lara Bonilla, one of the leaders of Galán's moralistic New Liberalism faction and minister of justice under the continued National Front practice of "equitable participation" by political factions in the Cabinet, decided to press the issue of money laundering by the drug barons. He moved against soccer teams and bullrings that had drug connections, and with support from the U.S. Drug Enforcement Administration he sent the national police to destroy Escobar's drug laboratories in the tropical forest of Caquetá. A few days later Lara was assassinated in Bogotá on Escobar's orders; in response Betancur decided to apply the extradition treaty, and one of the first people sent to face charges in the United States was a prominent Medellín businessman, president of one of the city's soccer teams.

A few weeks later a group of "extraditables," as the most prominent Medellín barons now called themselves, met with the former president López and with the attorney general in a Panama hotel. According to López, the group claimed drug earnings that exceeded the income from Colombia's coffee trade, and that was without the participation of the Cali cartel. The group handed López a "unilateral memorandum" in which they condemned Lara's killing, reiterated their support for the Colombian political system, denied any connections with the FARC (as the U.S. ambassador had alleged), and emphasized that their only political interest was the elimination of extradition. In return, they promised to abandon the drug business, deposit all their funds in Colombia, dismantle their processing laboratories, and sell (with official oversight) the elaborate transportation and chemical businesses that supported the trade. The government, perhaps under U.S. diplomatic pressure, did not continue the discussions. At that point Escobar declared all-out war. His organization had never shied away from killing judges and witnesses in legal cases against them or journalists who had investigated them, but their violence now became more generalized.

Drug trafficking reverberated in the peace negotiations between the government and the guerrillas. Despite the barons' support of MAS, the labyrinthine path of the drug trade had led many traffickers into fleeting alliances with individual guerrilla fronts in order to safeguard fields, airstrips, and arms supplies. In Caquetá, for example, the FARC reigned supreme in drug production and processing zones, and during the cocaine bonanza everyone from peasant producers of coca leaf to the most powerful drug barons had to work with them. In many drug regions, however, by the mid-1980s the dominant armed group was MAS itself, in association with the army, police, and local politicians.

The Tragedy of the Palace of Justice

In light of Betancur's policy of "political opening" and the La Uribe agreements, the FARC and the Communist Party created a new legal political movement in 1985, the Patriotic Union (UP). To the church hierarchy, business groups, and the political class, especially the Liberals, this was yet another sign of the government's weakness, since the FARC had not turned over its arms and the UP was thus the legal arm of an illegal organization. They also argued that social reforms should be debated openly in Congress rather than in clandestine meetings with groups that rejected the existing political process.

The tactic of combining armed and unarmed "legal" activity was not unique to the FARC; even the ELN, which rejected the Betancur peace process, gave up its exclusively military line and started to infiltrate labor unions and civic movements. This was all very ominous for the political right, which increasingly considered Betancur a Colombian Kerensky—a dupe of insincere and opportunist guerrillas. This attitude certainly translated into concrete action, since 165 UP leaders were killed in the group's first year of activity.

M-19 harmed its political stock by performing poorly in the few public "National Dialogue" sessions that were organized at the government's request by business, student, and technocratic groups. Many of its demobilized leaders were killed by urban hit squads associated with the security services. In mid-1985 the group announced that it was withdrawing from the peace process, and it organized a National Guerrilla Coordinating Group (CNG) that included the

EPL (which also withdrew from the process), the ELN, and two smaller groups, the Quintín Lame Front in Cauca (as the name suggests, largely an indigenous group) and the Ricardo Franco Front, a dissident FARC group.

In November 1985, an M-19 unit took over the Palace of Justice, directly opposite the Presidential Palace on the Plaza de Bolívar in Bogotá. They killed two doormen in the initial assault and took the occupants hostage, including twelve members of the Supreme Court. The assault was intended as armed theater, in early M-19 style: Betancur was to be tried for "betraying the peace process." But what began as propaganda, and potentially even comedy, ended in national tragedy. Half an hour after the building was seized, the world watched as an army tank smashed in the front door of the court building, which was framed by the words of Francisco de Paula Santander: "Colombians, arms have given you independence, but laws will give you freedom."

The military operation to retake the building lasted twenty-seven hours and followed a scorched-earth strategy, even though the minister of defense assured the Cabinet (meeting just across the plaza, in the Presidential Palace) that everything was being done to safeguard the hostages, in accordance with Betancur's orders. Much of the building was consumed by flames, and between the fire and the fighting over a hundred Colombians lost their lives, including eleven of the twelve judges. Only one of the guerrillas came out alive, and eleven people seen leaving the building under military custody eventually joined the ranks of the disappeared.

Although most of the population condemned the guerrilla assault, there also was widespread condemnation of the official response, especially given the broadcast appeals of the court's president for a cease-fire. The Palace of Justice tragedy demonstrated the weakness of Colombian presidents in dealing with the military and the professional incompetence of the military itself, including its intelligence operations. But it also laid bare the desperation and political incompetence of M-19, and to an extent that of all of Colombia's guerrilla groups.

Betancur tried to unify the political system by claiming sole responsibility, but a majority of the public believed that it was the military that "defended democracy" by taking unilateral and primitive action. The congressional debates that followed were further proof of the ineptitude of Colombia's political class when it came to discerning and analyzing the country's problems. One noteworthy participant in the debate was a young Liberal senator from Risaralda named César Gaviria, who would become president a few years later; he joined Galán's New Liberalism in seeking censure of the government. But the debate sparked little interest among the public.

The years since the tragedy have done little to dispel the fog surrounding what really happened. In 1991 a judge ordered the M-19's leadership to appear in court on the grounds that the attack constituted a crime against humanity, not covered under the amnesty that brought the group into legal politics in 1990; in response, the political class hurriedly passed a new law to ratify the amnesty's applicability. Three years later the attorney general's office ordered the firing of the general who directed the military's retaking of the building—the Senate had recently promoted him after hearing of the impending punishment—but many of the media attacked the notion of "punishing a soldier who did his duty." There was a rough logic to this, since the guerrillas enjoyed the benefits of an overall amnesty. But the Supreme Court (whose membership, of course, had to be entirely reconstituted) backed the firing in the strongest terms: "We cannot lead the new generation into the confusion of believing that the government forces were heroes rather than aggressors. What occurred [in the Palace of Justice] was a pitiless massacre of people whose lives meant nothing to those who ordered and took part in these actions."

While the ruins were still smoldering on the Plaza de Bolívar, an eruption of the Nevado del Ruiz volcano buried the bustling town of Armero, principal market town of northern Tolima. Some 25,000 people perished in the deadliest natural disaster in Colombian history. A country still reeling from the events of a few weeks earlier now had a new reason to mourn. But amidst all this tragedy, the government did manage to negotiate an important constitutional reform that introduced the popular election of mayors—eliminated in Núñez's 1886 document—and gave more fiscal autonomy to *municipios*, in accordance with a recent priority of the World Bank.

Well into 1985 Betancur continued the dialogue with the FARC, and he laid out a vast National Rehabilitation Plan (PNR) to channel investment into the poorest and most violent rural areas. By the end of Betancur's term the peace process had lost whatever modest support it initially had, but the armed guerrilla struggle lost credibility as well. Between the M-19's demented assault on the Palace of Justice and the Ricardo Franco Front's torture and murder of 170 of its own guerrillas in Tacueyó (Cauca) for allegedly betraying the cause, the notion of the altruistic and heroic guerrilla was buried forever.

Popular Mobilization and New Types of Violence

In the 1986 presidential elections the Liberal candidate, Virgilio Barco Vargas, defeated the Conservative Álvaro Gómez Hurtado by a wide margin, in a campaign that was largely peaceful but somewhat reminiscent of the old sectarian campaigns. Barco appealed only to Liberal voters, and while Gómez sought support beyond the ranks of Conservatives, he had always been a partisan figure and was the son of the most partisan Conservative of them all, Laureano Gómez. Although Barco may prove to be the last candidate to appeal effectively to the Colombian Liberal tradition, he also was a thinker who developed a comprehensive vision about how to address poverty in Colombia, both rural and urban.

For the first time in decades, a national development plan recognized that the extreme poverty of at least one-quarter of the population was one of the nation's most serious problems. Economic growth was, in effect, a question of social justice. Poverty and the skewed distribution of income seemed to Barco like facts of life that disrupted both social peace and democratic institutions. This line of reasoning, which ironically was made possible by Betancur's tough austerity package under the IMF's guidance, implied concrete goals. The vast health-care infrastructure developed over the preceding decades had to be used more efficiently, with emphasis on broadening basic coverage. In education the dropout rates in primary schools had to be reduced, along with the number of students who repeated a grade. For working mothers, the Barco plan designed a national system of child-care centers in poor neighborhoods, operated by "neighborhood mothers." The plan resurrected Betancur's ambitious housing policies, and added a sweat-equity element that harked back to the Alliance for Progress in the early 1960s.

The reasoning behind these policies and goals was a bit circular, and the effects of poverty were perhaps confused with its causes. The overall plan could also be criticized for not broaching the issue of Colombia's social structure — in other words, what created such widespread poverty. But the most important issue was how to harmonize these ambitious social spending goals with overall macroeconomic targets. The fall in coffee prices, which quickened in 1989 when negotiations for a new world coffee agreement broke down, as well as constant attacks on oil export pipelines by the ELN had an impact on government revenues. The Barco administration had to cut spending, devalue the peso, and stimulate domestic agriculture through subsidies. All of this left the government agencies responsible for implementing the social plan without the money to do so.

Renewed official attention to the "war on poverty" gave rise to social and protest movements throughout the country. ANUC briefly returned to the public eye, especially after the government passed a new agrarian reform in 1988, and the CUT labor confederation was also more active. Local general strikes and peasant marches took place, sometimes even with the president's tacit support; the usual demands for land, work, and public services were now accompanied by calls for "the right to life," and for good reason. According to the Jesuit think tank CINEP, in 1988 583 people were "massacred" (defined as a killing of more than three people, as opposed to a selective murder), and the following year the number was 429; 37 percent of these victims belonged to leftist organizations and over half were peasants or indigenous persons. The traditional parties and the political class were notably absent from these new mobilizations, and often they opposed them behind the scenes. Liberal political bosses were particularly concerned about the possibility that new social movements would destroy their electoral niches.

The landslide Liberal victory in 1986 enabled Barco to offer the Conservatives just three Cabinet posts, an offer they predictably refused. For the first time since the start of the National Front there was genuine single-party government (Liberals occupied all of the ministries except Defense, held by a general), and Conservatives had to oppose the government from a position outside it. The popular election of mayors, which began in 1988, further splintered the political class, since many from outside the established factions were elected even in the larger cities. To make matters worse, these new mayors and town councils enjoyed new resources and so could disregard local political barons in spending them.

Barco put new resources into Betancur's National Rehabilitation Plan and increased the decision-making power of technocrats, to the further disgust of the political class, which initially enjoyed substantial influence. But at the local level the PNR necessarily had to operate with the approval of the guerrillas, who approved individual projects.

In 1986 the rightist paramilitaries stepped up an extermination campaign against rural activists whom they considered communists and against the UP's local activists. In 1986 and 1987 some three hundred UP leaders were killed, among them the party's national leader, Jaime Pardo Leal. The paramilitary offensive extended to human rights organizations as well as union leaders, especially the teachers' union. It is estimated that some three thousand UP members were killed during this period.

The drug lords also increased their murderous activities during the Barco years. The Bogotá newspaper *El Espectador*, which had adopted a hard line against the influence of the drug trade in Colombian politics, was singled out for retribution, and its publisher was assassinated in late 1986. In response to this and other killings, the government established a commission to study the antiterrorist laws of several European countries and report back on how Colombia's laws could be strengthened. The killing of the UP's leader and of the attorney general, Carlos Mauro Hoyos, as well as the kidnappings of the Bogotá mayoral candidate Andrés Pastrana and the renowned sculptor Rodrigo Arenas Betancur, were all attributed to Pablo Escobar's organization. The government passed a new and more sophisticated version of Turbay's despised 1978 Security Statute, now called the Defense of Democracy Statute, but the violence did not let up.

By September 1988 the country had endured a long season of rural massacres and urban terrorism. On the heels of M-19's release of the former presidential candidate Álvaro Gómez after six months' captivity, Barco announced a new "peace initiative" which recognized that the drug trade was a political issue insofar as it now centered on the policy question of extradition. According to the Penal Code, political crimes were committed for altruistic motives. The decidedly nonaltruistic nature of the drug lords' violence put them in a different legal and moral category from the guerrillas. Ennobled by this official distinction, a militarily weakened M-19 agreed to restart negotiations. They were supported in this initiative by Gómez, who seemed to have succumbed to the Stockholm syndrome during his captivity. The man who had led the opposition to the lukewarm agrarian reform of 1961 now said that the failure of that reform was a source of Colombia's current problems.

Ideology counted for much less for M-19 than for the FARC or ELN, and with most of M-19's founders dead, the new generation of leaders saw a more promising future in party politics than in social movements, where their rivals had a better foothold after years of infiltration. On the government side, some of the peace negotiators saw successful negotiations as fodder for future politi-

212 An Elusive Legitimacy

cal stardom, and they handled the talks far more effectively than in the past. M-19's surrender of its arms was a public relations spectacular on which the Liberals sought to capitalize. Around this time the majority faction of the Maoist EPL also made peace with the government, but the FARC and ELN, which represented the vast majority of Colombia's leftist guerrillas, were stronger and better financed than ever, and they joined forces in the Simón Bolívar Guerrilla Coordinating Group (CGSB).

In August 1989 Luis Carlos Galán, the charismatic leader of the New Liberalism group and early favorite in the 1990 presidential elections, was killed at a political rally outside Bogotá. The killing was probably ordered by Pablo Escobar, possibly in cooperation with old-line politicians who saw Galán as a threat to their patronage networks. Galán's death ended any possibility of a dialogue with the cartels, and Barco immediately launched an unprecedented crusade against them. In the following two weeks the military arrested over 10,000 people (none of whom were leading figures in the drug trade), confiscated 550 properties, and seized hundreds of small planes. This sudden offensive created huge legal and administrative problems, and it also showed just how pervasive were the links between the illegal and legal economies: knowingly or not, many business people had contractual relationships of all sorts with drug traffickers. The overall picture was far more complex than a purely military strategy could handle effectively, especially since the military assistance provided by the United States seemed better suited to fighting guerrillas than reducing the drug trade.

The extraditables, a group that was largely coterminous with the Medellín cartel, now declared that they would cross the line from selective violence against government officials to total war: "We will not respect the families of those who have not respected our families. We will burn and destroy the oligarchy's industries and properties." In late 1989 their bombs destroyed *El Espectador* and the Bucaramanga *Vanguardia Liberal*, the headquarters of the national intelligence service, and an Avianca plane in mid-flight. At the same time they called in all their debts among the political class. In December 1989 Congress came very close to adopting a law that would have called for a national referendum on the extradition issue, something the government strongly opposed. The initiative fell short only when the police located and killed Gonzalo Rodríguez Gacha, one of the Medellín group's most feared leaders, thus showing that the official policy of confrontation had some chance of success.

Many other prominent figures died in the free-fire zone that was 1989–90, including the presidential candidates of the UP, Bernardo Jaramillo, and the M-19, Carlos Pizarro. In both cases the finger of blame pointed to the cartels, though M-19 alleged that the security services were responsible for the death of its leader. The UP abstained from the 1990 elections, which were won by the Liberal César Gaviria with a little less than half the vote. Before his death Galán had entrusted Gaviria with the leadership of his campaign precisely because of his strong ties to the traditional political barons; Gaviria's status as successor to Galán was unexpectedly enshrined by Galán's teenaged son in his funeral eulogy. Gaviria was the only candidate who promised to maintain Barco's hard line against the drug lords. In early 1990, during the last few months of Barco's government, the extraditables seemed to recognize the futility of their violent campaign and repeated their promise to give up their trafficking and turn over their laboratories and arms. At the same time, however, they kidnapped relatives of prominent political leaders, not for ransom but for a return to negotiations with a "commission of notables" to consist of three former presidents, the cardinal, and the leader of the UP.

Despite eight peaceful transfers of power from one presidency to another and the uninterrupted functioning of all three branches of government, the Colombian political system found itself at a crossroads, just as it had in 1957. But the society and the economy were not at all the same.

Chapter 6

GREAT TRANSFORMATIONS
WITHIN CONTINUITY

*T*he processes of social and economic modernization picked up speed in the second half of the twentieth century. All the conventional signs were there: declines in the birth and death rates, increases in life expectancy and literacy, the geographic expansion of financial and administrative services and of transportation and telecommunications networks, and an 8 percent annual growth rate in electricity production since mid-century. There were also increases in sewer and potable water systems, while homeownership increased among the urban middle class. In the countryside the standard of rural housing, while still low, showed improvement.

But the social and economic gaps between classes, between city and country, and between the capitalist core and the periphery became more apparent. The Colombian model as it developed during these decades included high concentration of income, conspicuous consumption by the middle and upper classes, low rates of investment and savings, very low rates of effective taxation, and capital flight. Evidence of these imbalances can be seen in the waves of emigration from Colombia: two million abroad in 1994, at least four million by 1999.

The great cities were in some sense ruralized by a massive influx of immigrants, and a new mass culture emerged which was spread throughout the country by the increasingly monopolized media, particularly radio and television. The culture of violence not only failed to disappear but took new forms. This culture would combine explosively with the aggressiveness of organized crime, whose most obvious and most menacing form was, and is, drug trafficking.

The Population

Today Colombia is the third most populous country of Latin America, after Brazil and Mexico. Between 1951 and 1993 the population rose from 11.6 million to 35.9 million. The increase was rapid between 1950 and 1970; then it began a gradual decline to a still significant annual rate of 2.2 percent between the censuses of 1985 and 1993.

Until 1950 Colombia's birth and mortality rates were high. The use of anti-biotics and a general improvement in hygienic conditions (including the pro-vision of piped water) brought about a fall in mortality rates, particularly for children. Birth rates also began to fall after a lag of around ten years, from 6.76 per thousand in 1950–65 to only 2.92 in 1990–95. The phenomenon cascaded from better-off and more educated urban women to those in the poorer neighborhoods, then to women in small towns, and finally to women in the countryside.

Women are at the heart of social change, whether we consider the initiative to migrate from country to city, the increase in school attendance at all levels, or participation in the labor force, both formal and informal. In the course of one generation, beliefs, values, and behaviors have been transformed. Women decided to use various contraceptive methods, and some resorted to abortion—as many as one in four Colombian women have taken that step, despite its illegality and its large contribution to female mortality, thanks to the clandestine conditions in which abortions are performed.

The marriage rate declined and the average age of starting a family went up; separations and divorces increased. Average family size declined from six to five members between 1970 and 1990. In the larger cities the proportion of women to men increased, a phenomenon previously noted in the poor neighborhoods of Bogotá in the late nineteenth century. This imbalance had two consequences: female participation in the labor force increased, from 20 percent in 1960 to 40 percent in 1990, and so did the number of single and adolescent mothers. In response to these changes, starting in the mid-1970s family law began to eliminate—at least on paper—the legal discrimination that still weighed heavily on women and on children born out of wedlock.

The demographic cycle had repercussions in the labor market and in the development of public services. The formal labor market, with its "burden" of social benefits, was shredded by the arrival of new cohorts in search of work who ended up in the growing urban informal economy. From 1960 on, Colombia has consistently registered urban unemployment levels above the Latin American average, while the rural sector is plagued by low productivity, unemployment, and underemployment. With the sudden increase in the proportion of young people in the population between 1950 and 1970 and the rural exodus to the cities, it was obvious that the health, education, and housing infrastructures could not absorb the new urban Colombians.

After becoming younger, the population began to age again: in 1985, the proportion of Colombians under 18 years of age was 43.5 percent, only to fall to 39.9 percent by 1993. The growth of the working-age population by over 3 percent a year puts further pressure on the labor market. The cities and the unskilled services sector absorb the labor supply, but the rise of the tertiary sector of the economy tells us little about living standards: as far as income, status, and access to social security are concerned, peasant smallholders, street merchants in the cities, and artisans in the slums are basically in the same unsatisfactory situation.

Colombia has become a nation of emigrants. While internal migrations have long been an escape valve for the rural pressure cooker, since around 1960 migration abroad has been a means of escaping the national one. It eases unemployment and demand for housing and public services. The remittances that Colombians working abroad send to their families back home improve the families' income and the country's balance of payments. The numbers of Colombians who leave in search of temporary employment or better opportunities grow day by day. By the early 1980s around 800,000 worked in Venezuela, Ecuador, and the United States, most of them illegally. By 1990 the total number of emigrants reached 1.3 million, and by 2000 it reached 4 million as the destinations multiplied to include Europe. The migrant profile is in keeping with the international norm — disproportionately young, male, single, and with above-average educational attainment. The net loss to Colombian society and the economy is incalculable and sometimes quite obvious. For instance, around half of the physicians graduated by Colombia's public universities between 1965 and 1978 ended up working in the United States, even though Colombia had only one physician for every 2,500 inhabitants. While this figure fell to one per 1,250 by 1985, it was still high in comparison with the Latin American average of 1 per 940.

Education

Although the shameful level of illiteracy registered in 1951 fell over the decades, from 39 percent to only 12 percent by 1993, it is difficult to measure the level and quality of education in Colombia. According to the results of language and mathematics examinations administered by the Ministry of Education in 1992 to students in the third and fifth grades, "the achievement of a majority of students does not match their grade level." Similar results have been reported at the secondary level, where the difference in official scores between elite private schools (usually with a bilingual curriculum) and other schools both public and private is even more glaring.

At the close of the twentieth century Colombia still did not have a mass education system. Despite the increase in school attendance at all levels, the percentages of the population who complete primary and secondary school are still too low. In the late 1980s only 86 percent of children who were supposed to begin their education did so; of those, only 49 percent would reach fifth grade and 31 percent would reach ninth grade. Increases in school attendance are usually attributed exclusively to the initiative of the state and the role of politicians. However, some studies have shown that a good part of the impulse comes from mothers in poor neighborhoods and regions, whose patient but tenacious efforts are what get their children into the classroom, in the hope of a better life.

While Colombia experienced the same enormous growth in the numbers of students, teachers, administrators, and school buildings as other countries, the gains were badly distributed geographically and accompanied by a decline in quality. The regional inequality is especially pathetic on the Caribbean coast, except for the islands of San Andrés and Providencia, which enjoy the highest literacy rates in the country as a distant historical legacy. The gap between urban and rural education continues to be alarming.

The model that developed has a dual profile, in which a public sector provides primary and secondary education of low quality while at least some of the private institutions offer something better. Since education is rightly seen as a privileged means of access to the modern sector of the economy, any family with even a remote possibility of paying private school fees chooses to do so, in the hope of better quality. Overall, despite continuing economic development and even rising individual incomes, the inequality of access to good-quality education seems to be increasing rather than decreasing. Colombian society has not realized the dream of providing quality education to the whole population, and the state has failed to fulfill its basic duty of unifying the nation via the classroom. Private education is not merely a supplement to the public sector, but a necessary alternative.

The increase in school attendance was not accompanied by changes in the functioning of educational institutions or by greater training of teachers and professors. Nor did it follow the norm of focusing first on making primary education universal, followed by emphasis on secondary education, and only then by expansion of the university system. Instead, the growth of enrollment at each level seems to reflect social stratification more than coherent public policy. Primary schooling increased until 1978 and then began to decline (probably because of the fiscal crisis that reached its peak in 1984–86), although it recovered somewhat at the end of the 1980s. According to the national planning office, the expansion of primary education slowed precisely when Colombia ranked next to last in the world, followed only by India, in equality of access to schooling.

Despite its growth, attendance in Colombia's secondary schools is still low in comparison with that of other countries of similar levels of economic development. Higher education is where the real growth occurred. Here the key factor is the growth of private institutions that offer night classes in disciplines with low costs per student, such as law, economics, and business. Many of these institutions function as family businesses and they constitute one of Colombia's greatest social frauds. Rates of postsecondary schooling have increased from 1.6 percent in 1960 to 14 percent in 1993. But as early as 1970, it was reported that university education was exhausting its potential as a means of social mobility, and that academic degrees were losing their value in the job market. As a result, we now see graduate programs with the same pattern of low quality and outright fraud.

The Continuing Centrality of Poverty

Just how wealth and income are distributed in Colombia is a question whose political and ideological implications guarantee a roaring debate. We actually know little about accumulated wealth, and so far as income distribution goes, the available statistics omit important factors such as emigration and remittances. Whatever the case, Colombia offers one of the worst pictures of income distribution in Latin America, and therefore the world. The World Bank estimated in 1989 that the average income of the top 10 percent of the population was 37 times greater than that of the bottom 10 percent. Measuring income distribution over time is necessarily an exercise in conjecture because of the poor quality of the historical data. Even today, it is impossible to know how much wealth is concentrated in the top 1 percent or 2 percent, because the data are offered only in deciles.

Using a methodology that focuses on the ranks of the poor rather than income distribution, the u.n. Economic Commission for Latin America has shown that the percentage of poor and indigent Colombians has declined. According to their studies, in 1970 around 45 percent of Colombians lacked enough income to purchase two typical "baskets" of foodstuffs (their definition of poverty) and 18 percent could not afford even one (their definition of indigence). By 1986 these groups were 38 percent and 17 percent of the population respectively, and in the countryside the change was even greater, a decline in poverty from 54 percent in 1970 to 42 percent in 1986.

Socioeconomic Transformations and New Roles for the State

The basis for the transformations summarized in Table 6 obviously is economic growth, which changed the profile of Colombia's GDP and employment structure. Between 1925–29 and 1988–90 GDP grew at a rate of 4.7 percent a year, or 2.2 percent per capita. Despite the changes brought about by this rhythm of growth, Colombia remains an example of capitalist underdevelopment. Until the mid–twentieth century its economy was dominated by an agricultural sector with very low productivity. At the end of the century, the dominant sector was a mixed bag of tertiary activities, also characterized by very low productivity. For the per capita income level achieved, around U.S. $1,400 in 1994, the size and level of technological development of Colombian industry was below international norms.

Nineteen seventy-four was a pivotal year in Colombia's long-term development: from 1945 through 1974 the economy grew by about 5 percent annually, but from that date through 1983 it fell to under 4 percent annually. The recession was most severe for industry, which for eight years grew more slowly than the overall economy, and in 1981–83 endured the worst crisis in its history. Subsequent growth through 1994 was the most erratic and anemic since the Second World War, and many analysts now wonder if the growth rates of the pre-1974 period will ever return.

TABLE 6

Principal Socioeconomic Indicators, 1951–93

	1951	1964	1974	1985	1993
Population (thousands)	11,548	17,484	22,915	30,062	37,422
Annual population growth rate (%)	2.10	2.23	3.20	2.96	2.45
Fertility rate[a]		6.7	4.7	3.5	3.1
Birth rate[a]		44.2	34.5	29.2	27.4
Life expectancy (years)		57.9	61.6	67.2	68.2
Child mortality per thousand (<5 years)[a]		92.1	73.0	41.2	39.7
Urban population as % of total	39.5	52.1	59.5	67.2	74.0
Population of four largest cities[b] as % of total	12.9	20.0	25.4	26.8	27.4
Population of Bogotá as % of total	5.4	8.3	12.5	13.8	14.6
Primary sector employment as % of labor force	55.0	48.9	35.2	33.8	
Secondary sector employment as % of labor force	15.8	17.1	22.4	21.4	
Tertiary sector employment as % of labor force	28.7	34.1	42.5	44.8	
Illiteracy rate (%)	38.5	26.6	17.7	12.5	12.0
Homes with piped water (%)	28.8	38.7	62.7	69.7	
Homes with electric service (%)	25.8	34.5	57.6	78.2	
Homes with sewer service (%)	32.4	40.7	68.1	77.0	

Sources: Census figures from the Departamento Administrativo Nacional de Estadística; Álvaro López Toro, *Análisis demográfico de los censos colombianos de 1951 y 1964* (Medellín, 1965); *Informe Final de la Misión de Empleo, Economía Colombiana,* offprint no. 10, August–December 1985; Miguel Urrutia, *Cuarenta años de desarrollo: Su impacto social* (Bogotá, 1990).

[a]1960–65, 1970–75, 1980–85, 1985–93.

[b]Bogotá, Medellín, Cali, Barranquilla.

Throughout this whole period, the basic conditions of Colombia's relation to the world economy remained the same: export of raw materials, import of manufactured goods, technology, and modern services, and an overall negative balance of trade. However, during the second half of the twentieth century the economic structure underwent four significant changes. The most important was the end of the coffee cycle, already evident by the end of the 1980s. This coincided with a rapid transition in Colombian coffee cultivation to a high-productivity model (measured in harvest per unit of area), which carried very high costs, exceeded only in Guatemala and Kenya. Coffee's participation in GDP declined from 10.3 percent in 1950–52 to 2.4 percent in 1988–90, and its role in agricultural production fell from 25 percent to 11 percent; perhaps most striking, coffee's place among Colombian exports fell from 80 percent all the way to 25 percent during this period.

The second big change was the emergence of an energy sector—oil and coal—whose share of total exports initially fell from 15 percent in the early 1960s to 4 percent by the late 1970s, only to rebound to 25 percent in 1986–90. Moreover, petroleum derivatives such as gasoline and lubricants increased their share in total exports from 3 percent to 12 percent, a relatively modest figure suggesting an official policy of reserving these products for local consumption. Third, the government promoted manufacturing exports, which between 1970 and 1990 grew from a mere 3 percent to fully 20 percent of total exports. During the 1970s the most dynamic sector was textiles and clothing, a more intensive user of unskilled labor than the technology- and skill-intensive metallurgical and plastics sectors, which took over in the 1980s. The fourth change, really more of a continuation of a dynamic process begun in the 1920s, was the maturation of import substitution by local production, made possible by importation of intermediate and capital goods.

All of these changes started to redraw the overwhelmingly rural and agrarian profile of Colombia that was still evident in the 1951 census and other statistical data from that period. Of course, these changes refer to the legal economy; the magnitude of the hidden economy, the illegal one that emerged in the 1970s, remains largely unknown. Some credible estimates have been developed for the value and relative importance of marihuana, cocaine, and heroin exports from 1980 to 1995. The enormous figures shown in Table 7 suggest a transformation that affected structures of savings and in the end had adverse effects on economic growth. Just as important, the highly concentrated capital flows of

TABLE 7

Legal Exports and Illegal Drug Exports as Percentage of
All Colombian Exports, 1980–95

	Coffee	Oil and derivatives	Other legal exports	All legal exports	Illegal drugs[a]
1980–84	50.1	9.5	40.4	100.0	65.4
1985–89	38.8	13.1	48.1	100.0	40.3
1990–95	17.7	18.4	63.9	100.0	30.6
Entire period, 1980–95	31.2	16.4	52.4	100.0	41.4

Sources: Alicia Puyana, *Políticas sectoriales en condiciones de bonanzas externas* (Bogotá, 1997); Roberto Steiner, "Los ingresos de Colombia producto de la exportación de drogas ilícitas," *Coyuntura Económica* 1 (1977): 1–33.
[a]Estimated.

drug trafficking distorted relative prices (especially for real estate), promoted smuggling, supported the tertiary sector at the expense of production, and corrupted public officials and public life in an atmosphere of organized extortion and violence.

From these figures we can see that from around 1980, Colombia's economy—or at least its export sector—has been supported by a tripod of illicit drugs (principally cocaine and heroin), coffee, and oil. From 1980 through 1995 their share of Colombia's GDP was 5.3 percent for the first, 4.5 percent for the second, and 1.9 percent for the third. During this period, some 36 billion laundered narcodollars entered the Colombian economy as nominally legal pesos. We still know little about the economic effects of this narcobonanza. We can assume that the rentier class has done well, as it always has, even at the cost of overall economic development. In the 1990s there was some change in the legs of the tripod: the share of illegal drugs in the GDP, according to estimates, fell to 4.7 percent, while coffee fell to 2.7 percent and oil shot up to 2.8 percent.

Oil is expected to continue to increase in importance through at least 2007. Whatever the economic effects of the petroleum bonanza, its political effects will be very different from those of past bonanzas, from gold to coffee to illegal drugs. Petroleum is a state asset, in the hands of the political class. This accounts, at least in part, for the fierce power struggles among Liberal factions—

which, like the battling Conservative factions of the 1920s, take their electoral majorities as a given. Unless the current political structure is reformed to suppress personal and mafia-style networks that see the state as booty, it is likely that the petroleum bonanza will be squandered under the legal guise of regional autonomy in the allocation of royalties. It will bring not modernity but a violent form of clientelism. Fiscal decentralization, as recommended by the World Bank and instituted in Colombia since 1986, has unwittingly provided a nurturing environment for this dangerous development.

Agriculture: Modernization, Poverty, and the Rural Middle Class

The mass movement of rural poor to Colombia's cities helped to boost agricultural productivity, to improve living standards in areas the migrants left, and even to transform the landscape. Rural–urban migration redefined the parameters of regionalism and eventually changed the patterns of urban life.

The rural exodus was a consequence of agricultural modernization after 1950 and of the Violencia. Industrial protection had been accompanied by agricultural protection, and a relatively capital-intensive agriculture developed behind tariff walls. Along with protection came public spending on infrastructure, cheap credit, and the spread of technology. Mechanization, the use of improved seeds, and massive employment of fertilizers were concentrated on the best lands. Production was oriented to export, to domestic industry, and to the new urban middle classes, who were rapidly acquiring a taste for supermarkets. The most dynamic products were cotton, sugar cane, African palm, rice, bananas, cacao, soybeans, sorghum, and sesame, as well as ornamental flowers, dairy products, and beef. Rice, soybeans, and cotton stagnated after the mid-1970s, just when technology was boosting coffee production.

One of the long-term effects of the coffee bonanza of the years from the mid-1970s through the early 1980s was an increase in production (from 7.6 million sacks in 1970–75 to 12.7 million in 1988–92), led by the most technologically advanced operations. The bonanza actually lessened the social importance of traditional family farms, while wealthier producers were able to join the coffee bourgeoisie and young urban professionals took out bank loans to invest in modernized coffee farms. The small producer did not disappear from the map: since coffee cultivation continued to represent his best option, the so-called marginal coffee regions (Cauca and Nariño, and the earlier coffee heartlands of the Santanders, Cundinamarca, and Tolima) actually saw an increase in *minifundios*.

Wheat was a different matter, as it had been threatened by North American imports since the late colonial period. Highland haciendas, more oriented to dairy cattle, stopped growing wheat, and it became a crop for small and midsized farmers. The government, seeking to bring down the cost of living for the urban poor, who prefer wheat flour to cornmeal (except in Antioquia), imported subsidized wheat from the United States under the Food for Peace program (Public Law 480). In only fifteen years, from 1960 to 1975, domestic wheat production almost disappeared.

The large properties that came out of the capitalist expansion of 1950–70 were not carved from public lands or assembled from small properties. They occupied underexploited and unproductive grazing lands and latifundios that came on the market during the expansion. In Tolima, Meta, Huila, and Magdalena, however, some captains of industry hired local political bosses and armed bands recruited in the Violencia environment to purge their new lands of peasant squatters and renters. The new landowners also benefited from a subproletariat of itinerant field hands who were paid very little. This situation did change somewhat after 1970, when census figures suggest a narrowing of the gap between rural and urban wages. In agribusiness and modernized coffee regions, poor neighborhoods arose on the outskirts of provincial cities to serve as recruitment centers for seasonal farm labor.

The overall reduction in the need for labor in agribusinesses — with exceptions such as coffee, bananas, and flowers — accelerated the flows of Colombians toward more dynamic regions, toward cities in general, and toward new agricultural frontiers. These migrations were especially significant in the Amazon region, where poor soils could not support the agricultural practices of new arrivals from the highlands.

The young people of the countryside, especially young women, reaffirmed their goal to become educated in order to emigrate to the cities for employment. The traditional precept of "honor thy father and thy mother" was weakened: emigration finally cut the Gordian knot of apportioning the family plot over the generations and assigning tasks within the family. The money economy so permeated labor relations, even within families that remained in the rural areas, that they had to pay for services or find ways to save work.

Rural poverty is exemplified by the persistence of sharecropping, voluntary communal labor, and underemployment on the eroded mountainsides and depleted soils of the Andes; on the Pacific coast, where living conditions have hardly changed since the seventeenth century; and even in the areas of post-1950s land colonization such as Urabá, Caquetá, Putumayo, and the Carare-Opón of Santander. In 1987 it was estimated that 80 percent of settlers in these regions were living beneath the levels of nutrition, education, health, and housing that would meet their basic needs.

Once more, rural migrations alleviated land pressure and raised productivity and wages in the areas from which people migrated, and rates of rural school attendance, electrification, housing, and road coverage improved. Social differentiation increased, but on the whole a more modern population emerged as measured by rates of voting, ability to secure bank credit, and interest in new and better agricultural supplies and techniques.

Between the highly capitalized modern agribusinesses and the precarious parcels of new settlers, a wide assortment of small and midsized farmers in the still densely populated mountain regions see their fortunes rise and fall. This so-called rural middle class has been identified by successive governments as the tipping point between successful capitalist development under the control of a unified Colombian state and a plunge into chaos. It represents around a third of the rural population and a fifth of arable land; its members account for around 30 percent of agricultural production and around 40 percent of the rural labor force.

Demand from Colombia's urban population and out-migration have helped to consolidate these rural middle sectors, who seem willing to take risks to introduce new technologies to make their holdings more productive, and who have been rewarded with improved living standards. Even so, a study in 1986 by the National Coffee Growers' Federation estimated that the annual income of a real-life Juan Valdez, the advertising archetype of the modern small-to-midsized coffee farmer, was still less than that of a minimum-wage urban worker—and that was without the miscellaneous benefits to which the full-time worker is entitled by law.

The ecological costs of this process of agricultural modernization are hard to estimate. We do know that the indiscriminate use of fertilizers and pesticides, the uncontrolled tapping of underground and surface water for irrigation in the more fertile valleys, and the destruction of traditional shade plantings when modernized "full sun" coffee is introduced, all degrade the soils and microclimates of rural Colombia. In addition, much high-quality agricultural land is lost outright to urbanization on the outskirts of Bogotá, the Aburrá Valley (Medellín), and the Cauca Valley (Cali).

A Nation of Cities

The transition from a rural society to an urban one is the defining social change of recent Colombian history. In two generations the urban population increased from 40 percent (1951) to 74 percent (1993). If the Colombia of 1950 could still be defined as a mosaic of regions, by 1970 it was more a network of cities, more connected with each other than with their rural hinterlands. Migration has been the principal factor of urban growth. Before we look at urban problems as the city dwellers themselves see them, a key theme of the closing chapters of this volume, it is appropriate to consider the problems of the urbanization process from a national perspective.

In 1950 a World Bank team headed by the economist Laughlin Currie concluded that Colombia still did not have a viable internal market. The country was divided into "four economic and commercial entities, clearly distinguished and separate from each other": the Caribbean coast, Antioquia, the southwest, and the center-east. Each of these four regions, whose distinctiveness reached back to the eighteenth century, had agricultural resources for self-sufficiency and raw materials to develop some industrial and energy-producing capacity. Interregional commerce involved only products able to withstand high transportation costs, such as salt, sugar, and petroleum and its derivatives.

Migration and industrialization transformed this picture. Migration overturned the rigid norms of regional cultural identity and strengthened the ideal of Colombian nationhood, while industrialization simultaneously benefited from and reinforced a network of trunk roads linking the metropolitan economies of Bogotá, Cali, Medellín, and Barranquilla, the centers of the four regions identified by Currie.

A central feature of Colombian urbanization is the relative weakness of the capital city's "primacy" (defined by demographers as share of the national population) and the strength of a national network of cities. Bogotá never reached the relative dimensions of other large Latin American capitals, although it is starting to show a tendency in that direction (see again Table 6): since around 1950 it has grown faster than the other three principal cities, and these in turn have grown faster than the rest. The four metropoles are at the top of a pyramid whose solidity comes from a network of 80 cities — 34 "larger" and 44 "intermediate," according to a 1988 classification. The base of the pyramid is made up of 230 smaller towns and 678 "basic" ones, which together account for only 10 percent of total municipal revenues.

Towns located in zones of colonization and agricultural modernization have grown especially rapidly, such as Valledupar, Villavicencio, and Montería in the 1950s and 1960s, and more recently Turbo, Florencia, and Puerto Berrío. Around these towns, just as around the largest cities, slums have sprung up which serve as a labor reserve for the seasonal needs of modernized agriculture.

All of this urbanization has left untouched the four macroregions noted by the Currie mission in 1950. Bogotá functions as the metropolis of the center and east, in a network with Ibagué, Neiva, Villavicencio, Bucaramanga, and Cúcuta, although the latter two have reconstructed a Santander regional economy in the northeast. Medellín is still the center of greater Antioquia, and the secondary cities of Manizales, Pereira, and Armenia anchor a coffee belt extending to the northern part of the Cauca Valley, providing socioeconomic, demographic, and cultural coherence to the macroregion. Cali is the primary city of the southwest, with Pasto and Popayán as secondary players, while on the Caribbean coast, Barranquilla maintains its primacy over Cartagena and Santa Marta (joined more recently by Montería, Sincelejo, Valledupar, and Maicao), despite the eclipse of the Magdalena River as a commercial artery. The urban network connects the labor market (formal and informal), public services, and the distribution of goods. Even so, the relative demographic equilibrium tends to obscure the significant administrative centralization of education, finance, and public services in Bogotá.

On the periphery of this network, poverty and backwardness persist. Although the gap was always there, it grew after 1950 as the rural–urban divide took precedence over the interregional one. By 1993, around half of Colombia's population lived in departmental capitals, and the place of each city within the urban hierarchy almost always depends on its region's place in the national economic hierarchy. Medellín, Montería, and Quibdó are all capitals, but while their poor neighborhoods may have some similarities, it is clear that the latter two cities depend on the first.

The rift within each of the macroregions is clearest with regard to the wages paid for unskilled labor and access to health and education. On the Atlantic coast, the inland strip, site of an unequal land struggle between settlers and old-style *latifundistas*, is in sharp contrast to the modern cities of the coast; in the west, the contrast is between the coffee belt, extending south into the prosperous north of the Cauca Valley, and the Pacific coast, one of the poorest and most abandoned regions of the country. In Antioquia, Medellín and its historical hinterland—the "white Antioquia" of lore, and to some extent of demographic reality—had the lion's share of income, services, and power, and assumed the political representation of the whole region. Urabá in the north and the old mining regions of the northeast of the department were marginalized: while they were integrated into the circuits of Antioquian capitalism early on, they were excluded from decision making, and until very recently the Medellín bourgeoisie thought of them as trouble spots full of blacks.

Cities without Citizens

If Colombia is noteworthy in Latin America for the relatively even geographic distribution of its urban population, the cities themselves are the best possible examples of the failure of the modern Western urbanization ideal. In a twenty-year period, from around 1950 to 1970, an avalanche of migrants overwhelmed the exquisite Cartesian rationality expressed in the urban planning of such European experts as Harland Bartholomew, Carlo Brunner, and Le Corbusier in Bogotá, José Luis Sert in Cali, and Paul Wiener (along with Sert) in Medellín. During the Liberal Republic the urban history of Colombia began to lose a social and spatial continuity that dated back to colonial times. A number of factors conspired to produce this break, including innovations in urban planning and municipal governance, wider cultural and ecological changes, and even the abilities of the inhabitants themselves.

In 1930 the Bolivian writer Alcides Arguedas, observing the disrepair of Bogotá's trash-strewn streets, described the Colombian capital as an enchanting city that lacked only a government. Thirty years later, one didn't need the discerning eye of Arguedas to notice that not only in Bogotá but in all of Colombia's major cities, the municipality (the *polis*, a form of political organization) was swamped by the city (the *civitas*, understood as a form of economic, social, and cultural life). To get a sense of the physical transformation and its repercussions on inhabitants' way of life, we need only look at the number of square blocks (*manzanas*) in Bogotá: 400 in the nineteenth century, 2,400 in 1950, 27,000 in 1980. This miracle of multiplication was replicated almost without exception in Colombia's thirty or forty largest cities. The legally established limits of urban expansion and the functional subdivisions of residential, industrial, service, and recreational zones were swamped by the realities of growth. Colombian cities represent a challenge to the definition of the city as "a physical framework politically organized."

Avenues, buses, and electrification provided the image of the modernizing city; they lent meaning to the development of the market plazas, stadiums, and networks of electricity, telephones, and clean water; and finally, they were the basis for new municipal interest groups and bureaucracies. The era of the old oligarchy, the patriciate that had dominated municipal councils since colonial times, came to an end. Starting in the 1940s that patriciate began to lose credibility on issues such as utility rates and public services. In some cities these conflicts took on a nationalist air, as in the disputes between cities on the Caribbean coast and the Cauca Valley and the American and Foreign Power Company; or an air of populism, as in the public takeover of buses in Bogotá during the dictatorship of Gustavo Rojas Pinilla.

Backed by World Bank credit programs, new interest groups tied to the expansion of urban public services such as electricity, water, and telephones began to crystallize in the 1950s, almost imperceptibly at first. The modernization process brought to the fore bankers, builders, urban planners, equipment importers, mass transport entrepreneurs and intermediaries, and technocrats, who as a group ended up displacing the old-line oligarchs and career politicians.

The urban professional middle class appeared to be the product of a happy marriage between personal effort and the education system. But in the last half-century the liberal professions have not been the center of the urban middle class; they have shared that space with middling landowners, merchants, and business people. The almost obsessive search for prestige has distanced them, physically and psychologically, from the lower classes. At the same time, there is a parallel phenomenon of downward mobility, of small farmers arrived from the countryside, petty merchants both urban and rural, and established artisans. They live shoulder to shoulder with the industrial proletariat, sharing with them a geographical segmentation and an inability to develop a distinctive social personality, a subculture.

This complex of urban transformations cannot be fully explained without a look at import-substitution industrialization and the peculiar form in which it occupied urban space. The composition of employment throws some light on the diversity of urban economic and social structures. A long-term view reveals two overlapping surges: of industry, between 1950 and 1973, and of services, starting around 1960. The so-called informal sector grew up on the backs of both.

Industry was concentrated in the four metropolitan areas (which in 1987 represented 73 percent of factories, 73 percent of employees, and 68 percent of value added), although there has been substantial activity in lower-tier cities such as Cartagena, Bucaramanga, Pereira, and Manizales. In addition, almost every town of more than 20,000 inhabitants possesses some small footwear, clothing, or food processing establishments.

Through 1965 or so, factories of more than 100 workers absorbed the labor supply. In the principal cities industry came to define the economic parameters, despite the fact that nowhere did factory workers surpass 10 percent of the economically active population. (Industrial employment peaked at around 480,000 in the mid-1970s and has stagnated or declined since then.) A wide range of services, from banking to transportation to electricity, depended on the rhythms of industrial production. New technologies created a demand for trained personnel in factories and service companies, and the National Training Service (SENA) and specialized secondary and postsecondary schools were assigned the task of training them. The social division of labor promoted and deepened by industry created the fundamental nexus between income level and rising labor productivity. Between 1950 and 1970 the average schooling of the labor force as a whole rose from two to seven years.

There were clear differences in styles of industrialization between the major cities. Bogotá, with its status as political-administrative center, a high concentration of financial services, and a well-educated population, offered the best opportunities for industry. By the 1950s, if not before, it was the most diversified industrial center. Large monopoly plants coexisted with tiny workshops. In between, highly competitive firms produced consumer goods or inputs for the two ends of the spectrum.

In Cali, which displaced Medellín as the second largest urban center between the 1985 and 1993 censuses, multinational manufacturers headquartered in nearby Yumbo reoriented an urban map which, as in some other cities, absorbed the surrounding old haciendas. In contrast, Medellín specialized in the production of consumer goods, and at mid-century observers were impressed by the relative order and functionality of its urban framework.

Alongside burgeoning public and private services and a bureaucratic stratum (most notably in Bogotá but on a smaller scale in departmental capitals), the informal sector expanded. By 1985 more than half of the working population of the largest cities was part of it. Here the heterogeneity of the urban working class forcefully asserted itself. The definition of the "informal sector" has a legal basis and is wider than commonly thought: it includes people who are self-employed (such as many professionals, shopkeepers, and artisans) and those who fall just short of the qualifications required for coverage by the labor and social security laws, such as domestic servants.

For the poorer members of this group, the many thousands of capitalists without capital, the issue is survival rather than how to achieve a certain target income level. In the 1960s the old fixtures of the city streets—hawkers of newspapers and lottery tickets, shoeshine men, and door-to-door salesmen—were submerged in a sea of sidewalk vendors, nominally independent but substantially controlled by wholesale suppliers. *Sanandresitos*—contraband markets, named for the duty-free Colombian island of San Andrés in the Caribbean—proliferated in neighborhood plazas. An even lower tier of vendors, dependent on the sidewalk sellers, seemed to rise out of the asphalt to sell cigarettes, fruit, and snacks in the street itself. At any downtown traffic light, groups of children sold chewing gum, windshield wipers, and rearview mirrors. And no such scene was complete without the politician, as intermediary for obtaining licenses and permits at city hall or the police station, or as adviser in the formation of associations that sought to mark off vendors' turf through their own form of zoning.

The "informals" are principal actors, though not the only ones, in the history of urban settlement, which is similar in some ways to the history of agrarian settlement. But the state and its housing policies were also key players.

The Institute of Territorial Credit (ICT), one of the creations of the Santos government in the early 1940s, designed and financed housing programs for the middle and lower classes. But at mid-century well over half of the urban population was paying rent, usually exorbitant in relation to their income. Public policy emphasized rent control and the large-scale construction of public housing. With proceeds of the coffee bonanza, the Gómez-Urdaneta and Rojas regimes constructed large public housing developments. Although the projects were spoken of in the language of modern reformism, the corrupt reality was apparent in land speculation and the stockpiling of building materials. Reformism, in effect, stimulated corruption.

Following the path of least resistance, the politically captive ICT paid full price for lands that were far from city centers, and sometimes outside the legally established city limits. The inhabitants of ICT housing therefore lived far from their workplaces and far from city administrative centers. The result was an excessive financing cost for the ICT, a relatively high price for the beneficiary, aggravation of transportation problems, and additional burdens on public services that had to extend their coverage.

The fall of coffee prices in 1956–57 put the brakes on the construction of public housing, which in any event was overwhelmed by the avalanche of migrants. It would be reactivated in the early 1960s under the Alliance for Progress, which emphasized the principle of "self-help": families and communities were to do their part. In practice their role was to plug into existing programs, which largely lost their funding once the scare generated by the Cuban Revolution passed and governments were persuaded that urban slums were not cauldrons of revolution. The ICT, still the principal builder of public housing and suffering liquidity problems, switched to middle-class housing in order to balance its books, and returned to true public housing only during the Betancur administration in the 1980s, which introduced no-down-payment mortgages. Slums often grew up around the ICT's projects.

As late as 1970 the Colombian government considered urbanization a good thing, so long as the regional balance was maintained. Official policy emphasized the development of "intermediate cities" in an effort to reduce the population pressure on the metropolitan areas and encourage growth in the surrounding regions.

The following year, the administration of Misael Pastrana offered a novel program of urban reform. Almost simultaneously it presented a "Four Strategies" development plan which contradicted that program, although it did salvage some of its regulatory aspects. The net result was a revisiting of Operation Colombia, the 1950 World Bank initiative, but limited to Bogotá. It was the first official attempt to take housing out of the realm of social policy and put it squarely into the capitalist market: urban construction was to be a motor of economic growth. Accelerated large-scale urbanization was now seen as a condition of modern life and of economic development, insofar as it brought economies of scale for businesses, more productive and therefore better-paid labor, and lower costs per capita for education, health, and clean water. This way of thinking seemed to forget that Colombia had by this time exhausted the process of labor-intensive industrialization.

The Pastrana strategy assumed that a directed process of urbanization would create a chain reaction of employment, demand for housing, and growing utilization of local productive resources. The centerpiece of the strategy was the establishment of a new financial instrument that would finance urban construction: the UPAC (unit of constant purchasing power), a bearer bond with unique tax advantages and a guaranteed return tied to the cost of living (the "indexing" that was to spread throughout the economy). A struggle broke out between financial firms eager to bring in money via the UPAC, and some industrial groups lost access to traditional investment funding through the equities market. Many economists identified with one interest group or another supplied arguments to politicians who discussed the "inflationary effects" of the UPAC. A considerable part of national savings went into the UPAC, and after one year there was a spectacular rise in building activity—and of interest rates.

The UPAC plan failed to meet its goals of housing construction, and the experts brought in from the United Nations and the World Bank were quick to figure out why: most families, especially the poorest, were actually dependent on informal housing markets, at the margins of recognized public- or private-sector programs, or those organized by labor unions. The "legal" housing supply was but a fraction of the total. It still was not clear exactly how the immense slums—or "subnormal neighborhoods"—of Ciudad Bolívar in Bogotá, the Comuna Oriental in Medellín, and Aguablanca in Cali actually came to be. What was clear was that the poor had carried out their own "urban reform." Politicians and experts agreed in the 1970s that the time had come to "normalize" these de facto neighborhoods.

The Illegal City

As in the case of rural land colonization, the occupation of urban territory varies according to the particular geography and culture of each region; but the overall sequence is much the same everywhere. Between 1920 and 1945 the principal cities developed one or more elegant and exclusive neighborhoods as the new generation of wealthy urbanites started to reside where they liked rather than stay near the colonial-era plazas, as tradition dictated. Their exodus resulted in the remodeling of the old center-city mansions into warrens of tiny *piezas* (rented rooms), somewhat like the *tiendas* in Bogotá a half-century earlier. According to the World Bank, in 1950 at least 200,000 Colombian families lived in spaces of twelve square meters or less.

As these spaces became saturated, the poor moved to vacant lands and created dispersed, precarious settlements, which over time would grow into neighborhoods. They did not develop into class-conscious communities along the lines of mining or industrial areas in Europe or the United States. Traditional criteria of mobility and stratification prevailed, bringing together blue-collar workers, white-collar employees, and the self-employed. Each family thus faced its own inflationary and employment cycles.

Urban property was governed by a peculiar set of market norms, inextricably linked to speculation and the steady arrival of new migrants from the countryside. High-sounding constitutional language about expropriation "for reasons of public use or social interest" was drowned out by private interests. Despite the doctrine of the "social function of property" which was the centerpiece of the constitutional reform of 1936, land speculation continued to enjoy the protection of local laws and the Code of Civil Procedure, which in its pertinent aspects remains a copy of Napoleon's 1804 code.

No sensible investor would undertake a lower-class housing project near the city center. Instead, in conjunction with the politicians who set the guidelines for urban development, builders bought up the most attractive vacant lots, the *lotes de engorde* ("fattening lots," so called because they often served as pasture for cattle while their owners awaited the sale that would fatten their wallets). They would later receive bank financing for multifamily housing projects for middle- or high-income buyers. In the 1970s the emphasis was on shopping centers, with costly housing built around them. Eventually the stable salaries of lower-level public employees and unionized workers made them attractive to mortgage lenders, and projects were built to their purchasing capacity. Urban land speculation was not a monopoly—in fact, these practices descended the social scale and could be found even in the outlying slum areas.

The pressure of new waves of migration created the "illegal city," formed by pirate neighborhoods and land invasions. Both are clandestine, and in general their first inhabitants are hard-bitten city folk. In the first case, the project does not meet regulatory requirements but the land titles themselves are legitimate, while in the second case everything is unofficial and illegal. City governments accept their inability to repress them through policing and prosecution, but since the 1970s there have been many forcible evictions and bloody confrontations with the police.

In Bogotá and some other cities, the proliferation of invasions was controlled through the toleration of pirate development. These neighborhoods brought positive assets into the clientelist system of the political parties, and the most successful pirate developers ended up with a seat on their respective city councils. Invasions, on the other hand, were promoted during the 1960s by the Central Nacional Provivienda, an organization under strong Communist Party influence.

It has been calculated that in Bogotá 4,000 hectares (close to 10,000 acres) were clandestinely occupied between 1958 and 1972, accounting for 220,000 lots and one million people. These were not separate cities; the integration of these poor and mobile populations into the larger urban structure was clear from the outset. They were accused of causing environmental deterioration, excessive population densities, the collapse of the planned urban framework, traffic congestion, the inadequacy of public transportation, and of course the increase in unemployment, underemployment, and crime. (In the 1980s a graffito in Bogotá asked, "Why don't they build cities out in the country?") On top of all this, unofficial urbanization aggravated the endemic bankruptcy of municipal finances.

But the slums did enter—and relatively quickly—the labyrinth of legalization. The net effect was to multiply the number of proprietors. The history of each housing unit seemed to parallel that of its neighborhood. Starting with walls of cardboard, cans, and scraps, they progressed to walls of brick with metal windows; the roofs, initially made of zinc, were replaced by reinforced concrete that would serve as the floors of upper stories, perhaps with balconies over the street to gain precious square footage. Meanwhile, the pirate settlement rose to the status of neighborhood, duly recognized as a subdivision of the municipality. The process of legalizing the property titles of the residents, laying out streets and sidewalks, building access lines for water, sewer, and electricity, opening schools and clinics, and connecting a neighborhood to the public transportation network usually took (and still takes) from ten to fifteen years.

The parties are tight-lipped about these processes, although the pirate builders who take risks can hope for patronage rewards, and the politicians who are willing to get involved in neighborhood organizations can hope for electoral rewards. The former dictator Rojas Pinilla benefited from the votes of these communities around 1970, but since then little can get them to the polls. Their few votes, prudent and splintered, have been channeled by the intermediaries of their legalization processes. Deliberately or not, the government seems to find their relative apathy convenient. In the largest slum neighborhoods (Ciudad Bolívar in Bogotá has well over a million inhabitants) public transportation always seems to be even scarcer than usual on election days. These areas always get the bare minimum number of voting tables, while in the neighborhoods of the middle and upper classes there are tables to spare, and election Sundays have the look of a carnival.

Urban Culture

The city, now more heterogeneous and ruralized, created a mass culture that colonized regional cultures. The hegemony of the elitist culture of letters, both religious and secular, went up in smoke. Several factors besides demographics helped to forge urban culture: Colombia's diminished isolation from the rest of the world since the Second World War, the increase in school attendance, and Colombians' integration into a web of mass communications, most notably radio and then television.

The children and adolescents of the population boom were the most receptive to the language and symbols of radio and soap operas, movies, sports, and popular music. These were the settings from which new cultural meanings emerged, new beliefs and even ways of expressing feelings, which broke with the prevailing Catholic rigidity, especially with regard to sexuality.

Radio broadcasts of soccer games (1947) and then of the Tour of Colombia bicycle race (1951), of musical and comedy programs, and of folklore festivals all began to create figures of local and regional pride: sports stars, singers, and beauty queens. Every important city had at least one or two soccer teams and a dozen beauty queens to offer. Bogotá's teams took the colors blue *and* red, symbolizing their wish to remain outside the realm of party conflicts.

As wide segments of the population began their apprenticeship, learning the ways of urban life, they contributed to changes in the existing rules. The first alarm bells about the coming of modernity and its superstitions were sounded by the traditionalist clergy. What to do in the face of the massive and commercialized eruption of images that represented a new paganism? In his Holy Week message of 1950, at the height of the Violencia, Bishop Miguel

Ángel Builes of Antioquia found time to relate "the advance of the communist revolution" to the "beauty pageants, nudity at the beach resorts, and the incitements of movies and dancing."

As far from the beach resorts as they were from communist influence, many rural folk found their encounter with city lights traumatizing. The most extreme cases were the young people who came to the cities dreaming of personal liberation and social advancement, only to find solitude, segregation, and discrimination. The suicides tell the story: the young people who killed themselves after the death of the Mexican singer and screen actor Jorge Negrete at mid-century, then the leaps from the Tequendama Falls near Bogotá, site of pre-Columbian Chibcha lore. Cheap rat poison also became a method of choice, with spikes around Holy Week and New Year's.

If suicide was the extreme response, the popularity of certain musical genres was arguably part of the same continuum. During the 1950s the popularity of tangos spread from the demimondes of Bogotá and Medellín to the working class and even to the middle class, despite their glorification of villainy both criminal and romantic. Mexican films brought the Cuban bolero (a musical genre whose lyrics seemed fixated on upper-class adultery, as noted by a character in Alfonso López Michelsen's 1955 novel *Los elegidos*), and two genuinely Mexican styles, the *corrido* and the *ranchera*. *Ranchera* lyrics in particular were full of romantic invocations of rural poverty, far from the noise, wealth, and social divisions of the big city—"that stuff about social classes," as José Alfredo Jiménez put it in song. The *ranchera* resonated in rural Colombia, in the new urban slums, and most of all in the central mountains where men wearing cartridge belts—a look that would have been at home in the genre's birthplace in northern Mexico—called the shots. Popular sentiments were also expressed in the popularity of Andean music, the sad and fatalistic sounds and lyrics of Ecuadorean *pasillos* and Peruvian *valses*. The middle class developed an appreciation for the Spanish *pasodoble*, and in more sophisticated circles, even the zarzuela. The Caribbean styles of *guaracha*, mambo, cha-cha-cha, and merengue were socially far more inclusive.

Around this time the Barranquilla Carnival, a longstanding popular musical celebration, began to take on not just economic but also electoral importance. Jorge Eliécer Gaitán benefited from a catchy tune based on his slogan "A la carga!" (Charge!) The indigenous and Afro-Colombian music and dance of the Caribbean coast, on display at the Carnival, were turned into accessible dance music that spread throughout Colombia both socially and spatially. *Cumbias* and *porros*, creatively arranged by composers such as Lucho Bermúdez and spread by recordings and radio broadcasts, offered Colombians a fuller sense of the richness of their mixed heritage. Andean folk music passed through a similar adaptive process and achieved similarly wide popularity. The *bambuco*, once a genre confined to Huila, was taken up by Colombians of all regions, now coexisting in new urban neighborhoods after migrations forged by poverty or by violence.

This musical explosion coincided, after all, with the bloodiest years of the Violencia. Perhaps it was an affirmation of life in the face of a tragedy that not even media censorship could hide. Colombia sang, danced, and evoked emotions with rhythms both home-grown and international. While *rancheras*, *corridos*, and tangos kept their places in popular taste, along with the *vallenatos* of the northeastern Cesar region, which took off in the early 1960s, the new middle classes took to rock-and-roll as early as the late 1950s, and would later embrace the Beatles. The Fab Four seemed to announce the coming of a youth subculture that did have some glancing impact on Colombian universities. But the students would soon rise in anger once they discovered the true extent of the Violencia and felt the effects of the political monopoly of the National Front, along with bourgeois and clerical hypocrisy in general. The young *nadaísta* poets of Medellín, rather than foreign rockers, captured their feelings and their attention.

The radio dramas of the 1940s and 1950s, first with Cuban scripts and later adapted specifically for Colombia, represented a new stage in the penchant for melodrama extending back to the *cancionero* or troubadour. It was an intermediate stage, as it turned out: the *telenovela*, the TV soap opera, was the end point. With some exceptions that only prove the rule, Colombian soap operas are mass-media injections of consumerist conformism. They transmit norms about sexual attitudes, fashions, and language. In their homogenization of cultural values, they exalt the hedonism of individual taste. The dominant message is one of happy modernity, within which the utilitarian narcissism of the protagonists is fed by denatured sentiment and instant but erratic attraction.

In the 1970s and 1980s the children of the middle classes and of first-generation migrants alike affirmed their personalities with few inhibitions and even less ideology. Reluctant to play the part of "the masses" which a moralizing and prefabricated elite culture sought to impose on them, they spread out across the urban map according to socioeconomic position. As pedestrians they helped define the symbols and rituals of the street; as spectators in sports stadiums or movie houses, or bound together in erotic poses on the dance floor, they revolutionized body language and overthrew the prevailing dullness of popular clothing. Brilliant and sometimes phosphorescent colors shone forth, rapidly picked up and promoted on television screens.

While these rites and expressions seemed to unite the younger generation regardless of class, other factors conspired to put them all in their place. There were the usual filters of money and connections with regard to education and employment, but also the new and dire filter of physical insecurity, which struck at the root of interpersonal relations. Ours is the golden age of the funeral industry, locksmiths, security companies, and bodyguards, of urban developers who both promote and cater to the growing demand for private streets in walled communities.

The new generations, unlike those of the 1957 student movement or the 1960s, were unresponsive to political theories and utopias: they were raised on everyday violence, on the idea of life as a series of (largely unwelcome) surprises, on the whiff of the forbidden given off by drugs and the drug business. Thus far they have expressed their nonconformity by staying away from the polls and affirming the values of personal autonomy and growth.

The epidemic of murders, assaults, and robberies during the last several years has been accompanied by a delirium of soccer, beauty pageants, and musical festivals in the mass media—just as in the Violencia years of the 1950s, though the technology has improved. *Colombia se derrumba y nosotros de rumba*, as a bumper sticker eloquently put it: Colombia is collapsing and we're partying. The "party" included 1970s protest music, rejection of the lyrics, orchestrations, and rhythms of the older generation, and an obsession with the erotic and unrestrained rhythms of salsa, a melding of Afro-Caribbean, Hispanic, jazz, and rock music forged by Latino composers in New York.

Changes in standards of taste and fashion are increasingly influenced by satellite television. In 1993 around one-third of Colombian viewers had access to foreign channels. While middle-class young people went for Spanish-language rock music (largely from Chile and Argentina), which to some extent inherited the role of 1970s protest music, the young people of the slums have remained faithful to strident heavy-metal music, with lyrics that are the radical negation of the sentimentalism of their parents and grandparents.

The Collapse

The collapse invoked by that bumper sticker was a confluence of many factors, including corruption at the top, anomie down below, the political disenchantment of the middle classes, and the vertiginous expansion of violent crime. The famous bank frauds of the 1980s and the dense network of complicities between drug traffickers and well-known politicians were the most obvious signs of corruption. We actually know little about anomie, because we know relatively little about how migrants adapted to the city. While some made incremental migrations via nearby towns and perhaps a departmental capital, perhaps half made the leap directly from countryside to metropolis. In the 1960s sociologists and anthropologists spoke of the "culture of poverty" to designate the political apathy, lack of organization, and "marginalization" of the new city dwellers of Latin America. These notions have undergone substantial revision, and today we know that the urban poor have gone through a whole gamut of experiences that no simple formula can capture, and that they have demonstrated an enormous ability to survive, to assimilate the rules of the game, and at least at certain moments to act collectively in defense of their most immediate interests.

But the idea of collapse also includes the growth of organized crime, its power to corrupt public institutions, and the state's inability to control it. The speed and scale with which the new urban way of life appeared and developed brought problems of social, cultural, and personal adjustment in migrants and their children. Overcrowding increased the perils of the streets and violence within families. Urban land speculation and the lack of modern mass transit systems reinforced a profound social segregation. The absence or weakness of the so-called traditional institutions—from family to full-day schooling to the church—without their replacement by new ones threw people into anonymity in an increasingly aggressive environment. For instance, many homicides have their origins in trivial episodes of verbal aggression or gestures. Why do Colombians seem to have such a short fuse? For as long as we have had halfway reliable statistics, we know that the probabilities of being either an agent or a victim of violence are greatest in the cities, among younger men who are either unemployed or holding jobs of low social status.

Homicide rates tend to go up in the poorest urban areas; those with the greatest heterogeneity in the cultures of regions of origin or even racial/ethnic origin, as in the neighborhoods of Cali and Medellín where Afro-Colombians are in the majority; those with the highest indices of family dissolution and female participation in the workforce, formal or informal; and those with the most exposure to the collective memory of the Violencia. That last factor produces hostility toward the police, though in view of the corruption among the police, it is certainly not the only factor in play.

In Colombia, perhaps more than in any other country in Latin America, the judicial system remains firmly in the artisan age while criminality has made the leap to the modern industrial age. The few available studies concerning 1980s juvenile delinquency and the notorious young assassins for hire in Medellín seem to confirm sociological ideas going back to Robert Merton and Emile Durkheim about the role of cultural values that demand social mobility by way of money even as the social structure blocks mobility.

Order and justice, not surprisingly, increasingly entered the realm of private arrangements. In 1993 the Ministry of Defense reported that valid firearms permits numbered two million, and estimated that at least as many arms were carried illegally. This suggests that as many as one-third of Colombian males between the ages of 14 and 45 may be armed. In this armed-to-the-teeth society, new kinds of criminal groups emerged, such as the gangs of boys who marked out their neighborhood as their turf. These groups are a recruiting ground for professional criminals, who use them for robberies and kidnappings. During the 1980s the most promising of these young criminals were trained in "hit man schools" in Medellín to join the elite triggermen of the drug cartels. However, these groups predated the cartels, and not all of them joined forces with the cartels.

As early as the 1970s death squads appeared in Cali, Medellín, and Pereira, dedicated to "social hygiene" — in other words, the extermination of so-called disposables, including street children (*gamines*), beggars, prostitutes, homosexuals, and petty criminals. The notion of *desechables* indicates a clearly fascist mind-set in certain sectors of the middle and even ruling classes. Meanwhile, by the late 1980s the lack of security and the arrival of guerrillas brought a new type of armed youth group to the urban slums, whose stated goal was to impose certain minimal rules of order. These "militias," which developed most notably in Medellín, laid bare the impotence and even the social illegitimacy of the state's official police forces, and they often enjoyed some local support.

Violence and the Weak State

Criminality reached a new organizational phase with the rise of drug trafficking, a crime born of urban society under hypercompetitive capitalism. If in the recent past the international archetypal image of Colombia was the sleepy (though fantastical) Macondo of Gabriel García Márquez's novel *One Hundred Years of Solitude*, now the image is of Colombia as cocaine, personified by Pablo Escobar. A circle of writers in Lisbon even coined the adverb *pabloescobariamente* (pabloescobarly) to denote, one supposes, someone who thrives in the twilight zone of marginality.

The increase in consumption of cocaine, particularly in the United States, encouraged the consolidation of criminal networks of unprecedented scope and sophistication. The drug trade employed thousands of people in organized networks: chemists, pilots, communications specialists, and security personnel, recruited from former police and military officers, former guerrillas, and street thugs. The business was controlled by a small number of mafias—Colombian, Peruvian, Bolivian, and Mexican—which arose in the late 1970s as they found markets in the United States; later they would seek markets in Europe.

Drug trafficking involved Colombians of all social classes, as can be seen from the lists of those accused of trafficking offenses in the United States and Europe. We still do not know much about the drug economy. The so-called cartels apparently are loose associations of smaller groups of drug entrepreneurs who supply the cocaine. The cartels sell protection, routes, and contacts for distribution of the product. Drug wars are fought throughout this web of services, which extends from the regions of Bolivia and Peru where coca leaf is produced and transformed into "paste" to the urban streets of consumer countries. Until 1993 the coca leaf produced in Colombia was reported to be marginal and of low quality, leaving little scope for eradication campaigns such as those waged in Bolivia and Peru. But since then that perception has changed, and it is now believed that Colombia's drug lords have broken loose from the Andean supply network by promoting cultivation in Colombia. Wherever the raw material comes from, the refining into cocaine is done in Colombia, whence it is exported by various air and sea routes. The next step is even more important: the laundering of the money. A network of discreet lawyers, accountants, and established stockbrokers and businessmen attends to that task, principally in Panama, Venezuela, and Argentina, but also in Colombia through smuggling, overinvoicing of exports, and fraudulent accounting of imports.

Cocaine trafficking took its organizational models from two principal sources. The first was the clandestine emerald mining business that developed in the 1960s, tied to a political culture that made the emerald zones of Muzo and Chivor in western Boyacá among the most violent in Colombia during and after the Violencia. The second was the marihuana trade, concentrated along the Caribbean coast from Barranquilla to Santa Marta to Maicao, and it is worth noting that the violence which developed in the Sierra Nevada de Santa Marta—a mix of the marihuana trade and multiple conflicts between indigenous people, land colonizers, and organized crime—prefigured similar situations that would develop in the cocaine era in Caquetá, Putumayo, and parts of Cauca.

The temptation to compare the violence of the late 1980s and early 1990s with the worst years of the Violencia is quite strong. The cynical observation that "the economy is doing well even though the country is doing badly" is a fixture of both eras. Certainly during the 1980s Colombia's economy contracted much less than others in Latin America, with the exception of Chile.

The norms of coexistence and justice collapsed, as revealed by indices of crimes of violence (murder, assault, kidnapping) and by the general impunity enjoyed by criminals. The national homicide rate (which masks large variations between regions) actually declined from 32 per 100,000 in 1960–65 to 23 in 1970–75, but then it rose steeply, to 32 in 1985, 63 in 1990, and 78 in 1991–93. The rate did fall to 56 in 1998, only to rise again to 63 in 1999–2000. Colombia is, by a wide margin, world champion in murder among countries not embroiled in full-scale civil war. As for impunity, it is enough to note that despite the increase in deaths by violence from 4,000 in 1960 to 30,000 in 1993, the number of individuals charged remained unchanged. From 1964 to 1994, 97 percent of homicides went unpunished, and even that figure springs from the dubious assumption that all of the convicted were actually guilty. Half of the prisoners in Colombian jails have not yet been tried or sentenced.

Just as during the Violencia, the dividing line between common crime and political crime is very indistinct. Perhaps 15 percent of homicides between 1986 and 1993 were motivated by politics. That percentage adds up to 20,200 who were killed or "disappeared." Less than a quarter of that number died in combat between any combination of the three armed groups: guerrillas, paramilitaries, and the Colombian armed forces. According to Amnesty International, the latter two groups bore principal responsibility for noncombat deaths during the 1980s and 1990s.

This sick society is presided over by an impotent state. The founders of the National Front in the late 1950s, led by its first president, Alberto Lleras Camargo, announced that their priority would be reconstruction of citizenship and of judicial power. The first goal would be achieved by peaceful elections without fraud, while the second required official recognition of the fragility and corruption of the existing judicial system and the need to undo the damage wrought by sectarian intrusion in its operations, especially since the 1940s.

Lleras Camargo and his successors dogmatically believed that the judicial system could be restructured through the nominal political independence of judges and the imaginary effects of increased sentences. The government purchased the beautiful island of Gorgona, off the Cauca coast in the Pacific, and turned it into a penitentiary for the most dangerous convicts. The state responded to rising criminality with policies inspired by the early-1900s Italian positivist school of criminology, which believed in a "scientific" approach. For instance, Rojas Pinillas's Social Security Statute of 1955—which meant the security of society rather than social security in the sense of benefits—defined thirty-two types of "social dangerousness" (a key concept to the Italian school) ranging from nineteenth-century fixtures such as "vagrancy, begging, pimping, and gambling" to the new phenomenon of "clandestine urban development."

Until the creation of the Ministry of Justice in 1945, judges were employees of the Interior Ministry. With the coming of the Violencia, the role of the judicial branch and of the police was redefined as preservation of "public order" rather than of Colombians' personal safety or individual liberties. The polarization created by the Cuban Revolution and by the guerrilla emergency of the 1960s made the task harder.

An essential element of the "defense of public order" has been the state of siege, or the "state of internal commotion," as the 1991 constitution calls it, which in effect grants legislative powers to the executive branch. From around 1948 to the present day, penal legislation has been brought in through these exceptional powers, permitting the establishment of multiple special and parallel jurisdictions, so that military justice was occasionally applied to civilians until that practice was proscribed in the constitution of 1991. Colombian justice, in its structures and in its overall rhetoric, has failed to grasp the distinction between crime and criminals as generic social phenomena, on the one hand, and the special problems of the security of a state with a traumatic and inconclusive history of political violence on the other.

The fascination of Colombian governments with draconian measures seems never ending. The Liberal regimes of Julio César Turbay (1974–78) and Virgilio Barco (1986–90) used the extraordinary powers that accompany a state of siege to bring in statutes that criminalized activities that in most democracies would be considered legitimate forms of social protest. The Barco reforms were incorporated into the permanent penal legislation in late 1991.

Until recently, the judicial system has gone without adequate resources, a situation that is now changing. But the issue is not just funding but construction of an appropriate technical-legal foundation, one that draws connecting lines between laws, judges, and the correctional system. What is lacking, really, is political will.

As far as social convention is concerned, crime is a negotiable category — as public opinion has recognized on the issue of drug trafficking, where policies have oscillated between extradition and voluntary "submission to justice" in return for reduced sentences. The idea is not easily accepted, nor can it be, by judges and police, who (at least in theory) are constrained by the legal-institutional order. Inasmuch as all Colombians are potential victims of crime and many are actual victims, they can hardly be expected to adopt a conciliatory approach. The citizen in the street is guided partly by retributive morality and partly by instinct. Both of these factors are seized upon by opinion makers, themselves often poorly informed, to create a clamor for justice that opportunistic politicians and governments codify into draconian laws under a state of siege, which give rise to a new public clamor, since they never resolve the problem. Colombia has lived through more than a half-century of this spiral of crime, public demand that something be done, repression, and more crime. If repression does not work, it is at least partly because the same people who call for it have little trust in their judges and even less in their police.

If there is any conclusion to be drawn from the years since 1950, it is the divorce between the dynamic though violent society described in this chapter and the fossilized politics discussed in Chapter 5. The dramatic events of 1988–90 were to lead to a rethinking of Colombia's institutions and ways to reform them. Colombia is still going through that process.

EPILOGUE

*T*he popular election of a constituent assembly in 1990 was one of the political highlights of late-twentieth-century Colombia. With the public in an uproar over violence and corruption, the assembly came up with constitutional precepts to encourage honest and competent leadership, end the armed conflict, do away with impunity, and widen the scope of democratic practices. It was said, with some disingenuousness, that Colombia was "moving beyond the stage of representative democracy" to "participative democracy."

The succession of violent incidents outlined in past chapters, the state's apparent inability to confront the various types of organized crime—private and political—and the elite's anxiety after the assassination of Luis Carlos Galán, all suggested that the social system and political order were fundamentally threatened. To understand the developments of 1990–91 one must start from the premise that the political process of the Constituent Assembly was in fact more important than its formal result, the constitution of 1991.

Several ministers in Barco's cabinet, including the future president César Gaviria, advanced the (unconstitutional) proposal to invite the electorate to approve via referendum the election of an assembly that would pass political reforms allegedly being blocked by the politicians in Congress. Under the banner of civil society a movement for the referendum launched in some of the country's private universities developed enough backing to achieve its goal, thanks to a dubiously legal proposal to add a seventh ballot to the 1990 national and regional elections. The Barco administration used its state-of-siege authority to legitimate this proposal, and its passage led to the election of a constituent assembly empowered to reform the 1886 constitution.

The political and business elites, which until now had controlled such matters of state organization and reform, either opposed the process or stayed on the sidelines. Almost imperceptibly they came on board as the movement gained popular support. Its young middle-class leaders declared themselves frustrated by the political system. This "opinion movement," which achieved all its objectives, represented the interplay of at least two factors: the perception, amplified by the media, that the country was in deep crisis, and the political skill of those young operatives who knew how to use their connections in the government to promote the idea that Colombia's crisis could be addressed through audacious constitutional reform. The parallel with the institutional crisis of 1956–57, which gave rise to the plebiscite and National Front, is readily apparent. In both cases, an ambitious group understood that its opportunity lay in substantial political reform, and that this in turn required a message first formulated in the late nineteenth century by Rafael Núñez: "Fundamental administrative regeneration or catastrophe."

The Constituent Assembly

The would-be reformers gave a stark depiction of the crisis: the Colombian ruling class was, quite literally, under threat of death. The three presidential candidates murdered by the traffickers' hit men were solid proof that Colombia was headed for the abyss. I hope the preceding chapters have shown that the roots of the crisis were in fact deeper than that. Perhaps it can be explained by the rapid pace of urbanization, "savage capitalism," political corruption, administrative sloth and venality, and last but not least, the gravitational pull of the Violencia on the memory and political culture of many parts of the country.

The Assembly was elected with one of the lowest voter turnouts in Colombian history: 26 percent, below even the turnout for the 1953 constituent assembly called by the Gómez-Urdaneta dictatorship and boycotted by the Liberals. Some intellectuals and academics argued that the low turnout was less important than the "quality" of the voters and the candidates. They emphasized the participation of social sectors that had previously been marginalized by the bipartisan political elite: indigenous peoples, unionists, former guerrillas, and the spokespeople of new social and religious movements. These arguments were part of the high-sounding but rather casual proposition that Colombians had somehow progressed beyond mere representative democracy.

Within the Assembly the tone was set by the recently demobilized M-19 (which captured 27 percent of the vote) and the National Salvation Movement

(MSN, with 15 percent of the vote), a heterogeneous group led by Álvaro Gómez Hurtado. This result was understandable given the skepticism and scant interest that politicians in both traditional parties displayed toward the Assembly, right up to the last minute; the government's propaganda campaign in favor of the peace process with M-19; and the mix of hope and curiosity with which the electorate viewed new faces and new movements. The M-19 and MSN forged an agreement that squeezed out the Liberals, whose plurality (33 percent of the vote) was diluted by the multiple competing lists fielded by regional party barons; this strategy, called Operation Swarm, usually worked for legislative elections because of Colombia's modified proportional representation system, but it was counterproductive this time. The Conservatives practically disappeared as a party.

The Assembly carried on in an atmosphere that could best be described as postmodernist relativism. The sessions did not take place in the neoclassical Congress building, still occupied by legislators who had been elected with far more votes than the new delegates, but who would soon have their mandates (though not their salaries) revoked by the Assembly; rather, the organizers chose a modern convention center, with rooms that could be divided to accommodate any assemblage. The Assembly's rules were similarly flexible, and they were applied opportunistically by the fleeting coalitions that came and went as the days passed.

What was lost in republican pomp was made up in histrionic performances, duly covered by radio and television. The Assembly met the expectations of audiences who, having lost the beliefs and sense of ritual that can come only from firmly internalized political traditions, now appreciated the fragmented language and signs of the actors who came onstage. From the 1960s on, media techniques had invaded the world of politics, and to the surprise of many, the traditional parties had no monopoly. This was the case of M-19, which, under the charismatic leadership of Jaime Batemán Cayón, had revealed a masterful talent for exploiting the logic of the small screen.

The delegates of 1991 were eager to separate themselves from the rituals of 1863 and 1886, and from the closed-door atmosphere in which the 1957 plebiscite was negotiated. Nevertheless, there was an abundance of private agreements between the principal figures of the Assembly and President Gaviria to introduce, modify, or quash one or another article of the developing constitution. The new document would enshrine, or so the participants hoped, a new political class that would be in a position to rule for the next forty years.

The Constituent Assembly almost immediately overstepped its mandate. Instead of revising the existing constitution, it produced a new one, a mosaic of 380 articles with another 60 provisional ones, unevenly and sometimes sloppily drafted. It broadened the scope of individual and political rights, expanded municipal and regional autonomy, strengthened the judicial branch, and recognized the country's cultural pluralism. To open the way for new political representation, it created a national electoral list to elect a senate of 102 members — the nice round number of 100, plus 2 seats reserved for indigenous peoples.

Before we examine the broad outlines of the 1991 constitution, it is worth noting the document's silence about the status of the police and the military and their relations with civil authority. The guerrilla wars, drug trafficking, general insecurity, and occasional border incidents with Venezuela all combined to justify an increase in military spending. In real terms the budget of the Ministry of Defense quintupled between 1985 and 1990, and it has continued to grow at the same pace. During that time the size of the army doubled; the national police remained under the control of the Ministry of Defense, and instead of modernizing its governance and resources, the government counted on internal reforms and the expanding private security business to fill the security gap. As in 1957, the political leadership of 1990 thought it imprudent to debate the core relationship between the military and civil power. Those themes were excluded from the agenda because the government was more interested in negotiating an agreement on shutting down the Congress that had been elected in 1990, and whose term ran through 1994. In any case, it was the former guerrilla movement M-19, the leading force in the Assembly, that preferred to respect the untouchability of the military and its legal jurisdiction over its members, which in attenuated form was still in force in Colombia.

The Constitution of 1991

The 1991 Constitution contained important provisions for developing the so-called third and fourth generations of human rights. It recognized ninety-nine specific rights, and it introduced important language about protecting the environment. Some rights that were quite controversial in the past, such as divorce, were approved almost without notice. Other more novel ones, such as the *tu-*

tela or right of redress against administrative and even judicial decisions, have found great public support and have brought people closer to the justice system, even though the poor design of the process has clogged tribunals all the way up to the Supreme Court. One noteworthy precept is laid down in Article 44: "The rights of children will prevail over the rights of others." Perhaps this was meant only as rhetorical and overdue recognition that child labor is still commonplace in many fields of Colombian economic life. Children are also the principal victims of Colombia's waves of political, criminal, and domestic violence. The rights of childhood, as commonly defined by the morality of our times, simply are out of reach for a majority of Colombian children because of the poverty of their families.

The new constitution provides fiscal support for municipal autonomy and sets wide horizons for decentralization, which had no legal basis for the previous 105 years but existed de facto throughout the period. The document contains the same tensions and ambiguities that characterized the political process that created it. Although the eight "national territories" under the central government's supervision were made full departments, the precariousness of control in these vast outlying regions placed most of them in the crosshairs of new turbulence. In the presence of guerrillas, paramilitaries, and the military itself, the backwardness of local administrations, which was all too conspicuous when the affluence of new fiscal resources converged with the old corrupt political culture, seemed to win out over the letter of the law.

The new municipal and departmental design called forth political actors who were unlikely to resolve their disputes without resorting to violence. Rising regional clans, particularly in the new departments, sought to consolidate their social and political dominance. Many of these groups appeared precisely in the zones of most recent violence such as Urabá in Antioquia, the Magdalena Medio region of Santander and Antioquia, southern Bolívar and Cesar, and the Yarí region of Caquetá.

Then there are the indigenous peoples. For the first time in the constitutional history of Colombia they came to Congress through a special electoral provision, and "indigenous territorial units" were created in which they could govern themselves and administer their own natural resources. This provision promises uncertain and perhaps stormy developments—with regard to petroleum resources, for instance. In many regions, mestizo peasants have sought to classify themselves as indigenous in an effort to get the government and the urban public to attend to their grievances. Indigenous peoples account for less than 2 percent of Colombia's population. But in Guajira, in the northeast, they constitute nearly 40 percent of the total. This department, thanks to its active coal-mining sector, had in 1990 the highest per capita income in the country, higher even than Bogotá—and it is located along a contested international border. In the extensive Amazonian departments of Guainía, Guaviare, Vaupés, and Vichada, all raised to departmental status by the new constitution, indigenous people are in the majority. Their potential mineral and petroleum riches cannot be explored or developed without prior agreements with the resident communities, in deference to their "cultural integrity."

A "Law of Afro-Colombian Communities" (*Ley de Negritudes*) passed under the new constitution created a national electoral district for those who identified themselves as members of that group. Very few did so, perhaps because of the strong historical identification of Afro-Colombians with the Liberal party, dating back to the sometimes violent actions of black Liberals against the formerly slaveholding elites of the southwest in the mid–nineteenth century. Such men as Luis Robles ("El Negro Robles") on the Caribbean coast in the late nineteenth century and the Chocó politician Diego Luis Córdoba in the mid–twentieth century were symbols of that identification. In addition, the possible significance of racial integration and the complex psychosocial phenomenon of "whitening," sought by many blacks and mulattos, deserve to be the subjects of future research.

On the judicial front, the 1991 constitution created a constitutional court to clarify and interpret the new doctrines. There will be, at least for a time, some confusion between this body and three other high courts: the Supreme Court, the Council of State, and the High Judicial Council (*Corte Suprema de Justicia, Consejo de Estado, Consejo Superior de la Judicatura*). To these should be added the all-powerful Prosecutor's Office (*Fiscalía*) and the ombudsman (*Defensoría del Pueblo*), which have functions close to those of the attorney general (*Procuraduría*). In the new internal balance of the Colombian state, the judicial apparatus came out strengthened, and with it the judges. The technocracy of economists finally met its institutional match. We can expect increasing conflict between the technocrats, working on a market model, and the courts, imbued with continental European ideas more social-democratic than neoliberal. This potential tension is implicit in the Constitution itself.

The Limits of the Constitution

If we can attribute a collective sentiment to the Constituent Assembly, it would be the wish to lay the institutional basis for modern political leadership. But the dichotomy between an "old" and "new" political class has been shown to be false. There was still no new republic, either in spirit or in basic institutions. The state continues in the hands of a generation only slightly younger than the old governing group, and like its predecessors it does not seem to think that the extremely high rate of electoral abstention—especially among the young and the poor, in a country full of guerrillas and other forms of organized violence—undermines the legitimacy of the political system.

But perhaps the key to the new constitution lies in its intent to accelerate turnover in the political class and to fragment it. The Constitution prohibits reelection of the president even after an intervening term, thus weakening the patriarchate of former presidents, whose influence and power depended in part on the possibility of their return to office. (A constitutional reform approved in 2005 permits direct reelection of the president—*Translator*.) We can also expect increased atomization, as representatives can no longer ride the coattails of senators elected to represent the nation at large (even if their support comes preponderantly from one region), and so on down the line, through departmental deputies to town council members. These departmental and local races will be more about local dynamics and local demands. The net effect will be to break up the vertical cohesion of the political class, already weakened by the 1986 reform that established the popular election of mayors.

The gravitational force of the political system continues to be presidential power. The president, as "head of state, head of government, and supreme administrative authority," maintains the powers and attributes enshrined in the previous constitution. He or she directs the armed forces, international relations, and economic policy, and enjoys the extraordinary powers that come with the state of siege—which has been renamed. As before, the president can name and remove functionaries, even governors, despite their direct popular election. Since there are no parties in the modern sense, much less in the parliamentary sense, they are in practice supplanted by the president and his team, ever more dominated by technocrats of the sort that the World Bank and International Monetary Fund consider essential to "good governance." Even if we set aside ideas of political modernity and think of parties only as organizations inspired by defined principles and maintained by loyalties, we must conclude that there really are no parties in Colombia. The new constitution has nothing to say about the internal organization of parties, even though they have certain constitutional prerogatives, such as the right to nominate candidates, receive public financing, and gain access to the airwaves.

The elections since 1991 have produced a lax and fragmented system of individualistic politicians, many of them neophytes and impromptu volunteers who leaped into the ring with improvised labels, supported under the table by economic interest groups or by traditional party patrons and their intermediaries, and seeking to negotiate with a future president, governor, or mayor for quotas of jobs to hand out.

M-19 and the National Salvation Movement lost support in the 1991 elections and were decimated in 1994. Congress and the political class changed only nominally: the Liberals strengthened their representation in Congress, but the recovery of the Conservative factions has been less certain, since they lost so much ground in the Constituent Assembly. At this point the return of the traditional two-party hegemony seems improbable.

Beneath all of this change and intrigue lurks a disquieting question: What role will the economic groups that finance the long and costly campaigns play in the new distribution of political power? What power can eventually rein in these groups that control the fate of so many candidates? The elimination of some mechanisms of formal patronage, such as "parliamentary assistance," did nothing to prevent them from sneaking back, despite the short-lived office of treasury overseer (*Veedor del Tesoro*), whose mission was to prevent the use of public funds in political contests. In any case, congressional hopefuls are now more in need of support from the economic groups than ever, given their control of so much of the print and electronic media. And this discussion does not even include the economic group par excellence, the drug lords, always in search of protection from (and therefore by) the state, and therefore always willing to support politicians who may better their chances.

Corruption, Drug Trafficking, Guerrillas: Worse than Before

Beyond the constitutional reform process, Gaviria reduced the project of modernizing and democratizing the state's institutions to a matter of applying, sometimes hurriedly, always dogmatically and compulsively, so-called economic restructuring along neoliberal lines: liberalization of imports, foreign investment, and the financial sector; privatization of the full range of state assets and entities, including social security and some basic services; and fiscal decentralization. The centerpiece of this vision was the preservation of economic stability. That goal colored even his dealings with Pablo Escobar, whom he saw as a disruptive influence on private investment.

Gaviria, contradicting his campaign rhetoric, defined drug trafficking as a global problem, on which all producing and consuming countries had to work together. The consuming countries had an obligation to suppress demand, since the costs in lives, instability, and disorder were being borne unfairly by countries like Colombia. Narcoterrorism, defined as that aspect of drug trafficking which attacked the security of the Colombian state, was what Gaviria really wanted to focus on. Succinctly put, the Medellín cartel were narcoterrorists and the Cali cartel were drug traffickers. This distinction was designed to reduce the perception that Colombia was entirely dependent on the United States in the war on drugs; it was a nationalist appeal to counter the state's ineptitude in its efforts to control drug trafficking. Besides, the campaign of urban terrorism launched by the drug lords convinced the middle classes and the Constituent Assembly that the security of Colombians and the defense of national sovereignty were more important than extradition, which was prohibited by the new constitution. It is a small irony of history that extradition returned to the constitutionally sanctioned list of options only under the administration of Ernesto Samper (1994–98), who was besieged by accusations of links to drug traffickers.

In the atmosphere created by the Constituent Assembly it was accepted that the taxonomy and categorization of crime provided wide scope for negotiation, based as it was on social conventions rather than immutable moral or legal truths. The Gaviria government, with the blessing of public opinion, offered drug traffickers the option of "submitting to justice" — voluntarily surrendering and making a full confession in exchange for a substantial reduction in sentence. What was negotiated was individual submission, not the dismantling of criminal organizations. It seemed implicit in the bargain that it was enough for these organizations to stop their urban terrorism and attacks on government officials.

Along with the prohibition of extradition by the Constituent Assembly, the country witnessed the surprising spectacle of a repentant Pablo Escobar behind bars.

But in mid-1992 Escobar and his inner circle staged a violent and spectacular breakout from their luxurious prison near Medellín, nicknamed "the Cathedral," which they had helped to construct, organize, and finance, and which they had largely administered. In fact, they had converted the prison into the Medellín cartel's center of operations, although formally the complex was under the government's direct control. In justifying their jailbreak, Escobar and his comrades cited the government's inability to defend them against their enemies, most notably the new group called the PEPES—Persecuted by Pablo Escobar—which had quickly become as effective and well organized a band of killers as the one led by Escobar himself.

One dies as one lives. In late 1993 Pablo Escobar, weakened militarily, logistically, and financially by the onslaught of the government and the PEPES, fell *pabloescobariamente*, riddled with bullets by the Medellín police on a rooftop in a nondescript middle-class neighborhood. The popularity of the government, which had plummeted since the jailbreak, shot back up. For the government, the war was won: with Escobar and his henchmen liquidated, Medellín and the country would return to peace and the drug trade would be thrown into crisis. But while the murder rate has not gone down significantly in Medellín or in Colombia as a whole, and there has been no decline in cocaine exports, the death of Pablo Escobar did indeed mark the end of a peculiar combination of politics, drugs, and terror. In the final analysis he was a product of that disordered, unjust, and chaotic amalgam that was the Colombian city of the late twentieth century, a new theater of capitalist accumulation but also of the culture of violence. Escobar's death debunked the myth of the all-powerful mafioso. But the myth refuses to die, as the Cali cartel continues business as usual while its leaders negotiate their "submission to justice" under conditions unacceptable to the U.S. government. The tension rises between the two countries, and politicians manipulate the genuine nationalism of the Colombian people.

Is the so-called Cali cartel really so powerful? Its power to corrupt politicians, judges, and the police seems unlimited. But it is hard to say whether it exercises such centralized and disciplined control over the drug business. All we know for sure is that cocaine and heroin will continue to flow from Colombia so long as there are consumers willing to pay for it in the streets of the United States or Europe. So long as consumption is penalized and the utopian myth of a society immunized to mind-altering drugs persists, we will witness the existence of well-organized bands of criminals with the power to kill, bribe, and corrupt in proportion to their illicit earnings.

The Gaviria government also left unresolved the political problem of the guerrillas, with even graver consequences. Peace talks between the government and the Simón Bolívar Guerrilla Coordination Group (CGSB, made up of the FARC, the ELN, and the remaining faction of the EPL), which took place in Mexico and Venezuela, broke down in mid-1992. The principal accomplishment during the Gaviria years was a peace agreement with an ELN faction, the Corriente de Renovación Socialista, and its return to civic life.

During the 1980s the variations in style among the guerrilla groups became apparent, and in the 1990s they continued to go their own way. But they differ very little on the ground: at the beginning a guerrilla detachment fills the vacuum of authority left by an absent state, finding sympathy and even support among the hitherto abandoned population. The farmers, usually land colonizers, see in the armed group the beginnings of political order, or perhaps an effective intermediary with the Colombian state. This kind of thinking is supported by events: if not for the guerrillas, there would never have been a national rehabilitation plan to offer assistance to isolated regions. Thus it is not hard for the guerrillas to consolidate a new "liberated zone."

The situation can be depicted this way as of the 1990s because in many regions the guerrillas have once again gained the sympathies of the poor; the extraordinary increases in the military budget and the political symbolism of having a civilian as minister of defense after several decades do not translate into operational efficiency. On the guerrilla side, extortion of money from ranchers (preferred by the EPL and FARC), the collection of a levy on cocaine and heroin transactions (typical of the FARC), payoffs from oil exploration firms (the specialty of the ELN), and kidnapping (practiced by all) take up most of their energies.

The guerrillas have demonstrated ever-increasing firepower, territorial expansion, and funding. As the political and state institutions have suffered functional and geographical fragmentation and ideological devaluation, the guerrillas seem to have renounced the supreme objective of taking power for the purpose of socialist revolution. The spirit of self-sacrifice and moral Puritanism associated with the combatant of Maoist or Guevarist extraction has given way to a pragmatic and professional model. Being a guerrilla has become an organized way of life, a career, with a political track available. Armed subversives who negotiate with drug traffickers or oil companies may succeed in political negotiation in the near future, as happened with the M-19, a chameleon organization not easily tagged with any specific ideology. But experience suggests that even if some groups evolve in this direction, others will appear that demonstrate—at least at the outset—greater congruence between their radicalism and the poverty, abandonment, and isolation of the rural or even urban population that serves as their base of support. If we consider the inefficiency of the army's strategy (which until recently was to keep troops in the cities and transport them by air in daylight supported by massive firepower), its search for support from right-wing paramilitary groups, and a tendency to electoral violence in agrarian frontier zones, we can assume that the guerrillas, as a sort of armed political class, will continue to enjoy a rich spawning ground.

The civilian population continues to be caught in the crossfire, and reports by the most reputable international human rights groups concluded in the 1990s that the Colombian situation was one of the worst in Latin America, comparable only to those of Haiti and Guatemala. The government's cynical claim that the guerrillas are the principal offenders is small comfort. Meanwhile, the government's lukewarm adherence to the Vienna Convention on control of illicit drugs, as evidenced by its negotiations with the Cali cartel and its reluctance to introduce strong money-laundering legislation, puts Colombia squarely in the sights of powerful international critics.

Ernesto Samper, candidate of a united Liberal Party, defeated his Conservative opponent, Andrés Pastrana, in the 1994 presidential elections—which for the first time were held over two rounds, and which for the first time in over eighty years included a ballot for vice president. Samper was an exceptional witness to Colombia's recent violence. With characteristic Bogotá humor Samper noted during the campaign that he was "the leaded candidate"—in 1989 he was chatting with the Communist youth leader, José Antequera, at the Bogotá airport when Antequera was assassinated in a hail of bullets that left Samper seriously wounded. He used the incident to present himself as a victim of drug-related violence even though his 1994 campaign is widely thought to have received financing from the Cali cartel.

Samper won a narrow victory, with a margin of only 3 percent, similar to

Turbay's victory over Betancur in 1978. The race demonstrated once again that the labels "Liberal" and "Conservative" had lost their ideological meaning, and that nothing remained of the historical parties apart from some residues of cultural identity among older Colombians. Even so, given the tightness of the race, a call from the bishop of Bucaramanga for the faithful not to support Samper because he had the support of Protestants might easily have decided the election against him—a curious episode that did not mark any return to the religious polarization of the past.

The elections went off smoothly, but less than a week later Pastrana attacked his rival's campaign on the grounds of alleged financing by drug traffickers. His charges were backed by tape recordings, apparently leaked by the U.S. Drug Enforcement Administration (DEA), which were in fact ambiguous with regard to the accusations. In the absence of legally valid evidence, Pastrana and his accusations lost credibility in the opinion polls. A few months later, a new chief prosecutor—a politician related to the assassinated Luis Carlos Galán— ordered the investigation reopened. New charges and evidence grew into the biggest political scandal in Colombia's twentieth-century history. The "8,000 case," so called for its felicitously round file number in the prosecutorial bureaucracy, implicated Samper, several cabinet members who had roles in his campaign, and a good number of Liberal legislators. While some of the legislators and other secondary figures ended up in jail, Samper escaped congressional censure and all legal consequences.

Summing Up

The twentieth century marked a fundamental change in Colombian history. Mass migrations to the cities and the cultural as well as demographic hegemony of urbanization broke down deep-rooted notions of localism and regionalism. This does not mean the end of the country's fragmentation, since the cities—which collectively are home to 70 percent of the population—are themselves increasingly focused on their own doings and identities. Nevertheless, between telecommunications, the expansion of education, and population dynamics, the mental map of Colombians has been redrawn. Just to cite one obvious example, the vast majority of today's schoolchildren would find the idea of the Magdalena River as "the Artery of the Fatherland" inconceivable or meaningless.

If Colombian history teaches anything, it is that Colombians and their political system have survived more than a century of weaving a tapestry of legitimacy and compromises, complicities and violence. Some conclusions:

1. The 1886 constitution, the coffee-based economy, and the hegemony of the two historical parties all sank more or less at once, toward the end of the twentieth century. But Colombian political culture has not freed itself from the symbiosis of clientelism and violence as the preferred formula for addressing conflict. Coffee, civilian supremacy, and the two-party system were at the heart of the collective identify of a country which, in spite of everything, was climbing the ladder of capitalist civilization. But it was really a collection of halfway modernizations, weighed down with privileges, conformity, impunity, and dead bodies.

   During the last decade of the century there arose an annoying consensus—annoying because it was merely rhetorical—on the virtues of peace, democracy, and progress as the characteristics of modernity and as the ideological glue of Colombian nationhood. To make any progress toward turning the rhetoric into reality, the Colombian state would have to exercise sovereignty over the whole of the national territory, and help to integrate a society dangerously divided between the very poor—largely in the informal sector, excluded from effective citizenship—and the rest of the Colombian population, who acted more as privileged subjects or protégés than as political actors with duties as well as rights.

2. Daily insecurity in the street, political assassinations, terrorism, drug wars, severe and prolonged electricity rationing (as in 1992–93, thanks to inefficiency and corruption), the human toll of natural disasters—everything confirms Colombians' ability to withstand adversity. The talent and tenacity of Colombia's painters and writers, cyclists, boxers, and soccer players and their success in entering the sophisticated machinery of international stardom reassures the country and its people that they really are part of the wider world.

3. The central problem of the Colombian state is more political than administrative or technical. To win the confidence and compliance of the people, the state must take back its public functions, promote a sense of responsibility among its personnel, and guarantee that basic services—whether supplied by the public or private sector—are delivered to the whole population. The task is much more arduous and complex than the routine and somewhat despotic exercises in macroeconomic adjustment and sectoral planning which

the Colombian state does reasonably well; and certainly more difficult than invoking the specter of chaos in order to forge ramshackle constitutions allegedly possessing magical powers.

4. A consistent population growth rate of about 2 percent and accelerated urbanization will continue to bring cultural, social, and political changes. In the last century cities tended to vote Liberal, but now their votes cannot be predicted. The Colombian electorate that lived through the sectarian strife of the Violencia and was held in sway by the charisma and prestige of traditional political leaders has been dying a natural and literal death since around the mid-1970s, coincidentally the beginning of the dismantling of the National Front.

The fate of the emerging political figures is as uncertain as the electorate is voluble and as the range of opinions is wide. The disenchantment of today's voters, to the extent that it does not simply become apathy (which is especially widespread among the young and the poor), seems to be channeled not into support of movements or parties but rather into casting blank ballots or protest votes for "new faces," "honorable men," self-declared independents, or anyone who can credibly claim opposition to the hypocrisy and corruption identified with the governing elites.

Even today, it is still possible to reconstruct the ethical bases of public action, to revitalize the ideas of just governance, and to recognize in deeds, not just in words, the importance of human rights and citizenship rights. If Colombia's history suggests anything, it is the need to construct a system able to predict, understand, and resolve the conflicts inherent in modern life, without myth-making or manipulation in the cause of an apocryphal consensus which has, in the end, proved as elusive as legitimacy.

Postscript: 2002

The perspective of the present may provide the reader with some orientation in confronting the panorama of Colombian history depicted in this book. It is said with increasing frequency that Colombia is about to fall apart. This notion can be developed in several ways. For instance, a report in *Time* on the 40,000-square-kilometer demilitarized zone which President Pastrana established in 1998 as part of his negotiations with the FARC sounded this alert: "Colombia risks being divided into three parts, along the geography of its mountains. The

Marxist guerrillas dominate the south; the government controls the center and the major cities; and the rightist paramilitaries, supported by the military, are well established in much of the north." [1]

The influential French political analyst Daniel Pécaut was equally emphatic about the dangers confronting Colombia: "This country has not yet been fully constructed as a country, as a society that accepts that there is a state, and that law is to be respected. This country prefers and is accustomed to the idea that everything is negotiable, and that law is an instrument for negotiation. It is also a country of intermediaries: . . . the local petty politicians and the lawyers are the ones who control the laws, and who impose their will in any negotiation." He adds: "Another reason why Colombians have become accustomed to violence is the lack of a founding national myth. Brazil has its unifying myth and the state there is quite strong. Argentina and Chile both have their unifying myths, while Mexico has its revolutionary myth. Colombia has no unifying myth. Colombia invented its only myth: that its entire history has been violence. And it is a myth, because there have been periods without extraordinary violence, as between 1910 and 1945 except for 1933 and 1934." [2] Certainly Pécaut has logic and the facts on his side: Colombians have known long periods of relative tranquility and progress, as I have sought to emphasize in several chapters of this book.

This idea of a unifying national myth as essential to a strong state is a complicated one. Sometimes competing national myths need to be unified, as in France, where Joan of Arc and Robespierre eventually won equal status. The historic defeat of the PRI in Mexico in 2000 made it clear that the myth of the Mexican Revolution was not as unifying as that of the Virgin of Guadalupe. And the current Argentine crisis illustrates the theoretical and practical difficulties of reconciling the myth of the nation's founding with the strength and relevance of a modern state.

Negotiation of the law, as a current practice that reflects the weakness of state institutions, has its roots in the colonial era, long before any need for a unifying myth on which to construct a modern nation. Ever since the Conquest, rulers have wanted to control the physical geography of a country that arrived at the twentieth century as a collection of dispersed pockets of population isolated from one another. That is why it has been so difficult to give a common political base to the local and provincial traditions and cultures. In this regard, on the cultural plane the role of the Habsburg and Bourbon

---

1 *Time*, Latin American ed., September 28, 1998.
2 *Revista Estrategia* (Bogotá), November 15, 1996.

monarchies and of Tridentine Catholicism in offering the inhabitants of New Granada a solid unifying base cannot be overstated. But with the partial destruction of this support in the wars of independence, civil and political obedience (in other words, governability) fed a new chain of conflicts. The task of governance was to make political tradition compatible with new liberal republican institutions, with the requirements of economic growth, and with the demands of an ever more modern and secular society. This problem was already apparent in the nineteenth century but would explode in the late twentieth when rapid population growth and urbanization began to erode social orders based on Catholic patriarchy and rural norms and values.

In addition, since the 1960s the deep-rooted local and family loyalties to the two traditional parties, which in many regions had continued uninterrupted since the 1830s, began to fray. These were loyalties forged in a series of civil wars fought between 1831 and 1902, wars that had clear social antecedents in the internecine strife of the early independence era (1811–16) and in the factional struggles of Bolívar-era Gran Colombia between 1826 and 1831. With the signing of the peace treaty that put an end to the War of the Thousand Days on November 21, 1902, the Colombian elite renounced warfare as a legitimate form of politics. They accepted the creation of a professional army (looking first to the Prussian example, then to the United States), which would be above the party struggle. In several trials by fire, from the disputed presidential elections of 1922 to the Liberal victory of 1930, which ended fifty years of Conservative rule, the elite kept to this golden rule. Later crises would prove to be the real challenges: the Conservative victory over a divided Liberal party in 1946, the popular insurrections in Bogotá and other cities in April 1948, the Liberals' boycotting of elections in 1949, and the unleashing of the Violencia. These extreme situations put the constitutional system to the test, particularly during the Conservative dictatorship of 1949–53, which was replaced with a civil-military dictatorship that lasted until 1958. During these years the most brutal partisanship was left to the local and regional political bosses; the ruling classes preferred to avoid direct confrontation, and they effectively stigmatized civil war in the name of civility, civilian rule, and republican values. This is important because in Colombia's dominant political discourse, the term "civil war" is narrowly defined: if the elites do not themselves take up arms (as they had done through 1902), it is not civil war, no matter the scale, intensity, or geographical spread of armed conflict, even on the scale of the Violencia.

The National Front and its consensual dismantling endorsed this notion of perpetual peace among the ruling class. This principle was of great relevance in the 1960s, when the elites faced two new problems. The first was whether the new system of electoral rules and distribution of governmental power, which was intended to civilize Colombians in their political practices, would prove viable; the second was the appearance of the Castro-inspired revolutionary model in the Western hemisphere, the most significant test to date of the apolitical armed forces.

The routinization of peaceful elections and the institutional loyalty of the armed forces (against the wave of Latin American military coups from the 1960s until the 1980s) were no small accomplishments. Ironically, it was this very success in making electoral politics "normal" that eventually led to tactical gambits that, in the context of pervasive clientelism, would throw the two-party system into crisis. The Conservative Party is about to disappear, and the Liberals, long divided, crossed a new line with the unprecedented victory of a dissident Liberal, Álvaro Uribe Vélez, in the presidential elections of 2002.

From the perspective of Colombia's armed conflict, *Time*'s claim would be more convincing if, instead of drawing borders between putatively sovereign proto-states, it had drawn lines of political legitimacy. Those lines, of course, would be more fluid and imprecise. If we briefly develop this exercise, we can see that the large cities—and not even all of them—would be islands of legitimacy, while the guerrilla south and the paramilitary north invoked by *Time* would be brought together functionally as niches of de facto power. That would leave the rest of Colombia to swing the national balance either way.

Political legitimacy is clearest in urban Colombia. The rules of representative democracy are more consistent; official business is becoming more transparent and public services are becoming more efficient and coherent; the idea of citizenship is being made more real. That said, it is a very fragile situation, as can be seen by the crime statistics of Cali and Medellín (in contrast to Bogotá, where the crime rate has fallen almost constantly for more than a decade), which put Colombia among the most violent countries in the world. Likewise, on the political side there are still reverses, which is hardly surprising given the fragmentation, violence, and corruption that the crisis of the two-party system has spawned. But all told, as a broad generalization we can say that in the cities legitimate state authority is respected—something that cannot be said for the territories of de facto power.

These territories include the major zones of recent land colonization, all with very low population densities. The failure of the agrarian reforms of the 1930s and 1960s led the land-hungry rural poor to head deeper into the forests. These colonization "fronts" of the late twentieth century can be grouped into nine regions: Urabá-Darién (Antioquia), Sincé–San Jorge (Sucre and Córdoba), Serranía del Perijá (Magdalena), Magdalena Medio (Santander, Antioquia, and to a lesser extent Boyacá and Caldas), the Pacific coast (Nariño and Chocó), Saravena (Arauca), the Andean foothills of Orinoquia (Meta and Casanare), Ariari (Meta), and nearly the entire departments of Caquetá and Putumayo. In all of these regions, it can truly be said that everything is negotiable.

These are the regions where we find entrenched de facto power constructed on the Hobbesian law of rule through strength. But there are many actors, ranging from the guerrillas and paramilitaries to traditional political networks and large latifundio interests (both traditional cattle ranchers and newer narco-landowners), and now the list must include all the interests that have sprung up around the immense drug cultivation and processing business. In many parts of this frontier there are well-established routes for global contraband, including arms. There are also buoyant regional economies based on oil, bananas, and gold. With high geographical mobility especially among the young, there is a constant process of social rooting and uprooting in which the state plays no role, through education or other means of benign upward mobility. The ingredients for conflict are readily apparent: there is wealth to be had, a population willing to move in order to have access to it, and a lack of structured and legitimate opportunities to gain that access.

These territories are full of transient alliances and private armies formed to combat the guerrillas. The paramilitaries, operating close to home, are gaining autonomy in the sense that they are not just an immediate response to guerrillas, and have sought (with mixed results thus far) to create a national-level organization to mirror the FARC.

In a country of de facto powers, the police, the judiciary, and the electoral system are facades. But the viability of the de facto powers depends, paradoxically, on the existence of a Colombian nation and state. The nation, as a nominally coherent entity, is what provides the intermediaries who give local networks meaning, and it is where the markets are located. The state is what provides legal cover and a cultural reference point: to a surprising extent, illegal actors adopt the forms of legality. Thanks to the constitution of 1991, a larger share of the resource-based revenues of these regions remains at the level of the *municipio* or department. This country, then, is a permanent framework of legitimacy and violence, and even though its institutions are facades, they provide resources and the rules of the game to everyone, even the guerrillas.

Although Colombia does not seem to be facing Balkanization, it is clear that the national balance of power is increasingly dependent on the "third country" located between the islands of legitimacy and the regions of de facto power. Most of the densely populated but nonurban areas fall into this category: the Caribbean coast, the eastern mountains, the coffee zone of Greater Caldas, the central departments of Tolima and Huila, and the southwestern departments of Cauca and Nariño. This is the part of Colombia that feeds the rest of the country, and where political and economic institutions function more or less normally, although on the basis of traditional patronage practices and under the insidious shadow of the drug traffickers. The "third country" also encompasses the more critical-minded members of the urban middle class, willing to make independent judgments and ready to join civil society.

There are, of course, other angles from which Colombian history can help us to understand the present. From the earliest colonial times, the basic characteristic of political authority in Colombia's territory has been its fragility, thanks to a physical and human geography that strengthened local strongmen, entrenched in their enclaves and often petulant in the face of distant royal authority. Contraband, whether gold in the sixteenth century or Marlboros today, is perhaps the best example of resistance to taxes and an overall antistate mentality raised to the level of a cultural tradition. Even in the centralized Bourbon era, late in the eighteenth century, large-scale smuggling was more the rule than the exception. Cartagena, the principal port of the New Kingdom of Granada, was in the hands of the great smugglers, who in time were the legitimate great merchants organized in the colony's only European-style merchant guild. During this period, in 1781, the most massive and dangerous social movement in Colombian colonial history broke out: the insurrection of the Comuneros (townspeople) of Socorro, which rapidly forged a formidable alliance of ethnicities, classes, provinces, and towns against the fiscal reforms of the Bourbons, all in the name of the king and against the "bad government" exercised in his name.

It is no wonder, then, that Colombians' tax burden, measured overall and across all classes, is among the lowest in Latin America—not because nominal taxes are low but because avoiding payment is easy. Nor is it a coincidence that the most powerful criminal organizations of the Latin American drug economy are Colombian, rather than Peruvian or Bolivian: they come from a long and well-developed tradition of smuggling and illegal trade in emeralds. This antistate tradition has a long past, and we can see its social ramifications and modes of legitimation at the local level. Something similar occurs with the illegal armed organizations: they have a past, if a more recent one, and deep roots in local populations.

Colombia's guerrillas are framed by the dates of the Cold War: they came out of the 1950s and 1960s, and the Soviet collapse and Cuban realpolitik of the 1980s and 1990s had a significant impact on them. We can look farther back to the radicalism that emerged from the last declared civil war (1899–1902) and returned half a century later during the Violencia, which left 200,000 dead, countless families displaced from their homes, and niches of rebellion and rage throughout the country. In the 1960s some of these niches provided assistance to the first guerrilla bands, Communist (FARC), Guevarist (ELN), and Maoist (EPL).

The guerrillas sought to build on two exclusions. First, the social exclusion of the rural poor, which the agrarian reform of the 1960s did nothing to address; second, the political exclusion represented by the two-party National Front, according to the radical politicians and intellectuals of the period. From the beginning the guerrillas chose to isolate themselves from the cultural and political trends of the cities (even the FARC, despite its close ties to the largely urban Colombian Communist Party); the Camilo Torres episode, when the Bogotá priest and other middle-class intellectuals left to join the ELN in the mid-1960s, was very much the exception. Guerrilla commanders have not tried to forge stable and systematic alliances with union members, university students, or cultural workers. They have therefore always been weak and marginal in what we might call national politics; but in parts of the countryside they have successfully woven networks of support and sympathy, as have their paramilitary enemies. This is the revenge of traditional rural society, in which ties of locality, family, and ritual kinship are joined to individual trajectories mediated by modern criteria of success or failure. From what we know of guerrillas' life stories, many of them joined after experiencing failure in their modest efforts at social advancement.

This phenomenon is even clear in the FARC, which took up the agrarian banners of the 1960s or earlier, and whose leaders (now mostly aged 45–50 or older) were socialized into the values and norms of the pro-Soviet and even Stalinist Colombian Communist Party. But the rural origins of most of them and their early efforts at upward mobility, cut short for political reasons, also identify them with the traditional practices of clientelism and political bossism. The secret of the longevity of the FARC's local organizations probably resides in a combination of guerrilla tactics, cemented by a half-century of experience, and armed extortion. The Leninist "democratic centralism" that the group inherited from the Communist Party and has ruthlessly maintained helps explain why the FARC has been able to maintain a solid unity of command, despite the extraordinary dispersion of its networks and combatants. This stands in marked contrast to the more federalist organization of the ELN and the complete dispersion of the paramilitaries, save for the press communiqués of their nominal leader, Carlos Castaño.

It would be naive to suppose that illegal activities such as the drug trade do not have strong social legitimacy in the communities where they are based, beyond the powerful political and commercial interests that directly underlie them. Clearly the drug economy feeds the conflict, or as is often said nowadays, it provides the conflict with an economic agenda. The same could be said of the economies of oil, bananas, and gold. Although the economic motive is important to an understanding of any and all illegal organizations (drug cartels, paramilitaries, guerrillas), it is no longer clear whether the guerrillas maintain a subversive subculture based on Marxist ideology. But they continue to express social resentments, rebelliousness, and a political anger whose rhetoric, despite the collapse of the Soviet bloc, has some resonance in the face of a political order assumed to be unjust and rotten.

Mapping the situations, participants, and interests reveals their fluidity. We can understand this chaotic hodgepodge only by investigating what goes on in local societies, which in turn suggests the impossibility of a military solution to the conflict: a conflict that is kept within Colombia's borders, and will stay that way unless and until it becomes a full-fledged civil war. In view of the country's geography and the guerrillas' capacity for political mobilization, it is hard to see this happening.

The current version of old counterinsurgency strategies (under the auspices of the U.S.-sponsored Plan Colombia) with a more efficient army has provoked a tactical fallback by the FARC since the collapse of the Pastrana peace process in early 2002. If the fallback is prolonged, there may be a possibility of a return to negotiations, this time with weakness on the guerrilla side. If the military pressure on the guerrillas is accompanied by pressure on the surrounding civilian population, as has historically been the case, we can expect the conflict to continue on the low-intensity model that observers have considered part of the Colombian landscape. This would be an ominous landscape indeed, especially for civil and political liberties, in a post–September 11 world.

Bibliographical Essay

Since the bulk of this book was written between 1990 and 1994, the works cited do not include those published after 1993.

General Works

Culture and geography provide the general framework for any historical narrative. The reader will find important keys to understanding Colombia in Gerardo and Alicia Reichel-Dolmatoff, *The People of Aritama: The Cultural Personality of a Colombian Mestizo Village* (London, 1961); in the overview by Ernesto Guhl, *Colombia: Bosquejo de su geografía tropical*, 2nd ed. (Bogotá, 1975); and in the more recent book by Fabio Zambrano Pantoja and Bernard Olivier, *Ciudad y territorio: El proceso de poblamiento en Colombia* (Bogotá, 1993). For the Magdalena River, central to any understanding of Colombian history, see Eduardo Acevedo Latorre, *El río grande de la Magdalena: Apuntes sobre su historia, su geografía y sus problemas* (Bogotá, 1981); E. C. Griffin, "The Changing Role of the Río Magdalena in Colombia's Growth," *Geographical Survey* 3, no. 1 (1974): 14–24; and Rafael Gómez Picón, *Magdalena río de Colombia* (Bogotá, 1945).

The *Revista Colombiana de Antropología*, published since 1953, and the publications of the Instituto Geográfico Agustín Codazzi, particularly its *Atlas de Colombia*, are indispensable to any understanding of their respective subjects.

For general histories of Colombia that examine the post-1875 period, see Álvaro Tirado Mejía, ed., *Nueva historia de Colombia*, 8 vols. (Bogotá, 1989), which includes Jaime Jaramillo Uribe, ed., *Manual de historia de Colombia*, 3 vols. (Bogotá, 1976). The chapters are of uneven quality and the overall compendium lacks thematic coherence. In English, see David Bushnell, *The Making of Modern Colombia: A Nation in Spite of Itself* (Berkeley, 1993); Malcolm Deas, "Colombia, Ecuador and Venezuela, c. 1880–1930," in *The Cambridge History of Latin America*, vol. 5 (New York, 1986), 641–63; and Christopher Abel and Marco Palacios, "Colombia, 1930–1958" and "Colombia since 1958," both in *The Cambridge History of Latin America*, vol. 8 (New York, 1991). Also worth mentioning are the panoramic introduction in Jenny Pearce, *Colombia: Inside the Labyrinth* (London, 1990), and, in French, Jean Pierre Minaudier, *Histoire de la Colombie: De la conquête a nos jours* (Paris, 1992).

The most important Colombian historical journals are the *Boletín de Historia y Antigüedades*, published since 1902 by the Academia Colombiana de la Historia, and the *Anuario Colombiano de Historia Social y de Cultura*, which since 1963 has been the domain of the so-called new historians.

There is no good general political history of the last century, but in a country where elections have always played a central role, the *Historia Electoral Colombiana, 1801–1988* (Bogotá, 1991), published by the Registraduría Nacional del Estado Civil, is a good starting point. For political thought, see Jaime Jaramillo Uribe, ed., *Antología del pensamiento político colombiano*, 2 vols. (Bogotá, 1970); and Gerardo Molina, *Las ideas liberales en Colombia*, 2 vols. (Bogotá, 1971–80). Although there is no general social history of the period, Virginia Gutiérrez de Piñeres, *Familia y cultura en Colombia: Tipologías, funciones y dinámica de la familia* (Bogotá, 1977) is very useful reading. For literature, see Antonio Curcio Altamar, *Evolución de la novela en Colombia* (Bogotá, 1975) and *Manual de la literatura colombiana*, 3 vols. (Bogotá, 1988); and Raymond Williams, *The Colombian Novel, 1844–1987* (Austin, 1991). The richness of Colombian music and dance and their roots in indigenous, Hispanic, and African cultures are treated in depth in George List, *Music and Poetry in a Colombian Village: A Tri-cultural Heritage* (Bloomington, 1983).

The works of Luis Eduardo Nieto Arteta, *Economía y cultura en la historia de Colombia* (Bogotá, 1942), and Luis Ospina Vázquez, *Industria y protección en Colombia* (Bogotá, 1955), are considered precursors of modern Colombian economic history. A noteworthy modern collection is José Antonio Ocampo, ed., *Historia económica de Colombia* (Bogotá, 1987). Entrepreneurial history has great and largely untapped potential, as demonstrated by Carlos Dávila L. de Guevara, *Historia empresarial de Colombia: Estudios, problemas y perspectivas* (Bogotá, 1991) and *El empresariado colombiano: Una perspectiva histórica* (Bogotá, 1986). On money and banking, the essential sources are Guillermo Torres Giraldo, *Historia de la moneda en Colombia* (Bogotá, 1954) and *El Banco de la República: Antecedentes, evolución y estructura* (Bogotá, 1990).

José Antonio Ocampo, *Colombia y la economía mundial, 1830–1910* (Bogotá, 1984), presents the most coherent panorama of the agro-export economy of the nineteenth century, but there is no similar study of the gold and silver export

Bibliographical Essay 271

economy of the second half of the century. Ocampo can be complemented by the Marxist approach of Salomón Kalmanovitz, *Economía y nación: Una breve historia de Colombia* (Bogotá, 1985), and by Jesús A. Bejarano, *El régimen agrario de la economía exportadora a la economía industrial* (Bogotá, 1979). Also recommended, with some reservations because of the questionable reliability of its sources, is Miguel Urrutia and Mario Arrubla, eds., *Compendio de estadísticas históricas de Colombia* (Bogotá, 1970).

Important works on agrarian history include Orlando Fals Borda, *El hombre y la tierra en Boyacá: Desarrollo histórico de una sociedad minifundista*, 2nd ed. (Bogotá, 1973); Francisco Leal Buitrago et al., *El agro en el desarrollo histórico colombiano* (Bogotá, 1977); and the useful survey by Emigdio Pinzón, *Historia de la ganadería bovina en Colombia* (Bogotá, 1984). The most complete study of agricultural interest groups is Jesús Antonio Bejarano, *Economía y poder: La SAC y el desarrollo agropecuario colombiano, 1871–1984* (Bogotá, 1985). The pioneering work on Colombia's coffee development is Robert C. Beyer, "The Coffee Industry in Colombia: Origins and Major Trends," Ph.D. dissertation, University of Minnesota, 1947, which unfortunately has not been published; subsequent works of value include Mariano Arango, *Café e industria, 1850–1930* (Bogotá, 1977); Absalón Machado, *El café: De la aparcería al capitalismo* (Bogotá, 1977); and Marco Palacios, *Coffee in Colombia, 1850–1970: An Economic, Social, and Political History* (New York, 1980).

Interpretive surveys of regional development include Alberto Pardo Pardo, *Geografía económica y humana de Colombia* (Bogotá, 1972), and Sandro Sideri and Margarita Jiménez, *Historia del desarrollo regional en Colombia* (Bogotá, 1984). The conference proceedings *Memorias del simposio: Los estudios regionales en Colombia: El caso de Antioquia* (Medellín, 1982) demonstrate that Antioquia is the most studied region in Colombia. The compendium edited by Jorge Orlando Melo, *Historia de Antioquia* (Medellín, 1988), is unmatched by other regional volumes. For studies of the Caribbean coast see Theodore Nichols, *Tres puertos colombianos* (Bogotá, 1973); Eduardo Posada Carbó, *The Colombian Caribbean: A Regional History, 1870–1950* (Oxford, 1996); and Gustavo Bell Lemus, *El Caribe colombiano: Selección de textos históricos* (Barranquilla, 1989); as well as the methodologically peculiar four-volume work by Orlando Fals Borda, *Historia doble de la Costa* (Bogotá, 1979–84). For the Cauca Valley see Richard Hyland, *El crédito y la economía en el Valle del Cauca, 1851–1880* (Bogotá, 1983), and José M. Rojas, *Empresarios y tecnología en la formación del sector azucarero en Colombia, 1860–1980* (Bogotá, 1983).

For the colonization of the agrarian frontier, see James Parsons, *Antioqueño*

Colonization in Western Colombia (Berkeley, 1949); Catherine LeGrand, *Frontier Expansion and Peasant Protest in Colombia, 1850–1936* (Albuquerque, 1986); and Jane Rausch, *The Llanos Frontier in Colombian History, 1830–1930* (Albuquerque, 1993).

Chapter 1

The current interpretive framework for understanding late-nineteenth-century Colombian political history was developed during the years of sectarianism and Violencia. Examples include Eduardo Rodríguez Piñeres, *Diez años de política liberal, 1892–1902* (Bogotá, 1945) and *El olimpo radical: Ensayos conocidos e inéditos sobre su época* (Bogotá, 1950); and Milton Puentes, *Historia del partido liberal colombiano,* 2nd ed. (Bogotá, 1961). These authors are sympathetic to the Radical Liberals and hostile to the Regeneration. A pro-Regeneration Liberal perspective is Indalecio Liévano Aguirre, *Rafael Núñez y su época* (Bogotá, 1944). There are many polemical works of legal/constitutional history, two of which are noteworthy for their relative conciseness and clarity: Tulio Enrique Tascón, *Historia del derecho constitucional colombiano* (Bogotá, 1953), and Gustavo Samper Bernal, *Breve historia constitucional y política de Colombia* (Bogotá, 1957). Hernando Valencia Villa, *Cartas de batalla: Una crítica del constitucionalismo colombiano* (Bogotá, 1987), is a suggestive revisiting of this genre, and can be complemented by two books by Fernando Guillén Martínez: *El poder político en Colombia* (Bogotá, 1975) and *La Regeneración, primer frente nacional* (Bogotá, 1986).

Liévano Aguirre's book on Núñez influenced subsequent works, including William P. McGreevy, *An Economic History of Colombia, 1845–1930* (Cambridge, 1973), with its controversial interpretation of 1890s economic development, and his less problematic chapter, "The Transition to Economic Growth in Colombia," 23–81, in Roberto Cortés Conde and Shane Hunt, eds., *The Latin American Economies* (New York, 1985). Two useful studies of Regeneration economic policy are Darío Bustamante, "Efectos económicos del papel moneda durante la Regeneración," *Cuadernos Colombianos* 4 (1974), and Miguel Urrutia, "El sector externo y la distribución del ingreso en Colombia en el siglo XIX," *Revista del Banco de la República* 541 (1972).

For the religious conflict, see Juan Pablo Restrepo, *La Iglesia y el Estado en Colombia* (London, 1885); Ramón Zapata, *Dámaso Zapata o la reforma educacionista en Colombia* (Bogotá, 1961); and Christopher Abel, *Política, Iglesia y partidos en Colombia* (Bogotá, 1987). Education in the Radical era is examined by Jane Rausch, *La educación durante el federalismo: La reforma escolar de 1870* (Bogotá, 1993); and for the Regeneration see Robert V. Farrell, "The Catholic Church and Colombian Education, 1886–1930: In Search of a Tradition," Ph.D. dissertation, Columbia University, 1974.

For Regeneration-era political thinkers see Rafael Núñez, *La reforma política en Colombia*, 7 vols. (Bogotá, 1946–50); Salvador Camacho Roldán, *Escritos varios*, 3 vols. (Bogotá, 1897); Rafael Uribe Uribe, *Discursos parlamentarios* (Bogotá, 1897); and Miguel Samper, *Escritos politico-económicos*, 3 vols. (Bogotá, 1925); as well as Gerardo Molina, *Las ideas liberales en Colombia*, vol. 1 (Bogotá, 1971); Jaime Jaramillo Uribe, ed., *Núñez y Caro* (Bogotá, 1986); Vincent Dunlap, "Tragedy of a Colombian Martyr: Rafael Uribe Uribe and the Liberal Party, 1896–1914," Ph.D. dissertation, University of North Carolina at Chapel Hill, 1979; and Manuel Américo Bretos, "From Banishment to Sainthood: A Study of the Image of Bolívar in Colombia, 1826–1883," Ph.D. dissertation, Vanderbilt University, 1976.

For an interesting contrast in interpretations of the causes of the civil war of 1885 and the later War of the Thousand Days, see Helen Delpar, *Red against Blue: The Liberal Party in Colombian Politics, 1863–1899* (Tuscaloosa, Ala., 1981), which emphasizes social and family aspects of the creation of a closed system of party loyalties; and the more economic approach of Charles Bergquist, *Coffee and Conflict in Colombia, 1886–1910* (Durham, 1978). Rafael Núñez's role as forger of the national state against regionalist pretensions is developed in somewhat idealized fashion by James Parks, *Rafael Núñez and the Politics of Colombian Regionalism, 1863–1885* (Baton Rouge, 1985). This debate continues in Colombian historiography, as in Guillén Martínez, *El poder político en Colombia*, and Lenin Flórez G. et al., *Estudios sobre la Regeneración* (Cali, 1987). For a general discussion of regionalism, see Marco Palacios, "La fragmentación de las clases dominantes en Colombia: Una perspectiva histórica," *Revista Mexicana de Sociología* 4 (1980).

Malcolm Deas examines the social and cultural significance of the nineteenth-century civil wars in "Poverty, Civil War and Politics: Ricardo Gaitán Obeso and His Magdalena River Campaign in Colombia, 1885," *Nova Americana* 2 (1979). For the War of the Thousand Days, see Carlos E. Jaramillo, *Los guerrilleros del novecientos* (Bogotá, 1991); Jorge Villegas and José Yunis, *La Guerra de los Mil Días* (Bogotá, 1979); Álvaro Tirado Mejía, *Aspectos sociales de las guerras civiles en Colombia*, (Bogotá, 1976); and Eduardo Lemaitre, *Panamá y su separación de Colombia* (Bogotá, 1972).

For eastern Colombia, Alfred Hettner's *Viajes por los Andes colombianos, 1882–1884* (Bogotá, 1976) is a classic. For the social structure of this region, Fals

Borda, *Historia doble de la Costa*, and David C. Johnson, *Santander siglo XIX: Cambios socioeconómicos* (Bogotá, 1984) are the best studies to date. For land colonization in the greater Antioquia region, in addition to Parsons, *Antioqueño Colonization in Western Colombia*, and LeGrand, *Frontier Expansion*, see the pioneering work of Antonio García, *Geografía económica de Caldas* (Bogotá, 1937); Álvaro López Toro, *Migración y cambio social en Antioquia durante el siglo XIX* (Bogotá, 1970); Roger Brew, *El desarrollo económico de Antioquia desde la independencia hasta 1920* (Bogotá, 1977); Keith Christie, *Oligarcas, campesinos y política en Colombia* (Bogotá, 1986); and Albeiro Valencia Llano, *Manizales en la dinámica colonizadora (1846–1930)* (Manizales, 1990).

The classic book by Medardo Rivas, *Los trabajadores de tierra caliente* (Bogotá, 1885), depicts the transition from colonization to coffee in central Colombia, a subject that is also studied by Malcolm Deas, "A Colombian Coffee Estate: Santa Bárbara, Cundinamarca, 1870–1912," 269–98, in Kenneth Duncan and Ian Rutledge, eds., *Land and Labour in Latin America* (Cambridge, 1977); see also Néstor Tobón, *La arquitectura de la colonización antioqueña*, 4 vols. (Bogotá, 1986–89), for one of the more idiosyncratic aspects of the process. Its urban aspects are examined by José Francisco Ocampo, *Dominio de clase en la ciudad colombiana* (Medellín, 1972); Luis Duque Gómez and Jaime Jaramillo Uribe, *Historia de Pereira* (Pereira, 1963); and A. Valencia Zapata, *Quindío histórico: Monografía de Armenia* (Armenia, 1955).

For nineteenth-century public finance, see Luis Fernando López Garavito, *Historia de la Hacienda y el Tesoro en Colombia, 1821–1900* (Bogotá, 1992), and Malcolm Deas, "The Fiscal Problems of Nineteenth-Century Colombia," *Journal of Latin American Studies* 14, no. 2 (1982). For transportation problems of the era, see Robert C. Beyer, "Transportation and the Coffee Industry in Colombia," *Inter-American Economic Affairs* 2 (1948); Hernán Horna, "Francisco Javier Cisneros: A Pioneer in Transport and Economic Development in Colombia," Ph.D. dissertation, Vanderbilt University, 1976, and by the same author, "Transportation, Modernization, and Entrepreneurship in Nineteenth-Century Colombia," *Journal of Latin American Studies* 14, no. 1 (1982). Luis Mauricio Cuervo González presents a valuable overview of Colombia's electrification process in *De la vela al apagón: Cien años de servicio eléctrico en Colombia* (Bogotá, 1992).

There is a lot of talk about artisans and their significance in Colombian history, but not a lot of published research. Miguel Urrutia devoted a chapter to them in *The Development of the Colombian Labor Movement* (New Haven, 1969), and more recently they have been the subject of a stimulating study by David Sowell, *The Early Latin American Labor Movement: Artisans and Politics in Bogotá, Colombia,*

1832–1919 (Philadelphia, 1992). Of particular interest is his analysis of similarities and differences between the artisans' movement of the nineteenth century and the Bogotá "workers' movement" of the early twentieth century.

Chapter 2

The era of the Conservative Republic has attracted less historiographical interest than the preceding period but some protagonists have left important writings, starting with Carlos E. Restrepo, *Orientación republicana*, 2 vols. (Bogotá, 1972), and Marco Fidel Suárez, *Obras*, 2 vols. (Bogotá, 1966), particularly "Los sueños de Luciano Pulgar." The political effects of Panama's secession in 1904 are discussed in Bergquist, *Coffee and Conflict*; Suárez, *Obras*; and Lemaitre, *Panamá y su separación*. Colombian-American relations are given an official treatment in Germán Cavelier, *La política internacional de Colombia*, 4 vols. (Bogotá, 1980), but see also E. T. Parks, *Colombia and the United States, 1765–1934* (Newark, 1935); Richard Lael, *Arrogant Diplomacy: U.S. Policy toward Colombia, 1903–1922* (Washington, 1987); and Stephen J. Randall, *The Diplomacy of Modernization: Colombian-American Relations, 1920–1940* (Toronto, 1977), as well as his *Colombia and the United States: Hegemony and Interdependence* (Athens, Ga., 1992), which takes the story through the 1980s.

U.S. investments in Colombia, particularly after the signing of the Panama Canal treaty, were described and analyzed by J. Fred Rippy, *The Capitalists and Colombia* (New York, 1931). For U.S. investments in Colombia's oil see Jorge Villegas, *Petróleo, oligarquía e imperio* (Bogotá, 1969), and the excellent study by René de la Pedraja, *Energy Politics in Colombia* (Boulder, 1989), which covers coal and electricity as well, sometimes with a strong component of populist conspiracy theory.

For elite racial attitudes, see the collection of essays by several intellectuals of the period, *Los problemas de la raza en Colombia* (Bogotá, 1920). Bogotá stereotypes of the surrounding regions abound in the descriptions of Rufino Gutiérrez, *Monografías*, 2 vols. (Bogotá, 1920–21), and in Congreso de Colombia, *Actas y documentos de la lucha antialcohólica* (Bogotá, 1928). Subtle observations about the political and social atmosphere of Bogotá in the late 1920s can be found in the work of the Bolivian writer and diplomat Alcides Arguedas, *La danza de las sombras* (Bogotá, 1983). For Medellín around the same time, see Constantine Payne, "Crecimiento y cambio social en Medellín: 1900–1930," *Estudios sociales* (Medellín) 1, no. 1 (September 1986): 111–94. In his *Rendón: Una fuente para la historia de la opinion pública* (Bogotá, 1984), Germán Colmenares offers the famous caricaturist's own take on 1920s politics. For the social environment of the era see Carlos Uribe Celis, *Los años veinte en Colombia: Ideología y cultura* (Bogotá, 1985). Marco Palacios, "La clase más ruidosa," *Eco, Revista de la Cultura de Occidente*, December 1982, looks at British diplomatic reports on Bogotá's social and political life between 1906 and 1940.

For political history Jorge Villegas and José Yunis, *Sucesos colombianos, 1900– 1924* (Medellín, 1976), provides a valuable chronicle from (mostly Bogotá) newspaper sources. Eduardo Lemaitre, *Rafael Reyes: Biografía de un gran colombiano*, 4th ed. (Bogotá, 1994), provides a conventional laudatory account of the general-turned-president. James Henderson, *Conservative Thought in Twentieth-Century Latin America: The Ideas of Laureano Gómez* (Athens, Ohio, 1988), examines the intellectual journey of the rightist leader of the mid–twentieth century; see also Gómez's *Obras completas*, 5 vols. (Bogotá, 1984–89). On the Liberal side see Gerardo Molina, *Las ideas liberales en Colombia, 1915–1934* (Bogotá, 1974). For the church-state dispute during the period, in addition to Abel, *Política, Iglesia y partidos*, see Aline Helg, *Civiliser le peuple et former les élites: L'education en Colombie, 1918–1957* (Paris, 1984).

For the indigenous movement during this period, see the pioneering work of Juan Friede, *El indio en la lucha por la tierra* (Bogotá, 1946). For Quintín Lame, see Gonzalo Castillo Cárdenas, *En defensa de mi raza* (Bogotá, 1978), and Roberto Pineda Camacho, "La reivindicación del indio en el pensamiento social colombiano," in Jaime Arocha and Nina S. Friedemann, *Un siglo de investigación social en Colombia* (Bogotá, 1984). For the Casa Arana, the most infamous protagonist in the rubber tappers' genocide against the native peoples of the Putumayo, see Michael Taussig, *Shamanism, Colonialism, and the Wild Man* (Chicago, 1984).

The economic and fiscal foundations of the early-twentieth-century Colombian state are comprehensively described in Bernardo Tovar, *La intervención económica del Estado en Colombia* (Bogotá, 1984). For the public debt in the 1920s, see the relevant chapter of Paul Drake, *The Money Doctor in the Andes: The Kemmerer Missions, 1923–1933* (Durham, 1989). Alejandro López, *Problemas colombianos* (Paris, 1927), offers the sharpest contemporary analysis of economic matters. For an excellent overview of 1920s economic problems and policies see Hugo López, "La inflación en Colombia en la década de los veintes," *Cuadernos Colombianos* 5 (1975), and for greater detail, Alfonso Patiño Roselli, *La prosperidad a debe y la gran crisis, 1925–1935* (Bogotá, 1981).

For a contemporary survey of industry, commerce, transportation, and economic practices see P. L. Bell, *Colombia: A Commercial and Industrial Handbook*

(Washington, 1921), from the U.S. Department of Commerce. Donald Barnhart, "Colombian Transportation Problems and Policies, 1923–1948," Ph.D. dissertation, University of Chicago, 1953, is a useful sectoral study, as are Enrique Echevarría, *Historia de los textiles en Antioquia* (Medellín, 1953), and Fernando Botero, *La industrialización en Antioquia: Genesis y consolidación, 1900–1930* (Medellín, 1984). Alberto Mayor Mora presents a suggestive picture of the role of an "Antioquian ethic" on the development of labor organization in the region's textile industry in *Etica, trabajo y productividad en Antioquia* (Bogotá, 1984). The pioneering work of Gabriela Peláez E., "La condición de la mujer en Colombia," undergraduate thesis, Universidad Nacional de Colombia, 1944, examines the civil status of female workers in textile mills and coffee processing plants. Ann Farnsworth Alvear employs more sophisticated methodology in her *Dulcinea in the Factory: Myths, Morals, Men, and Women in Colombia's Industrial Experiment, 1905–1960* (Durham, 2000). See also Luz G. Arango, *Mujer, religion e industria: Fabricato, 1923–1982* (Bogotá, 1991).

The union movement during this period has received significant attention and analysis: Ignacio Torres Giraldo, *Los inconformes*, 5 vols. (Bogotá, 1973), and Daniel Pécaut, *Política y sindicalismo en Colombia* (Medellín, 1973), which reinterprets Colombian politics from the 1920s through the 1940s. For the 1928 massacre in the banana zone of Santa Marta, see Judith White, *Historia de una ignominia: La United Fruit Co. en Colombia* (Bogotá, 1978), and for radical culture among river workers, see Mauricio Archila, *Barranquilla y el río: Una historia social de sus trabajadores* (Bogotá, 1987).

Michael Jiménez produced the most comprehensive studies of social life in a region of larger coffee estates in "Traveling Far in Grandfather's Car: The Life Cycle of Central Colombian Coffee Estates: The Case of Viotá, Cundinamarca (1900–1930)," *Hispanic American Historical Review* 69, no. 2 (May 1989): 185–219, and in "The Limits of Export Capitalism: Economic Structure, Class, and Politics in a Colombian Coffee Municipality, 1900–1930," Ph.D. dissertation, Harvard University, 1986. Agrarian issues are also examined in the relevant chapter of Albert Hirschmann, *Journeys toward Progress: Studies of Economic Policy-Making in Latin America* (New York, 1963); Pierre Gilhodes, "Agrarian Struggles in Colombia," in Rodolfo Stavenhagen, ed., *Agrarian Problems and Peasant Movements in Latin America* (New York, 1970); Gonzalo Sánchez, *Las ligas campesinas en Colombia* (Bogotá, 1977) and *Los "Bolcheviques" del Líbano (Tolima)* (Bogotá, 1976); and Elsy Marulanda, *Colonización y conflictos: Las lecciones del Sumapaz* (Bogotá, 1991).

Chapter 3

For economic structure around mid-century, the standard reference is the study by the United Nations Economic Commission for Latin America (CEPAL/ECLA), *The Economic Development of Colombia* (Geneva, 1957), which covers 1925–53 and contains reliable data on national accounts. See also Antonio García's *Geografía económica*; Mario Arrubla, ed., *La agricultura en Colombia en el siglo XX* (Bogotá, 1976); and Mariano Arango, *El café en Colombia, 1930–1958: Producción, circulación y política* (Bogotá, 1982).

For the Great Depression see David Chu, "The Great Depression and Industrialization in Latin America: Response to Relative Price Incentives in Argentina and Colombia, 1930–1945," Ph.D. dissertation, Yale University, 1972; José Antonio Ocampo and Santiago Montenegro, *Crisis mundial, protección e industrialización: Ensayos de historia económica colombiana* (Bogotá, 1984); Rosemary Thorp and Carlos Londoño, "The Effect of the Great Depression on the Economies of Perú and Colombia," and José Antonio Ocampo, "The Colombian Economy in the 1930s," both in Rosemary Thorp, ed., *Latin America in the 1930s: The Role of the Periphery in the World Crisis* (London, 1984); Donald Barnhart, "Colombian Transport and the Reforms of 1931: An Evaluation," *Hispanic American Historical Review* 38, no. 1 (February 1958): 1–24; and Oscar Rodríguez, *Efectos de la Gran Depresión sobre la industria colombiana* (Bogotá, 1973). For interest group politics during this period see Absalón Machado, *Políticas agrarias en Colombia, 1900–1960* (Bogotá, 1986). For other aspects of economic policy see Carlos Lleras Restrepo, *Política cafetera, 1937/1978* (Bogotá, 1980), and Robert Triffin, "La moneda y las instituciones bancarias en Colombia," *Revista del Banco de la República* 202 (1944).

The major interpretive work on the Liberal Republic and the subsequent Conservative regimes of Ospina and Gómez is Daniel Pécaut, *L'Ordre et la violence* (Paris, 1986), also available in Spanish as *Orden y violencia: Colombia, 1930–1954* (Bogotá, 1987). In a sophisticated analysis the author emphasizes the heterogeneity of both the ruling and working classes, and how the interplay of economically defined groups with the party system and partisan subcultures created the peculiar mix of "order and violence" that characterized Colombia in the 1940s and 1950s. For a comprehensive political history running from the Liberal Republic through the early years of the National Front, see Robert Dix, *Colombia: The Political Dimensions of Change* (New Haven, 1967), and the more recent study by Patricia Pinzón de Lewin, *Pueblos, regiones y partidos* (Bogotá, 1989); for electoral statistics from the period, Departamento Administrativo Nacional de Estadística, *Colombia política: Estadística* (Bogotá, 1972). James Payne, *Patterns of Conflict in Colombia* (New Haven, 1968), has been justly criticized for its formalism and ethnocentrism, but the author presents one of the most original and vigorous interpretations of the Colombian political elite and its oscillations between compromise and conflict. A similarly provocative book, amply criticized for its pro-Rojas line, is Vernon L. Fluharty, *Dance of the Millions: Military Rule and the Social Revolution in Colombia, 1930–1956* (Pittsburgh, 1957).

The basic unity of the Colombian ruling class and its conception of social and political coexistence is closely described and analyzed in Herbert Braun, *The Assassination of Gaitán: Public Life and Urban Violence in Colombia* (Madison, 1985); Christopher Abel, in his *Política, Iglesia y partidos*, also emphasizes elite unity. In the "Colombia" chapter of *Labor in Latin America: Comparative Essays on Chile, Argentina, Venezuela, and Colombia* (Stanford, 1986), Charles Bergquist argues that coffee smallholders were essentially the working class of Colombia's export sector, but were unable to act collectively because of the sociopolitical constraints of the party system and local bossism, property ownership, and state patronage.

For politics in the Liberal Republic, see Plinio Mendoza Neira, *El liberalismo en el Gobierno: Sus hombres, sus ideas, su obra*, 3 vols. (Bogotá, 1946), for the Liberals' case; for the contemporary Conservative version, see Abel Carbonell, *La quincena política*, 5 vols. (Bogotá, 1952). Other Liberal accounts and documents include Carlos Lleras Restrepo, *Borradores para una historia de la República Liberal* (Bogotá, 1975) and *Crónica de mi propia vida*, 11 vols. (Bogotá, 1983–93); Alfonso López Michelsen, *Los últimos días de López y cartas íntimas de tres campañas políticas* (Bogotá, 1961) and *Mensajes del presidente López al Congreso Nacional, 1934–38* (Bogotá, 1939); and Eduardo Santos, *Una política liberal para Colombia* (Bogotá, 1937). Germán Arciniegas, *El estudiante de la mesa redonda* (Bogotá, 1933), suggests how the iconoclastic Liberal/leftist student of the era was really a conformist in waiting.

Political biographies for this period are scarce, but contributions include Gustavo Humberto Rodríguez, *Olaya Herrera: Político, estadista, caudillo* (Bogotá, 1979); Eduardo Zuleta Ángel, *El presidente López* (Medellín, 1968); and Richard Sharpless, *Gaitán of Colombia: A Political Biography* (Pittsburgh, 1978). María Carrizosa de López, *Estudio sobre las tendencias ideológicas del liberalismo en Colombia, 1930–1946* (Bogotá, 1985), is a sympathetic study of Liberal trends during that period, while leftist accounts usually emphasize López's regime as a rupture from earlier conceptions of liberalism: Francisco Posada, *Colombia: Violencia y subde-*

sarrollo (Bogotá, 1969); Gerardo Molina, *Las ideas liberales en Colombia*, vol. 3 (Bogotá, 1980) and *Las ideas socialistas en Colombia* (Bogotá, 1987); and on a more speculative note, Marco Palacios, *El populismo en Colombia* (Bogotá, 1971). Orthodox Communist interpretations are of interest more for their shaping of the narrative to the party's dictates of the moment: Partido Comunista de Colombia, *Treinta años de lucha del Partido Comunista* (Bogotá, 1960), and Medófilo Medina, *Historia del Partido Comunista de Colombia* (Bogotá, 1980). Diego Montaña Cuéllar, *Colombia: País formal y país real* (Buenos Aires, 1963), provides a more heterodox and critical version.

For the Olaya years, Terrence Horgan, "The Liberals Come to Power in Colombia, *por debajo de la ruana*: A Study of the Enrique Olaya Administration, 1930–1934," Ph.D. dissertation, Vanderbilt University, 1983, is an excellent study supported by extensive primary research. Javier Guerrero, *Los años del olvido* (Bogotá, 1991), examines the political violence that followed Olaya's election in Boyacá. Alfonso López's first administration has been the subject of some debate, and sometimes that debate is between the evolving views of a single author: compare Álvaro Tirado Mejía's chapter in Mario Arrubla, ed., *Colombia hoy* (Bogotá, 1978), very much in a neo-Marxist vein, with his party-line Liberal version in *Aspectos políticos del primer gobierno de Alfonso López Pumarejo* (Bogotá, 1981). Richard Stoller, "Alfonso López Pumarejo and Liberal Radicalism in 1930s Colombia," *Journal of Latin American Studies* 27 (May 1995): 367–97, provocatively interprets the "Revolution on the March" as a questioning of the basic unity of the ruling classes: a challenge hurled by López at the Conservatives, whose response was a combination of abstention and mobilization that was a precursor of the Violencia.

For foreign policy during the Santos administration, particularly regarding the United States, see David Bushnell, *Eduardo Santos and the Good Neighbor, 1938–1942* (Gainesville, 1967), and John C. Kelser, "Spruille Braden as a Good Neighbor: The Latin American Policy of the U.S., 1930–1947," Ph.D. dissertation, Kent State University, 1991.

The second López Pumarejo administration is unanimously derided by historians; a good example is Renán Vega Cantor, *Crisis y caída de la República Liberal, 1942–1946* (Bogotá, 1988). For the Ospina regime and the end of elite cooperation across party lines, see Abel, *Política, Iglesia y partidos*, and Braun, *Assassination of Gaitán*, as well as Alexander W. Wilde, "Conversations among Gentlemen: Oligarchical Democracy in Colombia," 28–81, in Juan J. Linz and Alfred

Stepan, eds., *The Breakdown of Democratic Regimes: Latin America* (Baltimore, 1978). The Liberal-Conservative rupture is officially documented in *La oposición y el gobierno: Del 9 de abril de 1948 al 9 de abril de 1950* (Bogotá, 1950), and *Dos cartas* (Bogotá, 1950).

For the church and education during this period, see Ana María Bidegaín de Urán, *Iglesia, pueblo y política: Un estudio de conflictos de intereses: Colombia, 1930–1955* (Bogotá, 1985); Gustavo Pérez, *Anuario de la Iglesia Católica* (Bogotá, 1961); and Camilo Torres and Berta Corredor, *Las escuelas radiofónicas de Sutatenza* (Bogotá, 1961).

The literature on the Conservative years (1946–1953) is less extensive than for the previous Liberal period; two useful Conservative accounts are Hernán Jaramillo Ocampo, *1946–50: De la unidad nacional a la hegemonía conservadora* (Bogotá, 1980), which focuses on economic issues; and Rafael Azula Barrera, *De la revolución al orden nuevo: Proceso y drama de un pueblo* (Bogotá, 1956). A critical Liberal account from the period is Carlos Lleras Restrepo, *De la democracia a la dictadura* (Bogotá, 1955). Gómez's efforts to remake the Constitution along Iberian corporatavist lines can be found in the official volume *Comisión de Estudios Constitucionales*, 2 vols. (Bogotá, 1953), which includes the principal debates and the final bill that was to be studied by the National Constituent Assembly (ANAC).

For Rojas Pinilla, in addition to Dix, *Colombia*; Montaña Cuéllar, *Colombia*; and Fluharty, *Dance of the Millions*, see Silvia Galvis and Alberto Donadío, *El jefe supremo: Rojas Pinilla en la violencia y el poder* (Bogotá, 1988), and Carlos H. Urán, *Rojas y la manipulación del poder* (Bogotá, 1983). John D. Martz, *Colombia: A Contemporary Political Survey* (Chapel Hill, 1962), remains a useful account of the Rojas period and the early National Front years. The official volume *El proceso contra Gustavo Rojas Pinilla* (Bogotá, 1962) contains abundant material about Rojas's government and what led up to it; the brief references in *The Journals of David Lilienthal*, especially vols. 3 and 4 (New York, 1966), written during his visits to Colombia as a consultant, are of interest as well. For an official account of the transitional military junta, see *Itinerario histórico* (Bogotá, 1957).

The economy at mid-century is profiled by the International Bank for Reconstruction and Development (World Bank), *The Basis of a Development Plan for Colombia: Report from a Mission* (Washington, 1950), a study led by Laughlin Currie, who would become one of the most influential economic advisers to Colombian governments for the next twenty years. For Currie's career, see Roger Sandilands, *The Life and Political Economy of Laughlin Currie: New Dealer, Presidential Adviser and Development Economist* (Durham, 1990). For the role of advisers, we have Currie's own account: *The Role of Economic Advisors in Developing Countries* (London, 1981). For the Boyacá steel mill debate, see Eduardo Wiesner, *Paz del Río: Un estudio sobre sus orígenes, su financiación, su experiencia y sus relaciones con el BIRF* (Bogotá, 1963).

For the industralists' group, ANDI, see Gabriel Poveda Ramos, *ANDI y la industria en Colombia, 1944–1984* (Bogotá, 1984), which presents a glowing portrait; a more critical one, emphasizing the organic relationships between industrialists, politicians, and the media, is Eduardo Sáenz Rovner, *Colombia años 50: Industriales, políticos y diplomacia* (Bogotá, 2002). An even more scathing version, which links the economic model to political violence, is Renán Vega Cantor and Eduardo Rodríguez R., *Economía y violencia: El antidemocrático desarrollo capitalista de Colombia en los años cincuenta* (Bogotá, 1990). Manuel Rodríguez, *El empresario industrial del Viejo Caldas* (Bogotá, 1983), emphasizes the political and social connections among the business elite on a regional level. Miguel Urrutia, *Gremios, política económica y democracia* (Bogotá, 1983), presents an optimistic picture of technocrats' power to neutralize the influence of sectoral lobbying groups. The role of industrialists in mass media concentration is examined in Reinaldo Pareja, *Historia de la radio en Colombia, 1929–1980* (Bogotá, 1980), and Maria Teresa Herrán et al., *La industria de los medios masivos de comunicación en Colombia* (Bogotá, 1991). For transportation policy during the 1950–74 period see Richard Hartwig, *Roads to Reason: Transportation, Administration, and Rationality in Colombia* (Pittsburgh, 1983).

Chapter 4

Almost all of the works cited for Chapter 4 touch on the Violencia in some fashion. For *gaitanismo* and the *bogotazo* see Braun, *Assassination of Gaitán*, complemented by the interpretation of Antonio García, *Gaitán y el problema de la revolución colombiana* (Bogotá, 1955), and by Gonzalo Sánchez, *Los días de la revolución: Gaitanismo y el 9 de abril en provincia* (Bogotá, 1983). For unionism during this period, see Edgar Caicedo, *Historia de las luchas sindicales en Colombia* (Bogotá, 1977), and Almario Salazar, *Historia de los trabajadores petroleros* (Bogotá, 1984).

The Violencia was first treated as an autonomous subject of analysis in the well-documented and controversial book by Germán Guzmán Campo, Orlando Fals Borda, and Eduardo Umaña Luna, *La violencia en Colombia: Estudio de un proceso: Parte descriptiva* (Bogotá, 1962). Conservative versions include Alonso Moncada Abello, *Un aspecto de la violencia* (Bogotá, 1965); Jorge Enrique Gutiérrez Anzola, *Violencia y justicia* (Bogotá, 1962); and for the later "banditry" period,

Evelio Buitrago Salazar, *Zarpazo the Bandit: Memoirs of an Undercover Agent of the Colombian Army* (Tuscaloosa, Ala., 1977). Paul Oquist, *Violence, Conflict and Politics in Colombia* (New York, 1980), argues for the emergence of a modern state and its "partial collapse" as the key to understanding the Violencia. See also Charles Bergquist, Ricardo Peñaranda, and Gonzalo Sánchez, eds., *Violence in Colombia: The Contemporary Crisis in Historical Perspective* (Wilmington, Del.,1992), and Gonzalo Sánchez, "La Violencia in Colombia: New Research, New Questions," trans. Peter Bakewell, *Hispanic American Historical Review* 65, no. 4 (November 1985): 789–807.

Carlos M. Ortiz, in *Estado y subversion en Colombia: La violencia en el Quindío años 50* (Bogotá, 1985), takes a close look at the local mechanisms of politics and the utilitarian character of violence; see also Darío Betancourt and Martha García, *Matones y cuadrilleros: Orígen y evolución de la violencia en el occidente colombiano* (Bogotá, 1990). For Tolima, a region that suffered greatly throughout this period, see Roberto Pineda, *El impacto de la Violencia en el Tolima: El caso de El Líbano* (Bogotá, 1960); James Henderson, *When Colombia Bled: A History of the Violencia in Tolima* (Tuscaloosa, Ala., 1985); María Victoria Uribe, *Matar, rematar y contramatar: Las masacres de la violencia en el Tolima, 1948–1964* (Bogotá, 1990); and Darío Fajardo, "La violencia y las estructuras agrarias en tres municipios cafeteros del Tolima, 1933–1970," in Leal, *El agro en el desarrollo histórico*. For the insurgency on the eastern plains, Eduardo Franco Isaza's novelistic *Las guerrillas del llano* (Bogotá, 1959) was for many years the only readily available source, but more reliable works are now available, including Reinaldo Barbosa Estepa, *Guadalupe y sus centauros: Memorias de la insurrección llanera* (Bogotá, 1992); Eduardo Fonseca G., *Los combatientes del llano* (Bogotá, 1987); and Justo Casas Aguilar, *La violencia en los Llanos Orientales: Comando hermanos Bautista* (Bogotá, 1986).

The most complete study of the Violencia at the local level, and one that sheds light on the wider phenomenon, is Mary Roldán, *Blood and Fire: La Violencia in Antioquia, 1946–1953* (Durham, 2002). Roldán focuses on the Urrao region and argues that preexisting local rivalries and conflicts determined the course of the Violencia, especially when a new generation of upwardly mobile politicians upset the traditional order of an established patrician elite. See also her article "Guerrillas, contrachusma y caudillos durante la violencia en Antioquia, 1949–1953," *Estudios Sociales* 4 (March 1989): 57–85. Gonzalo Sánchez and Donny Meertens, *Bandits, Peasants, and Politics: The Case of La Violencia in Colombia* (Austin, 2001), delivers a rich analysis of the local fabric of political bossism operating through both elections and violence. In his *Guerra y política en la sociedad colombiana* (Bogotá, 1991), Sánchez, the dean of Violencia researchers, offers some measured reflections on several aspects of the phenomenon, including its impact on Colombians' "political imagination." For a much different and little-studied aspect, the Violencia's impact on Colombian poetry, see Juan Carlos Galeano, "La poesía de 'La violencia' en Colombia," Ph.D. dissertation, University of Kentucky, 1991. A bibliography on the Violencia, which captures only the first generation of works, can be found in Russell W. Ramsey, *Survey and Bibliography of La Violencia in Colombia* (Gainesville, 1974).

Chapter 5

For the National Front, see Daniel Pécaut, *Crónica de dos décadas de política colombiana, 1968–1988* (Bogotá, 1989). The most comprehensive works on the bipartisan agreement are Jonathan Hartlyn, *The Politics of Coalition Rule in Colombia* (New York, 1988), and Albert Berry, Ronald G. Hellman, and Mauricio Solaún, eds., *Politics of Compromise: Coalition Government in Colombia* (New Brunswick, 1980). The official volume *Historia de la Reforma Constitucional de 1968* (Bogotá, 1969) contains useful information on the role of the legislature and the problems of public administration in the 1960s; see also Francisco Leal et al., *Estudio del comportamiento legislativo en Colombia*, 2 vols. (Bogotá, 1973–75); Mario Latorre, *Elecciones y partidos políticos en Colombia* (Bogotá, 1974); and Camila Botero, ed., *Propuestas sobre descentralización en Colombia* (Bogotá, 1983).

For nonviolent opposition to the National Front, the Movimiento Revolucionario Liberal's MRL *Documentos 1961* (Bogotá, n.d.) is a good source for that group; for ANAPO, see Jorge Villaveces, *Vida y pasión de la Alianza Nacional Popular* (Bogotá, 1974), and the excellent study by Daniel L. Premo, "Alianza Nacional Popular: Populism and the Politics of Social Class in Colombia, 1961–1970," Ph.D. dissertation, University of Texas, 1972. For the Communists, see Filiberto Barrero, *Por un Partido Comunista de masas* (Bogotá, 1960).

Politics in the aftermath of the National Front, still very much marked by it, is analyzed in Francisco Leal Buitrago and León Zamosc, eds., *Al filo del caos: Crisis política en la Colombia de los años 80* (Bogotá, 1991), a book whose emphasis on catastrophe is suggested by its title; Francisco Leal Buitrago and Andrés Dávila Ladrón de Guevara explore the uses and abuses of officially sponsored grassroots development projects in their *Clientelismo: El sistema político y su expresión regional* (Bogotá, 1990). See also Gustavo Gallón, ed., *Entre movimien-*

tos y caudillos: Cincuenta años de bipartidismo, izquierda y alternativas populares en Colombia (Bogotá, 1989); Pedro Santana R., *Los movimientos sociales en Colombia* (Bogotá, 1989); Mónica Lanzeta et al., *Colombia en las urnas: ¿Qué pasó en 1986?* (Bogotá, 1987); Pontificia Universidad Javeriana, ed., *Mercado electoral: Elección de alcaldes* (Bogotá, 1988); Rubén Sánchez David, *Los nuevos retos electorales: Colombia 1990: Antesala del cambio* (Bogotá, 1991); and Pilar Gaitán et al., *Comunidad, alcaldes y recursos fiscals* (Bogotá, 1991).

The principal transformations and tensions within the Colombian church since 1960 can be studied in the works of Benjamin Haddox, *Sociedad y religión en Colombia* (Bogotá, 1965); Daniel H. Levine, *Religion and Politics in Latin America: The Catholic Church in Venezuela and Colombia* (Princeton, 1981); and in the documents of the Conferencia Episcopal Latinoamericana (CELAM), *La iglesia en la actual transformación de América Latina a la luz del Concilio*, 2 vols. (Bogotá, 1968–69). The writings of the guerrilla priest, Camilo Torres, are available in Oscar Maldonado, Guitemie Olivieri, and Germán Zabala, eds., *Cristianismo y revolución* (Mexico City, 1970). For liberation theology and its clerical supporters, see Anita Weiss and Octavio Belalcázar, *Golconda: El libro rojo de los "curas rebeldes"* (Bogotá, 1969); Dimensión Educativa Colombiana, ed., *Hemos vivido y damos testimonio: Comunidades eclesiásticas de base: Teología popular* (Bogotá, 1988); and the relevant sections of Daniel H. Levine, *Popular Voices in Latin American Catholicism* (Princeton, 1992).

For the union movement in the 1960s and 1970s, in addition to the works cited above, see Jaime Tenjo, "Aspectos cuantitativos del movimiento sindical colombiano," *Controversia* 35–36 (1975); Hernando Gómez Buendía, Rocío Londoño, and Guillermo Perry, *Sindicalismo y política económica* (Bogotá, 1986); and Victor M. Moncayo and Fernando Rojas, *Luchas obreras y política laboral en Colombia* (Bogotá, 1973).

Because of the special importance of coffee in the Colombian economy, economic thinking is dominated by a pragmatism that tempers the impact of doctrines such as monetarism and neoliberalism on the one hand and protectionism and economic nationalism on the other. There have nevertheless been intense debates about overall economic orientation over the last sixty or more years. U.S. Senate, Committee on Foreign Relations, *Survey of the Alliance for Progress: Colombia: A Case of U.S. Aid* (Washington, 1969), describes the electoral and bureaucratic politics of economic policy making; see also Carlos Díaz-Alejandro, *Foreign Trade Regimes and Economic Development: Colombia* (New York, 1976); Richard R. Nelson, T. Paul Schultz, and Robert L. Slighton, *Structural*

Change in a Developing Country: Colombia's Problems and Prospects (Princeton, 1971); and Richard M. Bird, *Taxation and Development: Lessons from the Colombian Experience* (Cambridge, 1970). For the 1970s and 1980s, see Roger W. Findley, Fernando Cepeda Ulloa, and Nicolás Gamboa Morales, *Intervención presidencial en la economía y el Estado de derecho en Colombia* (Bogotá, 1983); José A. Ocampo, "Crisis y política económica en Colombia, 1980–1985," in Rosemary Thorp and Laurence Whitehead, eds., *La crisis de la deuda en América Latina* (Bogotá, 1987); and José A. Ocampo and Eduardo Lora Torres, *Colombia y la deuda externa: De la moratoria de los treinta a la encrucijada de los ochenta* (Bogotá, 1989). Miguel Urrutia, *Winners and Losers in Colombian Economic Growth of the 70's* (New York, 1985), and Albert Berry and Miguel Urrutia, *Income Distribution in Colombia* (New Haven, 1976), offer two interpretations of the issue; see also Charles E. McClure et al., *Taxation of Income from Business and Capital in Colombia* (Durham, 1990). Rosemary Thorp, in *Economic Management and Economic Development in Peru and Colombia* (London, 1991), analyzes the importance of leadership in generating credibility for the institutions that formulate and manage economic policy.

The formation and operation of Colombia's internal market is not well studied; a rare exception is Emilio Latorre, *Transporte y crecimiento regional en Colombia* (Bogotá, 1986). As for the components of that market, studies of agriculture and industry are the most numerous. For the former, see the following works: Laughlin Currie, "La Operación Colombia," *Diario Oficial* (Bogotá), several issues in September 1961; Salomón Kalmanovitz, *La agricultura en Colombia, 1950–1972* (Bogotá, 1975); Pierre Gilhodes, *Politique et violence: La question agraire en Colombie* (Paris, 1974); Gonzalo Cataño, ed., *Colombia: Estructura política y agraria* (Medellín, 1975); and Darío Fajardo, *Haciendas, campesinos y políticas agrarias en Colombia, 1920–1980* (Bogotá, 1983). For peasant organizations, see Bruce M. Bagley, "Political Power, Public Policy, and the State in Colombia: Case Studies of Urban and Agrarian Reforms during the National Front, 1958–1974," Ph.D. dissertation, University of California at Los Angeles, 1979; CINEP, ed., *Campesinado y capitalismo en Colombia* (Bogotá, 1981); and León Zamosc, *The Agrarian Question and the Peasant Movement in Colombia: Struggles of the National Peasant Association, 1967–1981* (Cambridge, 1981). Other worthwhile studies include Nora Reinhardt, *Our Daily Bread: The Peasant Question and Family Farming in the Colombian Andes* (Berkeley, 1988); Absalón Machado, *Problemas agrarios colombianos* (Bogotá, 1986); María Errázuriz, *Cafeteros y cafetales de El Líbano* (Bogotá, 1986); and Luis Llorente, Armando Salazar, and Angela Gallo, *Distribución de la propiedad rural en Colombia, 1960–1984* (Bogotá, 1985).

For coffee, see Laughlin Currie, *La industria cafetera en la agricultura colombiana* (Bogotá,1962); FEDESARROLLO, *Economía cafetera colombiana* (Bogotá,1978); Mariano Arango et al., *Bonanza de precios y transformaciones en la industria cafetera: Antioquia, 1975–1980* (Medellín, 1983); and Roberto Junguito and Diego Pizano, eds., *Producción de café en Colombia* (Bogotá, 1991).

General studies of industrialization since 1950 include the relevant chapters of World Bank reports, especially *Economic Growth of Colombia: Problems and Prospects* (Baltimore, 1972); Albert Berry, ed., *Essays on Industrialization in Colombia* (Tempe,1983); Astrid Martínez, *La estructura arancelaria y las estrategias de industrialización en Colombia, 1950–1982* (Bogotá,1986); Francisco Thoumi, "Evolución de la industria manufacturera fabril, 1958–1967," *Boletín Mensual de Estadística* (Bogotá) 236 (1971); and Ricardo Chica, "El desarrollo industrial colombiano,1958–1980," *Desarrollo y Sociedad* 12 (1982).

For foreign investment, see CEPAL, *Las empresas transnacionales en el desarrollo colombiano* (Santiago,1986); Daniel Chudnovsky, *Empresas multinacionales y ganancias monopólicas en una economía latinoamericana* (Mexico City, 1977); and Konrad Matter, *Inversiones extranjeras en la economía colombiana* (Medellín,1977). For regional economic integration and the Andean Pact, see Alicia Puyana, *Economic Integration among Uneven Partners: The Andean Pact* (New York, 1982).

For Colombian foreign policy, see Gerhard Drekonja, *Retos de la política exterior colombiana*, 2nd ed. (Bogotá, 1983); Gerhard Drekonja and Juan Tokatlián, eds., *Teoría y práctica de la política exterior colombiana* (Bogotá, 1983); Martha Ardila, *¿Cambio de Norte? Momentos críticos en la política exterior colombiana* (Bogotá, 1991). The Betancur administration's foreign policy emphases and responses to them are covered in Marco Palacios, ed., *Colombia no alineada* (Bogotá, 1983); for Barco-era foreign policy, see Rodrigo Pardo and Juan Tokatlián, *Política exterior colombiana: ¿De la subordinación a la autonomía?* (Bogotá, 1988).

Colombia's relations with the United States in the 1980s were dominated by the drug trade; the most complete and valuable studies for this period are Juan Tokatlián and Bruce Bagley, eds., *Economía y política del narcotráfico* (Bogotá, 1990); Juan Gabriel Tokatlián, "The Political Economy of Colombian-U.S. Narcodiplomacy: A Case Study of Colombian Foreign Policy Decision-Making, 1978–1990," Ph.D. dissertation, Johns Hopkins University,1991; Carlos Arrieta, Luis Orjuela, Eduardo Sarmiento, and Juan Tokatlián, *Narcotráfico en Colombia: Dimensiones políticas, económicas, jurídicas e internacionales* (Bogotá, 1990); Bruce Bagley, "Colombia and the War on Drugs," *Foreign Affairs* 83 (1988), and by the same author, "Colombia: The Wrong Strategy," *Foreign Policy* 77 (1989–90).

The drug economy in Colombia is surveyed in Luis F. Sarmiento and Ciro Krauthausen, *Cocaína y Co.: Un mercado ilegal por dentro* (Bogotá, 1991); Hernando J. Gómez, "La economía ilegal en Colombia: Tamaño, características, e impacto económico," *Coyuntura Económica* 3 (1988); Francisco E. Thoumi, "Some Implications of the Growth of the Underground Economy in Colombia," *Journal of Interamerican Studies and World Affairs* 2 (1989); Roberto Junguito and Carlos Caballero Argáez, "Illegal Trade Transactions and the Underground Economy in Colombia," in V. Tanzi, ed., *The Underground Economy in the United States and Abroad* (New York, 1982); and in many other works. For the regional impact, see Hermes Tovar Pinzón, "La coca y las economías exportadoras en América Latina: El paradigma colombiano," *Análisis Político* 18 (1993).

The wider role of the drug trade in Colombian society is analyzed in Álvaro Camacho Guizado, *Droga y sociedad en Colombia: El poder y el estigma* (Bogotá, 1988). Before the rise of cocaine, marihuana was Colombia's principal drug export and there was some debate about how to address the problem; see Ernesto Samper Pizano et al., *Legalización de la marihuana* (Bogotá, 1980). The pioneering work of Jaime Jaramillo, Leonidas Mora, and Fernando Cubides, *Colonización, coca y guerrilla* (Bogotá, 1986), is a good introduction to the bibliography on political violence in the 1980s. Perhaps a better word would be "violences," a plurality underlined in Gonzalo Sánchez et al., *Colombia: Violencia y democracia: Informe presentado al Ministerio de Gobierno* (Bogotá, 1987). See also Myriam Jimeno Santoyo, ed., *Conflicto social y Violencia: Notas para una discusión* (Bogotá, 1993); and Human Rights Watch, *The "Drug War" in Colombia: The Neglected Tragedy of Political Violence* (Washington, 1990).

Fernando Landazábal Reyes, *Política y táctica de la guerrilla revolucionaria* (Bogotá, 1966), and Richard L. Maullin, *Soldiers, Guerrillas, and Politics in Colombia* (Santa Monica, 1973), provide general introductions to 1960s guerrilla groups. For the origins of the ELN, see Jaime Arenas Reyes, *La guerrilla por dentro: Análisis del E.L.N. colombiano* (Bogotá, 1971). For the early history of the FARC, see Eduardo Pizarro Leongómez, *Las FARC (1949–1966): De la autodefensa a la combinación de todas las formas de lucha* (Bogotá, 1991); Arturo Alape, *Tirofijo: Las vidas de Pedro Antonio Marín, Manuel Marulanda Vélez* (Bogotá, 1989); and José Jairo González Arias, *El estigma de las repúblicas independientes, 1955–1965* (Bogotá, 1992). For the M-19, see Patricia Lara, *Siembra vientos y recogerás tempestades* (Bogotá, 1982), and Germán Castro Caycedo, *Del ELN al M-19: Once años de lucha guerrillera* (Bogotá, 1980). For civil-military relations see J. Mark Ruhl, *Colombia: Armed Forces and Society* (Syracuse, 1980), and

Gustavo Gallón Giraldo, *La república de las armas: Relaciones entre Fuerzas Armadas y Estado en Colombia* (Bogotá, 1983).

Chapter 6 and Epilogue

Colombia's 1950s socioeconomic situation is covered in the CEPAL/ECLA and World Bank reports and in Louis Lebret, *Estudio sobre las condiciones del desarrollo en Colombia* (Bogotá, 1958). See also the study by CEPAL/ECLA and the U.N. Food and Agriculture Organization, *Coffee in Latin America: Productivity Problems and Future Prospects*, vol. 1, *Colombia and El Salvador* (1958); Departamento Nacional de Planeación, "La economía colombiana, 1950–1975," *Revista de Planeación y Desarrollo* 3 (1977); and Miguel Urrutia, ed., *Cuarenta años de desarrollo: Su impacto social* (Bogotá, 1990).

For population studies and the role of women, see Ramiro Cardona, ed., *Las migraciones internas* (Bogotá, 1971); Carmen E. Flórez Nieto et al., *La transición demográfica en Colombia: Efectos en la formación de la familia* (Bogotá, 1990); Elssy Bonilla C., *Mujer y familia en Colombia* (Bogotá, 1985); and Magdalena León, ed., *Debate sobre la mujer en América Latina y el Caribe: La realidad colombiana*, vol. 1 (Bogotá, 1982). There is no overall study of Colombian migration abroad, but for Colombians in Venezuela see Gabriel Murillo, *La migración de trabajadores colombianos a Venezuela* (Bogotá, 1979), and Ramiro Cardona et al., *Migraciones colombianas a Venezuela* (Bogotá, 1983).

There is an abundant bibliography on urban and regional development; for an account of shifting official policies see Departamento Nacional de Planeación, "Política de desarrollo regional y urbano: Modelo de regionalización," *Revista de Planeación y Desarrollo* 2 (October 1970); and *Ciudades dentro de la ciudad: La política urbana y el plan de desarrollo en Colombia* (Bogotá, 1974).

For employment and housing policies, see International Labour Office, *Towards Full Employment: A Programme for Colombia* (Geneva, 1971); *El problema laboral colombiano: Diagnóstico perspectivas y políticas: Informe final de la Misión de Empleo*, in *Economía colombiana*, offprint no. 10 (August–September 1986); Francisco Uribe Echvarría and Edgar Forero, *El sector informal en las ciudades intermedias* (Bogotá, 1986), about Pereira and Bucaramanga; Harold Lubell and Douglas McCallum, *Bogotá: Urban Development and Employment* (Geneva, 1968); Alan Gilbert, "Urban and Regional Development Programs in Colombia since 1951," in W. A. Cornelius and F. M. Trueblood, *Latin American Urban Research*, vol. 5 (London, 1975); Alan Gilbert and Peter M. Ward, *Housing, the State, and the Poor: Policy and Practice in Three Latin American Cities* (Cambridge, 1985); Gabriel Murillo C. and Elizabeth B. Ungar, *Política, vivienda popular y el proceso de toma de decisiones en Colombia* (Bogotá, 1978); and Laughlin Currie, *Una política urbana para los países en desarrollo* (Bogotá, 1965). For the emergence of the "illegal city," see Alfonso Torres Castillo, *La ciudad en la sombra: Barrios y luchas populares en Bogotá, 1950–1977* (Bogotá, 1993).

For a broader cultural perspective on urban life, see Fernando Viviescas M., *Urbanización y ciudad en Colombia* (Bogotá, 1989), and by the same author, "Medellín: Del terror a la ciudad," *Gaceta Colcultura* 4 (1989): 24–26. For urban problems, see Ulpiano Ayala et al., *La problemática urbana hoy en Colombia* (Bogotá, n.d.); Jaime Carrillo, *Los paros cívicos en Colombia* (Bogotá, 1981); Medófilo Medina, *La protesta urbana en Colombia* (Bogotá, 1984); and Álvaro Camacho and Álvaro Guzmán, *Ciudad y violencia* (Bogotá, 1990). Two testimonial accounts of youth violence in Medellín are Alonso Salazar, *Born to Die in Medellín*, trans. Nick Caistor (London, 1992), and Diego A. Bedoya Marín, *De la barra a la banda* (Medellín, 1991); see also Carlos Miguel Ortíz, "El sicariato en Medellín: Entre la violencia política y el crímen organizado," *Análisis Político* 14 (1991): 60–73; and Seminario sobre la Comuna Nor-Occidental de Medellín, *Violencia juvenil: Diagnóstico y alternativas* (Medellín, 1990). Alejandro Ulloa, *La salsa en Cali* (Cali, 1992), and Pilar Riaño, *Descifrando la cultura popular* (Bogotá, 1991), focus on the festive side of urban youth culture. Pilar Gaitán Pavia and Carlos Moreno Ospina, *Poder local: Realidad y utopía de la descentralización en Colombia* (Bogotá, 1992), examines the tensions, possibilities, and conflicts arising from the direct popular election of mayors starting in 1986.

For land colonizations in the second half of the twentieth century, basic works include Instituto Colombiano de la Reforma Agraria (INCORA), *La colonización en Colombia*, 2 vols. (Bogotá, 1974); Instituto Geográfico Agustín Codazzi, *Problemas de la colonización del Putumayo* (Bogotá, 1978); Ronald L. Tinnermaiaer, "New Land Settlement in the Eastern Lowlands of Colombia," Ph.D. dissertation, University of Wisconsin, 1965; and the oral histories gathered by Alfredo Molano, *Selva adentro: Una historia oral de la colonización del Guaviare* (Bogotá, 1987). See also the valuable contributions of Roberto Pineda Camacho and Myriam Jimeno Santoyo in *Colombia amazónica* (Bogotá, 1987), and the collected writings of Raymond Crist, *Por los países de América tropical, 1942–1975: Aspectos sociales, geográficos e históricos* (Bogotá, 1987). For the colonization of Urabá in the northwest, see the early account of James Parsons, *Antioquia's Corridor to the Sea: An Historical Geography of the Settlement of Urabá* (Berkeley, 1967), and the later study by Fernando Botero Herrera, *Urabá: Colonización, violencia y crisis del Estado* (Medellín, 1990).

For native peoples since the mid–twentieth century, see Departamento Administrativo Nacional de Estadística, *Ayer y hoy de los indígenas colombianos* (Bogotá, 1971) and *Elementos para el estudio de los resguardos indígenas del Cauca* (Bogotá, 1978); Instituto Colombiano de Antropología, *Introducción a la Colombia amerindia* (Bogotá, 1987); François Correa R., ed., *Encrucijadas de la Colombia amerindia* (Bogotá, 1993); Ernesto Guhl et al., *Indios y blancos en la Guajira* (Bogotá, 1963); Myriam Jimeno and Adolfo Triana, *Estado y minorías étnicas en Colombia* (Bogotá, 1985); Gerardo Ardila et al., *La Guajira* (Bogotá, 1991); and Christian Gros, *Colombia indígena: Identidad cultural y cambio social* (Bogotá, 1991).

For Afro-Colombian and mulatto minorities, see Aquiles Escalante, *El negro en Colombia* (Bogotá, 1964); Nina Friedemann, *Criele criele son: Del Pacífico Negro* (Bogotá, 1989); and on the racial identity of the people of Chocó in their home region and as migrants in Medellín, see Peter Wade, *Blackness and Race Mixture: The Dynamics of Racial Identity in Colombia* (Baltimore, 1993).

There is a vast literature on education issues and a good journal, the *Revista Colombiana de Educación*. Noteworthy overviews include Gonzalo Cataño, ed., *Educación y sociedad en Colombia: Lecturas de sociología de la educación* (Bogotá, 1973) and *Educación y estructura social* (Bogotá, 1989); Rodrigo Parra Sandoval, *Ausencia de futuro: La juventud colombiana* (Bogotá, 1985); Ángel Facundo Díaz, "Crecimiento y desarrollo educativo en Colombia: Análisis del sector educativo, 1968–1993," Misión Ciencia Educación y Desarrollo (Bogotá, 1994); and Jesús Hernando Duarte Agudelo, "Education in Colombia during the 1980s: Plans and Achievements," M.Sc. thesis, Oxford University, 1992. Jeanne Marie Hamilton, "Women in Movement: The Expansion of Education in Urban Colombia, 1950–1980," Ph.D. dissertation, Johns Hopkins University, 1985, convincingly analyzes the decisive role of mothers in pressing for increased educational opportunities.

For higher education, see Germán Rama, *El sistema universitario en Colombia* (Bogotá, 1970); Luis E. Orozco, Rodrigo Parra, and Humberto Serna, *La universidad, ¿a la deriva?* (Bogotá, 1988); and Ricardo Lucio and Mariana Serrano, *La educación superior: Tendencias y políticas estatales* (Bogotá, 1992).

Finally, for some early studies of the Constitution of 1991 (no doubt superseded by a decade or more of subsequent works not cited here), see Gustavo Gallón G., ed., *Guerra y Constituyente* (Bogotá, 1991), and Carlos Lleras de la Fuente et al., *Interpretación y génesis de la Constitución de Colombia* (Bogotá, 1992), whose principal author was a member of the Constituent Assembly but takes a dim view of what it produced.

Index

Marco Palacios is a professor at the Colegio de México in Mexico City. He is the author and editor of many books, including *Coffee in Colombia, 1850–1970: An Economic, Social, and Political History* (New York, 1980), and (with Frank Safford) *Colombia: Fragmented Land, Divided Society* (New York, 2002).

Library of Congress Cataloging-in-Publication Data
Palacios, Marco.
[Entre la legitimidad y la violencia. English]
Between legitimacy and violence : a history of Colombia, 1875–2002 / Marco Palacios ; translated by Richard Stoller.
p. cm. — (Latin America in translation/en traducción/em tradução)
Translation of: 2nd ed., rev. and aug.
Includes bibliographical references and index.
ISBN 0-8223-3754-1 (cloth : alk. paper)
ISBN 0-8223-3767-3 (pbk. : alk. paper)
1. Colombia—History—1832–1886. 2. Colombia—History—1886–1903.
3. Colombia—History—20th century. I. Title. II. Series.
F2276.P2413 2006
986.106′3—dc22   2005034055